"SADDLE UP FOR A WILD RIDE."
—*NEW YORK DAILY NEWS*

"Brilliant! ABSOLUTELY HAUNTING. The medical, investigative, and historical details of Lincoln's assassination make you feel as if you were there, watching every second of John Wilkes Booth's cunningly calculated violence and a great president's inevitable and horrific death. Swanson's AMAZING account places you in the room as Lincoln lies dying and carries you across the countryside as Booth escapes. This historical book is ALMOST IMPOSSIBLE TO PUT DOWN."
—PATRICIA CORNWELL

"James Swanson has written A TERRIFIC NARRATIVE of the hunt for Lincoln's killers that WILL MESMERIZE THE READER FROM START TO FINISH just as the actual manhunt mesmerized the entire nation. It is A TRIUMPHANT BOOK."
—DORIS KEARNS GOODWIN

"EXTRAORDINARY. . . . As GRIPPING as any tightly scripted crime drama. . . . Booth remains ONE OF HISTORY'S GREAT VILLAINS."
—*BOSTON GLOBE*

"A HAIR-RAISING ACCOUNT."
—*CHICAGO SUN-TIMES*

"I CHALLENGE ANYONE TO BEGIN THE CHASE AND NOT BECOME COMPLETELY ENGROSSED."
—John Hope Franklin

"Brilliantly re-creat[es] the twelve anxious days when a grieving nation awaited the capture of the first man to assassinate an American president. This story is as gripping as any tightly scripted crime drama yet Swanson doesn't play fast and loose with historical facts. A noted Lincoln scholar, he constructs his narrative from letters, manuscripts, trial transcripts, and other original sources." —*Boston Globe*

"This riveting hour-by-hour account of Lincoln's assassination, Booth's escape, and the pursuit that finally ran down and killed him is a truly remarkable narrative. Even those familiar with the story will find fascinating new details here." —James M. McPherson

"*Manhunt* infuses the historical events with a sense of adventure. It takes the reader down dusty roads and into teeming swamps in the company of soldiers and scoundrels alike. Swanson illuminates the characters of his story with a wealth of personal detail usually found in fiction. He binds them to his narrative, which gallops along at the pace of a page-turning thriller." —CNN.com

"An amazing and entertaining book." —Liz Smith

"An engrossing blend of history and thriller that pulls off the heady feat of creating edge-of-your-seat narrative even as its conclusion is inevitable. And the ride? Like the TV show *24*, James L. Swanson's tale of the search for President Abraham Lincoln's killer rivets because of its pacing.... This tale is anything but common. Grade: A." —*Christian Science Monitor*

"Swanson reminds us that history is ultimately governed not by impersonal, economic, and social forces but by all the emotions that make up individual human beings." —David A. Price, *Wall Street Journal*

"Riveting.... Swanson makes the characters in this great American tragedy actually seem human. Even Booth comes across as viscerally real. Grade: A." —*Entertainment Weekly*

"It was the most horrific assassination that the nation had ever witnessed. With verve and no little drama, James L. Swanson re-creates John Wilkes Booth's murder of Abraham Lincoln and takes the reader into the mind-numbing twists and turns of the twelve-day manhunt that ensued. What a rollicking ride!" —Jay Winik, author of *April 1865: The Month That Saved America*

"Vividly readable ... managed with *CSI* immediacy." —*Washington Post*

"Gripping.... With his cinematically vivid writing and novelistic flair, Swanson makes the story suspenseful despite the fact that we all know the ending." —*American Heritage*

"Swanson deftly peels back the hitherto mostly hidden layers of this complex moment in our nation's history with panache, verve, and a compelling command of narrative and suspense, meticulously detailing the plot and the aftermath. . . . Swanson paints the scene at Ford's Theatre brilliantly and vividly. . . . *Manhunt* is full of the small, stranger-than-fiction details that give Swanson's narrative the ring of truth."　　*—American Spectator*

"James L. Swanson brings vividly to life one of the greatest stories in American history: the thrilling manhunt for John Wilkes Booth. His beautifully crafted narrative commands the reader's interest from start to finish—and, most important, he gets it right, down to the smallest detail."　　*—Edward Steers Jr., author of Blood on the Moon:*
The Assassination of Abraham Lincoln

"A rousing good read. . . . Booth's flawed, flamboyant character pushes the tale along. . . . Suspenseful."　　*—USA Today*

"So suspenseful that it's hard to put down. . . . Swanson takes the reader along on the chase with a riveting narrative, much of it told in authentic quotes from the many principals involved. . . . There are fascinating twists and revelations."　　*—Sacramento Bee*

"An incredible account. . . . Though this book reads like a page-turning suspense novel, every word of it is true. Swanson blows the dust off of more than 140 years of history to bring both the murder and its fragile place in our national history into sharp focus. . . . Simply put, exceptional."　　*—King Features Syndicate*

"The lucky reader will require mere hours to race along the taut narrative of *Manhunt*, an accomplished new thriller that reconstructs the massive search for the murderer of Abraham Lincoln. Following Booth's trail through these 448 pages is akin to galloping on horseback through the dark Maryland countryside. . . . Poetic. . . . Riveting. . . . A ripping story and a cautionary tale."　　*—Cleveland Plain Dealer*

"If the assassination of President Lincoln happened in today's world, the subsequent search for his killer would have been reported with breathless detail, complete with its own logo and theme music on twenty-four-hour cable news, not to mention blogs. Fortunately, we can rely, instead, on James L. Swanson's gripping, fact-filled thriller, *Manhunt*. Scrupulously researched, he follows the trail from D.C. into the Maryland swamps, down to the Virginia woods, and on to the capture of John Wilkes Booth."　　*—New York Post*

"In reading Swanson's detailed account, it will occur to readers that the events of April 14, 1865, shook the fragile, war-weary nation as much as the September 11, 2001, attacks stunned the United States. Both attacks were only partly successful but were terrible enough. Grade: A."　　*—Rocky Mountain News*

"Detail-rich. . . . A vivid and compelling portrait of the assassin."　　*—Pittsburgh Post-Gazette*

"A vividly rendered account. . . . *Manhunt* makes for a gripping read, all the more so because the events really happened. Even the most knowledgeable reader will feel the suspense of it."　　*—Washington Times*

"*Manhunt* is the historical equivalent of a chase movie. And a fast-paced one it is. . . . A fascinating read."
—*Fort Lauderdale Sun-Sentinel*

"When Booth shot the president in Ford's Theatre, his journey was just beginning. In his superb book, Lincoln historian James L. Swanson takes readers along for the ride. . . . Thrilling. It takes work to keep a book suspenseful when the outcome has been known for more than a century, but *Manhunt* keeps pages turning and delivers a generous helping of history without bogging down, just as good nonfiction should do."
—*Charleston Post and Courier*

"Recounts the tale with the detail of a true-crime book and the gripping tension of a crime novel."
—*The Winnipeg Sun* (Canada)

"A true-adventure tale of the first rank. . . . Vividly wrought."
—*BookPage*

"A thrilling murder mystery. . . . *Manhunt* is an exciting, unfailingly gripping account. . . . Impossible to leave before the last page. . . . Swanson's methods and resulting story may remind the reader of Truman Capote's *In Cold Blood*, the classic of narrative history that reads like the best fiction."
—*Deseret Morning News*

"Swanson presents the full story, in thrilling vignettes worthy of the drama of the actual events. . . . Swanson's well-documented and vivid account allows its readers to retain Abraham Lincoln as the object of our admiration, and John Wilkes Booth as an object of intense curiosity."
—*National Review*

"A riveting, you-are-there narrative. . . . Swanson humanizes actor Booth and his quest for one last dramatic triumph."
—Tony Mauro, *Legal Times*

"With great power, passion, and at a thrilling, breakneck pace, Swanson conjures up an exhausted yet jubilant nation ruptured by grief, stunned by tragedy, and hell-bent on revenge. . . . Vivid. . . . With a deft, probing style and no small amount of swagger, Swanson . . . has crafted pure narrative pleasure, sure to satisfy the casual reader and Civil War afficionado alike."
—*Publishers Weekly* (starred review)

"Reads like a full-throttle thriller."
—*Birmingham Post*

"A meticulously researched and thrilling account of the twelve-day chase."
—*Melbourne Herald Sun* (Australia)

"A pure page-turner."
—*Arizona Republic*

"A fast-paced, well-researched, and tightly written account [of] the greatest manhunt in American history."
—*Baltimore Sun*

MANHUNT

MANHUNT

The

TWELVE-DAY CHASE

for

LINCOLN'S KILLER

James L. Swanson

HARPER ● PERENNIAL

NEW YORK ● LONDON ● TORONTO ● SYDNEY

HARPER ● PERENNIAL

A hardcover edition of this book was published in 2006 by William Morrow, an imprint of HarperCollins Publishers.

P.S.™ is a trademark of HarperCollins Publishers.

FIRST HARPER PERENNIAL EDITION PUBLISHED 2007.

Maps by Paul Pugliese

Designed by Betty Lew

The Library of Congress has catalogued the hardcover edition as follows:

Swanson, James L.
    Manhunt : the twelve-day chase for Lincoln's killer / James L. Swanson.— 1st ed.
      p.   cm.
    Includes bibliographical references and index.
    ISBN: 978-0-06-051849-3 (acid-free paper)
    ISBN-10: 0-06-051849-9 (acid-free paper)
      1. Lincoln, Abraham, 1809–1865—Assassination.   2. Booth, John Wilkes, 1838–1865.   3. Fugitives from justice—United States—Case studies.
    4. Assassination—Investigation—United States—Case studies.   5. Criminal investigation—United States—Case studies.   I. Title.

    E457.5.S993   2006
    364.152'4'0973'09034—dc22   2005044911

ISBN: 978-0-06-051850-9 (pbk.)
ISBN-10: 0-06-051850-2 (pbk.)

07 08 09 10 11 ❖/RRD 10 9 8 7 6

For my parents,

Lennart and Dianne Swanson

I have never had a feeling politically that did not spring from the Declaration of Independence...that which gave promise that in due time the weights should be lifted from the shoulders of all men, and that *all* should have an equal chance....Now, my friends, can this country be saved upon that basis?...If it can't be saved upon that principle...if this country cannot be saved without giving up on that principle...I would rather be assassinated on this spot than to surrender it.

—PRESIDENT-ELECT ABRAHAM LINCOLN DURING
A SPEECH ON FEBRUARY 22, 1861, TEN DAYS
BEFORE TAKING THE OATH OF OFFICE AS THE
SIXTEENTH PRESIDENT OF THE UNITED STATES

This man's appearance, his pedigree, his coarse jokes and anecdotes, his vulgar similes, and his policy are a disgrace to the seat he holds...
he is...the tool of the North, to crush out, or try to crush out slavery, by robbery, rapine, slaughter and bought armies...a false president yearning for a kingly succession...

—JOHN WILKES BOOTH TO HIS SISTER AT A PRIVATE
HOME SHORTLY BEFORE PRESIDENT LINCOLN'S
REELECTION IN NOVEMBER 1864

Contents

List of Illustrations

A Note to the Reader

This story is true. All the characters are real and were alive during the great manhunt of April 1865. Their words are authentic. Indeed, all text appearing within quotation marks comes from original sources: letters, manuscripts, affidavits, trial transcripts, newspapers, government reports, pamphlets, books, memoirs, and other documents. What happened in Washington, D.C., in the spring of 1865, and in the swamps and rivers, and the forests and fields, of Maryland and Virginia during the next twelve days, is far too incredible to have ever been made up.

—JAMES L. SWANSON

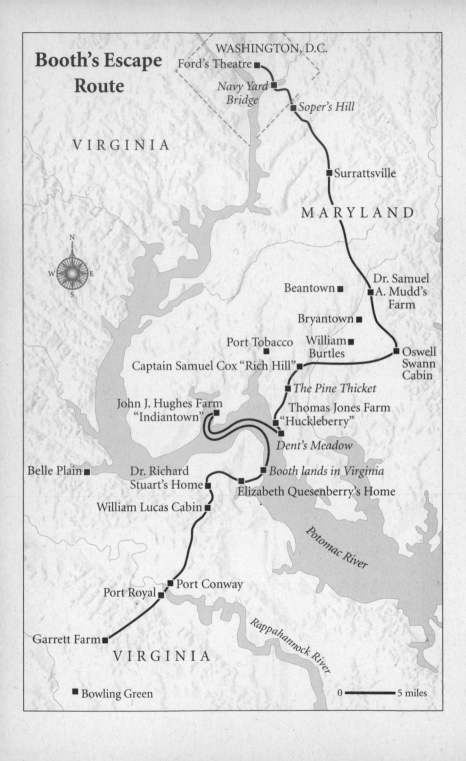

Booth's Escape Route

WASHINGTON, D.C.

Ford's Theatre

Navy Yard Bridge

Soper's Hill

VIRGINIA

Surrattsville

MARYLAND

Beantown

Dr. Samuel A. Mudd's Farm

Bryantown

Port Tobacco

William Burtles

Oswell Swann Cabin

Captain Samuel Cox "Rich Hill"

The Pine Thicket

John J. Hughes Farm "Indiantown"

Thomas Jones Farm "Huckleberry"

Dent's Meadow

Belle Plain

Dr. Richard Stuart's Home

Booth lands in Virginia

Elizabeth Quesenberry's Home

William Lucas Cabin

Potomac River

Port Conway

Port Royal

Rappahannock River

Garrett Farm

VIRGINIA

Bowling Green

0 — 5 miles

MANHUNT

Prologue

❦

I
T LOOKED LIKE A BAD DAY FOR PHOTOGRAPHERS. TERRIFIC
winds and thunderstorms had swept through Washington early that
morning, dissolving the dirt streets into a sticky muck of soil, garbage,
and horse droppings. Women, for their own safety, were advised to stay
indoors. The ugly gray sky of the morning of March 4, 1865, threatened
to spoil the great day. One block east of the Capitol Building, a patent
lawyer and part-time photographer named William M. Smith set up his
camera and pointed its lens at the temporary wood platform that had
been hastily erected over the East Front steps. His job was to make a historic photograph—the first image ever taken during a presidential inauguration of the recently completed great dome. Smith adjusted his
apparatus until his lens framed the panoramic, vertical view, from the
low-lying plinth of Horatio Greenough's marble statue of George
Washington on the lawn to the tip top of the dome, crowned by Thomas
Crawford's bronze statue of "Freedom." Abraham Lincoln had ordered
that work on the dome continue during the war as a sign that the Union
would go on.

Closer to the Capitol, and standing on another platform, Alexander
Gardner set up his camera to photograph the ceremony. Gardner's
large, glass-plate negatives captured not only images of the president, vice president, chief justice, and other dignitaries occupying the

stands, but also the anonymous faces of hundreds of spectators who crowded the East Front scene. One face among them stands out. On a balcony above the stands, standing near an iron railing, a young, black-mustachioed man wearing a top hat gazes down on the president. It is the celebrated actor John Wilkes Booth.

Abraham Lincoln rose from his chair and advanced toward the podium. He was now at the height of his power, with the Civil War nearly won. In one hand he held a single sheet of paper, typeset and printed in double columns. The foreboding clouds threatened another downpour. Then, reported Noah Brooks, journalist and friend of the president, the strangest thing happened: "Just at that moment the sun, which had been obscured all day, burst forth in its unclouded meridian splendor, and flooded the spectacle with glory and light. Every heart beat quicker at the unexpected omen...so might the darkness which had obscured the past four years be now dissipated." The president's text was brief—just 701 words.

"Fondly do we hope—fervently do we pray—that this mighty scourge of war may speedily pass away....With malice toward none; with charity for all; with firmness in the right, as God gives us to see the right, let us strive on to finish the work we are in; to bind up the nation's wounds; to care for him who shall have borne the battle, and for his widow, and his orphan—to do all which may achieve and cherish a just and lasting peace, among ourselves, and with all nations."

Subsequent events would soon change how witnesses recalled Lincoln's greatest day. To Noah Brooks, "Chiefly memorable in the mind of those who saw that second inauguration must still remain the tall, pathetic, melancholy figure of the man who...illuminated by the deceptive brilliance of a March sunburst, was already standing in the shadow of death."

On April 3, 1865, Richmond, Virginia, capital city of the Confederate States of America, fell to Union forces. It was only a matter of time now before the war would finally be over. The rebellion had been crushed, and the North held a jubilee. Children ran through the streets

NEGATIVE BY WM. M. SMITH.   POSITIVE BY A. GAR

Re-Inauguration of President Lincoln,
4th March, 1865.

William M. Smith's historic photograph of Lincoln's second inaugural.

waving little paper flags that read "Richmond Has Fallen," "We Cele-
brate the Fall of Richmond," or "Victory Will Lead to Peace: The Right
Stripe." Across the country, people built bonfires, organized parades,
fired guns, shot cannons, and sang patriotic songs. Four days later, John
Wilkes Booth was drinking with a friend, the actor Samuel Knapp Ches-
ter, at the House of Lords saloon, on Houston Street in New York City.
Booth struck the bar table with his fist and regretted a lost opportunity.
"What an excellent chance I had, if I wished, to kill the President on
Inauguration day! I was on the stand, as close to him nearly as I am
to you."

IN RESPONSE TO A THRONG OF SERENADERS WHO MARCHED
onto the White House grounds and begged him to address them,
Abraham Lincoln appeared at a second-floor window below the North
Portico on April 10 to greet this crowd of citizens celebrating General
Grant's victory at Appomattox the previous day. Lincoln did not have
a prepared text, and he was unwilling to speak on a subject of any consequence, including his postwar policy for the South. He resorted to
his favorite oratorical device to distract and disarm an audience—
humor.

"I see that you have a band of music with you....I have always
thought 'Dixie' one of the best tunes I have ever heard. Our adversaries
over the way attempted to appropriate it, but I insisted yesterday we
fairly captured it. I presented this question to the Attorney General, and
he gave it as his legal opinion that it is our lawful prize. I now request
the band to favor me with its performance."

CRUSHED BY THE FALL OF RICHMOND, AND BY THE FIRE THAT
consumed much of the rebel capital, John Wilkes Booth had left New
York City on April 8 and returned to Washington. The news there was
worse. On April 9, Lee and the Army of Northern Virginia surrendered

to Grant at Appomattox. The cause was lost. Booth wandered the streets in despair until he encountered Henry B. Phillips, who invited him to walk to Birch's saloon and share a drink. Inconsolable, Booth accepted.

"Yes, anything to drive away the blues." Lee's surrender, Booth says, "was enough to give anyone the blues."

ON THE NIGHT OF APRIL 11, A TORCHLIGHT PARADE OF A FEW thousand citizens, with bands and banners, assembled on the semicircular driveway in front of the Executive Mansion. Journalist Noah Brooks, a favorite of Lincoln's, was with the president and watched the throng from a window below the North Portico: "After repeated calls, loud and enthusiastic, the president appeared at the window, which was a signal for a great outburst. There was something terrible in the enthusiasm with which the beloved Chief Magistrate was received." Elizabeth Keckley, Mary Lincoln's black dressmaker and confidante, felt the mood too. "Close to the house the faces were plainly discernible, but they faded into mere ghostly outlines on the outskirts of the assembly; and what added to the weird, spectral beauty of the scene, was the confused hum of voices that rose above the sea of forms, sounding like the subdued, sullen roar of an ocean storm."

This time Lincoln was ready. He had written a long text, short on exultation and designed to prepare the people for reconstruction. When someone in the crowd shouted that he couldn't see the President—"A light! A light!"—Tad Lincoln volunteered to illuminate his father: "Let me hold the light, Papa!" Lincoln dropped each page of his manuscript to the floor when he finished reading it, and Tad scooped them up.

"We meet this evening, not in sorrow, but in gladness of heart. The evacuation of Petersburg and Richmond, and the surrender of the principal insurgent army, give hope of a righteous and speedy peace whose joyous expression can not be restrained. In the midst of this, however, He from Whom all blessings flow, must not be forgotten...no part of the honor...is mine. To General Grant, his skilful officers, and brave

men, all belongs." Lincoln then discussed the newly organized state government of Louisiana: "It is also unsatisfactory to some that the elective
franchise is not given to the colored man. I would myself prefer that it
were now conferred on the very intelligent, and on those who serve our
cause as soldiers."

As Lincoln spoke, Elizabeth Keckley, standing a few steps from him,
observed that the lamplight made him "stand out boldly in the darkness." She feared he was the perfect target. "What an easy matter would
it be to kill the President, as he stands there! He could be shot down
from the crowd," she whispered, "and no one would be able to tell who
fired the shot."

In that crowd, standing amidst the throng below Lincoln's window,
was John Wilkes Booth. He turned to his companion, David Herold,
and denounced the speech.

"That means nigger citizenship," he said, "now, by God, I'll put him
through."

As Booth left the White House grounds and walked toward Lafayette Square, he spoke to another companion, Lewis Powell: "That is the
last speech he will ever give."

ON THE EVENING OF APRIL 13, THE CITY CELEBRATED THE END
of the war with a grand illumination. Public buildings and private
homes glowed from candles, torches, gaslights, and fireworks. It was the
most beautiful night in the history of the capital. The next *Evening Star*
newspaper reported the wondrous display:

> Last night Washington was all ablaze with glory. The very
> heavens seemed to have come down, and the stars twinkled
> in a sort of faded way, as if the solar system was out of order
> and the earth had become the great luminary....Far as the
> vision extended were brilliant lights, the rows of illuminated
> windows at a distance blending into one, and presenting an

unbroken wall of flame…high above all towered the Capitol, glowing as if on fire and seeming to stud the city below with gems of reflected glory as stars light upon the sea. Away to the right a halo hung over the roofs, rockets flashed to and fro in fiery lines, and the banners waved above the tumultuous throng, where shouts and cheers rolled up in a dense volume from the city, and with the incense of the grand conflagration, drifted away to the darkness of the surrounding hills.

John Wilkes Booth had seen all of this—the grand illumination, the crowds delirious with joy, the taunting insults to the fallen Confederacy and her leaders. He returned to his room at the National Hotel after midnight. He could not sleep. He reached for pen and paper and wrote a melancholy letter to his mother, Mary Ann Holmes Booth. It was early in the morning of April 14.

Dearest Mother:

> *I know you expect a letter from me, and am sure you will hardly forgive me. But indeed I have nothing to write about. Everything is dull; that is, has been till last night. (The illumination.)*
>
> *Everything was bright and splendid. More so in my eyes if it had been a display in a nobler cause. But so goes the world. Might makes right. I only drop you these few lines to let you know I am well, and to say I have not heard from you. Excuse brevity; am in haste. Had one from Rose. With best love to you all, I am your affectionate son ever,*
>
> *John*

Chapter One

"I Had This Strange Dream Again Last Night"

JOHN WILKES BOOTH AWOKE GOOD FRIDAY MORNING, APRIL 14, 1865, hungover and depressed. The Confederacy was dead. His cause was lost and his dreams of glory over. He did not know that this day, after enduring more than a week of bad news and bitter disappointments, he would enjoy a stunning reversal of fortune. No, all he knew this morning when he crawled out of bed in room 228 at the National Hotel, one of Washington's finest and naturally his favorite, was that he could not stand another day of Union victory celebrations.

Booth assumed that April 14 would unfold as the latest in a blur of eleven bad days that began on April 3 when Richmond, the Confederacy's citadel, fell to the Union. The very next day the tyrant, Abraham Lincoln, visited his captive prize and had the audacity to sit behind the desk occupied by the first and last president of the Confederate States of America, Jefferson Davis. Then, on April 9, at Appomattox Court House, Robert E. Lee and his glorious Army of Northern Virginia surrendered. Two days later Lincoln made a speech proposing to give blacks the right to vote, and last night, April 13, all of Washington celebrated with a grand illumination of the city. And today, in Charleston harbor, the Union planned to stage a gala celebration to mark the retaking of Fort Sumter, where the war began four years ago. These past eleven days had been the worst of Booth's young life.

He was the son of the legendary actor and tragedian Junius Brutus Booth, and brother to Edwin Booth, one of the finest actors of his generation. Twenty-six years old, impossibly vain, preening, emotionally flamboyant, possessed of raw talent and splendid élan, and a star member of this celebrated theatrical family—the Barrymores of their day—John Wilkes Booth was willing to throw away fame, wealth, and promise for his cause. Handsome and charismatic, he was instantly recognizable to thousands of fans in both the North and the South. His physical beauty astonished all who beheld it. A fellow actor once described him: "Picture to yourself Adonis, with high forehead, sweeping black hair, a figure of perfect youthful proportions and the most wonderful black eyes in the world. Such was John Wilkes Booth. At all times his eyes were his striking features but when his emotions were aroused they were like living jewels." Booth's passions included fine clothing, delectable women, and the romance of lost causes.

Booth's day began in the dining room of the National, where he was seen eating breakfast with Miss Carrie Bean. Nothing unusual about that—Booth, a voluptuous connoisseur of young women, never had trouble finding female company. Around noon he walked over to Ford's Theatre on Tenth Street between E and F, a block above Pennsylvania Avenue, to pick up his mail. Accepting correspondence on behalf of itinerant actors was a customary privilege Ford's offered to friends of the house. Earlier that morning Henry Clay Ford, one of the three brothers who ran the theatre, ate breakfast and then walked to the big marble post office at Seventh and F and picked up the mail. There was a letter for Booth.

That morning another letter arrived at the theatre. There had been no time to mail it, so its sender, Mary Lincoln, used the president's messenger to bypass the post office and hand-deliver it. The Fords did not even have to read the note to know the good news it contained. The mere arrival of the White House messenger told them that the president was coming tonight! It was a coup against their chief rival, Grover's Theatre, which was offering a more exciting entertainment: *Aladdin! Or*

"The most beautiful black eyes in the world."
John Wilkes Booth at the height of his fame.

His Wonderful Lamp. Master Tad Lincoln and chaperone would represent the family there. The letter, once opened, announced even greater news. Yes, the president and Mrs. Lincoln would attend this evening's performance of Tom Taylor's popular if tired comedy *Our American Cousin.* But the big news was that General Ulysses S. Grant was coming with them. The Lincolns' timing delighted the Fords. Good Friday was traditionally a slow night, and news that not only the president—after four years a familiar sight to Washingtonians—but also General Grant, a rare visitor to town and fresh from his victory at Appomattox, would attend, was sure to spur ticket sales. This would please Laura Keene, who was making her one thousandth performance in the play; tonight's show was a customary "benefit," awarding her a rich share of the proceeds. The Lincolns had given the Fords the courtesy of notification early enough in the day for the brothers to promote their appearance and to decorate and join together the two boxes—seven and eight—that, by removal of a simple partition, formed the president's box.

By the time Booth arrived at Ford's, the president's messenger had come and gone. Sometime between noon and 12:30 P.M. as he sat outside on the top step in front of the main entrance to Ford's reading his letter, Booth heard the galvanizing news. In just eight hours the subject of all of his brooding, hating, and plotting would stand on the very stone steps where he now sat. This was the catalyst Booth needed to prompt him to action. Here. Of all places, Lincoln was coming here. Booth knew the layout of Ford's intimately: the exact spot on Tenth Street where Lincoln would step out of his carriage; the place the president sat every time he came to the theatre; the route through the theatre that Lincoln would walk and the staircase he would ascend to the box; the dark, subterranean passageway beneath the stage; the narrow hallway behind the stage that led to the back door that opened to Baptist Alley; and how the president's box hung directly above the stage. Booth had played here before, most recently in a March 18 performance as Pescara in *The Apostate.*

And Booth, although he had never acted in it, also knew *Our*

American Cousin—its duration, its scenes, its players, and, most important, as it would turn out, the number of actors onstage at any given moment during the performance. It was perfect. He would not have to hunt Lincoln. The president was coming to him. But was there enough time to make all the arrangements? The checklist was substantial: horses; weapons; supplies; alerting his fellow conspirators; casing the theatre; so many other things. He had only eight hours. But it was possible. If luck was on his side, there was just enough time. Whoever told Booth about the president's theatre party had unknowingly activated in his mind an imaginary clock that, even as he sat on the front step of Ford's, chuckling aloud as he read his letter, began ticking down, minute by minute. He would have a busy afternoon.

AT THE EXECUTIVE MANSION, ABRAHAM LINCOLN ATE breakfast with his family and planned his day. The president's eldest son, Robert, a junior officer on General Grant's staff, was home from the war. Robert had been at Appomattox, and his father was eager to hear details of Lee's surrender. Lincoln had scheduled a meeting with Grant at 9:00 A.M. at the White House. He wanted to talk more with Robert, so he postponed the meeting and sent a messenger over to the Willard Hotel with a handwritten note for his special guest: "General Grant, Please call at 11. A.M. to-day instead of 9. as agreed last evening. Yours truly, A. Lincoln." The president decided that Grant should join the cabinet meeting set for that later hour.

At the cabinet meeting Lincoln was jubilant—everyone in attendance, Secretary of War Edwin M. Stanton, Secretary of the Navy Gideon Welles, and the secretaries of the Treasury, the Interior, and the Post Office and the attorney general—noticed Lincoln's good mood. Welles, a faithful diarist, preserved an account of the gathering. Lincoln expected more good news from other battle fronts.

"The President remarked that it would, he had no doubt, come soon, and come favorable, for he had last night the usual dream which he had preceding nearly every great and important event of the War. Generally the news has been favorable which succeeded this dream, and the dream itself was always the same. I inquired what this remarkable dream could be. He said it related to your (my) element, the water; that he seemed to be in some singular, indescribable vessel, and that was moving with great rapidity towards an indefinite shore. That he had this dream preceding Sumter, Bull Run, Antietam, Gettysburg, Stone River, Vicksburg, Wilmington, etc."

General Grant interrupted Lincoln and joked that Stone River was no victory, and that "a few such fights would have ruined us."

"I had," the president continued, "this strange dream again last night, and we shall, judging from the past, have great news very soon. I think it must be from Sherman. My thoughts are in that direction, as are most of yours."

Lincoln had always believed in, and sometimes feared, the power of dreams. On June 9, 1863, while he was visiting Philadelphia, he sent an urgent telegram to Mary Lincoln at the White House, warning of danger to their youngest son: "Think you better put 'Tad's' pistol away. I had an ugly dream about him." And in April 1848, when he was a congressman in Washington, he wrote to Mary about their oldest son, Robert: "I did not get rid of the impression of that foolish dream about dear Bobby till I got your letter."

After the meeting adjourned, the president followed his usual routine: receiving a variety of friends, supplicants, and favor seekers; reading his mail; and catching up on correspondence and paperwork. He was eager to wind up business by 3:00 P.M. for an appointment he had with his wife, Mary. There was something he wanted to tell her.

At THE THEATRE, HENRY CLAY FORD WROTE OUT AN ADVERtisement to place in the evening papers, which would start coming off the press at around 2:00 P.M. He delivered the notice to the *Evening Star* personally and sent another via messenger to at least two of the other papers. That afternoon an advertisement appeared in the *Evening Star:* "LIEUT. GENERAL GRANT, PRESIDENT and Mrs. Lincoln have secured the State Box at Ford's Theatre TO NIGHT, to witness Miss Laura Keene's American Cousin." Around 1:00 P.M., Ford walked next door and delivered notice in person to his neighbor James P. Ferguson at his restaurant at 452 Tenth Street, one door north of the theatre.

"Your favorite, General Grant, is going to be in the theatre tonight; and if you want to see him," Ford cautioned, "you had better to go get a seat."

Ferguson took advantage of the tip: "I went and secured a seat directly opposite the President's box, in the front of the dress circle." Ferguson booked seats 58 and 59 at the front corner of the house near stage right. The restaurateur didn't want the best view of the play, but the best view of Lincoln and Grant.

James Ford walked to the Treasury Department a few blocks away to borrow several flags to decorate the president's box. Returning to the theatre, his arms wrapped around a bundle of brightly colored cotton and silk bunting, he bumped into Booth, who had just left Ford's, at the corner of Tenth and Pennsylvania, where they exchanged pleasantries. Booth saw the red, white, and blue flags, confirmation of the president's visit tonight.

A few blocks away, on D Street near Seventh, at J. H. Polkinhorn and Son, Printers, pressmen began setting the type for the playbill that would advertise tonight's performance. Once newsboys hit the streets with the afternoon and evening papers, the ad for *Our American Cousin* caught the eye of many Washingtonians eager to see General Grant.

Dr. Charles A. Leale, a twenty-three-year-old U.S. Army surgeon on duty at the wounded commissioned officers' ward at the Armory Square Hospital in Washington, heard that President Lincoln and General Grant would be attending the play. He decided to attend. Three days prior, on the night of April 11, Leale, while taking a walk on Pennsylvania Avenue, encountered crowds of people walking toward the White House. He followed them there and arrived just as Lincoln commenced his remarks. Leale was moved: "I could distinctly hear every word he uttered, and I was profoundly impressed with his divine appearance as he stood in the rays of light which penetrated the windows." The news that Lincoln was coming to Ford's Theatre gave the surgeon "an intense desire again to behold his face and study the characteristics of the 'Savior of his Country.'"

Lincoln's box at Ford's was festooned with flags and a framed engraving of George Washington. The box office manager prepared for a run on tickets when he went on duty at 6:30 P.M.

Later, witnesses remembered seeing Booth at several places in the city that day, but none of his movements created suspicion. Why should they? Nothing Booth did seemed out of the ordinary that afternoon. He talked to people in the street. He arranged to pick up his rented horse. Between 2:00 and 4:00 P.M., Booth rode up to Ferguson's restaurant, stopping just below the front door. Ferguson stepped outside onto his front porch and found his friend sitting on a small, bay mare. James L. Maddox, property man at Ford's, stood beside the horse, one hand on its mane, talking to Booth. "See what a nice horse I have got!" boasted the actor. Ferguson stepped forward for a closer look. "Now, watch," said Booth, "he can run just like a cat!" At that, Ferguson observed, Booth "struck his spurs into the horse, and off he went down the street."

At about 4:00 P.M., Booth returned to the National Hotel, walked to the front desk, and spoke to clerks George W. Bunker and Henry Merrick. Three days later a *New York Tribune* reporter described the encounter:

> [He] made his appearance at the counter…and with a nervous air called for a sheet of paper and an envelope. He was about to write when the thought seemed to strike him that someone around him might overlook his letter, and, approaching the door of the office, he requested admittance. On reaching the inside of the office, he immediately commenced his letter. He had written but a few words when he

said earnestly, "Merrick, is the year 1864 or '65?" "You are surely joking, John," replied Mr. Merrick, "you certainly know what year it is." "Sincerely, I am not," he rejoined, and on being told, resumed writing. It was then that Mr. Merrick noticed something troubled and agitated in Booth's appearance, which was entirely at variance with his usual quiet deportment. Sealing the letter, he placed it in his pocket and left the hotel.

On his way out of the National, Booth asked George Bunker if he was planning on seeing *Our American Cousin* at Ford's, and urged Bunker to attend: "There is going to be some splendid acting tonight."

Around 4:00 P.M., the actor John Matthews, who would be playing the part of Mr. Coyle in tonight's performance, met Booth on horseback on Pennsylvania Avenue, at the triangular enclosure between Thirteenth and Fourteenth streets, not far from the Willard Hotel. "We met," recalled Matthews, "shook hands, and passed the compliments of the day." A column of Confederate prisoners of war had just marched past, stirring up a dust cloud in their wake.

"John, have you seen the prisoners?" Matthews asked. "Have you seen Lee's officers, just brought in?"

"Yes, Johnny, I have." Booth raised one hand to his forehead in disbelief and then exclaimed, "Great God, I have no longer a country!"

Matthews, observing Booth's "paleness, nervousness, and agitation," asked, "John, how nervous you are, what is the matter?"

"Oh no, it is nothing. Johnny, I have a little favor to ask of you, will you grant it?"

"Why certainly," Matthews replied. "What is it?"

"Perhaps I may have to leave town tonight, and I have a letter here which I desire to be published in the *National Intelligencer;* please attend to it for me, unless I see you before ten o'clock tomorrow; in that case I will see to it myself." Matthews accepted the sealed envelope and slipped it into a coat pocket.

As Booth and Matthews talked, Matthews spotted General Grant riding past them in an open carriage with his baggage. He appeared to be leaving town.

"There goes Grant. I thought he was to be coming to the theatre this evening with the President."

"Where?" Booth exclaimed.

Matthews recalled: "I pointed to the carriage; he looked toward it, grasped my hand tightly, and galloped down the avenue after the carriage."

When Booth caught up to the Grants and rode past their carriage, Julia Grant thought of something that had happened earlier in the day. She was at lunch at the Willard Hotel with General Rawlins—one of Grant's top aides—Mrs. Rawlins, and the Rawlinses' daughter, when four men entered the dining room and occupied a nearby table. One of the men would not stop staring at her, and Julia and Mrs. Rawlins both found the whole group "peculiar." Now, a few hours later, Booth reminded her of the unpleasant incident when he caught up to their carriage. "As General Grant and I rode to the depot, this same dark, pale man rode past us at a sweeping gallop on a dark horse.... He rode twenty yards ahead of us, wheeled and returned, and as he passed us both going and returning, he thrust his face quite near the General's and glared in a disagreeable manner." She was sure that it was the same man from Willard's.

The sight of the Grants must have disappointed Booth. Their carriage, loaded with baggage, was heading toward the train station. They were leaving town. They must have canceled their engagement at Ford's Theatre. If General Grant was not attending *Our American Cousin* tonight, did that mean the Lincolns had canceled, too? Curtain call, approximately 8:30 P.M., was in less than five hours, and John Wilkes Booth did not know whether the Lincolns still planned to attend the play or who might be in the box with them.

Booth rode over to the Kirkwood House, where he accomplished his strangest errand of the day. The Kirkwood was the residence of the new vice president, Andrew Johnson, former military governor of Tennessee. Johnson did not own a house in Washington, and the job did not include official quarters, so he lodged at a hotel. Johnson's room was unguarded, and, if Booth had wanted to, he could have walked upstairs and knocked on the door. But he did not want to see the vice president. He just wanted to leave him a note. Booth approached the front desk and requested a small, blank calling card. He wrote a brief note and handed it to the desk clerk, who placed it in Johnson's mail slot. The mysterious message, which soon became the object of intense speculation, read: "Don't wish to disturb you. Are you at home? J. Wilkes Booth."

He visited a boardinghouse at 541 H Street, a few blocks from Ford's Theatre, to pay what looked like an innocent social call on the proprietor, Mary E. Surratt, a forty-two-year-old Maryland widow and the mother of his friend John Harrison Surratt Jr., a Confederate courier. Over the last several months, Booth had become a frequent caller at Mrs. Surratt's town house. Her son John wasn't home—he was out of the city on rebel business—and would not be back tonight. Mary told Booth that she was riding out that afternoon to her country tavern in Surrattsville, Maryland, several miles south of Washington, and Booth asked if she would mind delivering a small package wrapped in newspaper to her destination. Conveniently, Booth had the package with him.

There was one more thing. Booth informed Mary that he would be riding out of Washington this evening. Sometime that night, he said, he would stop at her tavern to pick up not only this package, but also the guns, ammunition, and other supplies that her son John had secreted there for him. Booth asked Mary to tell the tavern keeper John Lloyd—a heavy-drinking former Washington policeman to whom she had rented her country place—to get everything ready for the actor's visit this evening. She agreed, and soon she and one of her boarders, Louis Weichmann, an old school chum of John Surratt's, drove down to Surrattsville by carriage.

Booth returned to Ford's Theatre around 5:00 or 6:00 P.M., where Edman "Ned" Spangler, a scene shifter and stagehand—"stage carpenter," he called himself—saw the actor come up behind the theatre through Baptist Alley, named for the church that once occupied the site. Spangler had known Booth and his family for about a dozen years and had done odd jobs for them, most recently helping the actor outfit a small, private stable in the alley behind Ford's, about fifty yards from the back door. Spangler had seen Booth use a variety of horses: tonight he rode what Ned described as "a little bay mare." Booth and Spangler walked to the stable, where the actor removed the saddle and the yellow-trimmed saddlecloth. He didn't like the look of the cloth, he told Ned, and said he might use his shawl instead. Booth asked Ned not to remove the mare's bridle. "She is a bad little bitch," Booth said, and she should remain bridled. Booth locked the stable door, took the key, and went for a drink.

At some point, most likely by late afternoon or early evening, Booth must have secluded himself, probably in room 228 at the National, and made his final preparations. There were two elements, practical and psychological. First, the weapons. Booth chose as his primary weapon a .44-caliber, single-shot, muzzle-loading percussion cap pistol manufactured by Henry Deringer of Philadelphia. It was a small, short-barreled, pocket-size handgun designed for stealth and concealment, not combat, and favored by gamblers and other unsavory types. Unlike military pistols such as the .44-caliber Colt or Remington Army revolvers, or the lighter-weight .36-caliber Colt Navy revolver, all of which could fire up to six rounds before reloading, the Deringer could be fired just once. Reloading was a laborious process that called for two hands and twenty to forty seconds. Booth knew that his first shot would be his last. If he missed, he wouldn't have time to reload. Because the Deringer fired a round ball and not a rifled conical bullet, it was most effective at short range. Its big .44-caliber ball, weighing in at nearly an ounce, was a solid, deadly round.

If Booth missed, or failed to inflict a fatal wound with the pistol, he would turn to his secondary, backup weapon, a "Rio Grande Camp Knife," a handsome and extremely sharp type of Bowie knife. Booth left behind no explanation for why he chose the Deringer over a revolver. Pistols misfire occasionally. Either the copper percussion cap might fail to spark, or the black powder in the barrel might be spoiled from dampness and fail to ignite. Three decades earlier, on January 30, 1835, Richard Lawrence, a crazed, unemployed British house painter who fancied himself of royal blood, failed to assassinate Andrew Jackson on the East Front of the U.S. Capitol when not one, but both, of his single-shot, black powder, percussion cap pistols misfired. And even if Booth's pistol worked, how certain was he that he could kill Lincoln with one shot? Plenty of veteran combat soldiers who had survived multiple gunshot wounds were getting drunk in the saloons of Washington that night. Booth couldn't have chosen the Deringer because he could not obtain a revolver. He had already purchased at least four, and if he did not have any in his hotel room within easy reach, he could have gone out and bought another one. In the war capital of the Union, thousands of guns, including small, lightweight pocket-sized revolvers, were for sale in the shops of Washington.

Booth was a thrill seeker, and perhaps he wanted to enhance his excitement by risking the use of a single-shot pistol. Or did he believe it more heroic, honorable—even gentlemanly—to take his prey with a single bullet? Perhaps he preferred a stylish coup de grâce to blazing away at Lincoln with a six-shooter.

Given Washington's damp spring air and Booth's knowledge that he would have just one shot, he probably did not arm the pistol with a fresh copper cap and black powder charge until late in the afternoon. Better to be sure than rely on a stale load that might have been languishing in the barrel for weeks. Before wrapping the bullet with a small swatch of cloth wadding and ramming the round down the barrel, did he roll the ball between his fingertips, scrutinizing it for flaws in the casting and perhaps contemplating how this little round, dull gray one-ounce piece of metal would soon change history?

Before leaving the National, Booth slid the knife and pistol into his pockets and gathered the rest of his belongings. He planned to travel light tonight, without baggage. In addition to the weapons and his garments—a black felt slouch hat, black wool frock coat, black pants, big, knee-high black leather riding boots with spurs—he took only a velvet-cased compass, keys, a whistle, a datebook, a pencil, some money, a bank draft or bill of exchange, a small switchblade, and a few other small items including carte-de-visite photographs of five of his favorite girl-friends. His valise and big traveling trunk would have to stay behind; he would not be coming back. About 7:00 P.M., room clerk George Bunker saw Booth leave the National for the last time that day:

"He spoke to me and went off."

𝒲HEN MARY SURRATT AND LOUIS WEICHMANN ARRIVED IN Surrattsville, John Lloyd wasn't there. He had gone to pick up some foodstuffs. Mary waited for him. She could not leave without delivering Booth's message. When Lloyd returned he parked his wagon near the wood yard, climbed down, and began unloading his cargo of fish and oysters. Mary walked over to him.

"Talk about the devil, and his imps will appear," she teased her tenant.

"I was not aware that I was a devil before."

"Well, Mr. Lloyd," Mary went on once she was sure that she was out of Weichmann's earshot, "I want you to have those shooting-irons ready; there will be parties here to-night who will call for them."

She handed him the package wrapped in newspaper. The evening callers will want this too, she explained. And, she added, give them a couple bottles of whiskey. Her mission accomplished, Mary prepared to drive back to Washington. But the front spring bolts of her buggy had broken, and the spring had become detached from the axle. Lloyd tied them tightly with cord—the best he could do without proper spare parts. After Mrs. Surratt departed, Lloyd followed her instructions. He carried the package upstairs, unwrapped it, and discovered Booth's field glasses. Then he went to the unfinished room where, several weeks ago, John Surratt had shown him how to conceal two Spencer carbines under the joists. Lloyd retrieved them and placed them in his bedchamber. He had been drinking, and he was tired. Indeed, he confessed, "I was right smart in liquer that afternoon, and after night I got more so. I went to bed between 8 and 9 o'clock, and slept very soundly until 12 o'clock."

AT THE HERNDON HOUSE AT THE SOUTHWEST CORNER OF Ninth and F streets, around the corner from Ford's, at around 8:00 P.M. Booth presided over a conclave of some of the coconspirators he had assembled over the previous months to strike against President Lincoln. He must have hoped that this would be their last meeting before a great success. They had failed at least once before and then dispersed amid suspicion and fear. Tonight they needed to get ready for action in less than two hours. It was not the first time they had assembled to move against the president. Beginning in 1864, the last full year of the Civil War, the young stage star had marshaled his cash, celebrity, and connections in service of a bold plan. He hatched a harebrained scheme to kidnap President Lincoln, spirit him to Richmond, hold him as a hostage for the Confederacy, and turn the tide of the war. The origins of the plot remain murky. From the time of Lincoln's election in 1860, there arose several conspiracies to kidnap or murder him. Secessionist hotheads began posting numerous death threats to Springfield before Lincoln took office on March 4, 1861, and some even sent him jars of poisoned fruit. In the notorious Baltimore plot of 1861, local rebels schemed to assassinate the president-elect when his railroad train passed through the city en route to Washington for his inauguration. But Detective Allan Pinkerton thwarted the scheme by persuading Lincoln to pass through Baltimore incognito hours ahead of schedule. Other Lincoln haters threatened to assassinate him on the East Front of the Capitol the moment he commenced reading his inaugural address. During the war, several Southern military officers, as well as a handful of officials in the Confederate Secret Service, considered various actions against Lincoln. At some point, John Wilkes Booth came into contact with these circles and operatives, in Canada, New York City, Washington, D.C., Maryland, and Virginia.

In late 1864 and early 1865 Booth organized his own little band of conspirators, loyal to him and not Richmond, to plot against the president. He recruited a gang who, after he clothed and fed them, plied them with drink, and allowed them to bask in his fame and favor, would, he hoped, follow him anywhere—even into a plot to kidnap the president of the United States. But big talk was cheap in wartime Washington and as late as January 1865, with the Confederacy in danger of imminent collapse, not one of the several overlapping conspiracies had ever attempted decisive action against Abraham Lincoln.

Booth and his gang of acolytes—Lewis Powell, David Herold, John H. Surratt Jr., Samuel Arnold, Michael O'Laughlen, and George Atzerodt, plus others lost to history who drifted in and out of his orbit— would change that by kidnapping the president.

O'Laughlen, born in 1834, had known Booth since 1845, when their families lived across the street from each other in Baltimore. In 1861, the first year of the war, Michael enlisted in the First Maryland Infantry, but soon illness ended his military service. Restless, and looking for excitement, he signed on to the plot. Samuel Arnold, who was thirty-one, met Booth in 1848 when they were students at St. Timothy's Hall, a boys' school near Baltimore. He joined the First Maryland too in April 1861, but after the first battle of Bull Run in July 1861 he was, like O'Laughlen, discharged. Arnold's family operated a prominent Baltimore bakery at the corner of Fayette and Liberty streets. In August 1864, Booth wrote to Sam, suggesting they meet. They hadn't seen each other since 1852, thirteen years ago. Arnold visited Booth's room at Barnum's Hotel in Baltimore, where the actor offered him cigars and wine, and introduced him to O'Laughlen. Arnold joined the conspiracy. But

Booth needed to recruit more men than these two boyhood chums, who possessed scant military experience. An introduction to John Harrison Surratt Jr., a wily, twenty-year-old courier for the Confederate Secret Service who lived in Washington at his mother's boardinghouse, gave Booth the men he needed. Surratt had traveled the rebel underground's secret routes to the South, essential knowledge if they were going to transport Lincoln across Union lines. Surratt brought George Atzerodt into the plot. George, a hard-drinking, twenty-nine-year-old Prussian immigrant who worked as a carriage painter in Port Tobacco, Maryland, knew boats and the waters of Charles County. David Herold, a twenty-two-year-old pharmacist's assistant who lived with his mother near the Washington Navy Yard, joined the conspiracy. He was an avid hunter and outdoorsman who knew the country through which they would have to carry the president. Lewis Powell, twenty-one-year-old son of a Baptist minister, enlisted in May 1861 as a private in the Second Florida Infantry. An attractive, well-muscled six-footer, Powell exemplified the best that the Confederate army could muster. A loyal, obedient, and hard-fighting soldier, he saw plenty of action until he was wounded and taken prisoner at Gettysburg in July 1863. Paroled, he made his way to Baltimore and fell into the orbit of Surratt and Booth. Powell had the size and strength necessary to physically subdue Abraham Lincoln.

On March 17, 1865, Booth and his coconspirators planned to, like eighteenth-century British highwaymen, ambush Lincoln's carriage on a deserted road as he rode back to the Executive Mansion after attending a performance of the play *Still Waters Run Deep* at Campbell Military Hospital. They would seize the president at gunpoint and make him their hostage. Booth's intelligence sources proved faulty, however, and Lincoln did not attend. Instead, unbelievably, while Booth and his gang lurked on the Seventh Street road on the outskirts of the city, several miles from downtown Washington, Lincoln was giving a speech at Booth's own hotel, the National. What a chance that would have presented, the actor mourned. If only the kidnapping plot had worked.

Then there would be no torchlight parades, thunderous cannonades, mobs serenading Lincoln at the Executive Mansion, citywide illuminations, or children scampering through the streets holding colorful little paper flags decorated with red, white, and blue stars and stripes and elephants and imprinted with slogans like "Richmond Has Fallen" and "We Celebrate the Fall of Richmond." He could—should—have prevented all of this, he admonished himself.

Although his panicked followers scattered after that ludicrous failure, Booth hoped to try again, but events overtook him just eighteen days later when Richmond fell, and six days after that when Lee surrendered. Dejected, Booth remonstrated himself for not acting more boldly, even fantasizing aloud that he should have shot the president at the Capitol on inauguration day, March 4, 1865, an event he attended with his fiancée, Lucy Hale, daughter of U.S. Senator John Parker Hale. "What an excellent chance I had, if I wished, to kill the President on Inauguration day!" he boasted later to a friend.

Lincoln's April 11 speech provoked more violent talk. The president's proposal for a limited black suffrage had enraged the actor, a passionate devotee of white supremacy. But Booth did nothing. If he was serious about assassinating Lincoln, all he had to do was stroll over to the Executive Mansion, announce that the famous and talented thespian John Wilkes Booth wished to see the president, await his turn—which nearly always resulted in a private talk with Lincoln—and then shoot him at his desk. Incredibly, presidential security was lax in that era, even during the Civil War, and almost anyone could walk into the Executive Mansion without being searched and request a brief audience with the president. It was a miracle that no one had yet tried to murder Lincoln in his own office.

There can be no doubt that Booth had been fantasizing about killing Abraham Lincoln. But was he serious, or was it merely extravagant but harmless bravado? Booth had never killed a man. Was he capable of doing it? On April 13, on the afternoon of illumination day, Booth took what might have been his first step toward answering that question. He visited Grover's Theatre, along with Ford's one of the two most popular establishments in the city. He asked the manager, C. Dwight Hess, if he had invited the president to attend a performance of *Aladdin!*, the current production. No, he had forgotten, Hess replied, but he would attend to it now. Lincoln did not come to Grover's. That night, Booth, as he had on countless previous nights, drank away the blues, watched the illumination, and before collapsing in his bed, wrote his mother a letter.

Booth's gang was not at full strength on April 14. Rebel courier John Surratt was in Elmira, New York, and it was impossible to command his return on a few hours' notice. Surratt had been away since March 25, the day he left for Richmond. The Confederacy's days were numbered, but Secretary of State Judah Benjamin had a final mission for the courier: Go North once more, pass undetected through Union territory, cross the border into Canada, and deliver dispatches to General Edwin Gray Lee, a cousin of Robert E. Lee, and head of Confederate Secret Service operations in Montreal. Surratt left Richmond on March 31 and on April 6 checked in at St. Lawrence Hall, unofficial headquarters of the South's covert operations there. Lee gave Surratt another mission: Go to New York to spy on the Union's prisoner-of-war camp at Elmira, in preparation for a raid to break out the Confederate soldiers languishing there. Surratt arrived in Elmira on April 13 and devoted the next two days to spying and shopping. He drew detailed sketches of the prison, counted the guards, tallied their small arms and cannon, and estimated the number of prisoners. He also made time for a personal mission. Surratt, a fastidious dresser—although not in the same league as Booth—visited clothiers in search of suits and shirts. On April 14, while Booth was planning the assassination, Surratt's most pressing concern was finding some fresh, white shirts to spruce up his wardrobe.

Booth's boyhood chums, Samuel Arnold and Michael O'Laughlen, were not on hand to help with the assassination either. Arnold was back home in Baltimore. O'Laughlen was somewhere in Washington but not under Booth's command. O'Laughlen had taken in the illumination

with friends and then gone on a drinking spree. Later, evidence suggested that he might have met secretly with Booth in the actor's hotel
room sometime on the thirteenth or fourteenth.

Present at the Herndon House were Lewis Powell, David Herold,
and George Atzerodt. Booth had put Powell up at the Herndon, and he
sent Herold over to the Kirkwood House, Atzerodt's hotel, to summon
him to the meeting. Before returning to the Herndon, Herold went up
to Atzerodt's room and placed a revolver, knife, and a coat there. Then
both men rendezvoused with Booth and Powell. Booth spoke in a con-
fidential tone barely above a whisper. No one in the halls or in an adjoining room must overhear what he was about to say. The cause was
almost lost, stated Booth. Capturing the president would no longer be
enough to turn the tide of the war. It would take something bolder,
something so daring and shocking that he had never even thought of it
before. They would target not only President Lincoln, but also Vice
President Andrew Johnson and Secretary of State William H. Seward.
The secretary of state was not, after the vice president, next in line for
the presidency. But Seward, a longtime abolitionist, was viewed as a
forceful advocate of Lincoln's policies, including the suppression of dis-
sent, the suspension of the writ of habeas corpus, and the imprisonment without trial of several thousand citizens suspected of disloyalty.
Booth had had his eye on General Grant, too, but unfortunately Grant
broke his engagement with the president. Booth probably told his gang
that he had spotted the Grants in their carriage earlier that afternoon,
heading toward the train station. Perhaps it was for the best. The commanding general might have been accompanied by an entourage of
staff officers, messengers, and other factotums. No, Booth explained,
they would not kidnap Lincoln, Johnson, and Seward. How could a
skeleton crew of only four conspirators possibly kidnap three men in
different parts of the city?

But Booth did have just enough men to accomplish another mission. "Booth proposed," Atzerodt recalled, "that we should kill the president." It would, said Booth, "be the greatest thing in the world." Tonight,

at exactly 10:00 P.M., they would strike simultaneously and murder Lincoln, Johnson, and Seward. Armed with a revolver and a knife, George Atzerodt's assignment was to assassinate the vice president in his residence at the Kirkwood House. "You must kill Johnson," Booth told him. Powell, also armed with a revolver and a knife, would murder the secretary of state in his bed at his mansion. David Herold would accompany Powell, direct him to Seward's home, and then guide the assassin, unfamiliar with the capital's streets, out of the city. Booth claimed the greatest prize for himself. He would slip into Ford's Theatre and assassinate the president in the middle of the play. Powell and Herold, Booth's two most loyal servants, agreed to the plan. Atzerodt noticed that Powell "had a wild look in his eyes." Atzerodt balked at his assignment. He would not do it, he said. "Then we will do it," Booth said, "but what will become of you?" Kidnapping was one thing, but murder? Booth threatened him, implying that he might as well do it because if he didn't, Booth would implicate him anyway and get him hanged. The actor promised him "if I did not I would suffer for it," and said he would blow Atzerodt's brains out. The German did not know it, but Booth had implicated all of them several hours ago when he entrusted that sealed envelope to John Matthews. In his letter to the *National Intelligencer,* not only did Booth justify the triple assassination, he signed his coconspirators' names to the document:

> For a long time I have devoted my energies, my time and money, to the accomplishment of a certain end. I have been disappointed. The moment has arrived when I must change my plans. Many will blame me for what I am about to do, but posterity, I am sure, will justify me. Men who love their country better than gold and life.
>
> John W. Booth, Payne, Herold, Atzerodt.

Atzerodt's reluctance jeopardized the entire enterprise. If he left that meeting and went to the authorities, Booth, Powell, and Herold would be finished. Guards would rush to protect those marked for death, and the conspirators would be hunted down. "You had better come along and get your horse," Booth suggested. Booth adjourned the meeting.

AT THE EXECUTIVE MANSION, THE LINCOLNS WERE BEHIND schedule. It was past 8:00 P.M. and they still had not gotten into their carriage. As the curtain rose at Ford's, coachman Francis Burke and valet Charles Forbes were waiting atop the carriage box. The Lincolns' private, afternoon carriage ride and absence from the mansion had frustrated several politicians who wanted to see the president, and they would not be denied.

Earlier that afternoon, Lincoln was happy to be free of them and all the burdens of his office. It was one of the happiest days of his life. At breakfast his eldest son, Robert, regaled his parents with his personal observations of Lee's surrender. For once, the cabinet meeting was free of crises, battle news, casualty figures, and innumerable problems requiring the president's immediate attention. Victory had elated him, and ever since Lee's surrender Lincoln had been more buoyant than at any other time during his presidency. He expected more good news from General Sherman about the expected surrender of Confederate General Joe Johnston's army.

But first he wanted to ride with Mary. He had made the appointment two days ago when he sent her a note, "written from his office...a few lines, playfully and tenderly worded, notifying, the hour, of the day, *he* would drive with me!" The war had increased their estrangement. Official Washington, under a heavy Southern influence, had snubbed her as a gatecrasher and a western parvenu from the start, despite her aristocratic Kentucky slaveholding origins. She had been emotionally distraught since the death of their favorite son, eleven-year-old William Wallace Lincoln—"Willie"—in February 1862, and she had fallen under the spell of mediums and spiritualists at White House séances. The president, who scorned her infatuation with the spirit world, once attended one of her supernatural events. It was enough to entice a music publisher to issue a sheet-music parody, "The Dark Séance Polka," the cover art depicting a wild Executive Mansion séance with objects flying through the air. Mary was at heart a kind woman, but her critics preferred to criticize her personal eccentricities—her expensive shopping habits both for the White House and for herself, and her raging, jealous temper—rather than to praise her good works for soldiers or her absolute loyalty to husband, liberty, and Union. And the demands of the war had been so great that the president spent less and less time with her.

Lincoln knew he had to change that now. He wanted to talk to Mary about their future. He escorted her to the open carriage, and before the coachman drove on she asked him if anyone should accompany them on their ride.

"No," he replied, "I prefer to ride by ourselves today."

Lincoln's joy was irrepressible. Mary Lincoln had noticed it on their recent river cruise: "Down the Potomac, he was almost boyish, in his mirth and reminded me, of his original nature, what I have always remembered of him, in our own home—free from care, surrounded by those he loved so well and *by whom,* he was so idolized."

Now, during their afternoon carriage ride, Mary spoke to him about his happy mood.

"Dear husband, you almost startle me by your great cheerfulness."

"And well I may feel so, Mary," the president replied. "I consider *this* day, the war has come to a close."

"We must *both,* be more cheerful in the future—between the war and the loss of our darling Willie—we have both, been very miserable."

During their leisurely ride, which took them, among other places, down to the Navy Yard near Capitol Hill, where they inspected an ironclad naval vessel, the monitor *Montauk,* the president told his wife that they must try to be happy again. That he would like to see the Pacific Ocean. That perhaps at the end of his second term in office, they would move to Chicago and he would practice his trade again. Freed from the vexations of war and death—he would send no more armies of young men to die—Lincoln dreamed of the future. Yes, they would be happy again. Later, Mary remembered that on *"The Friday,* I never saw him so supremely cheerful—his manner was even playful."

At Lafayette Park near the White House, Major Henry Rathbone and his fiancée, Clara Harris, awaited their hosts at the residence of Senator Harris, at Fifteenth and H streets. The Lincolns had promised to pick them up on the way to the theatre, but they were almost twenty minutes late. The major and Miss Harris hoped that the president had not forgotten them. Then, about 8:20 P.M., the carriage appeared. The popular young couple, although known to the Lincolns, was not their first choice. After the Grants changed their plans, the Lincolns invited several people to join them, but all declined. Finally they settled on Rathbone and Harris who, ignorant of how many others had declined before them, were delighted to accept. There was happy talk during the ten-minute ride to the theatre, Miss Harris remembered, reflecting the spirit of a week of joy and celebration: "They drove to our door in the gayest spirits; chatting on our way." At Ford's the management decided not to hold the curtain for the presidential party, and the play began without them.

Dr. Charles Leale was behind schedule, too. "After the completion of my daily hospital duties, I told my ward master that I would be absent for a short time....I changed to civilian's dress and hurried to Ford's Theatre." Leale hoped there was still time to purchase a good seat. "I arrived late at the theatre, at 8.15 P.M., and requested a seat in the orchestra, whence I could view the occupants of the President's box....As the building was crowded, the last place vacant was in the dress circle. I was greatly disappointed, but accepted this seat, which was near the front on the same side and about forty feet from the President's box."

Finally the lookout at Ford's spotted the big black carriage turning down Tenth Street. It slowed to a halt beside the elevated wood platform in front of the theatre, constructed especially to assist carriage riders in getting out of their vehicles and avoiding the muddy street. The Lincolns, Rathbone, and Harris disembarked, and the chief usher escorted them through the lobby, up the winding staircase, and across the dress circle—the first balcony—to their box. Abraham Lincoln's entry to Ford's Theatre at 8:30 P.M. on April 14, 1865, was majestic in its simplicity. He arrived with no entourage, no armed guards, and no announcement to the crowd.

Before the presidential party reached the box, the actors, musicians, and patrons became aware that the Lincolns had arrived. The audience shouted and cheered. The actors onstage stopped performing. Orchestra conductor William Withers was looking forward to leading his players in a special patriotic song, "Honor to Our Soldiers," that he had composed just for the occasion. That would come later. Now, he led his orchestra in a stirring rendition of "Hail to the Chief." The audience went wild.

Charles Leale had arrived in time to witness it all: "Many in the audience rose to their feet in enthusiasm and vociferously cheered while looking around." Leale looked around, too, and saw Abraham Lincoln standing nearby. "Turning, I saw in the aisle a few feet behind me, President Lincoln, Mrs. Lincoln, Major Rathbone, and Miss Harris. Mrs. Lincoln smiled very happily in acknowledgment of the loyal greeting, gracefully curtsied several times, and seemed to be overflowing with good cheer and thankfulness." But it was the president who Leale desired to behold. "I had the best opportunity to see distinctly the full face of the President, as the light shone directly upon him. After he had walked a few feet he stopped for a moment, looked upon the people he loved, and acknowledged their salutations with a solemn bow."

At the supreme moment of victory they cheered their Father Abraham, the man who, after a shaky start in office, learned how to command armies, grew in vision and eloquence, brought down slavery, and who, just six weeks ago, had given the most graceful and emotionally stunning inaugural address in the history of the American presidency. And as he promised he would, he had saved the Union. Lincoln stood in the box and bowed to the audience.

The spontaneous homage, the band, the hissing gaslights, the packed house, the fresh, moist scent of spring in the air, the recent and joyous news from the front—all combined to create a singular and magical moment. "The President," remembered Clara Harris, "was received with the greatest enthusiasm."

James Ferguson was not so impressed. He had seen Lincoln before. Where was the man who Harry Ford had promised would be there, the one whom he had come to see? "I supposed that probably Grant had remained outside, so as not to create any excitement in the theatre, and would come in alone, and come in the box." Ferguson was so determined to see the general that, for the next hour and a half, he would spend as much time staring at the president's box as he would watching the stage. "I made up my mind that I would see him...and I watched everyone that passed around on that side of the dress circle towards the box." No one, he promised himself, was going to enter that box unobserved.

Chapter Two

"I Have Done It"

---◆❧❧◆---

LEGEND HAS IT THAT JOHN WILKES BOOTH WAS HIDING OUT-side in the shadows near the front door of Ford's as the presidential carriage rocked down the uneven dirt street and slowed to a stop, but no one really knows where he was at that precise moment. On April 29, 1865, Clara Harris wrote in a letter, "They say we were watched by the assassins; ay, as we alighted from the carriage...and when I think of that fiend barring himself in with us, my blood runs cold." Wherever Booth was it is almost certain that somehow he verified with his own eyes that the Lincolns were actually inside the theatre. And he probably wondered at the identity of Lincoln's guests and gauged whether Major Rathbone looked like the type who could pose a threat to his plans. It didn't matter, really; no one was going to stop him from going through with it.

Next door at Peter Taltavul's bar, the Star Saloon, it was a night like any other when the lights were on at Ford's. Some playgoers downed a quick one before the show; others would come in during intermission to fortify themselves.

It was now about 9:00 P.M. Time for Booth to go inside the theatre for the first time since the Lincolns had arrived. Although the actor, like the Lincolns, entered Ford's after *Our American Cousin* started, he was still on schedule. The play was like a clock, every word spoken was another tick of the second hand. After hearing just one snippet of dialogue, Booth would know, to the minute, how much time had elapsed from curtain raising, and how much time remained in the performance. He knew that he had at least another hour. He left Ford's.

In a little while, he returned to his alley stable, where he and Spangler had left the bay mare. Booth unlocked the door, threw his shawl over the horse's back, and saddled her. He led his rented horse down Baptist Alley by the reins, up to the back door of Ford's. He would have tied the animal to a hitching post behind the theatre, but he remembered the stable man's warning that this horse did not like to be tied. She would pull at the post to break free. And anyway, what if he left the horse unattended and when he came back later discovered that someone had stolen her? Better to have someone hold the reins until he returned. He called through the open back door: "Ned. Ned Spangler!" There was no reply.

Inside Ford's, employee John Debonay tracked down Ned: "Booth is calling you." Spangler stepped into the alley.

"Hold this mare for ten or fifteen minutes," Booth instructed him.

"I have not time," Ned replied. The play was going on. He could not neglect his backstage duties and waste time holding a horse. He was needed at his post in the wings to shift scenery. He offered to summon another employee, John Burroughs, nicknamed "John Peanut" by his fellow staff members after the snack he sold to patrons.

Spangler sent for John Peanut. Booth gave Ned the reins, cautioning him that this horse would not stand tying and that she had to be held. Booth went into the theatre. When John Peanut came out he demurred, saying he was needed at the front of the theatre to make sure that people didn't sneak in without paying. After a minute or two of bickering, he gave in and accepted the reins from Spangler. Ned went back to work. Mary Jane Anderson, a black woman who lived in an alley house behind the theatre, watched Booth lead his horse up the alley, walk past her front door, and call Ned Spangler. Once Booth went inside Ford's, she couldn't see the horse anymore but could hear how restless it was. "It kept up a great deal of stamping on the stones, and I said 'I wonder what is the matter with that horse,' it kept stamping so." It was the second time Mrs. Anderson had seen Booth that day. In the afternoon, between 2:00 and 3:00 P.M., she watched him and a woman standing behind the theatre "for a considerable while," having a conversation. Mary Anderson could not take her eyes off the handsome star: "I stood in my gate, and I looked right wishful at him."

Booth, once inside Ford's, wanted to cross behind the stage all the way to the other side of the building, where a small door led to a narrow passageway that ran west to Tenth Street and the front of the theatre. Booth asked an employee if he could walk across the stage, hidden behind the scenery. That was impossible, he was told. The "dairy scene," a deep scene that required the full stage, was on, and there was no room to hide from the audience by creeping along behind the scenery. Instead, Booth would have to cross under the stage through a passageway and emerge on the other side.

Booth lifted the trapdoor and dropped below into darkness. Walking along the hard-packed dirt floor, he could hear the wooden planks of the stage creaking overhead, and the distant, muffled voices of the actors and laughter from the audience. He ascended the stairs at the end of the passageway, nudged open the trapdoor, and entered the passageway that ran lengthwise between Ford's and the Star Saloon next door. He walked the length of the building and emerged on Tenth. Anyone who saw him now would assume he had come down Tenth on foot to take in the play. No one in the theatre, save a few employees, knew he had a horse waiting out back. There was time for one last drink.

Booth walked into the Star Saloon at around 10:00 P.M. The cramped, narrow, dimly lit establishment catered to the actors, stagehands, and playgoers who frequented Ford's Theatre. Booth was alone. A regular, he nodded to owner Peter Taltavul and called for his pleasure: whiskey. The bartender poured him a glass and set the bottle on the counter within Booth's reach. Water, too, please, Booth reminded him: Taltavul had neglected to serve the customary companion beverage.

Booth's pale, delicate fingers squeezed the glass, raised it to his lips, and he downed the drink the way a more temperate, thirsty man might swallow the glass of water. Booth savored the warming spirits. It might be a while before he could enjoy another one. Any customers who recognized the handsomest, best-dressed man in Washington kept it to themselves and did not disturb the famous actor. Booth slapped a few coins on the bar and left without saying a word. He exited onto Tenth Street, turned to his right, walked a few paces, and saw the president's carriage still parked on the near side of Tenth several yards beyond the main door, the coachman and horse waiting to take Lincoln back home. Burke had gone for a drink after he dropped off the Lincolns and their guests, and then returned to the coach.

In the alley behind Ford's, Mary Anderson watched John Peanut walking Booth's impatient horse back and forth.

This was it. Booth tarried in the lobby, soaking in the atmosphere and listening to the dialogue. He was still on schedule. No need to rush. Walking to the lobby's north end, he ascended the curving staircase to the dress circle, following the same path the Lincolns took to their box. Booth paused at the head of the stairs to take advantage of the best view of the president's box, a vista that caused him to look slightly down, and diagonally across the width and length of the house. He walked slowly along the west wall. James Ferguson, still hoping to witness General Grant's arrival, looked up from his first-floor seat and saw, on the other side of the theatre, another man—not Grant—approaching the box. He recognized John Wilkes Booth: "Somewhere near ten o'clock…I saw Booth pass along near the box, and then stop, and lean against the wall. He stood there a moment."

Booth could see the door that opened to the vestibule that led directly into the president's box. What he saw—or more accurately what he did not see—surprised him. The door was unguarded. He expected to find an officer, a soldier, or at least a civilian policeman seated there. Instead, seated near but not blocking the door was Lincoln's valet, Charles Forbes, who had ridden to Ford's atop the coach beside the driver. Booth paused to speak to Forbes, showing him some kind of card or piece of paper. To this day no one knows what words they exchanged, or what document Booth displayed. Was it a letter? Or merely the actor's calling card? A card with Booth's name on it would open almost any door in Washington. Forbes did not attempt to stop him. Booth proceeded to the door, realizing that, unless a hidden guard was perched inside the small vestibule, no one was going to stop him. He seized the knob, turned it, and pushed open the door. James Ferguson looked up again and watched Booth enter the box: "I looked back and saw him step down one step, put his hands to the door, and his knee against it, and push the door open. I did not see any more of him." Yellow gaslight from the dress circle illuminated the dark vestibule. Booth peered inside. Empty. There was no guard. No one stood between him and the president of the United States.

Inside the box, the Lincolns were enjoying themselves, not because of the play but simply from being together, out of the White House, during their happiest week in Washington. At one point the president stood up to put on his coat—the cool night air had chilled him. Back in his rocking chair, perhaps thinking of their carriage ride that afternoon, Lincoln reached out and held Mary's hand. In mock embarrassment she chided her husband for his boldness: "What will Miss Harris think of my hanging on to you so?" Lincoln replied to the last words he would ever hear his wife speak: "She won't think anything about it," and he smiled affectionately at her. Booth closed the outer vestibule door behind him so quietly that the occupants of the box heard nothing. He had been prepared to cut his way in with the knife if necessary. Instead, he had strolled in unmolested, as though he had reserved the box this night, as he often had on prior occasions. Bending down, he felt along the edge of the carpet near the wall for the pine bar—part of a music stand—he had hidden there that afternoon. When no one was watching he had returned to Ford's that day, slipped unseen into the vestibule and box, and made his preparations. Hoping that no one had discovered it and tossed it into the trash as an odd piece of leftover lumber, he ran his fingers across the carpet. It was still there. He lifted the bar, first inserting one end into the awaiting mortise he had incised in the plaster wall and concealed behind a flap of wallpaper. He lowered the other end to nearly a parallel position, until it made contact with the door. He was careful not to hammer the bar into place by pounding it with the bottoms of two clenched fists. The noise might alert the theatre party sitting just a few yards away. Instead, he grasped the bar with both hands, using his weight to apply gradual, increasing downward pressure until the fit was tight. It took only a few seconds, just as he had planned. Now no one could follow him into the vestibule and prevent him from entering the president's box.

Booth turned to face the two paneled wood doors—one to his left and the other directly in front of him—that opened into boxes seven and eight, now combined into one box for the Lincolns.

The actor's black pupils flared wide, adjusting to the darkness, while also fixing on the only available light in the dim, claustrophobic chamber—a faint pinpoint emanating from the peephole that somebody, probably Booth, had bored through a right-hand panel of the door to box number seven. A cylindrical beam shone through from the illuminated box on the other side of the door, but it was so weak that it failed to span the narrow vestibule and put a small spot of light on the opposite wall. Instead the ray faltered in midair, diffused into the absorbing darkness.

Booth peeked through the dot of light on the door, giving himself a partial view of the interior of the box. He saw what he was looking for—a high-backed, upholstered rocking chair, just a few feet away on the other side of the door.

The seating arrangement in the box was perfect for an assassin. Lincoln sat at the far left, his rocker wedged nearly against the wall of the box. At this angle the president's left side faced the audience, his right the interior of the box, and, to his front, the stage below. Lincoln was close to the door through which Booth would spring. Mary Lincoln sat to the president's right, perched on a wood, caned-bottom chair. Next to her right was Clara Harris on another chair, and at the far right was Major Rathbone on a sofa. Booth could enter the box and move on Lincoln without having to get past the major.

Onstage, it was the beginning of act 3, scene 2. There were four scenes left before the end of the play. Mrs. Mountchessington and her daughter Augusta, a pair of English gold diggers, were conniving about how to marry off the girl to Asa Trenchard, a rich American bumpkin played by the celebrated comic actor Harry Hawk.

"*Yes, my child, while Mr. De Boots and Mr. Trenchard are both here, you must ask yourself seriously, as to the state of your affections. Remember, your happiness for life will depend on the choice you make.*"

"*What would you advise, Mamma? You know I am always advised by you.*"

"*Dear, obedient child. De Boots has excellent expectations, but they are only expectations after all. This American is rich, and on the whole I think a well regulated affection ought to incline to Asa Trenchard.*"

It was approximately 10:11 P.M. Booth plunged both hands into the deep, copious pockets of his black frock coat and withdrew his weapons. In his right hand was the .44-caliber single-shot Deringer pistol, in his left the shiny and sharp Rio Grande Camp Knife. He steadied himself. Harry Hawk entered the scene from stage left. No, not yet. Too many characters—Mrs. Mountchessington, Augusta, and Asa Trenchard—were still onstage. Booth listened keenly to the dialogue of the play for his cue, the actors' voices rising to the president's box and echoing through the doors and into the vestibule where he remained hidden. Booth heard Asa Trenchard confess to Mrs. Mountchessington that he is not rich.

"*Not heir to the fortune, Mr. Trenchard.*"

"*Oh, no.*"

After a few more lines, Harry Hawk would hold the stage alone and would speak a line guaranteed to produce such uproarious laughter that it would smother the sound of just about anything including, Booth hoped, the report of a pistol.

Booth's thumb pulled back the hammer of the Deringer until he heard it cock into firing position. His hand dropped to the porcelain doorknob.

"*Mr. Trenchard, you will please recollect you are addressing my daughter, and in my presence.*"

"*Yes, I'm offering her my heart and hand just as she wants them, with nothing in 'em.*"

"*Augusta, dear, to your room.*"

"*Yes, Ma, the nasty beast.*"

Now, Booth knew, only two actors remained onstage.

The tension was unbearable. The syllables being spoken onstage sounded no longer like words but like the last ticks of a dying clock winding down. It was 10:13 P.M.

"*I am aware, Mr. Trenchard, you are not used to the manners of good society, and that, alone, will excuse the impertinence of which you have been guilty.*" Mrs. Mountchessington exited in a huff.

Harry Hawk was alone onstage now.

Booth opened the door and stepped into the president's box. Hawk began reciting the last sentence Lincoln would ever hear, a corny broadside of comic insults that delighted the audience.

"*Don't know the manners of good society, eh? Wal, I guess I know enough to turn you inside out, old gal…*"

Lincoln was so near. If Booth desired, he could reach out and tap him on the shoulder with the Deringer's muzzle. No one in the box had seen or heard him enter. The Lincolns, Harris, and Rathbone all continued watching the action onstage. Booth began the performance he had rehearsed in his mind again and again since that afternoon. He stepped toward Lincoln who was stationary—not rolling back and forth on the rockers of his chair. Booth focused his eyes on the back of the president's head. He raised his right arm to shoulder height and extended it forward, aiming the pistol at Lincoln's head. He didn't even really have to aim—aiming suggests a marksman's skill—he was so close to the president now that all he had to do was point the Deringer.

The factory had not set the pistol with a hair trigger, so until Booth increased his finger pressure to a few pounds the Deringer would not fire. He squeezed harder.

"*...you sockdologizing old mantrap...*"

As the audience exploded in laughter, at that instant, at the last possible moment before the pistol discharged, Abraham Lincoln jerked his head away from Booth, low and to the left, as though trying to evade the shot. The black powder charge exploded and spit the bullet toward Lincoln's head. James Ferguson saw Lincoln move just before he saw the muzzle flash illuminate the box momentarily like a miniature lightning bolt. The president's movement and the shot were simultaneous. Had Booth missed?

If he had, the assassin was suddenly at great risk because he didn't have the twenty to forty seconds needed to reload—and, anyway, he hadn't even bothered to carry more gunpowder and bullets in his coat. Now he was trapped between Lincoln and Rathbone, armed with nothing but the knife. If Lincoln's peripheral vision had alerted him to the presence of an intruder creeping stealthily toward him, or if he had caught the blur of Booth's arm moving into firing position, the president might have ducked the shot, or at worst suffered a nonfatal grazing head, neck, or shoulder wound. If only that had happened, then Lincoln, even at fifty-six years old, would have been a formidable opponent. The idea of venerable Father Abraham fighting back against the gymnastic, leaping, and sword-fighting stage star is not as farfetched as it sounds.

It was widely held in 1865, and certainly today, that the toil of the Civil War had transformed Lincoln into a ruined old man. Lincoln's beard, his slow, ambling gait, and his careworn face, captured so movingly in the last photographs by Alexander Gardner in February 1865 and by Henry Warren in March 1865, gave credence to the myth of Father Abraham, the ancient, Moses-like figure leading his people. But there was another Abraham Lincoln that no one in Washington had ever seen: the vigorous, muscular Rail-splitter of the West. That image was more than a brilliant slogan from the presidential campaign of 1860. Lincoln had really been a rail-splitter, and a man hardened by years of brutal physical toil. With his creased apple doll-like head sitting atop a thin, six-foot-four-inch frame, President Lincoln might have looked old and weak. The wartime demands of the presidency had taken their toll, and Lincoln had lost twenty or thirty pounds during four years in office. But beneath that ever-present baggy frock coat and ill-fitting trousers, there remained a lean and formidable physique. Too soon doctors would discover and marvel at the age difference between his face and his body.

Had Booth missed, Lincoln could have risen from his chair to confront his assassin. At that moment the president, cornered, with not only his own life in danger but also Mary's, would almost certainly have fought back. If he did, Booth would have found himself outmatched facing not kindly Father Abraham, but the aroused fury of the Mississippi River flatboatman who fought off a gang of murderous river pirates in the dead of night, the champion wrestler who, years before, humbled the Clary's Grove boys in New Salem in a still legendary match, or even the fifty-six-year-old president who could still pick up a long, splitting-axe by his fingertips, raise it, extend his arm out parallel with the ground, and suspend the axe in midair. Lincoln could have choked the life out of the five-foot-eight-inch, 150-pound thespian, or wrestled him over the side of the box, launching Booth on a crippling dive to the stage almost twelve feet below.

But Lincoln had not seen Booth coming. He had not moved to avoid being shot. Instead, just as Booth was about to fire, Lincoln leaned forward and to the left to look down into the audience on the main floor. James Ferguson saw it all: "The President, at the time he was shot, was sitting in this position: he was leaning his hand on the rail, and was looking down at a person in the [theatre],—not looking on the stage.

He had the flag that decorated the box pulled around, and he was look-ing between the post and the flag."

The pistol, a fine, expensive weapon, had functioned perfectly. The trigger freed the cocked hammer from its tension spring. The hammer snapped forward, striking the copper percussion cap resting over the hollow steel nipple mounted on the barrel. The resulting spark flashed into the chamber, igniting the load of black powder. The explosion pro-pelled the .44-caliber ball at a muzzle velocity slow by modern stan-dards, but fast enough. Still, Booth had almost missed. If the president had leaned forward a little more, the bullet might have whistled just over his head.

Instead it struck him in the head, on the lower left side, a little below the ear. The ball ripped through his chestnut-colored hair, cut the skin, perforated the skull, and, because of the angle of Lincoln's head at the moment of impact, drove a diagonal tunnel through Lincoln's brain from left to right. The wet brain matter slowed the ball's velocity, ab-sorbing enough of its energy to prevent it from penetrating the other side of the skull and exiting through the president's face. The ball came to rest in Lincoln's brain, lodged behind his right eye.

Lincoln never knew what happened to him. His head dropped for-ward until his chin hit his chest, and his body lost all muscular control and sagged against the richly upholstered rocking chair. He did not fall to the floor. He looked as though he was bored with the play and had fallen asleep. It happened so fast that Lincoln lost consciousness before he heard the report of the pistol, smelled the burnt gunpowder, or was enveloped by the voluminous cloud of blue-gray smoke, the sig-nature of all black-powder weapons. The sound of the pistol, more like the hollow "poof" of fireworks than the hard cracking of a modern firearm—another characteristic of nineteenth-century black-powder weapons with low muzzle velocities—echoed and hung in the box for several seconds. Then it traveled to the ceiling and the stage below and reverberated throughout the theatre.

Nobody moved. The president, Mary Lincoln, Clara Harris, Major Rathbone, and Booth remained perfectly still, as though posed in the studio for one of Alexander Gardner's wet-plate albumen photographs that required a motionless exposure of several seconds. Time stopped.

The pistol's report did startle a number of people in the audience. Some thought it was part of the play; others, an unscripted surprise in honor of the president's visit. Some people didn't hear it at all.

Rathbone, an experienced army officer who had heard gunfire before, was the first to realize that something was amiss. He turned to his left. The smoke, now tinted red from the gaslights, and the crimson upholstery and wallpaper that combined to give the box a fiery, devilish glow, partly obscured his vision. Rathbone rose from his seat, stepping in the direction of the president. At that instant he saw a wild-eyed man, his face ghostly against his black clothes, hair, and moustache. Like a demon, Booth emerged from the black-powder haze and sprang at him. Simultaneously Rathbone lunged for Booth, grabbing him by the coat. The assassin broke free, shouting but one word, "Freedom!" and thrust his right arm up, as high as he could reach. Rathbone's eyes were drawn up by the gesture, and he saw what Booth clenched in his fist: a big, shiny knife, its menacing blade pointed directly down at him. Booth moved too quickly for Rathbone to read the patriotic slogans acid-etched into the blade: "Land of the Free/Home of the Brave"; "Liberty/Independence." Booth was not going to try to fend off Rathbone with a few, puny forward jabs of the knife. Instead, he sought the death blow. He was going to deliver an arcing, theatrical swing pivoting from his shoulder that would drive the blade through Rathbone's ribs and into his heart. Booth's arm was already in motion, and at the last moment Rathbone raised his arm to parry Booth's strike. The major grunted in pain. His reflexive, lightning-fast defensive maneuver saved his life, but the assassin's blade sliced through his coat sleeve and into his upper arm. Blood gushed from the long, deep wound.

Booth had no more time to waste on finishing off Rathbone. The clock in his head was still ticking down. If he was going to escape the theatre, he had to get out of the box at once. He turned to the balustrade and swung one leg over the side. By now some members of the audience had looked up. Was that a man climbing out of the president's box, preparing to leap to the stage? As Booth positioned for his leap, Rathbone came at him again, grabbing at his coattail. Distracted, Booth got tangled in the framed portrait of George Washington hanging from the front of the box, and one of his riding spurs snagged one of the flags that just a few hours before Harry Clay Ford had cradled in his arms when he ran into Booth on the street. It was the revenge of "Old Glory," soon went the popular myth. Still he managed to free himself and imperfectly leapt forward to the stage. Booth hit the stage unevenly but still on his feet. He knew something was wrong. He could feel it in his left leg, near the ankle, but there was nothing he could do about it now.

Booth clambered to center stage, turned to the audience, and rose erect to his full height. His splendid chest had always made him appear taller than he was. Every second was precious to his escape, but he had rehearsed this part too well to forsake it now. He knew that this was his

The great crime. A fanciful print published shortly after the assassination.

last performance on the American stage, and for this he would be re-membered for eternity. He must not blow his lines. All eyes were upon him. He stood motionless, paused momentarily for dramatic effect, and thrust his bloody dagger triumphantly into the air. The gas footlights danced on the shiny blade now speckled with red and exaggerated his wild countenance. "Sic semper tyrannis," he thundered. It was the state motto of Virginia—"Thus always to tyrants." Then Booth shouted, "The South is avenged."

DR. CHARLES LEALE HAD WITNESSED THE LEAP: "I SAW A MAN with dark hair and bright black eyes, leap from the box to the stage be-low...and [he] raised his shining dagger in the air, which reflected the light as though it had been a diamond."

Harry Hawk, the only actor onstage when Booth made the leap, could not understand what was happening. Hawk, more than anyone else in the theatre, was in the best position to hear the shot, see the smoky cloud, and observe a familiar-looking figure climb onto the bal-ustrade. Why, if he didn't know better, he would swear that the man who landed hard on the stage, gathered himself, and was now approach-ing him rapidly with an unsheathed dagger looked an awful lot like John Wilkes Booth. Hawk had known Booth for a year and wasn't likely to make a false identification. Hawk lingered indecisively, standing di-rectly in Booth's escape path. When Booth was nearly upon him, Hawk fled: "[H]e was rushing towards me with a dagger and I turned and run." As Booth moved across the stage heading for the wings, James Ferguson, sitting just a few feet away, heard him exult to himself—"I have done it!"

Booth fled into the wings off stage right, slashing his dagger wildly at anyone—actor, orchestra conductor, or employee—who got in his way. William Withers said he felt Booth's hot breath as the assassin pushed past him and struck at him with the knife. The conductor did not try to stop him. No one in the cast did. Booth had taken all the actors backstage by surprise and rushed past them.

Then a voice cried out from the president's box. "Stop that man!" From the time Booth shot Lincoln, wounded Rathbone, fought his way out of the box, leapt to the stage, claimed center stage, uttered his cry of vengeance, and vanished into the wings, no one in the audience had done a thing. It was just as Booth had planned. Some in the audience gasped with fright and delight—they still thought it was part of the play. Others, including the actors near the stage and in the wings, were too shocked to obstruct or pursue Booth.

"Will no one stop that man?" an anguished Rathbone again pleaded to the crowd below. Clara Harris echoed his cry.

"He has shot the President!"

$\mathcal{L}$ESS THAN A MILE AWAY, ON MADISON PLACE, NEAR THE WHITE House on the east side of Lafayette Park, all was quiet at the home of Secretary of State William H. Seward. Bedridden since a terrible carriage accident on April 5, Seward drifted in and out of consciousness. Nine days before, when out riding with his daughter, Frances "Fanny" Adeline Seward; his son Frederick; and a family friend, the coachman, Henry Key, dismounted to fix a stubborn door that wouldn't stay shut. The horses bolted, running madly through the city with the unmanned reins swinging wildly in the air. The secretary of state sprang from the moving carriage to try for the reins or horses, but he caught his shoe on the way out, tore off the heel, and was spun facedown into the street. The fall almost killed him, but he survived with a concussion, his jaw broken in two places, right arm broken between the shoulder and elbow, and deep bruises too numerous to count. Fanny rushed to his crumpled body, fearing he was dead.

That night Seward's disfigured face swelled so badly that his own children could barely recognize him, and the blood pouring through his nose almost suffocated him. Seward's personal physician, Dr. T. S. Verdi; Dr. Basil Norris, an army medical officer; and Surgeon General Joseph K. Barnes attended him and cautioned the family to keep their patient under constant watch.

On April 9, Secretary of War Edwin M. Stanton visited Seward three times. The diplomat liked Lincoln's fierce, iron-willed war leader.

"God bless you Stanton—I can never tell you half..."

Stanton hushed him: "Don't try to speak."

Early that evening Abraham Lincoln rushed to Seward's big brick mansion, known as the "Clubhouse" among Washington insiders. The accident worried Lincoln. Carriage accidents were not trifling affairs in wartime Washington and could prove deadly. Mary Lincoln had nearly been killed when her carriage broke down and flung her headlong into the street. She hit her head hard on the ground and was lucky to survive. The sight of Seward, alive if not well, relieved Lincoln tremendously. They were great rivals once, when in 1860 the emerging rail-splitter from the west challenged Seward, the odds-on favorite for the Republican nomination, and later, when Seward tried to usurp him early in his presidency. But they made peace, and Seward evolved into a trusted adviser and confidant. Just back from Grant's headquarters at City Point, Virginia, the president reclined on the foot of Seward's bed and regaled him with the news—his remarkable visit to Richmond, and how he had gone to a military hospital and shook the hands of thousands of wounded soldiers. Then the president confided the best news of all. According to Grant, Lee's surrender was imminent. After chatting quietly with Seward for nearly an hour, Abraham Lincoln departed. They never saw each other again. Lincoln's prophecy proved true when a little later, Secretary Stanton visited the Clubhouse so he could tell Seward the news in person. Lee had surrendered. The war was over.

Now, on the fourteenth, Fanny watched over her father and listened to the sights and sounds of the never-ending celebrations in the streets. A torchlight procession marched to the White House. A band played "Rally Round the Flag." Fanny was a tall, slender, brown-haired girl precociously conversant in literature and politics, and, at twenty, her father's prize. With her mother Frances often away at their Auburn, New York, homestead, Fanny grew up in a world of political receptions, dinners, and historical personages and events. An avid and talented writer with an eye for detail, her secret diary that she began at age fourteen brimmed with subtle observations and trenchant character sketches of her encounters with the political, military, and diplomatic elites.

Around 10:00 P.M. she put down her book, *Legends of Charlemagne,* turned down the gaslights, and, along with Sergeant George Robinson, a wounded veteran now serving as an army nurse, kept watch over her recovering father.

Outside in the shadows, Lewis Powell and David Herold were keeping the Clubhouse under surveillance. The street was quiet. They saw no guards at the front door, or anywhere on Madison Place. Two hours ago, when they'd met with Booth at the Herndon House, their leader assured them that they would find their target at home. The newspapers reported the carriage accident days ago, and the extent of Seward's serious injuries, and noted that he was recuperating at home, bedridden. That made Seward, of all of Lincoln's cabinet officers, Booth's most attractive target tonight. The others might prove difficult to track, and could be anywhere—dinner parties, entertainments, or traveling. Seward, alone, helplessly anchored to his bed, was sure to be home at 10:00 this evening. The actor issued simple instructions: invade the house, locate the secretary of state's bedroom, and kill the defenseless victim with pistol fire and, if required, the knife. This was a difficult mission even for a man like Powell, a battle-hardened and extremely strong ex-Confederate soldier. Powell had three problems. First, how could he get inside Seward's house? He couldn't just walk in unannounced. By 10:00 P.M. the front door would certainly be locked. He would have to ring the bell. When—if—someone answered, he could not just shoot or slash his way through the threshold. That might attract the attention of passersby or rouse the occupants from their beds to defend themselves.

Cunning deception, not brute force, was the key. Booth concocted, probably with David Herold's help, a brilliant plan. He told Powell to impersonate a messenger delivering important medicine from Seward's physician, Dr. Verdi. To add the final touch of verisimilitude to the ruse, Powell would actually carry a small package wrapped in butcher's paper and tied with string. Herold, the former pharmacist's assistant experienced in making similar deliveries, probably tutored Booth and Powell in the appearance of such packages and then wrapped an empty box to mimic an authentic delivery from Dr. Verdi.

But then what? Once inside it was Powell's job to track down Secretary Seward in the sprawling, three-story mansion. Booth did not provide him with a floor plan. He could rule out the first floor. But Seward might lie in one of a number of upper rooms. Powell faced a third challenge: he did not know how many occupants—family members, State Department messengers, nurses, doctors, servants, maids, and guards—were on the premises. Certainly several, but perhaps up to a dozen. A more cautious man might have told Booth he was mad. But Powell, a slavishly loyal one who called his hero "captain," agreed. Anything for his master. David Herold also complied, as long as he did not have to bloody his hands by killing somebody and could wait for Powell outside, holding their horses.

From the shadows, Powell and Herold had watched Dr. Verdi leave around 9:30 P.M. After him had come Dr. Norris, who visited briefly and departed around 10:00 P.M.—just in time, according to Booth's preset timetable. The house was quiet now. They watched the gaslights go dim in several rooms, a signal that the occupants were settling in for the night. A short while later Powell handed his horse to Herold and strode across the street to the secretary of state's front door. He rang the bell. Herold's dull, hooded eyes warily scanned up and down the block as he stood watch, safeguarding their mounts.

Upstairs, on the third floor, Fanny Seward was watching over her sleeping father, and did not hear the bell. She did not know that outside a man waited to, like Macbeth, murder sleep.

Down on the first floor, William Bell, a nineteen-year-old black servant, hurried to answer the door. Late-night callers were not unusual at the Seward home. At moments of crisis State Department messengers bearing telegraph dispatches might arrive at any hour of the day or night. And ever since the carriage accident, members of the cabinet, military officers, and three different doctors called frequently. There was no reason at all why William Bell should not open that door.

Before him stood a tall, attractive, solidly built man, well dressed in fine leather boots, black pants, a straw-colored duster, and a felt-brimmed hat; he was holding a small package in his hands. The masquerade worked. Nothing about Powell's conventional appearance raised Bell's suspicions. Bell greeted Powell and asked politely, as Seward had trained him, how he could help the visitor. Powell explained his mission: he was a messenger with medicine from Dr. Verdi. That sounded satisfactory to Bell. Dr. Verdi had left his patient within the hour and lived only two blocks from the Sewards. Obviously, Bell reasoned, the doctor must have prescribed some medicine but did not have it with him in his well-worn doctor's bag. When Verdi got home he probably summoned a messenger to deliver the healing product. Up to this moment Powell did nothing to call undue attention to himself. He even pronounced Dr. Verdi's name correctly, with the proper Italian accent. Powell stepped into the hall and closed the door behind him. Bell reached out to accept the delivery. No, Powell said, he could not give it to a servant. The doctor said he had to deliver it personally to the secretary of state and instruct him how to take the medicine. Bell countered that he was qualified to receive deliveries on Seward's behalf. Powell was adamant. "I must go up." He must see the secretary personally—those were his instructions. For five minutes, the assassin and the servant bickered about whether Powell would leave the medicine with Bell. "I must go up," he repeated like a mantra. "I must go up."

Powell, growing impatient, inched relentlessly toward the staircase, backing Bell up to the landing. Bell was in grave danger now. Powell's patience was almost out, and he knew how to deal with a recalcitrant, disobedient Negro like this, just as he had in Baltimore a few months back, when, as a houseguest of the mysterious and attractive rebel Branson sisters, he struck and nearly stomped to death a black female servant who sassed him. He didn't have a knife or pistol then. Now Powell turned away from Bell and lifted a foot to the first stair, then another to the second. Bell chattered on, but Powell kept pounding up the staircase slowly, his boots striking the stairs with dull, methodical thuds that echoed like a ticking case clock to the floors above. If Bell interfered now, he would face Powell's knife. Luckily for him, he did not attempt to block Powell's path. Instead, he ascended the stairs with him. The assassin warned Bell that if he didn't allow him to deliver this medicine, he would report him to his master and get him in big trouble. Cowed, Bell, like a schoolmarm, warned Powell not to tread so heavily on the stairs. He might wake Mr. Seward.

At the top of the staircase Frederick Seward, who served his father as assistant secretary of state, confronted Bell and the stranger. Powell did not know it, but Frederick stood only a few feet from the closed door to his father's sickroom. The stranger explained his mission again. Frederick told him that his father was asleep and that he would take delivery of the medicine for him. Again Powell refused, arguing that he must see the secretary. Incredibly, Powell, thanks to that little package he prominently displayed as a prop, had still not aroused suspicion about his true intentions. To Frederick he seemed merely like a stupid messenger, a man so dull-witted that he took instructions literally, believing that Dr. Verdi meant for him to actually place the package into the secretary of state's hands. Soon Powell would make Frederick regret his assuming condescension.

Inside the bedroom, Fanny sensed a presence in the hall. Perhaps President Lincoln had come for another visit, she thought. Such a late-night call would not be unusual. Lincoln was famous for his nighttime walks. Perhaps he had strolled to the telegraph office at the nearby War Department for the latest news and then decided to call on the secretary. Fanny hurried to the door and opened it only a little to shield her father from the bright gaslight that would otherwise flood the bed-chamber. She saw her brother and, to his right, the tall stranger in the light hat and long overcoat. She whispered, "Fred, Father is awake now." She knew in an instant that she had done wrong. "Something in Fred's manner led me at once to think that he did not wish me to say so, and that I had better not have opened the door." Powell leaned forward and tried to peer into the dark room, but Fanny held the door tight to her body, and the assassin was not able to see his target. He stared at Fanny and, in a harsh and impatient tone, demanded, "Is the Secretary asleep?" Then Fanny made a terrible mistake. She glanced back into the room in the direction of her father, and replied, "Almost." Fred Seward grabbed the door and shut it quickly.

It was too late. Innocently, Fanny had given Powell the priceless in-formation he needed. Secretary of State William H. Seward was in that room, lying helpless in a bed against the wall, to the right of the door, defended by no one, Powell probably assumed, but a frail-looking girl. Powell did not know that Sergeant Robinson was in the bedroom too. Powell resisted the impulse to draw his knife that instant and burst through the door. With William Bell and Frederick Seward hovering close, his wit restrained his body and he calculated his next move. The pair was no match for him, but together, they could delay by precious seconds his entry to the bedroom. Trickery had taken him this far—time for one more charade.

Powell continued to argue with Frederick outside the door. Finally Fred, exasperated, gave Powell an ultimatum: surrender that medicine now, or take it back to Dr. Verdi. Powell glared at the young Seward, still refusing to yield the medicine. Finally, the persistent messenger feigned surrender in this battle of wills. He stuffed the package into his pocket, turned around, and began his descent. He did not remove his hand from the pocket. Bell, walking down ahead of Powell, turned over his shoulder and chided him again about walking so loudly. Bell continued down the stairs, his eyes looking ahead now to the front door through which, in a few moments, he would, with pleasure, conduct the ill-

"I'm mad, I'm mad!" Lewis Powell,
Secretary of State Seward's assassin.

mannered stranger into the street. At the top of the stairs Frederick
Seward, satisfied at turning away an annoying pest, took his eyes off
Powell's back and headed for his room. In a flash, Powell reversed course
and bounded up the stairs. Before Seward could turn around, Powell
already stood behind him. Seward whirled but too late: Powell was
pointing a Whitney revolver at him, the muzzle inches from his face. In

another moment a .36-caliber conical lead round would explode his face, and the hot black powder would, at this range, not only kill him instantly but also burn and disfigure his flesh a hideous black.

Powell, staring into Seward's eyes, squeezed the trigger. The hammer fell and struck the percussion cap. Seward had no time to move—he knew he was dead. Then he heard…a metallic click. Misfire! Either the copper percussion cap malfunctioned or the faulty powder charge in the chamber did not ignite. The reason did not matter: Seward was still alive. But Powell, unlike his master Booth, had five more rounds in his revolver. He could draw the hammer back with his thumb, cock the pistol, rotate the revolver's cylinder to bring a fresh round into firing position, and shoot again. It would take just a moment. Then Powell made the first of two miscalculations that jeopardized his mission.

Instead of trying to fire again, Powell raised the pistol high in the air and brought down a crushing blow to Seward's head. He hit him so hard that he broke the pistol's steel ramrod, jamming the cylinder and making it impossible to fire the weapon again. In a fury, Powell, using all his might, clubbed Seward repeatedly with the barrel of the broken Whitney. William Bell ran down the stairs and into the street, shouting, "Murder!" Watching from across the street, a skittish David Herold knew this was not part of the plan.

Fanny, ignorant of the mayhem on the other side of the door, sat down in her chair beside her father. A few minutes after her encounter with the determined stranger, she heard "the sound of blows—it seemed to me as many as half a dozen—sharp and heavy, with lighter ones between." She thought the servants were chasing a rat. When the sounds continued, Fanny turned to Sergeant Robinson: "What can be the matter? Do go and see." Suddenly afraid, she rose and accompanied him. While Fanny was puzzling about the sound, Lewis Powell stood on the other side of the door, beating in her brother's brains. As soon as Robinson opened the door, Fanny saw a horrible sight—her brother's face, wild-eyed, covered with blood. Powell moved lightning fast. He shoved Fred aside and struck Robinson in the forehead hard with the knife, stunning him with the blow. The assassin pushed past the reeling sergeant and the waiflike girl blocking his path and sprinted to the bed with his arms outstretched, clutching the knife in his right hand and the pistol in his left, brushing Fanny with it as he passed.

In near darkness, Fanny raced Powell to the bed, trying to throw her slender body between the huge assassin and her helpless father. Unable to get ahead of him, she could do no better than run beside him. The assassin reached the bed and pounced upon Seward. Fanny shouted, "Don't kill him!" Seward awoke, tried feebly to raise himself, turned to the left, and saw Fanny. Then he looked up. He glimpsed Powell's unforgettable rugged face, lantern jaw, and searing eyes. The assassin's left hand pushed down hard on the secretary's chest, pinning him to the bed. Powell's right hand clutching the knife rose high until he exerted every ounce of strength he possessed to swing down a tremendous blow. The knife flashed past Seward's face, cutting into the sheets and plunging into the mattress. Powell had missed. Inflamed, Powell thrust the knife above his head again and delivered another powerful blow. He missed again. In the dim light, and with Seward positioned by his doctors on the far side of the bed so that his broken arm could hang free over the side, Powell's aim was off. His style of attack was wrong. The theatrical arcing swing of the knife that Booth employed against Major Rathbone had no place in an almost pitch-black room. The darkness made it too hard to aim the pivoting strike. Moreover, Powell, unlike Booth—renowned for his expertise with swords and daggers—was not a knife fighter. As a Confederate soldier, his primary tools were firearms—the musket and the pistol—not edged weapons. Powell needed to get in close and slice across Seward's throat, or stab through an eye socket into the brain, or sink the blade into the soft stomach tissue.

Determined not to miss again, Powell adjusted himself and delivered a third mighty blow aimed at Seward's throat. The agonized groan that rose from the bed told Powell he had finally baptized his knife. The blade slashed open Seward's cheek so viciously that the skin hung from a flap, exposing his teeth and fractured jawbone. His cheek resembled a fish gill. Seward choked on the warm, metallic tasting syrup that spurted from his mouth and poured down his throat. The bedsheets, stained with blood and scarred by the blade, and preserved to this day as holy relics at Seward's home in Auburn, New York, survive as mute testimony to the power of Powell's striking arm.

Across the room Sergeant Robinson regained his senses and made a split-second decision: he would fight to the death before he allowed the assassin to murder the secretary of state and Miss Fanny. He rushed Powell. In an instant the two battle-hardened Civil War veterans grappled in a death struggle. Powell's strength surprised Robinson—he could barely hold on to him as Powell went for the bed again. Fanny, temporarily dazed, thought for a moment that it was all a "fearful dream." Then she knew. She screamed, not once, but in a ceaseless, howling, and terrifying wail that woke her brother Augustus, or "Gus," who was asleep in a room nearby. Fanny then opened a window and screamed to the street below. That was enough for David Herold. He kicked his horse and fled, abandoning Powell to fate. Undeterred by Fanny's screaming, Powell kept fighting. His adventures at Gettysburg and with Mosby's Rangers made him cool under fire. His resolve stiffened. He would not permit one man and a screaming girl to scare him off.

Gus Seward, dressed in his nightshirt, raced to his father's room and saw the shadows of two men fighting. Confused, he thought his father had become delirious and the male nurse was trying to restrain him. As soon as Gus seized the shadowy figure he believed was his father, he knew it was someone else. Now combating two men, Powell fought harder, slashing wildly with the knife. When Robinson got behind him and wrapped him in a bear hug, Powell reversed the knife, thrust it blindly over his shoulder, and stabbed Robinson twice in the shoulder, deeply and to the bone. Robinson ignored the wounds and kept fighting. In the dark it was hard to see the knife coming clearly enough to parry the blows. Throughout the battle Powell hadn't said a word. When the sergeant and Gus wrestled Powell into the hall and into the bright gaslight, Powell and Gus, their faces inches apart, locked eyes. Then

Powell spoke for the first time during the attack. In an intense but eerily calm voice, the assassin confided to Gus, as though trying to persuade him, the strangest thing: "I'm mad. I'm mad!"

Secretary Seward's wife, alarmed by Fanny's screams, emerged from her third-floor, back bedroom in time to witness the climax of the hallway struggle between Powell and her son Gus. Uncomprehending, she assumed that her husband had become delirious and was running amok. Fred's wife, Anna, rushed to the scene, and Fanny ran out of her father's bedroom and shouted, "Is that man gone?" Bewildered, Mrs. Seward and Anna replied, "What man?"

Powell wound his arm around Robinson's neck in a choke hold, and the sergeant braced himself for the knife that was sure to follow at any moment. Then, in a curious act of mercy, Powell let him go and, instead of stabbing him again, punched him with his fist. Powell fled down the stairs. On his way out, he caught up with Emerick Hansell, who was running down the staircase, trying to stay ahead of the assassin. The State Department messenger, on duty at Seward's home, was fleeing rather than joining the battle. But Powell gave Hansell a parting gift as he ran past him—an inglorious stab in the back. Hansell crumpled to the floor. He had been stabbed over the sixth rib, from the spine obliquely toward the right side. The cut was an inch wide and between two and a half and three inches deep, but the blade had not penetrated the lungs. Powell ran into the street, his eyes searching desperately for David Herold, but found nothing more than his lone horse. Powell tossed his knife to the ground, mounted his horse, and, instead of galloping into the night, calmly and inconspicuously trotted away. William Bell, flailing in the street, pursued Powell on foot for a few blocks, yelling all the way. Unable to keep pace with the horse, he gave up and returned to the Clubhouse.

Fanny ran back to her father's room only to find the bed empty. "Where's father?" she cried in panic. She spotted what she thought was no more than a pile of discarded bedclothes on the floor—but it was the secretary of state, bloody and disheveled. To save his life he had rolled out of bed during the attack and crashed to the floor, hoping to escape Powell's reach in the dark room. That agonizing tumble aggravated his broken bones and sent spasms of pain through his body. Fanny slipped on a big puddle of blood and tumbled to the floor beside her father. He looked "ghastly…white, and very thin." And that made her scream: "O my God, father's dead." Sergeant Robinson, ignoring his own wounds, flew to her side, lifted the broken Seward from the floor, and laid him tenderly in his bed. Seward opened his eyes, looked up at his terrified daughter, and, in unimaginable pain and fighting off the effects of shock, concentrated his mind, spit the blood out of his mouth, and whispered: "I am not dead; send for a doctor, send for the police, close the house."

Chapter Three

"His Sacred Blood"

———————— ✦❀✦ ————————

BACK AT FORD'S THEATRE THE MANHUNT FOR BOOTH ALMOST ended before it began when one man, an army major and lawyer named Joseph B. Stewart, rose from his front-row seat to pursue the assassin. Stewart, long-limbed at six foot five, and rumored to be the tallest man in Washington, decided to leap from the first row across the orchestra pit to the stage. But the wide opening served as Booth's moat, sealing off any pursuit by the audience. Stewart slipped before he could make his leap. It was too far. He regained his balance and then, in an acrobatic display, danced across the pit by tiptoeing along the chair tops. In a few moments he reached the stage and followed Booth into the wings. Within days, newspaper woodcuts immortalized Stewart as the solitary audience member who thought of chasing after Booth.

Booth continued rushing through the wings and down the passageway leading to the back door that opened to Baptist Alley. A few more seconds, and he would be in the saddle. But he knew he wouldn't be safe even then. Alert audience members from the rear of the theatre, guessing that the assassin would head for the alley, might sprint out onto Tenth Street to cut off his escape. At this moment, as Booth reached for the back door, interceptors might be running right on Tenth, then right again on F, to cut him off at the mouth of F and Baptist Alley. Even worse, someone might have already mounted a horse to chase him down.

Booth may have been focused on the alley, but the more immediate danger lay behind him, closing fast. Stewart, following him into the wings and down the passageway, was shortening the distance between them with every stride.

Booth prayed that Ned Spangler or John Peanut stood on the other side of that door, still holding his horse. If either one had tired of holding the animal and taken it back to the actor's stable a few yards down the alley, or had tied her off behind the theatre, only to have her break free, Booth was doomed. He burst through the alley door, sucked his lungs full of fresh, spring night air, and slammed it shut behind him. Mrs. Anderson saw him run out "with something in his hand glittering." Where was the bay mare? She wasn't where he left her. Was Booth trapped, about to suffer the same fate as Shakespeare's Richard III— abandoned on enemy ground without his steed? But when Booth turned his head to the right he saw salvation: his horse, standing quietly in the alley, just a few steps away. In a split second Booth's eyes raced the length of the leather reins, following them into the hands of a man reclining on the wood carpenter's bench near Ford's back wall. It was John Peanut! "Give me my horse, boy!" Booth commanded as he lunged for the animal. There was no wood stepping box nearby to elevate him to the stirrups. With brute strength, he yanked himself onto the black-legged bay mare with a white star on her forehead and grabbed the reins. John Peanut rose to surrender them. As thanks, Booth, still clutching his dagger stained with Major Rathbone's blood, popped Peanut in the head with the pommel, then kicked the youth away hard with his boot heel. Better that than a cut to the throat of the harmless Peanut. Booth balanced himself in the saddle, and at that moment Stewart swung open the theatre door and saw Booth about to gallop away.

From the ground Stewart looked up and saw the assassin, illuminated by the rising moon. Stewart reached for the reins, but Booth, an experienced rider, spurred and pulled the horse in a tight, quick circle away from Stewart. The horse really could move like a cat. Stewart tried for the reins again, but once more Booth outmaneuvered him from the saddle. Stomping hooves pounded the ground until Booth finally broke free, settled low, and kicked the bay horse hard. She exploded into a gallop that Booth steered down the alley, then guided left toward F Street, vanishing from sight.

Mary Anderson, standing no more than twenty-five feet away, witnessed the assassin's escape: "He had come out of the theatre-door so quick, that it seemed like as if he had but touched the horse, and it was gone in a flash of lightning." Mary Ann Turner, her next-door neighbor, heard the commotion but wasn't quick enough to witness Booth's escape: "I only heard the horse going very rapidly out of the alley; and I ran immediately to my door and opened it, but he was gone."

With F Street coming up fast, Booth looked ahead to the alley's mouth. Had his pursuers reached it before him? No one blocked his way. He emerged onto F Street and reined his mount hard to the right. No one was chasing him. Booth galloped east down F Street. He had escaped from Ford's Theatre—barely. But now he faced an even more difficult challenge. Could he escape from Washington, war capital of the Union, its streets filled with thousands of soldiers and loyal citizens, all there to celebrate the end of the Civil War?

By now, back in the alley, a number of people had poured out the door in pursuit of the assassin. "Which way did he go?" they asked Mrs. Anderson. "Which way did he go?" She asked a man what was the matter. "The president was shot," he answered. "Why, who shot him?" "The man who went out on that horse: did you see him?"

A block down F and to his right, Booth rode past the Herndon House, where just two hours ago he had met with his gang and dreamed of this moment. As Booth continued another block east on F he approached two of Washington's grandest landmarks. To his left he saw the Patent Office, his dark figure silhouetted by the white glow of the huge marble building that was the scene of Walt Whitman's ministrations to wounded soldiers and, just six weeks ago, Lincoln's inaugural

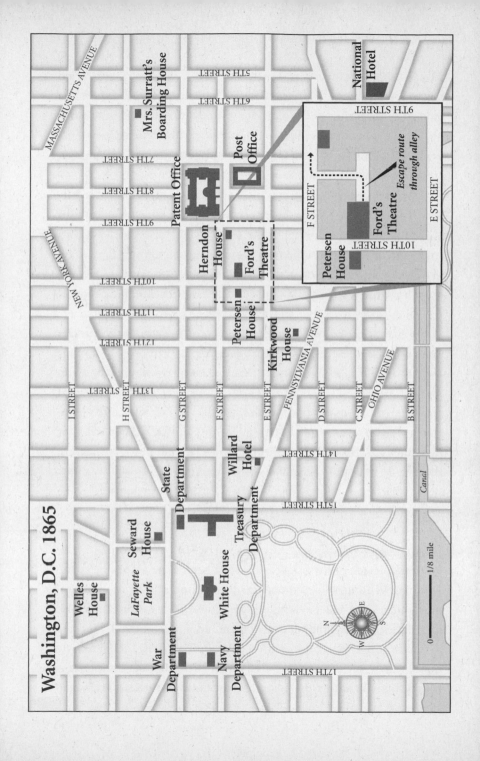

Washington, D.C. 1865

Massachusetts Avenue

New York Avenue

Mrs. Surratt's Boarding House

5TH STREET
6TH STREET
7TH STREET
8TH STREET
9TH STREET
10TH STREET
11TH STREET
12TH STREET
13TH STREET
14TH STREET
15TH STREET
17TH STREET

Post Office

Patent Office

Herndon House

Ford's Theatre

Petersen House

Kirkwood House

Pennsylvania Avenue

Ohio Avenue

National Hotel

Welles House

Seward House

LaFayette Park

War Department

White House

Navy Department

Treasury Department

State Department

Willard Hotel

I STREET
H STREET
G STREET
F STREET
E STREET
D STREET
C STREET
B STREET

Canal

N
E
W
S

0   1/8 mile

9TH STREET

F STREET

10TH STREET

E STREET

Petersen House

Ford's Theatre

Escape route through alley

ball. To Booth's right, he saw the massive marble pile of the Post Office, where just ten hours ago Harry Clay Ford picked up the letter that he handed to the actor on the front step of the theatre. Gaslight bounced off the slick, polished walls of both buildings and bathed Booth in a searching glow. Past the buildings in seconds, Booth galloped right and cut across Judiciary Square to Pennsylvania Avenue.

Few people saw him as he fled through downtown Washington. That was understandable, however, because Booth rode away from the celebrating crowds that clogged the upper avenue. He rode east, then southeast, in the opposite direction from the throng, aiming for Capitol Hill. And what interest was one man on a horse to thousands of jubilant men? Booth crossed the Capitol grounds, riding beneath the shadow of the great dome, completed in time for Lincoln's second inauguration. Booth then cut over to the southeast part of Pennsylvania Avenue. He galloped on to Eleventh Street and turned right, swinging south in the direction of the Navy Yard Bridge that led out of Washington and into Maryland. One thought possessed him. Could he reach that bridge and cross the Potomac's eastern branch (now the Anacostia) before pursuers, or news of the assassination, caught up with him? Luck was with him that night. His hard riding kept him ahead of the news. As he neared the river he reined his horse and slowed to a trot. He saw guards ahead. Be natural, he instinctively thought. Don't arouse suspicion.

SERGEANT SILAS T. COBB WAS STANDING WATCH AT THE Washington side of the bridgehead. He'd been there since sunset and was on duty until 1:00 A.M. Looking off into the distance, he saw an approaching rider. Cobb knew his orders: allow no one to cross the bridge after dark. Cobb and the handful of men under his command prepared to challenge the rider. Booth, with the flair only a master thespian could muster under such duress, prepared for an impromptu performance— talking his way across the bridge. The time was between 10:35 and 10:45 P.M.

"Who goes there?" Cobb challenged.

"A friend," the actor replied. Perhaps Cobb would recognize the stage star and wave him across with a smile, his horse not even breaking stride. No such luck.

"Where are you from?"

"From the city," Booth said vaguely.

Cobb asked his destination.

"I am going down home, down in Charles County."

The sergeant noticed that the horse's coat was wet and had been ridden hard. He studied Booth's features: "Clear white skin...his hands were very white and he had no gloves on...[he] seemed to be gentlemanly in his address and style and appearance." Cobb also noted that while Booth carried himself nonchalantly, he seemed to possess reserves of muscular power. Cobb continued to press the matter, asking Booth if he knew that the bridge leaving Washington closed at 9:00 P.M.

The actor claimed he didn't and said he'd chosen a late start on purpose because "it is a dark road ahead and I thought if I waited a spell I would have the moon."

Cobb pondered for a moment. Booth was at his wit's end. Every second was precious, and this fool was wasting time with his stupid questions. Then Cobb agreed reluctantly to allow Booth to pass.

Booth adopted a reassuring, theatrical voice to calm the dutiful sergeant: "Hell, I guess there'll be no trouble about that."

Booth gave his horse a gentle tap with the spurs. Then Cobb noticed something unusual. Unlike its cool and collected rider, the horse was restive and nervous, so much that Booth had to rein her in so that she would walk, and not gallop, across the bridge. Cobb wondered why. Booth had handled Cobb perfectly. Except for two things. When the sergeant asked his name he responded, inexplicably, "Booth." And when Cobb asked where he was going, Booth answered, "Beantown."

This was a lucky moment for the assassin. If Cobb denied him passage, he had no alternate route of escape. He could not turn back to the city. He had to cross the river now, at this spot, into Maryland. Open, isolated country beckoned him from the other side of the bridge. He would find friends there. He had to cross. Armed with only a knife, Booth could never have fought his way across. Had he tried, the sergeant and his sentinels would have shot him out of his saddle, and the manhunt would have ended that night, less than an hour after John Wilkes Booth assassinated Abraham Lincoln.

Once over the bridge, Booth turned to see if his cat's-paws—David Herold, Lewis Powell, or George Atzerodt—followed in the distance. This was their route, too. Booth saw no one, neither conspirators nor pursuers, behind him, but as he gazed across the river he saw a beautiful scene. The moon, two days past full, rose high over Washington, and under its cool, lunar light the great dome glowed like a twin moon descended upon the earth.

Like Lot's wife, who paused, turned, and dared look upon the destruction of Sodom and Gomorrah, Booth could see the sleeping city from which he fled, and he knew it would awaken soon and hear of the destruction he had wrought. He had done it. And he had escaped.

$\mathcal{B}$OOTH AND LEWIS POWELL HAD LEFT BEHIND SO MUCH blood. Sergeant Robinson and Fanny Seward worked feverishly to save the secretary of state's life. Seward had more wounds than the sergeant had hands, and Robinson had to teach Fanny how to stanch the flow of blood with cloths and water. "I did not know what should be done," she said. "Robinson told me everything." Sprawled across sheets sheared by Powell's knife, she knelt beside her father and, with all of her strength, pressed the ersatz bandages tightly against the cuts. Robinson played doctor and examined Seward's body for additional wounds. Punctures to the lungs, stomach, or heart? No. Any nicked or severed arteries? No. If they could stop the bleeding and Seward could just hold on until Dr. Verdi, Dr. Norris, or Surgeon General Barnes arrived, he might live.

Within minutes messengers returned with the doctors, who relieved Fanny and Robinson. Their examination confirmed it. Despite their

Secretary of State William H. Seward and daughter Fanny.

hideous appearance, the wounds were not fatal. Seward—who to Dr. Verdi looked like "an exsanguinated corpse"—would live. Verdi turned to the family and spoke: "I congratulate you all that the wounds are not mortal." Robinson finally allowed himself to be treated by the doctors. He, too, would live, along with Gus Seward and Hansell. But Powell had inflicted a grievous and potentially fatal wound upon Frederick Seward. The Whitney revolver fractured his skull and exposed his brain. Fred wandered about the house like a zombie, babbling the same phrase, "It is…it is," over and over unable to complete the thought, while touching the back of his head with his finger. Fred smiled at Dr. Verdi and seemed to recognize him.

Verdi, interpreting Fred's hand gesture, asked: "You want to know whether your skull is broken or not?"

"Yes," Fred replied.

Within half an hour Fred passed out for fifteen or twenty minutes, then woke up. Verdi and others helped him to bed, where he passed out again. When he awakened three days later, he had been unconscious for sixty hours. But he would live.

As the evening wore on, Fanny became increasingly fearful that Powell might return, or other assassins might be lurking in the house. Her mother ordered her not to wander off alone in the big mansion, but Fanny disobeyed and, prowling from room to room, searched alone— until others joined her—for concealed assassins. Finding none, she returned to her father's bed and sat beside him. Weakly, Seward lifted his left arm and opened a soothing hand to Fanny to calm and reassure her. His good, brave girl had done well this night.

The house became quiet again. Everywhere she looked Fanny saw signs of the horror that she and her family had just survived. "All the white woodwork of the entry was covered with great dashes of blood," she wrote in her diary, "the drugget on the stairs was sprinkled with it, all the way down to the floor below…on the inner side of the door of father's room there was, in blood, the distinct impression of a hand…blood, blood, my thoughts seem drenched in it—I seemed to breathe its sickening odor…the bed had been covered with blood—the blankets and sheets chopped with several blows of the knife." Then she looked at herself: her hands, her arms, her long pretty dress, all drenched in blood. She could not stop screaming.

Sergeant Robinson, too, could not forget the blood, and later he sought a bizarre, gruesome relic of the battle that night. Might he, the fearless nurse queried the secretary of war, have the knife that Powell used to stab him and Secretary Seward? Stanton granted the unusual request:

*War Department/Bureau of Military Justice, Washington,
D.C., July 10th, 1866. Sir. Your application for the knife used
by Payne* [one of Powell's pseudonyms], *in his attempt to
assassinate the Honorable William H. Seward, Secretary of
State of the United States, at Washington D.C. on the night of
the 14th of April 1865, having been referred to the Secretary
of War, has been by him approved, and I am directed by him
to comply with your request. Your conduct on the occasion
mentioned is now a matter of history, and none will hereafter
doubt but that by your self possession and courage in grappling
with the assassin, you contributed largely to saving the life of
the Secretary of State, at the extreme hazard of your own—
a most meritorious public service, nobly rendered, and of
which the weapon now committed to your keeping will be an
enduring memento. Very respectfully, Your obedient Servt. J.
Holt. Judge Advocate General.*

Congress went one step further and proffered a generous and more conventional award: a gold medal was struck in Robinson's honor, and he was given $5,000 in cash. The obverse of the medal included a bust portrait of Robinson's profile in high relief, and the legend: "For his Heroic Conduct on the 14 Day of April 1865. In Saving the Life of Wm. H. Seward." On the reverse, the engraver froze Robinson and Powell in perpetual combat, the assassin raising the knife high in the air while the sergeant held the striking arm at bay. Behind them, Seward lay helpless in bed, and Powell's revolver lay broken on the floor.

THE PRESIDENT'S BOX AT FORD'S THEATRE WAS ALSO DRENCHED in blood.

After Booth's leap to the stage, the women attended to their men. Mary Lincoln turned to her left and stared at the president. He was motionless in the rocker, his head hung low, eyes shut, his chin resting on his chest. He did not return her imploring gaze. She spoke to him, but he did not answer. She touched him; he did not stir. "Father…father!" she shouted into his right ear from just a few inches away. Lincoln did not react. Now frantic, Mary moved closer and tried to push his body into a more upright position. The muscles in his neck, shoulders, chest, and arms, all limp, offered no resistance. Lincoln had no visible wounds. There was no blood on his face or neck. His white linen shirt was unstained. Her touch left no wet, red spots upon her hands. But her loving hands had overlooked the back of his head. Mary Lincoln, terrified, uncomprehending, and by now nearly hysterical, clutched her husband's body and supported it in a sitting position in the chair.

Clara Harris lifted her eyes from the stage below and looked back into the box. She beheld Rathbone, wild-eyed, staggering, and clutching his upper left arm with his right hand. He could not suppress the copious flow of blood that flooded over his hand, and dripped on the luxurious Turkish carpet. Booth had struck him hard, and the knife had penetrated deep. Clara, who had seen the whole thing, never forgot the forceful swing of Booth's "practiced and powerful arm." Superficially, Rathbone's wound appeared small—just a narrow puncture of the skin near the elbow, no more than about one and a half inches wide, mimicking the dimensions of the blade. But the knife had sliced deep inside the major's raised, parrying arm, parallel to the bone, and nearly to the shoulder, cutting an artery, nerves, and veins. Most of the damage was beneath the skin. Clara rushed to attend to her fiancé's wound.

Down in the audience, more than fifteen hundred people went wild. Some playgoers climbed to the stage, looked up to the box, and shouted desperate queries to its occupants. "What has happened?" "Is the president alive?" Throughout the theatre hundreds of people turned to friends, spouses, and total strangers, all repeating the same questions: "Has the president been shot?" "Who was that man onstage?" "Was that a knife?" "What did he say?" Some women fainted. Innumerable, half-crazed voices cried out from all corners of the theatre in a frightening chorus of vengeance: "Kill the murderer!"; "Hang him!"; "Shoot him!";

"Cut his heart out!"; "Catch him!"; "Don't let him escape!" None of them realized that the assassin was already out the back door, safe from the reach of their vigilante howls. Like a violent spring storm, the climate inside Ford's became dark, ugly, and menacing. Under the dim glow of the hissing gaslights, people pushed one another to get to the stage. Others, in a panic to flee, shoved men, women, and children out of the aisles. The voices grew louder until nearly all fifteen hundred of them came together to create an angry roar. This was a mob.

Other voices, these pleading for assistance, not roaring for vengeance, arose from the mob. "Water!" "Has anyone any stimulants?" "Stand back!" "Give him air!" "Is there a doctor in the house?"

In the dress circle, sitting just a few yards from the door to the president's box, Charles Leale jumped up from his seat. Disregarding the aisles and customary route to the box, he raced there in a direct line, and, like a hurdler gone haywire, staggered and half vaulted over the cane-bottomed chairs obstructing his path as he shouldered his way past dazed playgoers. He joined a number of other men who were trying to get inside the box. But the door was locked.

Inside, Major Rathbone walked toward the sound of the beating fists. The men were pounding on the door like it was a drumhead, but their fists and shoulders could not break it open. They shouted to the occupants, if any of them were still alive, to unlock the door. Rathbone staggered forward, already feeling the effects of blood loss and shock. He cupped the hand of his good arm under the wooden music stand that Booth used to bar the door, and tried to pull it up. It wouldn't budge. He tried harder, then realized that the harder the men on the other side pushed, the more effective Booth's device became. It was too thick to snap, so every push created a tighter seal between the door panel and the head of the bar. "For God's sake open the door," the voices pleaded. Rathbone shouted through the door to stop pushing—the door was barred. The men obeyed Rathbone's order and stepped back. Weakening rapidly, Rathbone pulled up with his remaining strength. The music stand popped free and nearly a dozen men rushed inside.

Dr. Leale, not in uniform, announced his rank and profession and stepped ahead of them. Immediately he saw all four occupants. Like an officer under enemy fire, he needed to regain his composure. "Halt!" he commanded himself silently. Do not panic. "Be calm," he chided himself. Do your duty. Major Rathbone, standing between Leale and Lincoln, beseeched the doctor to treat him first, and as proof of his injury, he ostentatiously used his right hand to hold up his wounded left arm. Leale lifted Rathbone's chin, peered into his eyes, and, when "an almost instantaneous glance revealed the fact that he was in no immediate danger," ignored the emotional major and rushed to the president's side.

Leale approached Mary Lincoln and introduced himself as a United States Army surgeon. Wordlessly, she thrust out her hand, and he grasped it tightly. Then she unleashed a torrent of pitiful pleas: "Oh, Doctor, is he dead? Can he recover? Will you take charge of him? Do what you can for him. Oh, my dear husband." The doctor assured the first lady that he would do everything possible for her husband. As Mary wept bitterly, Leale released her hand and began his examination.

Lincoln looked dead. His eyes were closed, he was unconscious, and his head had fallen forward. Leale concluded, from Lincoln's "crouched-down sitting posture," that if Mary had not held his body upright in the rocking chair, the president would have already tumbled to the floor. Leale took Lincoln's right radial pulse, but felt no movement of the artery. Just to be sure, Leale and others lifted Lincoln from the rocker and laid him in a recumbent position on the floor. While Leale held the president's head and shoulders, one of his hands felt a wet spot, invisible to the eye, on the left shoulder of Lincoln's black frock coat. It was a clot of blood. Leale, remembering Booth's flashing dagger onstage and noting Rathbone's severely bleeding wound, assumed that Lincoln had been stabbed. Leale called for a knife. He brought no surgeon's tools to a social night at the theatre. If Lincoln had been stabbed, how could he suture the wounds without needles and thread? By now several men had joined Rathbone in the box, and hands began fishing wildly in pants pockets until William Kent, a government employee, produced a pocketknife. Leale removed Lincoln's custom-made, black wool frock coat, trimmed at the collar, lapels, and cuffs with grosgrain piping. The box was too dimly lit to read the tailor's label sewn inside the collar— Brooks Brothers, New York—or to admire the black silk lining embossed with a large American eagle, a shield of stars and stripes, and the motto "One Country, One Destiny." Leale cut open Lincoln's collar, shirt, and coat to examine him for knife wounds. There were none. Then Leale lifted each of the president's eyelids, studied the pupils, and reeled in dismay: it was a brain injury. Leale separated his fingers, weaved both of his hands gently through Lincoln's hair, and as he worked them thoroughly around the head, he discovered that the hair was matted with blood. Leale's fingers probed rapidly for its source and found it within seconds, behind the left ear. A neat, round hole, about the diameter of a man's fingertip, clotted with a plug of wine-red, coagulated blood. Leale's heart sank.

In the theatre below, the audience would soon be past control. In a valiant attempt to calm them, the actress Laura Keene marched to the front of the stage, close to the footlights, and begged the crowd to remain calm. "For God's sake, have presence of mind and keep your places, and all will be well." The president was not dead, she assured them, without knowing whether that was really true. Then the mayor of the District of Columbia took to the stage to try to keep the crowd under control. An angry voice shouted, "Burn the theatre!" and others echoed him. Yes, burn it down. Others remembered that on Capitol Hill, not more than a fifteen-minute march from Ford's, the Old Capitol prison was filled with disloyal rebel prisoners. The assassin may have escaped, but they could take their revenge there. And walking in the very streets of Washington this night were ex-Confederate soldiers and officers, some of them still wearing their rebel uniforms. This would be a dangerous night for anyone who came into the proximity of the mob.

In a few hours, when the telegraph spread the horrible news to the other great cities of the North, dangerous mobs would take to the streets across the country.

Dr. Charles Sabin Taft, an army doctor seated on the main floor near the orchestra pit, heard voices shout for "a doctor!" He rose and headed for the stage. His wife begged him to stay: "You sha'n't go! They'll kill you too—I know they will!" He got onstage in moments and stood helplessly below the president's box. The distance from the stage to the balustrade overhead was too far—eleven feet six inches—to jump. It was one thing to leap down from the box—not an easy move even for an athlete like John Wilkes Booth—but it was impossible to jump up to it. There had to be another way up there. Perhaps other men could lift him and launch him into the box. Taft corralled a few of the men standing onstage to form a human catapult. Men bent low and shaped their interlocked fingers into improvised stirrups. Taft dug his boot heels into their cupped palms and fastened his hands to their shoulders for balance. Then, with one rapid, fluid motion the men's twitching leg, arm, and shoulder muscles exploded in a burst of strength and propelled Taft skyward. On the way up, he shot his arms above his head as high as they could reach, ready to grab anything he could get his hands on. The catapult launched him just high enough. His fingertips grasped wildly for the balustrade, for the framed engraving of George Washington hanging from a thin wire, for the flags, for the bunting—anything that would save him from a plummet to the polished, hardwood stage. His blue army officer's cape unraveled from his neck and floated back to the stage. Taft swung momentarily from a piece of bunting until others who followed Dr. Leale into the box reached over the side and pulled him up and into the box. But by now Dr. Leale was already attending the president. Under customary medical tradition, Lincoln was Leale's patient.

Although Leale feared that Lincoln might already be dead, he made a split-second decision to revive him. To relieve pressure on the brain, he used his fingers to pull the clot from the bullet hole. Then he dropped to his knees, straddled Lincoln, opened the president's mouth, stuck two fingers down his throat, pressed hard on the base of his paralyzed tongue, and opened the larynx. Air could now reach Lincoln's lungs, and to draw life-sustaining oxygen into them, Leale pressed the diaphragm upward and ordered two men to manipulate Lincoln's arms like levers on a water pump. Then Leale stimulated the apex of the heart by pressing hard under the ribs. To everyone in the box, including Dr. Leale, the situation seemed hopeless. Then the president's reluctant heart began to beat and his lungs sucked in a breath. The heartbeat was feeble, the breathing irregular, but Abraham Lincoln was still alive. Barely. However, unless Leale could stabilize him immediately, Lincoln would expire within a few minutes. The doctor raced against the clock. Death hovered near, impatient to claim the president and escort him on the voyage to that dark and distant shore that had beckoned Lincoln so often in his dreams.

Leale leaned forward until his chest met Lincoln's and their faces nearly touched. Leale sucked in as much air as his lungs could hold, until he felt like they would burst, and then he breathed air directly into Lincoln's mouth and nostrils. Lincoln's lungs expanded and his respiration improved. After forcing several more lungfuls of air into the president, Leale paused, studied his patient's face for a moment, placed his ear over Lincoln's thorax, and, amid the cacophony of shrieks, moans, cries, and threats that filled the theatre, along with Mary's deep sobs a few feet way, he listened keenly. Then he heard it, almost inaudible at first, then louder: Lincoln's heart, stronger, sustaining a regular beat. Leale leaned back and monitored Lincoln's mouth and rising chest. The president's lungs started filling on their own. Leale's quick thinking saved the president from immediate death.

Time seemed to stop again, just as it did the moment after Booth fired his pistol. Mary Lincoln sank into the sofa and was comforted by Clara Harris, whose face, hair, hands, and dress were smeared with her fiancé's blood. Major Rathbone continued to apply pressure to his wound and tried to remain conscious. Sensing that Dr. Leale's work was done, the occupants of the box hushed to a breathless silence. Still on his knees, with all eyes fixed upon him, Dr. Leale intoned his diagnosis and prognosis simultaneously: "His wound is mortal; it is impossible for him to recover."

A̲T THE KIRKWOOD HOUSE, GEORGE ATZERODT HAD YET TO inflict a mortal wound upon Vice President Johnson. Around 10:00 P.M., as Booth closed in on Lincoln and Powell on Seward, Atzerodt showed up at T. Naylor's livery stable and talked to the foreman, John Fletcher. He wanted to pick up the horse that he and David Herold had dropped off there that afternoon. But first Atzerodt invited Fletcher to join him for a drink at the nearby Union Hotel, at 13½ and E streets. Fletcher ordered a glass of beer and Atzerodt had a whiskey. After they left the hotel, Atzerodt said a strange thing: "If this thing happens tonight, you will get a present." Fletcher didn't know what he was talking about and assumed that the German was drunk: "He seemed to be about half-tight, and was very excited-looking. I did not pay much attention to him." When they got back to the stable and Atzerodt mounted the horse, Fletcher cautioned him that the mare seemed as nervous as he did.

"I would not like to ride that mare through the city in the night, for she looks so skittish."

"Well," Atzerodt replied, "she's good upon a retreat."

Fletcher remembered that Atzerodt's friend, David Herold, was overdue in returning the horse he had rented that day. "Your acquaintance is staying out very late with our horse."

"Oh, he'll be back after a while," Atzerodt assured him.

Fletcher watched Atzerodt go down E Street, pass 13½ Street, and enter the Kirkwood House. Like Powell, Atzerodt was armed with a knife and a pistol—a six-shot revolver. Indeed, he was better armed than Powell, for he had in his room upstairs a second revolver and knife. His room, number 126, was one floor above Johnson's. The vice president—alone and unguarded—had retired for the night. All Atzerodt had to do was knock on his door and, the moment Johnson opened it, plunge the knife into his chest or shoot him dead. Compared with the tasks that faced Booth and Powell, Atzerodt had the easiest job of all.

Atzerodt hunkered down over the Kirkwood bar, hoping to drink enough courage to carry him up the stairs to Andrew Johnson's room. John Fletcher had kept an eye on the Kirkwood ever since Atzerodt went inside. Perhaps something about the garrulous German's behavior had aroused his curiosity, or his suspicion. Fletcher watched Atzerodt walk out of the Kirkwood a few minutes after he went in, mount his horse, and ride toward D and Tenth streets, near Ford's Theatre. He did not appear to be in a hurry.

John Fletcher could not stop fretting about his overdue horse. Herold knew that he wasn't supposed to keep "Charlie" past 8:00 P.M.—9:00 at the latest. "At about 10 o'clock [I was] having a suspicion that Herold was going to take the horse away." Fletcher feared the worst—the horse had been stolen. He wasn't going to wait any longer. He decided to search the streets of downtown Washington for the Naylor stables' property.

Andrew Johnson had escaped the reaper's knock on his door. Atzerodt couldn't do it. The more he drank, the worse the plan sounded. He did not call on Andrew Johnson. He left the bar and walked out. Abandoning his mission, Atzerodt got on the mare and rode away. He wasn't sure what to do now. He didn't know it yet, but he was about to undertake a comical escape journey.

In the saddle, a few blocks from Ford's, David Herold relished his escape from the Seward house disaster. He had gotten away just in time, before the fleeing Powell could rejoin him on the street or call out his name. No one in the house realized that Powell had an accomplice waiting in the wings. Fanny Seward possessed the right instincts in suspecting that Powell was not alone, but she feared a companion assassin lurking in the house, not on the street outside. For the moment, Davey was safe. No one pursued him when he fled the scene, and no one at the Seward house saw or could implicate him. At the moment he was just another man on a horse on a happy night in Washington. He regretted abandoning Powell, but when the titan botched his assignment, Herold decided to save himself.

For half an hour, between about 10:15 and 10:45 P.M., David Herold was a man with options. He could go home to his widowed mother's house on Eighth Street, pretend that nothing had happened, and hope for the best, a risky strategy if the manhunters captured Booth, Powell, Atzerodt, Arnold, O'Laughlen, or the Surratts. Any one of them could implicate him. Even if they did not, too many people in Washington had seen him in Booth's company too many times. Someone would remember that. It was only a matter of time before the police or soldiers came to question him. No, going home was a bad idea. Alternatively, he could run away and lose himself in the isolation of a small town or the anonymity of a big city like New York, Boston, or Philadelphia. Or he could outfit himself and take to the backwoods of Maryland for months, living by his wits and his hunting and fishing skills. Or he could cleave unto Booth, his master, who would soon approach the Navy Yard Bridge and then close in on their prearranged rendezvous point on the other side of the river.

Between 10:20 and 10:30 P.M., Herold rode down Pennsylvania Avenue, leaving the Seward mansion behind, and now heading away from the Treasury building and approaching Fourteenth Street. At the same time, Fletcher was walking up Fourteenth toward Pennsylvania. Herold and Fletcher reached the intersection, near Willard's hotel, simultaneously. Instinctively, Charlie pulled against the reins, trying to get off Pennsylvania and turn onto Fourteenth. Fletcher recognized the action—the horse was heading home. The roan, Fletcher knew, "was a horse very well acquainted with the stable," and he "seemed as if he wanted to go to the stable." Fletcher, eager to make that happen, prepared to dash after Herold and unseat him from the saddle: "I thought, if I could get close enough to him…I would take the horse away from him." As Fletcher closed the distance Herold spotted him—"I expect he knew me by the light of the gas, the lamp from Willard's corner," Fletcher concluded. Herold yanked on the reins and spun Charlie around. Fletcher yelled at him to stop: "You get off that horse now! You have had that horse out long enough."

Herold didn't say a word. Fletcher, on foot, watched helplessly as Herold "put spurs to the horse, and went, as fast as the horse could go, up Fourteenth Street." Fletcher lost sight of him when Herold turned right on F Street from Fourteenth. It was about 10:25 P.M. The foreman hurried back to Naylor's stable, saddled a mount, and went after Herold. Fletcher described his route of pursuit: "[I] went along... [Pennsylvania] Avenue until I came to Thirteenth Street; went up Thirteenth to E until I came to Ninth, and turned down Ninth Street to Pennsylvania Avenue again. I went along the avenue to the south side of the Capitol. I there met a gentleman, and asked him if he had passed any one riding on horseback. He said yes, and that they were riding very fast."

In a few minutes, Herold, mimicking Booth's route, approached the bridgehead at Eleventh Street. Sergeant Cobb and his guards were not inclined to let another man pass.

"I halted him," Cobb reported, "and when challenged he answered 'a friend.'" The sergeant asked where he was going.

"Home to White Plains."

Cobb vetoed Davey's crossing: "You can't pass it is after nine-o'clock, it is against the rules."

Herold challenged him back: "How long have these rules been out?" He hoped that pleading ignorance of the law might gain an exception.

For a while, Cobb replied, unmoved: "Some time ever since I have been here."

Davey persisted: "I didn't know that before."

Just as Cobb had questioned Booth, he asked Herold why he had left Washington so late: "Why weren't you out of the city before?"

Davey fabricated the perfect reply, one that any soldier might forgive: "I couldn't very well, I stopped to see a woman on Capitol Hill and couldn't get off before."

Herold waited for Cobb's reply and did not ask him if another rider matching Booth's description had crossed recently. Sergeant Cobb waved Herold across.

Fifteen minutes later, a third rider approached the bridge. It was Fletcher. He wasn't going to give up. "I followed on until I got to the Navy Yard bridge." One of the soldiers stopped him and called for his sergeant. When Cobb emerged from the guardhouse Fletcher asked if a horse matching this description had crossed: "A light roan horse; black tail, black legs, black mane, and close on fifteen hands high." The stolen animal had special characteristics: "He was a lady's saddle-horse; and any one could ride him, he was so gentle and nice." Then Fletcher described the saddle, bridle, and rider.

"Yes, he has gone across the bridge," Cobb replied.

"Did he stay long here?" "Did he tell you his name?"

"Yes," Cobb divulged, "he said his name was Smith."

Fletcher wanted to chase Herold into Maryland, and asked Cobb if he could continue the pursuit.

"Yes, you can cross the bridge; but you cannot return back." Those were the rules, Cobb insisted. He had already bent them twice. He would not do it again.

Fletcher wanted to return to Washington tonight. Dejected, the self-appointed manhunter gave up. "If that is so, I will not go." He turned around and rode back to the city. When he got to Third Street he looked at his watch. It was 11:50 P.M. He stopped at another stable, Murphy's, and the foreman told him the news: "You had better keep in, for President Lincoln is shot and Secretary Seward almost dead." Fletcher returned to Naylor's, put up his horse, and, at about 1:30 A.M., sat down in front of the office window. He didn't know that his private manhunt had almost captured one of the accomplices of Lincoln's killer.

Somewhere east of the Capitol building, Lewis Powell was not having as easy a time as Booth and Herold in fleeing the city. He had evaded William Bell and the others, and no one was chasing him now. But he did not know where he was. It got worse. He had lost or abandoned his surest and swiftest means of escape, the one-eyed horse that Booth bought for his gang. As midnight approached on the night of April 14, Lewis Powell was in trouble: he was a solitary figure standing in the moonlight, lost and unarmed, and wearing a coat stained with another man's blood. He did not know where to go or what to do. For the next two nights he slept in a tree. Without Booth to command him, he became confused and began thinking about some of the places he knew in Washington, places where Booth had taken him before. There was one in particular. He might be safe there—if he could just remember the address.

In Surrattsville, Maryland, thirteen miles southeast of Washington, John Lloyd, the proprietor of Surratt's tavern, retired for the night. He had been pretty tight in liquor that evening—really since the afternoon, if he were to be honest about it—and he was tired. Although Mary Surratt had told him that afternoon to expect some nighttime callers, they had never shown up. It made no difference to him.

Several miles south of Surrattsville, on an isolated farm near Bryantown, Maryland, Dr. Samuel A. Mudd, his wife, and their four young children were also in bed. Beantown, where Booth told Sergeant Cobb he was headed, was not far away.

ℰBRAHAM LINCOLN SLEPT, TOO. MORE THAN FIFTEEN MINutes after he was shot, he still lay prone on the floor of boxes seven and eight at Ford's Theatre. Although Dr. Leale had averted the president's immediate death and stabilized his patient, the novice surgeon wasn't sure what to do next. Lincoln could not be left to die on the floor of a theatre gone mad. As Leale contemplated his next move, a woman rushed through Ford's to get to the president. She knew that history was being made in that box, and she had convinced herself that she must be part of it. From her vantage point onstage, she saw that swift passage through the main floor was impossible. She would have to push through the throng on the main floor, and then go up the stairs against a panicked mob coursing down them. They might sweep her off her feet and

crush her. But her expert knowledge of the theatre's architecture allowed her to bypass almost the entire audience that stood between her
and Abraham Lincoln. Thomas Gourlay, father of the actress Jennie
Gourlay, led Keene to the box. Carrying a pitcher of water that would
serve as her passport to the president's box—she dare not spill it—she
slipped through a door near the stage and scurried up a hidden staircase that took her straight up to a private office near the box. In less
than a minute, she traversed the entire length of Ford's and emerged on
the second floor on the same side as Lincoln's box. She fought her way
to the door, through the vestibule, and into the box. No one thought to
bar the way to the great actress Laura Keene, star of tonight's performance.

The scene riveted Keene and excited her theatrical instincts. Mesmerized by the image of the stricken president, Keene imagined a fantastic tableaux with her as its central figure. It was a once-in-a-lifetime
opportunity, impossible to resist. Might she, the actress asked Dr. Leale,
cradle the dying president's head in her lap? It was a shocking request,
and of no possible physical comfort or medical benefit to Lincoln. Under normal circumstances, its brazenness would have provoked the vol-
canic Mary Lincoln into paroxysms of jealous anger. Recently Mary had
embarrassed herself and her husband when she raged viciously in public against the lovely wife of General Ord. Mrs. Ord's crime? Riding too
close to President Lincoln during a military review, and, in Mary's opinion, masquerading as the first lady. To all who witnessed it, the ugly incident opened a portal into the workings of Mary Lincoln's troubled
and sometimes pathetic mind. But now, delirious with grief and fear,
Mary Lincoln, sitting on the sofa a few feet away, uttered no objection to
Keene's intimate request. She probably did not even hear it. Dr. Leale
consented.

Laura Keene knelt beside Lincoln and formed her lap into a natural
pillow. She lifted his head, exposing the bloodstained linen handkerchief that Dr. Leale had placed below the wound. Leale removed it, and
Keene rested Lincoln's head in her lap. Bloodstains and tiny bits of gray

matter oozed onto the cream silk fabric, spreading and adding color to the frock's bright and festive red, yellow, green, and blue floral pattern. The wound did not bleed profusely, and of the trio of dresses bloodied that night, Laura's dress alone was spared the drenching that saturated the garments of Fanny Seward and Clara Harris.

Fanny's and Clara's dresses did not survive. But Laura Keene, like a Victorian bride who lovingly preserved her wedding dress as a sacred memento of her happiest day, cherished the blood- and brain-speckled frock from this terrible night. In the days ahead, people begged to see the dress, to caress its silken folds, and to marvel at the stains and the scenes of high drama they evoked. Soon it became the object of morbid curiosity. Others even asked Keene to model the dress and made surreptitious attempts to cut coveted swatches as bizarre keepsakes. In time, Keene banished the haunted artifact from her sight. But she could not bear to destroy it and instead exiled it into the care of her family so that she would never have to look at it again. The dress vanished long ago, but miraculously a few remnants—five treasured swatches— survived. Their gay floral pattern remains almost as bright as the day the dress was fashioned nearly a century and a half ago by Jamie Bullock of Chicago. But long ago the stains, once red, faded to a rust-colored, pale brown. Laura Keene became forever known for the Pietà-like improvisational scene she staged in the president's box. We remember her not for her deep talent, diverse repertoire, or lifetime of great performances, but for a single unscripted act that played out for only a few minutes in the box at Ford's Theatre on April 14, 1865. Her great contemporaries from the nineteenth-century American stage have faded into oblivion, forgotten by all except a tiny fraternity of theater scholars. But Keene's name lives on, forever linked to Abraham Lincoln's by the macabre, supporting role she played that night.

Her presence in the box also highlighted an uncomfortable fact. She was an actress, this was a theatre, and it was Good Friday, the most solemn day on the Christian calendar. But the president of the United States was not worshiping in church. Instead, he was dying on the floor of a secular and morally illicit landmark. The great Civil War journalist George Alfred Townsend spoke for many when he wrote, "The Chief Magistrate of thirty millions of people—beloved, honored, revered,— lay in the pent up closet of a play-house, dabbling with his sacred blood the robes of an actress."

Indeed, in two days a number of ministers would admonish Lincoln in their Sunday sermons for spending Good Friday in a theatre. So did John Wilkes Booth's devoted sister, Asia Booth Clarke: "It was the moan of the religious people, the one throb of anguish to hero-worshippers, that the President had not gone first to a place of worship or have remained at home on this jubilant occasion. It desecrated his idea to have his end come in a devil's den—a theatre.... That fatal visit to the theatre had no pity in it; it was jubilation over fields of unburied dead, over miles of desecrated homes."

THE SCENE IN THE PRESIDENT'S BOX WOULD HAVE AMUSED Asia's brother John. Leave it to Laura Keene to try to upstage his spectacular performance. Just like an actress to ride his coattails. Now safely across the Eleventh Street Bridge, Booth looked toward Maryland and plunged ahead into the dark. Of his three cohorts, he needed Davey Herold the most right now, more than Atzerodt or Powell. Once Booth escaped downtown Washington, reached the city limits, and crossed the river into Maryland, he sidestepped immediate danger. The countryside was dark and quiet, with few travelers using the empty roads. He trotted over the route he had rehearsed over the previous year for the kidnapping plot. No need to gallop now, with no pursuers in sight when Sergeant Cobb let him pass. Better to let the horse rest and regain her strength for later. As Booth rode on, he searched the horizon for Soper's Hill, the chosen rendezvous place. In daylight it seemed simple, but nightfall had leveled the hills. Alone in the country, he was out of his milieu. Booth was a creature of the city and its fancy hotel lobbies, hard liquor saloons, oyster bars, back alleys, and gaslit shadows. He did not have the skills he'd need to survive in the coming days, those of out-doorsman, hunter, or river boatman. But Herold was all of those things, and that's why Booth chose him, above all the others, to guide him.

Now that Booth had slowed down, the pain in his left leg bloomed under the moonlight. Near desperation after his hard ride, he gazed into the horizon just before midnight—he was about eight miles from Washington's city limits. Davey and the others might be a few minutes ahead or behind him, depending on exactly how they had timed their attacks on Seward and Johnson. Booth saw nothing ahead of him. When he turned to look behind him, he heard a noise trailing in the distance. Horses' hooves pounding the earth. Was it the first warning of a cavalry patrol in hot pursuit? As the noise increased in volume, it sounded, to Booth's relief, like one horse, not many. Then his solitary pursuer came within sight—a small man on a large gray horse. His eyes held Booth's for a long, suspicious moment, then relief trickled down the wounded assassin's spine. It was David Herold.

The actor was jubilant. He was on safe ground, and now he had his guide. Maryland, although it did not secede from the Union in 1861, remained a hotbed of secessionism. Maryland was as Confederate as a state could be without actually joining the Confederacy. If Maryland had become the twelfth star on the Confederate flag, the Union would have been in grave danger. Washington, D.C., would be surrounded by rebel states, isolated from the rest of the North. Thousands of its citizens joined the Confederate army, marching off to war to the tune of "Maryland, My Maryland." Rebel spies and couriers infested the state, and James McPhail, the U.S. Army provost marshal stationed there, had his hands full suppressing Confederate schemes in Baltimore. It was in Baltimore that the citizens plotted to assassinate Abraham Lincoln in February 1861 when he traveled through their city on the way to his inauguration, and a Baltimore mob had attacked Union troops—the Sixth Massachusetts Infantry—as the unit marched through the city. It was from Maryland that Booth drew several of the conspirators for his kidnapping plot. And it was in Bel Air that Booth grew from boy to young adult. Maryland was his ground, and, he was certain, its people would shelter him and wish him Godspeed on his journey to the Deep South.

Booth and Herold spurred their horses, riding southeast to their first safe house just a few miles away in Maryland. Booth likely grilled Herold with questions: Why was he alone? Where is Powell? Did he kill Seward? Had he seen Atzerodt? Did he murder Vice President Johnson? No, Herold would have answered, he hadn't seen Atzerodt since the conspirators broke up earlier in the evening to carry out the three assassinations. He had no idea whether Johnson was dead. Herold recounted what had happened at the Seward residence: the entry plan worked perfectly, and Powell and his little package were admitted to the mansion. All seemed quiet in the house. Herold heard no gunshots. About ten minutes later, a black servant ran out the front door into the street screaming "murder," and then a girl threw open an upstairs window and started yelling, too.

This news seemed to prove to Booth that the faithful Powell had carried out his mission. But the actor must have been displeased with Herold for abandoning Powell, for whom he had a special fondness. And Powell would have come in handy if they had to do to any fighting during their escape. Booth guessed that Powell, who never learned the geography of the capital city, was a lost man. Herold explained how he almost got caught, not by the police or the army, but by John Fletcher, the stable man who rented Herold his horse. Booth certainly told Herold of his success at Ford's Theatre. This was the assassin's first opportunity to describe his deed, and the irrepressible thespian in him probably laid it on thick.

ℬETWEEN 11:30 P.M. AND MIDNIGHT, GEORGE ATZERODT appeared on Sixth Street, without his horse, and boarded a streetcar headed for the Navy Yard. By chance, one of the passengers was someone he'd known for the past seven or eight years, a man named Washington Briscoe. Atzerodt failed to recognize him until Briscoe spoke to him. Briscoe asked him if he'd heard the news—Lincoln had been assassinated. Yes, he had, George replied. Atzerodt asked if he could spend the night at Briscoe's store at the Navy Yard. When Briscoe said no, Atzerodt became agitated: "His manner was excited, and he was very anxious to sleep there; he urged me to let him." Briscoe explained that someone else was already sleeping there, too, and he could not impose upon the man. Atzerodt stayed on the car and got off with Briscoe on I Street, near Briscoe's store. He asked a third time if he could spend the night. Briscoe refused again, but he waited with Atzerodt at the corner of I and Garrison streets for the streetcar to return. George told Briscoe that he was heading to the Pennsylvania House, also known as the Kimmell House, on C Street. Atzerodt got on the next car and headed back to downtown Washington. He still had his room key to the Kirkwood in his pocket. When he left there, he failed to surrender it to a front-desk clerk.

Luckily, Atzerodt did not return to the Kirkwood House. By late Saturday morning, John Lee, a member of the military police force, was breaking down the door to room 126. After the assassination, Major James O'Beirne, provost marshal of Washington, ordered Lee to rush to the vice president's hotel. He, too, might be a target. When Lee got there, a bartender, Michael Henry, informed him that a suspicious-looking man had rented a room the previous day. Lee scanned the hotel register until he spotted it: "a name written very badly—G. A. Atzerodt." Desk clerks Robert R. Jones and Lyman Sprague could not find the room key. Sprague escorted Lee upstairs. Atzerodt's door was locked. Lee broke it open and searched the room. Under the pillow he found a revolver, loaded and capped; between the sheets and mattress he discovered a large Bowie knife.

The room was filled with clues: a brass spur, a pair of socks, two shirt collars, a pair of new gauntlets, three boxes of cartridges, a piece of licorice, and a toothbrush. A black coat hung from a hook on the wall. Lee searched it and found a map of Virginia and three handkerchiefs.

One was embroidered with the name "Mary R. Booth." Lee found a bankbook from the Ontario Bank in Montreal, showing a credit of $455.00. The name of the account holder was "Mr. J. Wilkes Booth."

D<small>R</small>. L<small>EALE</small> <small>KNEW</small> <small>THERE</small> <small>WERE</small> <small>ALL</small> <small>KINDS</small> <small>OF</small> <small>REASONS</small> <small>HE</small> couldn't leave Abraham Lincoln to die on a theatre floor. The president was going to die—it was just a matter of time—and Leale had never seen a man with such a wound survive more than an hour. He was helpless to save Lincoln's life, but, now that he had stabilized him, he did have power over the place and manner of the president's passing. George Washington, the nation's first president, and the first former one to die, and William Henry Harrison and Zachary Taylor, the only presidents who had died in office, did not expire under tawdry circumstances, in shredded clothes on a boot-tracked, soiled floor, and neither would Abraham Lincoln. Leale's instincts issued another silent command: "Remove to safety." The president of the United States would die with dignity, in a proper bed. "Take him to the White House," someone in the box implored. Yes, take him home. Impossible, Leale explained, and the other two doctors who had joined him in the box, Charles Sabin Taft and the improbably named Albert Freeman Africanus King, who had arrived just after Taft, concurred. Even the brief carriage trip between Ford's and the Executive Mansion over unpaved, muddy streets, gouged deeply with ruts and tracks from hundreds of carriage wheels, would be too much for Lincoln to endure. The bumpy ride would jostle the head wound and instantly kill him. No, they must take him someplace closer. Another voice suggested Peter Taltavul's saloon next door, where Booth enjoyed his last drink. Others vetoed that suggestion at once: it was bad enough that Lincoln might die in a theatre, but a tavern? Unthinkable. Even obscene.

They prepared to lift Lincoln's body without knowing where they would take him. First Dr. Leale closed the curtain on Laura Keene's maudlin, private drama. Her fame guaranteed, her dress sanctified by gore, she released her hold on the martyr, rose from the floor, and stepped back. Leale told Dr. Taft to support Lincoln's right shoulder and Dr. King the left. Leale ordered other men in the box to place their hands under the torso, the pelvis, the legs. Leale bent down and cradled the head. On his order, their hands worked in unison and lifted the president from the floor. They inched toward the vestibule. Clara Harris and Major Rathbone got Mary Lincoln on her feet and supported her unsteady gait. The trio, accompanied by Keene, followed the body. They carried Lincoln through the vestibule headfirst. Creeping backward and looking over his shoulder at the door leading to the dress circle, Leale observed a crush of humanity blocking the way and straining to get a glimpse of the president. Leale's voice blasted at them twice like a battlefield trumpet: "Guards, clear the passage! Guards, clear the passage!"

The bearers emerged from the vestibule with their precious, fragile cargo and walked north to the curved staircase that, two and a half hours before, the president had ascended. A small force of officers and soldiers shoved the gawkers aside. Leale reversed course at the landing and choreographed Lincoln's descent feetfirst, to avoid tilting Lincoln's head down and increasing the pressure on the brain. The descent seemed to take forever. But Lincoln was barely alive and Leale wanted no sudden movements that might jostle the president and disrupt the heartbeat or respiration. Seaton Munroe, an assistant secretary at the Treasury Department, rushed from his seat to find out what had happened to Lincoln. "I now made my way towards the box exit to await the descent of Miss Keene, hoping to learn from her the President's condition." Munroe intercepted her, dress in disarray, hair disheveled, and stage makeup smeared, at the foot of the staircase leading from the box. "I begged her to tell me if Mr. Lincoln was still alive."

"God only knows," she shrieked.

The actress who began the night in a light comic role now looked to Munroe like an apparition from a nightmare. "Attired, as I had so often seen her, in the costume of her part in 'Our American Cousin,' her hair and dress were in disorder, and not only was her gown soaked in Lincoln's blood, but her hands, and even her cheeks where her fingers had strayed, were bedaubed with the sorry stains."

Outside Ford's on Tenth Street, an anxious crowd of theatre patrons, swelled by bewildered passersby, hovered near the front doors and awaited the president. Leale's team carried Lincoln through the lobby, out the doors, and across the top stone step where, just eleven hours earlier, John Wilkes Booth sat under the midday sun laughing and reading his letter, and calculating if he had enough time. The crowd gasped at the sight of the prostrate figure and pushed forward. Some men darted forward and dared to lay their hands upon Lincoln. In a few seconds they would swarm and surround the president. Leale, dismayed, searched for an open seam through the hundreds of pressing bodies that blocked his way. Paralyzed, Leale and the doctors and soldiers assisting him froze at the threshold of Ford's, cradling the body of the dying president in their arms.

Nearby, just a few yards to the right, Lincoln's carriage, its polished, black enameled surface glinting under the light of the big gas lantern atop the tall iron pole anchored in front of Ford's, offered sanctuary from the mob and safe transport to the Executive Mansion. The president's coachman Burke grasped the reins and tensed at the ready atop the carriage box, expecting in another moment to crack his whip for the mad dash up Tenth Street and then the quick turn west to the mansion. "For God's sake, take him home to the White House to die," an anonymous voice from the crowd cried, echoing the plea first voiced in the theatre. "To the White House," other voices begged. A reporter who went to the White House found citizens assembling there: "An immense crowd was gathered in front of the President's house, and a strong guard was also stationed there, many persons evidently supposing that he would be brought to his home."

No, Dr. Leale ordered again, the president would never survive the trip. At that moment an army officer pushed through the half-insane crowd, faced Leale with steely resolve in his eyes, and drew his sword from its scabbard: "Surgeon, give me your commands and I will see that they are obeyed," he bellowed.

The officer fought his way forward, cut a seam through the mob, and led Lincoln's bearers into the dirt street. Leale's eyes raced from side to side, scanning across Tenth Street for refuge. Straining his voice to communicate above the din to the sword-bearing officer, he shouted a succinct command. Take the president straight across the street and into the nearest house. A soldier sprinted ahead and pounded on the door, demanding entry. Then, incredibly, Leale halted the procession in the middle of the muddy street, and in full view of the horrified mob, yanked a blood clot from the hole in Lincoln's head to relieve the pressure on the brain, and tossed the gooey mass into the street. Fresh blood and brain matter oozed through Leale's fingers. The procession continued several more feet. Another clot. Then the same process all over again. When Leale was halfway across the street, soldiers on the far side made a beeline straight at him and yelled that the house was locked and no one answered the door. The scene was incredible, impossible. Shipwrecked, stranded in the middle of a muddy street with no place to go, the president of the United States was dying in the presence of hundreds, if not by now more than a thousand, frenzied witnesses.

From an upper window on the far side of Tenth Street, Carl Bersch, an artist, looked down on the drama playing out in the street below. His practiced observer's eyes captured, like a camera, every detail—the big, glowing gaslight, the prostrate president borne by many hands, the swarming crowd. What a fine subject this scene would make for an oil painting, he mused.

Up until this moment no one had paid attention to William Petersen's neat, three-story brick row house next door to the home that denied entry to the president. Inside, one of Petersen's boarders, Henry Safford, sat quietly reading a book in the front first-floor parlor. Dr. Leale was trying to figure out what to do next when he saw somebody open the front door of 454 Tenth Street. Safford had heard the shouting mob and ventured outside to see what was happening. He stepped out onto the top step of the high, curved staircase, and raised high a sole candle. "Bring him in here!" he shouted above the human sea that coursed between him and the president. "Bring him in here!"

Leale changed course. He'd found a safe house, at last.

Chapter Four

"We Have Assassinated the President"

RIDING IN OPEN COUNTRY ABOUT TEN MILES SOUTH FROM Washington, John Wilkes Booth and David Herold had not yet reached their safe house. Surrattsville was almost an hour's ride away, but they didn't expect any trouble along the route. Just as Booth hoped, the assassination had thrown Washington into chaos. As they pressed on, Booth and Herold didn't encounter any soldiers on the road ahead, and even if they had, there was no danger because they were riding in advance of the news. At this moment the assassin could ride unmolested past an entire regiment of Union cavalry. Not a soul in Maryland knew that Abraham Lincoln had been shot.

Within a few minutes of the assassination, however, the news began spreading from Ford's by word of mouth, but it went no faster than a man could run on foot or ride on horseback. Between 10:30 and 11:00 P.M. more than fifteen hundred mouths poured from the theatre onto Tenth Street. Some maintained a vigil in front of Ford's or the Petersen house, but many fanned out in all directions, like an unpaid army of newsboys shouting "Extra!" House by house, block by block, they spread the news. Men ran or galloped to the White House, the War Department, the homes of cabinet officers, Pennsylvania Avenue, and newspaper row. They invaded the lobbies of the Willard, Kirkwood, and National hotels, and threw open the doors of oyster houses, saloons, and houses of ill repute. They rushed home and roused families and boarders, knocked on neighbors' doors, roused children from their beds.

Washingtonians were used to getting important news this way. When the telegraph arrived at the War Department announcing that the Union had taken Richmond on April 3, War Department clerks, without permission or command, exploded into the street and ran in every direction shouting tidings of joy. Again on April 9, they rocketed from their desks to spread the news of Appomattox. Tonight, like a terrible inferno burning outward in all directions from a single flashpoint of origin, the news spread from Ford's in ever-widening concentric circles. At Grover's Theatre the manager interrupted the performance of *Aladdin* and told the audience that Abraham Lincoln had just been shot. A frightened twelve-year-old boy screamed in horror. Tad Lincoln, the president's youngest boy, was rushed home to the White House by his chaperon, the president's doorman, Alphonso Donn.

Simultaneously, word of another assassination spread from the Seward mansion and into the streets. Neighbors, soldiers, State Department employees, and even a few fleet-footed reporters tried to gain entry to the house. Messengers—some self-appointed—fanned out in all directions barking word of the Seward assassination just as their counterparts from Ford's proclaimed the president's. It was only a matter of time before two armies of town criers, bearing word of separate attacks, collided in the streets. The same exchange happened countless times that night: No, I tell you, it was Lincoln who was assassinated. Impossible, it was Seward. I just came from his house. And I just came from Ford's. It was Lincoln. It was Seward. Then the terrible truth emerged—it was both.

At 1325 K Street someone rang the bell at the home of the most powerful man in Washington, aside from the president: Secretary of War Edwin M. Stanton, "Mars," Lincoln's god of war. A brilliant lawyer with a distinguished record of public service, Stanton did not suffer fools. He couldn't. The president placed in his hands the most awesome task of the war: raising, training, equipping, and sending into battle the army of the Union. Creating that army was the most monumental logistical achievement in American history up to that time. Stanton weeded out incompetent, unfit, or scoundrel officers; battled fraudulent government contractors who foisted shoddy uniforms, rotting equipment, and defective weapons upon the troops; and suffered along with Lincoln an epidemic of general officers who would not fight. If any man sat at Lincoln's right hand during the war of the rebellion, it was Edwin McMasters Stanton.

Their relationship got off to a rocky start. Before the war the two had crossed paths in an important lawsuit. Stanton, a nationally known attorney, scoffed at Lincoln and dismissed him as an uncouth, country idiot. Lincoln never held a man's high opinion of himself against him, as he had proven by appointing William Henry Seward, his great rival for the presidency, secretary of state. So, too, when he made Stanton his secretary of war in 1862. The business of the war brought them into intimate, daily contact at the Executive Mansion, the War Department, the telegraph office, or the Soldiers' Home, a summer refuge for the Lincoln and Stanton families. They grew close, and each developed a profound respect for the other's talents. And both knew that when they gave orders, men died. In their private lives, both had suffered tragedies that affected them more deeply than they would care to let most men know. By April 1865 the butcher's bill was high: more than three hundred thousand Union dead. Lincoln once bestowed on Stanton the highest compliment he paid to any cabinet officer during the entire war: Stanton, he said, was the great rock upon which the mighty waves of the rebellion crashed and were broken.

Stanton had looked forward to a low-key evening at home on April 14. After the grand celebrations on April 3 and 9, and the previous evening's astonishing illumination of the capital city, Stanton sought quiet relief. He turned down the president's invitation to join him and Mary at Ford's Theatre tonight. Instead, he left his office at the War Department and went home for dinner with his wife, Ellen. Around 8:00 P.M., not long before the curtain rose on *Our American Cousin* at Ford's, Stanton left his house to visit William H. Seward's sickbed again. Ever since the carriage accident, the secretary of war had been a faithful bed-side presence, a kindness that touched Seward's daughter, Fanny. Stanton returned home a little before 9:00 P.M. to keep an unusual appointment, a patriotic custom that augmented the effervescence of victory week: the serenade.

Since the fall of Richmond, and more so since Lee's surrender, bands of citizens intoxicated with joy—and often more—would roam the streets at night bearing torches, waving flags and banners, playing musical instruments, and singing songs. Wandering from place to place, they visited the White House, where, to their delight, the president appeared and addressed them. They visited hotels, theatres, and public houses, and sometimes they wandered aimlessly. Some serenades came together spontaneously, pulled together, it seems, by random gravitational forces. Others were organized in advance with military precision by government workers. Tonight the War Department clerks, the first men in Washington privileged to learn the news of Richmond and Appomattox, would, by prior arrangement, call upon their boss. By the time Stanton got home, he could already see the approaching torches bobbing in the street. "Mars" played his part and welcomed them graciously. After he addressed the crowd a little after 9:00 P.M., it marched to its next destination: Ford's Theatre. The serenaders wanted to surprise President Lincoln after the play, when he stepped out onto Tenth Street.

After Stanton bid some army officers good night, he closed his front door and locked it. It was 10:00 P.M., and he walked upstairs and began undressing for bed. Not long after the doorbell rang. His wife, Ellen, still downstairs, unlocked and opened the door. If Ellen Stanton had known that murder was afoot in Washington that night, she most likely would not have answered the door. When Ellen heard the news from the messenger, she screamed, "Mr. Seward is murdered!"

Her piercing cry echoed upstairs to her husband, who scoffed at the tale. "Humbug," he shouted down, "I left him only an hour ago."

When a dubious Stanton came downstairs, he found not only the excited messenger but several other highly agitated men. Alarmed by the insistence and vividness of their accounts, he decided to investigate the rumor personally. Within a few minutes, he was racing in a carriage to the Seward home. It could not be true, Stanton tried to convince himself. In four years of Civil War, countless incredible—and false—rumors swept in and out of Washington as predictably as the tide and the phases of the moon. But assassination? Impossible. Yes, Stanton had scolded the president regularly for his inattention to his own safety. But perhaps he was an alarmist. After all, as William Seward himself had written in 1862, political murder was alien to our customs: "Assassination is not an American practice or habit, and one so vicious and desperate cannot be engrafted into our political system. This conviction of mine has steadily gained strength since the civil war began. Every day's experience confirms it."

Stanton's ride took only a few minutes, and the first sign was not good—people filled the street and crowded around Seward's front door. An hour ago, when Stanton left the Seward home, the street was deserted. What were all these people doing here? As soon as the carriage halted, an army sergeant named Koerth babbled that he had just come from Ford's Theatre and had terrible news: the president had been assassinated. Stanton had arrived moments before the secretary of the navy, Gideon Welles, reached Seward's house.

Welles had retired to bed around 10:30 P.M. and was just falling asleep when his wife, Mary Jane, said someone was at their front door. The secretary heard a man's voice yelling for his son, John, whose second-floor bedroom was at the front of the house. Welles got out of bed, raised a window, poked his head through the opening, and peered down at the man standing at his door. It was James Smith, his Navy Department messenger. Smith looked up at his boss and shouted the news:

Secretary of War Edwin McMasters Stanton.

President Lincoln has been shot, and Secretary Seward and his son, Frederick, have been assassinated.

Welles told him his story was "very incoherent and improbable." To Welles, Smith looked "much alarmed and excited." Where, asked the navy secretary, "was the president shot?" At Ford's Theatre, Smith replied, adding that the Sewards had been attacked at home. "Damn the Rebels," Welles cursed, "this is their work." He dressed immediately and walked with Smith to Seward's house.

Stanton, just behind Welles, charged upstairs to Seward's bedroom. It was true. A scene of mayhem replaced the domestic tranquility Stanton had seen little more than an hour ago. "The bed," Welles saw, "was saturated with blood." Several doctors hovered over the bloody secretary of state, working feverishly to save his life. Then the rest of the nightmare came into focus: Fanny Seward, wandering like a pale ghost, her dress dripping with blood; Augustus Seward stabbed and his brother unconscious from a crushed skull; Sergeant Robinson with multiple stab wounds; and the messenger Hansell sliced through the back.

Recovering from their initial shock, Stanton and Welles realized that there was nothing they could do now for the victims at the Seward slaughter pen; it was in the hands of the doctors, and God. They turned their thoughts to the president: "As we descended the stairs, I asked Stanton what he had heard in regard to the President that was reliable. He said the President was shot at Ford's Theatre, that he had seen a man who was present and witnessed the occurrence." Welles proposed that they go immediately to the White House. But, Stanton said, Lincoln wasn't there. He was still at Ford's. "Then let us go immediately there," Welles said. Stanton agreed, but first he gave orders to rush military guards to the home of every member of the cabinet and to Vice President Johnson's hotel. On their way out of Seward's house, Stanton and Welles ran into Montgomery Meigs, quartermaster general of the United States Army, who warned them that the trip to Ford's could be dangerous. Meigs begged Stanton not to go down to Tenth Street. What if assassins had marked the president and every officer in his cabinet for death that night? Stanton had no entourage or army escort to protect him, but still he ignored Meigs and called for a carriage to transport him and Welles to the theatre at once. They would ride alone—if they left now, they could make it in less than five minutes. The quartermaster general insisted on joining them, as did Judge David Cartter of the Supreme Court of the District of Columbia, who had rushed to Seward's as soon as he heard the news.

On Tenth Street, Dr. Leale ordered Lincoln's bearers and the officer spearheading the procession to head straight for the man with the candle. They carried the president up the curved staircase. In this elevated position, for the first time since he was carried into the street, the near lifeless body of Abraham Lincoln became visible to the entire crowd. Awestruck, the people watched as their president disappeared into the Petersen house. Except for a handful of doctors, government officials, and family friends who would, in the hours to come, be granted access to the closely guarded house, that glimpse of the president, ascending the stairs of the Petersen house, was the last time Americans saw Abraham Lincoln alive.

As Stanton and Welles were leaving the Seward house, a lone man on horseback raced up and tried to stop the carriage. It was Major Thomas Eckert, one of Stanton's most trusted aides, head of the War Department's telegraph office, and a favorite of Abraham Lincoln, who marveled at the major's physical strength. Eckert implored Stanton to turn around and not approach the theatre. "At this moment," Welles recalled, "Major Eckert rode up on horseback and protested vehemently against Stanton's going to Tenth Street." Eckert had just come from there. The mob in the streets had already grown to thousands, and by the minute it was swelling in size—and danger—as news spread and citizens from all over the city converged on the site. Stanton and Welles defied him—nothing would stop them from attending the president. Meigs, in a concession to Eckert, ordered two soldiers to accompany the carriage. Eckert spurred his horse around, got in front of their carriage, and escorted it in the direction of Tenth Street. If he couldn't stop them, at least he could try to protect them. Ford's stood five blocks east and two blocks south of the Seward place.

As the carriage clipped along, it passed the indistinct shapes of men running haywire in all directions, some away from Ford's and others right to it. At first, there were not enough people in the street to stop Stanton's progress, but the closer the carriage got to Ford's, the thicker the crowds became. Welles described the scene: "The streets were full of people. Not only the sidewalk but the carriage-way was occupied, all…hurrying towards Tenth Street." As the carriage came down F Street and neared Tenth, Major Eckert, in the lead, was the first to see it, right ahead: a roaring, unruly, frenzied, and angry mob of thousands of people teeming at the corner of Tenth and F. Eckert spurred his horse forward.

ALMOST THIRTEEN MILES OUT OF WASHINGTON, BOOTH AND Herold had the road to themselves. An inconsequential encounter with two men and a broken-down wagon proved harmless and hardly slowed their escape. They rode quietly as they closed on their destination: Surrattsville, Maryland, not a real town of any size and little more than a crossroads outpost, named after the family that owned the tavern there. Before they could continue south, where they would seek medical treatment for Booth's injured leg, they had business at that tavern.

The dark outline of a building appeared vaguely on the horizon. Surratt's place was hard to spot at night—the two-story, frame structure was unpainted, and the dull wood boards, unlike a pigmented surface, reflected no light. Built in 1852, the tavern had served three functions in its heyday: saloon, inn, and post office. It was not a high example of the carpenter's art: the structure was plain, boxy, and finished roughly. Indeed, the doorframe was even crooked. The original owner, John Surratt Sr., sold whiskey by the finger, rented out rooms by the night, and served as U.S. postmaster. When John died in 1862, his widow, Mary Surratt, inherited the place and stayed on with her children. One son, John Jr., won the appointment of postmaster, replacing his father.

The government issued him an impressive, oversize commission, measuring fifteen by eleven inches, engraved with a handsome patriotic eagle and the boldly printed legend: "Post Office Department/Montgomery Blair Postmaster General of the United States of America." The document continued in the flowery language typical of executive branch appointments in that day: "To all who shall see these Presents, Greeting…on the 1st day of September 1862, John H. Surratt was appointed Postmaster at Surratt's in the County of Prince George, State of Maryland; and whereas he did, on the 8th day of September 1862…[take] the oath of office…know ye, that confiding in the integrity, ability and punctuality of the said John H. Surratt, I do commission him as a Postmaster." Surratt's commission was signed by Montgomery Blair on September 10, 1862.

Eventually, the government caught on to the questionable status of Surratt's loyalty and integrity and revoked his commission. In 1864, Mary moved her family to her Washington, D.C., boardinghouse and rented the tavern to a man named John Lloyd.

The tavern operated in the usual fashion of a nineteenth-century roadside establishment. The premises were divided into private and public spaces. Paying customers entered, not through the front door and center hall, but through a side door that led directly into the bar and post office. The room smelled like wax candles, oil lamps, tobacco, burning stove wood, whiskey, soiled clothes, and boot leather. Drink and meal prices were posted on a wall or chalked on a board. Nighttime callers were not unusual. During the war, the Surratts and Lloyd grew accustomed to them.

Booth and Herold rode their horses to the side entrance. The night was still, and, inside, the tavern was quiet and dark. They had to make this quick. Herold dismounted and strode to the door while Booth remained in the saddle. They had no time to tarry, and it would hurt Booth too much to dismount and put weight on his foot. The stirrup was painful enough; dismounting and then mounting the horse again would be excruciating. Herold's pounding fist finally awakened the hard-drinking Lloyd. He climbed out of bed, went downstairs, and opened the side door. He recognized David Herold, a friend of John Surratt. Herold, impatient, hissed at him: "Lloyd, for God's sake, make haste and get those things."

Davey did not have to be more specific. Lloyd knew what they wanted. After Mary Surratt's afternoon visit, he took the "shooting irons" from their hiding place so they would be ready for the callers. Lloyd left Herold in the bar with a bottle of whiskey and went into the house. Herold poured himself a glass. Lloyd returned in a moment, bearing a small package wrapped in twine—the field glasses—and a loaded Spencer repeating carbine. Herold seized the weapon and carried the bottle outside to Booth. While sitting on his horse the actor swallowed several big gulps to steady his nerves and dull the pain. Lloyd offered the second Spencer to Booth but he declined it. With his broken leg, he didn't want to carry any more. He needed his hands to hold on to the saddle. His pistols would have to do. He would pick them up at his next stop.

Herold retrieved the bottle from Booth and brought it back to Lloyd. "I owe you a couple of dollars," he said. "Here." Herold handed him a one-dollar note that, Lloyd calculated, "just about paid for the bottle of liquor that [they] had just pretty nearly drank." As Herold and his master prepared to ride off, Booth could not resist the temptation any longer. The boastful, impulsive thespian had to tell someone or he would burst.

"I will tell some news, if you want to hear it," Booth offered.

Lloyd responded indifferently. "I am not particular; use your own pleasure about telling it."

"Well," continued Booth, "I am pretty certain that we have assassinated the President and Secretary Seward."

Lloyd, "very much excited and unnerved" by his own account, said nothing. He watched them ride off into the night "at a pretty rapid gait," not understanding exactly what Booth had meant. Then he went back to bed. Booth and Herold had spent less than five minutes in Surrattsville.

They continued on to the south and east for an unplanned but necessary detour.

Booth's leg was throbbing painfully. He needed a doctor. And he knew just where to find one, a four hours' ride away.

At the Petersen house, Abraham Lincoln would soon have more doctors than he could ever want, but little use for any of them.

As soon as the president was carried across the threshold, Dr. Leale commanded Henry Safford to "take us to your best room." To his right Leale saw a narrow staircase leading up to the second- and third-floor bedrooms. To his immediate left was the front parlor where, just a few minutes earlier, Safford read quietly until he heard the commotion in the street. In front of Leale a dim hallway led to the rear of the house. Safford told the doctor to follow him there. Leale, and as many of Lincoln's bearers as could squeeze their bodies into the tight passageway, carried the president behind their host. As they shuffled along, they passed a second parlor on the left situated directly behind the first. They could not see the bed until they actually stepped into the back room, glanced to the right, and found it wedged into the northeast corner, its side running along the north wall and the headboard pushed against the east wall, close to the door. Leale's eyes cast about the chamber. The occupant, William Clark, was out for the evening, celebrating the end of the war. This would do. It would have to.

Chasing after the president, Mary Lincoln, escorted by Clara Harris and Major Rathbone, with Laura Keene trailing at their heels, burst into the Petersen boardinghouse. Wringing her hands in anguish, Mary looked "perfectly frantic" to George Francis, one of the tenants. "Where is my husband? Where is my husband?" she pleaded to no one in particular. Behind the first lady's party, a number of opportunistic strangers scampered up the stairs, and, taking advantage of the confusion, slipped into the house before any guards could be posted at the door. The interlopers were probably no more than heedless curiosity seekers, but who could guarantee that more assassins were not lurking among them, intent on finishing Booth's work? The strangers invaded the first-floor parlors and worked their way down the hallway, inching closer to the president. If someone did not take command soon, the situation in the Petersen house would break down into utter chaos.

At the corner of Tenth and F streets, Secretary of War Stanton's carriage approached the surging mob. Apprehensive, Major Eckert doubted whether the horses would drive through it. Wary of the crowd's size and sensing its mood, they might balk. And there was the possibility that the throng, refusing to yield, might overwhelm them. But Stanton and Welles were determined to ignore the danger. They must push on.

In the back bedroom, Dr. Leale ignored the chaos around him. Only one person mattered now. Someone tore back the coverlet and top sheet. Someone else turned up the valve of the gas jet protruding from the wall to full flame. In an instant the hissing, burning vapor illuminated the grotesque scene. The others laid the unconscious body upon the mattress. Mary Lincoln burst into the room, and the bright gaslight confirmed to her that this was not the nightmare she hoped it was—this was real.

Leale held the president's head steady and ordered his helpers to stretch Lincoln's body out to its full length, in preparation for a complete examination. When Lincoln's heavy boots kicked the footboard, his legs were still not straight. The bed was too short, and his bent knees stuck up in the air. Break the footboard off the bed, Leale demanded. But it wouldn't budge. Try again, exhorted Leale. Impossible, Doctors Taft and King explained. It was integral to the construction of the bed, and if they broke it off, the whole bed would collapse to the floor with

Lincoln in it. Frustrated, Leale laid Lincoln out across the bed diagonally, with his head on the corner of the mattress closest to the door and his feet on the corner closest to the wall.

Leale leaned in close to the president's face. He was still alive. Leale decided to give the president a few minutes to gather what strength he still possessed before undertaking a complete examination. At this moment of temporary repose, Leale seemed, for the first time, to take in his surroundings. He sniffed the moist and stifling air. There were too many people in the little room, raising the temperature and sucking the oxygen that Lincoln needed to live. Leale ordered the windows opened. Then he ordered everyone but doctors and friends of the president out. Still too many people. Leale asked all but the doctors to leave. Mary Lincoln remained and hovered over her husband. Dr. Leale prodded her gently. He explained that he and the other doctors must examine the president now. After that, she could return to his side. Mary agreed to leave the room and went to a sofa in the front parlor, where she remained throughout the night whenever she was not at the bedside. Alone with their patient, Leale, Taft, and King worked quickly, stripping Abraham Lincoln naked, head to toe.

Maunsell B. Field, assistant secretary of the treasury, pushed through the masses packed in front of the Petersen house and forced his way inside. The first person he saw, Clara Harris, told him that the president was dying but admonished him not to tell Mary Lincoln. It was obvious to everyone that Mary was coming apart and no one wanted to push her over the edge into total breakdown. Field entered the parlor and found Mary "in a state of indescribable agitation." He heard her ask the same question "over and over again": "Why didn't he kill me? Why didn't he kill me?" To Clara Harris, Mary Lincoln chanted another lament throughout the night. Whenever Mary laid eyes upon Clara's crimson-streaked dress, she recoiled in horror. "My husband's blood," she moaned again and again. "My husband's blood." Clara chose not to correct her. It was not the president's blood that soaked her dress, but that of her fiancé, Henry. And his supply was running low: "The wound which I had received was bleeding profusely, and, on reaching the house…feeling very faint from the loss of blood, I seated myself in the hall, and soon after fainted away, and was laid upon the floor. Upon the return of consciousness, I was taken to my residence."

A few hundred feet away, Stanton's carriage came to a standstill, unable to penetrate the crowd. The coachman simply could not drive the horses through the mob. Stanton decided that if they could not ride, they would walk. He opened the door and dismounted the carriage, joined by his passengers Secretary of the Navy Welles, Judge Cartter, and General Meigs. Eckert could not believe his eyes. Sitting in their carriage, elevated above the crowd, the officials were relatively safe, like passengers in a lifeboat riding atop a tumultuous sea. But on foot, in the dark, in the midst of thousands of people, anything could happen that night. Indeed, it already had. But now Stanton's entourage, which included the two cabinet secretaries responsible for the entire, combined armed forces of the United States on land and at sea, headed into the mob and vanished from sight.

ON THE ROAD SOUTH AND EAST FROM SURRATTSVILLE, BOOTH and Herold had the road to themselves—they saw and were seen by no one. Although desperate to put as much distance as possible between themselves and Washington, they had to be careful to not ride their horses too fast or hard. They had a long way to go and could not risk having the horses break down during a prolonged and dangerous sprint. Booth had pushed his horse to the limit when he galloped through downtown Washington, but escaping Baptist Alley and putting that first mile or two between himself and Ford's Theatre was vital. Once he left Lloyd's tavern, he paced the animal more carefully.

DRS. LEALE, TAFT, AND KING SCRUTINIZED LINCOLN'S ENTIRE body front and back for knife or gunshot wounds but found nothing other than the bullet hole in the head. During their examination they noticed that the president's lower extremities—his feet and legs—were already getting cold. Lincoln's eyes were closed. The lids and surrounding tissue were so filled with blood that to Dr. Taft they looked bruised, like someone had punched the president in the face. The doctors lifted the lid covering Lincoln's left eye: the pupil was very contracted. They lifted the lid over the right eye: the pupil was widely dilated, and both pupils were totally insensitive to light—all signs consistent with a catastrophic, irreversible injury to the brain. On the doctors' orders, a hospital steward from Lincoln Hospital, a nearby military facility, sprinted from the bedside and returned with hot water, brandy, blankets, and a large sinapism, or mustard plaster. Soon the surgeons covered the whole anterior surface of Lincoln's body, from the neck to the toes, with mustard plasters to keep him warm. Then they covered him up to his chin with a sheet, blankets, and a coverlet. His breathing was regular but heavy, interrupted by an occasional sigh. They laid a clean, white napkin over the bloodstains on the pillow. They placed a small chair at the head of the bed, near Lincoln's face. Now the president was ready for Mary to see him again. Leale sent an officer to the front parlor to inform her. She rushed to the bedroom and sat beside her husband. "Love, live but for one moment to speak to me once—to speak to our children." Lincoln was deaf to her pleas.

With the president's condition stable for now, or at least as stable as that of a dying man shot through the brain could be, Dr. Leale diverted his attention from medical to practical concerns. He sent messengers summoning Robert Todd Lincoln, the president's eldest son; Surgeon General Joseph K. Barnes; Surgeon D. Willard Bliss at the Armory Square Hospital; Lincoln's family physician, Dr. Robert King Stone; and the president's pastor, the Reverend Dr. Phineas T. Gurley. He also sent a hospital steward in search of a special piece of medical equipment, a Nelaton probe. There was work to do inside Lincoln's brain.

Secretary of War Stanton pushed through the crowd, clambered up the stairs of the Petersen house and rushed down the hall. The sight of the president shocked him. He did not need doctors to tell him what would happen: Abraham Lincoln was going to die, and there was nothing that anyone could do about it. But he could do something: in the president's absence, he could protect and defend the country.

Stanton took charge of the Petersen house and commandeered the back parlor, the one closest to the bedroom, as his field office. He made a quick executive decision. He would not return to the War Department tonight but instead would remain with the president. The Petersen boardinghouse was the War Department now. Edwin Stanton assumed that the Lincoln and Seward assassinations had exposed the existence of a devilish Confederate plot to kill the leadership of the national government, reverse the verdict of the battlefield, and, in one last desperate assault, win the Civil War. Stanton and his lieutenants assumed that all the cabinet heads had been marked for death tonight. And a rebel army might be advancing on Washington at this moment.

Stanton wanted his commanding general back in Washington immediately and ordered his aides to track down U. S. Grant. It was the first telegram issued from the ersatz War Department headquarters at the Petersen house.

April 14th 12 P.M. 1865
Washington DC

To Lt. Genl Grant
On Night Train to Burlington
The President was assassinated tonight at Ford's Theatre
at 10 30 tonight & cannot live. The wound is a pistol shot
through the head. Secretary Seward & his son Frederick,
were also assassinated at their residence & are in a dangerous
condition. The Secretary of War desires that you return to
Washington immediately. Please answer on receipt of this.
Thos. T. Eckert, Maj.

It occurred to Charles A. Dana, assistant secretary of war, that Grant might be in danger. The newspapers had advertised his appearance at Ford's Theatre, and perhaps he, too, was on Booth's death list. Dana sent a telegram to Philadelphia, warning the commanding general of assassins or sabotage on the railroad: "Permit me to suggest to you to keep a close watch on all persons who come near you in the cars or otherwise; also, that an engine be sent in front of the train to guard against anything being on the track." Stanton rushed guards to the homes of all the cabinet secretaries to protect them from imminent assassination, if they were not dead already. He ordered military units to take to the streets. At midnight Quartermaster General Meigs, who had ridden with Stanton to the Petersen house, dispatched an urgent message to Major General Christopher Columbus Augur (who signed his name "C. C." for the obvious reasons), commander of the military district of Washington: "The Secretary directs that the troops turn out; the guards be doubled, the forts be alert; guns manned; special vigilance and guard about the Capitol Prison I advise, if your men are not sufficiently numerous, call upon General Rucker for assistance in furnishing guards." The troops must maintain order and be ready for anything on this wild night. And clear away the mob from the street in front of this house, Stanton ordered. Soldiers tried to push back the insistent throng that pressed forward and obstructed Petersen's staircase.

Stanton then turned to his second mission, launching an investigation that would ascertain what had happened at Ford's Theatre and the Seward house. He was determined to apprehend the criminals. He set up around his table a three-member court of inquiry—Judge Abram B. Olin, attorney Britten A. Hill, and chief justice of the D.C. courts David K. Cartter—to question witnesses. The secretary of war made it clear that he was in charge. Later, when Vice President Johnson arrived at the deathbed, he remained in the background and chose not to assert himself. In the days ahead the new president left it to Stanton to bring Lincoln's killer and his accomplices to justice.

Stanton had witnesses from Ford's Theatre dragooned and brought before him. They spoke so fast that he recruited a legless Union army veteran who lived next door, James Tanner, to take it down in shorthand. One witness after another swore that it was Booth, John Wilkes Booth. Stanton barked orders by telegraph—his operators could wire news and orders all over the country—and soon telegraph lines across the nation were singing the same frequency: the president and the secretary of state have been assassinated. Messages went from the War Department to Baltimore, New York, and beyond. Search the trains. Guard the bridges. Watch for suspicious characters. Question witnesses. Identify suspects. Make arrests.

Stanton did not have time to write out every order and telegram personally on Petersen's round parlor table. Soon the command structure took over as his trusted subordinates issued a blizzard of instructions. All through the first hours of April 15, the telegraph wires carried messages between Washington and commanders in the field. At 12:20 A.M., General James A. Hardie sent an order to the U.S. Military Railroad at Alexandria: "It is reported that the assassin of the President has gone out hence to Alexandria, thence on the train to Fairfax. Stop all trains in that direction. Apply to military commander at Alexandria for guard to arrest all persons on train or on the road not known. By order of the Secretary of War."

At Winchester, Virginia, General Stevenson received an urgent message about the trains: "Have any trains reached Harper's Ferry this morning?...[It] is possible that the assassins may endeavor to escape south through your lines at some point." In a 1:00 A.M. telegram, Augur informed Major General Winfield Scott Hancock, commanding the Middle Military Division at Winchester, that he could spare no troops: "The President, Mr. Lincoln, was assassinated at Ford's Theatre...and is now dying. The Secretary of State, Mr. Seward, was also stabbed in his bed, and is not expected to recover. I shall not be able to send cavalry as you ordered, as I wish to use them scouring the countryside for the assassins." Around the same time Augur ordered General Gamble, commanding at Fairfax Court House, to "at daylight take your cavalry and scatter it along the river toward Leesburg to arrest and send in all suspicious persons; also along your whole line between it and Washington."

$\mathcal{A}$T 1:10 A.M., APRIL 15, STANTON SENT A HURRIED TELEGRAM to John Kennedy, New York City's chief of police, asking him to rush detectives to Washington: "Send here immediately three or four of your best detectives to investigate the facts as to the assassination of the President and Secretary Seward. They are still alive, but the president's case is hopeless, and that of Mr. Seward's nearly the same."

$\mathcal{S}$OMETIME BETWEEN MIDNIGHT AND 1:00 A.M., GEORGE ATZE-rodt arrived at the Pennsylvania House. James Walker, a black employee whose job it was to "make fires, carry water, and to wait on gentlemen that come in late and early," greeted him. Atzerodt was on a horse again, and he told Walker to hold the animal while he went into the bar to drink. When he emerged from the bar he rode away but returned on foot around 2:00 A.M. He wanted a bed and asked for room 51, where he had stayed in the past. Walker and the innkeeper, John Greenawalt, told him that his old room was occupied—he'd have to stay in 53, a room with several beds that he would have to share with other occupants. As George headed to his room Greenawalt told him to come back:

"Atzerodt, you have not registered."

"Do you want my name?" He was reluctant to sign the book.

"Certainly," Greenawalt replied.

The innkeeper thought that the German behaved oddly. "He hesitated some, but stepped back and registered, and went to his room. He had never before hesitated to register his name."

After Atzerodt had settled into his room, another guest, Lieutenant W. R. Keim, climbed into the bed opposite his. They had a passing acquaintance, having shared room 51 a week or ten days ago. Keim mentioned the news: "I asked him if he had heard of the assassination of the President, and he said he had; that it was an awful affair."

At 1:30 A.M., STANTON SENT A TELEGRAM TO MAJOR GENERAL John A. Dix in New York. It contained the first details of the assassination:

> Last evening about 10:30 P.M. at Ford's Theatre the President while sitting in his private box with Mrs. Lincoln, Miss Harris and Major Rathbun [sic] was shot by an assassin who suddenly entered the box and approached behind the President. The assassin then leaped upon the Stage brandishing a large dagger or knife and made his escape in the rear of the theater. The Pistol ball entered the back of the President's head and penetrated nearly through the head. The wound is mortal. The President has been insensible ever since it was inflicted and is now dying.
>
> About the same hour an assassin (whether the same or another) entered Mr. Seward's house and under pretense of having a prescription, was shown to the Secretary's sick chamber, the Secretary was in bed a nurse and Miss Seward with him. The assassin immediately rushed to the bed inflicted two or three stabs on the throat and two on the face. It is hoped the wounds may not be mortal my apprehension is that they will prove fatal. The noise alarmed Mr. Frederick Seward who was in an adjoining room & hastened to the door of his father's room, where he met the assassin who inflicted upon him one or more dangerous wounds. The recovery of Frederick Seward is doubtful. It is not probable that the President will live through the night. General Grant & wife were advertised to be at the theater this evening, but he started to Burlington at 6 o'clock this evening.

At a cabinet meeting yesterday at which General Grant
was present, the subject of the State of the Country & the
prospect of speedy peace was discussed. The President was very
cheerful & hopeful spoke very kindly of General Lee and others
of the Confederacy, and the prospect of establishment of
government in Virginia.

The members of the Cabinet except Mr. Seward are now in
attendance upon the President. I have seen Mr. Seward but he
& Frederick were both unconscious.

Soon the wires sang back with messages to Stanton from military
commanders. We have received your news. We are obeying your orders.
John Wilkes Booth could be heading anywhere: to Baltimore, the city
where Lincoln was almost murdered in 1861, to his friends and old
haunts there. To New York, disloyal capital of American commerce. Or
farther north, to Canada, seat of operations for the Confederate Secret
Service. Booth could be anywhere. The government would have to
search for him everywhere. At 2:00 A.M., Major General Halleck, the army's chief of staff, telegraphed General W. W. Morris, commanding the
District of Baltimore: "Attempts have been made to-night to assassinate
the President and Secretary of State. Arrest all persons who leave Washington to-night on any road or by water, and hold them till further orders. In the meantime report as to each person arrested." At 3:00 A.M.,
Stanton wrote out another telegram to General Morris from his post
at the Petersen house: "Make immediate arrangements for guarding
thoroughly every avenue leading into Baltimore, and if possible arrest
J. Wilkes Booth, the murderer of Abraham Lincoln. You will acknowledge the receipt of this telegram, giving time, & c. Edwin M. Stanton,
Secretary of War." Before Major Eckert handed the order over to a messenger to run over to the War Department telegraph office, he added a
quick postscript in his own hand, addressed to the operators: "Bates,
Stewart, or Maynard: Rush this through and order the immediate delivery." Despite Eckert's demand, it took fifty-five minutes for the message

to travel from Stanton's table in the back parlor at the Petersen house into Morris's hands in Baltimore. He wrote his response at 4:15 A.M.: "Your dispatch received. The most vigourous measures will be taken. Every avenue is guarded. No trains or boats will be permitted to leave."

From Baltimore, Provost Marshal James L. McPhail sent an order to B. B. Hough at Saint Inigoes, Maryland: "The President is murdered: Mr. Seward and son nearly so. One of the murderers, J. Wilkes Booth, actor, played at Holliday Street a year ago. Twenty-five years old, five feet eight inches high, dark hair and mustache. He took the direction from Washington toward Saint Mary's and Calvert Counties. Use all attempts to secure him."

Back in Washington, General Halleck, perhaps overly optimistic, made plans to imprison the assassins. In Halleck's defense, if Booth was captured, the army would have to sequester him carefully to protect him from Lincoln's avengers—rampaging mobs of vigilantes who might storm the Old Capitol prison—should they discover that the assassin was jailed there. It was too risky to imprison Booth anywhere on land. Halleck issued an order to General Augur: "Should either of the assassins of last night be caught put them in double irons and convey them, under a strong escort, to the commander of the navy-yard, who has orders to receive them and to confine them on a monitor to be anchored in the stream." A watery moat would protect Booth from the angry citizens of Washington.

Water was the secretary of the navy's element, so Gideon Welles issued instructions personally to Commodore J. B. Montgomery at the Navy Yard: "If the military authorities arrest the murderer of the President and take him to the yard, put him on a monitor and anchor her in the stream, with strong guard on vessel, wharf, and in yard. Call upon commandant of Marine Corps for guard. Have vessel immediately prepared to receive him at any hour, day or night, with necessary instructions. He will be heavily ironed and so guarded as to prevent escape or injury to himself." Welles could hardly allow Booth to commit suicide aboard one of his ships. Just to be sure, Welles also sent an order to

Colonel Zeilin, commandant of the Marine Corps: "Have extra strong and careful guard ready for special service, if called for." The army, the navy, and the marine corps were ready. Now all they had to do was catch John Wilkes Booth, Lewis Powell, John H. Surratt, David Herold, and George Atzerodt.

Halleck telegrammed Major General Ord in Richmond: "Attempts have been made to-night to assassinate the President and Secretary of State. Arrest all persons who may enter your lines by water or land." Late that day General Grant, now back in Washington, sent Ord a telegram ordering him to arrest all paroled Confederate officers and surgeons. "Extreme rigor," Grant warned, "will have to be observed whilst assassination remains the order of the day with the rebels."

Arrest everyone? a skeptical Ord wired back to Grant—even General Lee and his staff? That would be dangerous and unwise, Ord cautioned, and might incite a violent uprising in the former Confederate capital if rebel soldiers and the local citizenry feared that their hero Robert E. Lee was in danger: "Should I arrest them under the circumstances," Ord continued, "I think the rebellion here would be reopened." Grant relented: "On reflection I withdraw my dispatch."

*T*HE DOCTORS CONTINUED THEIR USELESS MINISTRATIONS TO the dying president. They probed the wound with their bare, unsanitary fingers, sticking their pinkies inside Lincoln's brain. They deployed the Nelaton probe to locate the bullet for possible extraction, as if that would have helped Lincoln. They poured a little brandy into their patient's mouth to see if he could retain and swallow it. That unnecessary experiment sent Lincoln into a spasm of coughing that almost choked him to death. Eventually the assembled physicians gave up their tinkering and contented themselves to observe, monitoring Lincoln's vital signs. Dr. Ezra Abbott, one of a dozen physicians who rushed to Lincoln's deathbed, took notes on his pulse and respiration.

An emotional Dr. Leale held the president's hand: "Knowledge that frequently just before departure recognition and reason return to those who have been unconscious, caused me for several hours to hold the president's right hand firmly within my grasp, to let him in his blindness know, if possible, that he was in touch with humanity and had a friend."

While Lincoln yet lived, the manhunt began. Soldiers and detectives rushed to Booth's room, number 228, at the National Hotel. Of course Booth was gone, but they searched his trunk and discovered an incredible and mysterious letter signed only "Sam" that pointed to a large conspiracy against the government.

Several blocks from the National, just a few hours after the assassination, a raiding party showed up at Mary Surratt's boardinghouse. In the bedlam in the streets outside Ford's Theatre and the Petersen house, one or more anonymous tipsters reported that John Wilkes Booth and John H. Surratt Jr. were intimates, and that Mrs. Surratt's boardinghouse was just a few blocks away. Louis J. Weichmann, a boarder and school friend of John Surratt, was the first to respond to the patrol's arrival.

"I heard the front door bell ring very violently." Weichmann pulled on a pair of pants and went to the front door. Without opening the door, he spoke to the caller on the other side.

"Who is there?"

"Detectives," was the reply, "come to search the house for John Wilkes Booth and John Surratt."

"They are not here," Weichmann answered.

"Let us in anyhow." They wanted to search the house.

Weichmann retreated from the front door and knocked on Mary Surratt's first-floor bedroom door.

"Here, Mrs. Surratt, are detectives who have come to search the house."

"For God's sake! Let them come in. I expected the house to be searched."

Weichmann returned to the front hall and unlocked the door.

John Clarvoe, James A. McDevitt, Daniel R. P. Bigley, and John F. Kelly entered the house. "They explored the house from top to bottom," recalled Weichmann, "going into the rooms occupied by the young ladies and looking to see who they were."

When the detectives got to Weichmann's room, he asked, "Gentlemen, what is the matter? What does this searching of the house mean?"

Clarvoe replied: "Do you pretend that you do not know what has happened?"

Weichmann said he did not.

"Then I will tell you. John Wilkes Booth has shot the President and John Surratt has assassinated the Secretary of State."

"My God, I see it all," Weichmann blurted out.

Weichmann told the detectives that John Surratt was in Canada, and he offered to do anything in his power to assist their investigation.

When Clarvoe asked Mary where her son was, she said she did not know. When he responded skeptically, she retorted that during this war, many mothers did not know where their sons were.

Weichmann asked McDevitt how they came to Mrs. Surratt's so soon after the assassination. The detective said that a man on the street said, "If you want to find out all about this business go to Mrs. Surratt's house on H Street."

Out of earshot from the detectives, Anna Surratt revealed her fear. "Oh, Ma! Mr. Weichmann is right; just think of that man having been here an hour before the assassination. I am afraid it will bring suspicion upon us."

"Anna, come what will. I am resigned," Mary replied. "I think that J. Wilkes Booth was only an instrument in the hands of the Almighty to punish this proud and licentious people."

After the detectives left, Weichmann returned to his room and did not sleep any more that night.

At breakfast with the Surratts the next morning, Weichmann deplored the assassination, and suggested that Booth's many visits to their home would provoke an official investigation. Anna Surratt interrupted him, saying that the death of Lincoln "was no worse than that of the meanest nigger in the army." Weichmann disagreed. "I told her that I thought she would find out differently."

𝒯HROUGHOUT THE NIGHT AND INTO THE EARLY MORNING, Mary Lincoln made regular pilgrimages from the front parlor to her husband's bedside. Around 3:00 A.M., as Mary sat beside him, the president emitted a horrible, loud sound, and he gasped for breath. Frightened, Mary wailed: "Oh! That my little Taddy might see his father before he died!" Then, according to a witness, "she sprang up suddenly with a piercing cry and fell fainting upon the floor." Stanton, unnerved by her cry (and fearing that the president had just died), rushed in from the adjoining room and with raised arms called out loudly, "Take that woman out and do not let her in again." She did not deserve that cruelty. It did not matter: Stanton was obeyed.

Stanton returned to the back parlor and drafted another telegram:

> *Washington City,*
> *No. 458 Tenth Street, Apl 15, 1865—3 A.M.*
> *Major-General Dix:*
> *New York,*
>
> *The President still breathes, but is quite insensible, as he has been ever since he was shot. He evidently did not see the person who shot him but was looking on the stage as he was approached from behind.*
> *Mr. Seward has rallied, and it is hoped that he may live. Frederick Seward's condition is very critical. The attendant who was present was stabbed through the lungs, and is not expected to live. The wounds of Major Seward are not serious. Investigation strongly indicates J. Wilkes Booth as the assassin*

of the President. Whether it was the same or a different person
that attempted to murder Mr. Seward remains in doubt.
Chief Justice Cartter is engaged in taking the evidence. Every
exertion has been made to prevent the escape of the murderer.
His horse has been found on the road, near Washington.

Edwin M. Stanton
Sec. Of War

Stanton reached for a clean sheet of paper and wrote another telegram.

WAR DEPARTMENT
Washington, April 15, 1865—3 A.M.
Brigadier-General MORRIS
Commanding District of Baltimore:

> *Make immediate arrangements for guarding thoroughly*
> *every avenue leading into Baltimore, and if possible arrest*
> *J. Wilkes Booth, the murderer of President Lincoln. You will*
> *acknowledge the receipt of this telegram, giving time, &c.*

EDWIN M. STANTON
Secretary of War

BOOTH NEEDED A FRIEND ON THE LONELY ROAD FROM SUR-
rattsville to points south. After riding half the night, he and David Herold neared their destination—an isolated farmhouse in Charles County, Maryland, a few miles north of a small village named Bryantown. A city-dwelling night rider unfamiliar with the sparsely populated region might have continued down the road and missed the turnoff to the house in the dark, predawn hours of April 15, but Booth spurred his mount forward confidently, found the way, and guided Davey up the path toward the handsome, well-built, two-story frame dwelling that

glowed a pale, ghostly white in the distance. Booth recognized their sanctuary at once. He had been here before.

It was 4:00 A.M., fewer than six hours since Booth shot the president, and he and David Herold hadn't seen a soul in miles. This was an auspicious omen for a man who, within a few hours, would be damned in the morning newspapers as the most wanted man in America. They could rest here, the assassin reassured his faithful companion. This would not be like their rushed, five-minute interlude at Surratt's tavern, which was much too close to Washington and possible pursuers. Here, farther south, and deeper into the night of this remote countryside, they could tarry, rest, eat, and even sleep. And Booth could obtain medical care for his injured leg, plagued, he was now certain, by a broken bone. He also needed desperately to renew his strength after having been awake for almost twenty-four hours. He was dog tired, and his weary body ached from five bumpy hours on horseback.

By this time, the War Department had expanded the search beyond the vicinity of Washington, activating manhunters in places as distant as Delaware and Pennsylvania. In Wilmington, the commanding officer, Brigadier General J. R. Kenly, received this telegram: "J. Wilkes Booth, tragedian, is the murderer of Mr. Lincoln. No trains will be permitted to leave this city. Do your utmost to preserve order and keep a sharp lookout for Booth. Report your action." In Philadelphia, Major General George Cadwalader was warned by Halleck: "Attempts have been made to-night to assassinate the President and Secretary of State. Arrest all persons who leave Washington to-night and hold them till further orders."

Closer to Washington, General Augur ordered General J. P. Slough, military governor of Alexandria, Virginia, to join the hunt: "The murderer of the President is undoubtedly J. Wilkes Booth, the actor. The other party is a smooth-faced man, quite stout. You had better have a squad of cavalry sent down toward the Occoquan to intercept anything crossing the river. The fisherman along the river should be notified and kept on the lookout." Slough complied within the hour: "All of the orders received during the night from you have been obeyed, except the sending of cavalry toward the Occoquan, which will be done as soon as a sufficient number can be assembled. The river and shore from Alexandria to Washington are abundantly patrolled, and are all active and vigilant. A tug-boat will start soon to notify the fisheries." Augur emphasized the river's importance in a second order to Slough: "It is possible that the parties have crossed the river. Patrol the river. Intercept all boats and vessels. Allow no one to pass down the river unless well known."

Booth and Herold left the main road and approached the farmhouse, a quarter mile ahead. The moist, spring night air was still and eerily silent. No barking dogs warned of their approach, and the slow, quiet pacing of their horses' hooves failed to arouse the six occupants—a man and wife and their four young children—or the three hired hands who slept nearby in the dependencies.

Herold dismounted, handed his reins off to Booth, and walked toward the house. The assassin remained in his saddle, alert for any sounds of danger. No lamplight shone through the window glass into the front yard. Davey would have to wake up the people inside. He knocked on the front door and listened for signs of life. Nothing. No one answered. Herold pounded the door harder, then returned to Booth's side. This time his knocking penetrated the stout barrier and echoed through the five first-floor rooms and pricked the ears of the couple slumbering in the back bedroom.

The loud rapping worried the farmer: "I was very much alarmed at this, fearing it might be somebody who had come there not for any good purpose"—or so he would claim later. He rose from his bed and, without lighting a telltale candle or oil lamp, walked to the front door. "Who's there?" he called to the person on the other side. Two strangers, replied a young man's voice, hailing from St. Mary's County and on their way to Washington. One of their horses had fallen, the man claimed, throwing the rider and breaking his leg. Hesitating, the farmer peered through a window and, satisfied, unlocked the door.

In the front yard he found two men about twenty paces away, standing under a cedar tree, "one on a horse led by the other man who had tied his horse to a tree near by." John Wilkes Booth watched as the door opened, and a man stepped toward him. The assassin eyed him warily until the figure got close, and then relaxed at the sight of a familiar face. The farmer helped Booth get down from his horse, offering support when the fugitive's body weight bore down on his injured leg. Booth's feet touched the ground. Exhausted and grimacing in pain, but relieved and grateful, Booth staggered into the arms of Dr. Samuel A. Mudd.

Their faces now inches apart, Mudd helped Booth limp up the front steps and ushered him into his home. Davey stayed outside, proposing to take charge of the horses until they could be stabled. Mudd woke Frank Washington, his hired "colored man"—emancipation had robbed the doctor of his slaves months ago—and ordered him to put the animals in the stable. In a few minutes, Herold trailed Booth into Dr. Mudd's farmhouse. Herold was a stranger to Mudd—the doctor had never laid eyes on him before—but Davey's master was not.

THE CHAIN OF EVENTS THAT LED JOHN WILKES BOOTH TO THE threshold of Dr. Samuel A. Mudd in the predawn hours of April 15, 1865, began six months earlier in faraway Montreal, Canada. By late 1864, Booth had taken steps to consummate his fantastic scheme to kidnap President Lincoln. He attempted to recruit conspirators in disloyal, wartime New York City, a Copperhead stronghold that Walt Whitman described as corrupted by the "scent of thievery, druggies, foul play, and prostitution gangrened." Naturally, Booth knew the city well. New York was the national capital of the American stage, and he was on intimate terms with its players—the actors, managers, and employees of the theatre, along with the establishments—and female fans—who catered to them.

North of New York was Canada, a major base of operations for the Confederate Secret Service. In Montreal, nests of rebel agents armed with plans and gold were busy fomenting anti-Union conspiracies. The promise of aid and comfort beckoned Booth across the border. But more than cash, the actor sought contacts. He wanted to tap into the established network of Confederate operatives and couriers stretching from Washington to Richmond, and points beyond. He and his own little band could manage to snatch Lincoln, but kidnapping the president would not be enough. They would have to get him out of Washington. And to spirit Lincoln south to Richmond on horseback or by carriage, a distance of nearly one hundred miles, Booth needed help. He needed no less than a rebel version of the hated "underground railroad" that transported runaway slaves north to freedom. Booth's railroad, however, would run in reverse, by taking south the tyrant who dared free the slaves. To pull off his daring plan to kidnap the president, Booth needed loyal Confederate agents and safe houses located at strategic points along the route.

In October 1864, Booth ventured north into Canada to find the Confederate agents who could ensure his success. On October 18, he checked into the St. Lawrence Hall hotel. During his nine nights in the city, he met secretly with a number of rebels, foremost among them Patrick Charles Martin. Martin, a blockade runner, was once a liquor dealer in Baltimore, a city that Booth knew well and would soon turn to for recruits. The actor entrusted Martin with his theatrical wardrobe, an extremely valuable property in an age when all the great thespians traveled with trunks overflowing with fabulous, custom-made costumes. Booth wanted the wardrobe sent south aboard a sailing vessel. Once he kidnapped Lincoln, he could hardly return to the North to reclaim the professional tools of his trade. Martin agreed to handle the matter.

Martin also provided an infinitely more valuable service—the names of two prominent residents of Charles County, Maryland, who would help Booth execute his plan. Even better, Martin offered to write letters of introduction vouchsafing the actor's devotion to the Confederacy and requesting aid. Before John Wilkes Booth left Montreal for New York City on October 27, 1864, Patrick Martin gave him two letters, one addressed to Dr. William Queen, and the other to Dr. Samuel A. Mudd.

Mudd was thirty-two years old and had attended Georgetown College. He received his M.D. from the University of Maryland in 1858. He and his thirty-year-old wife, Sarah Frances, lived on a 218-acre farm with their four young children, three boys and a girl, aged between one and six years old. In 1859, he built a handsome new farmhouse and enjoyed life as a physician-farmer. He was anti-Union, antiblack, and the owner of up to eleven slaves before emancipation freed them.

By November 9, Booth was back in Washington at his primary lair, the National Hotel. Two days later, eager to pursue Patrick Martin's contacts, he traveled by stage to the Bryantown Tavern in Charles County, Maryland. A combination saloon, inn, and post office—not unlike Surratt's Tavern—the establishment was known among Confederate operatives and sympathizers as a reliable safe house and place to exchange information. To the curious, the actor explained the trip as merely an exploration for real estate to purchase on speculation. Booth was known for his speculative investments in Pennsylvania oil fields, so it was credible when he passed himself off as merely a real estate investor. He found Dr. Queen quickly and spent the night of November 12 at his farm.

Booth told Queen about the kidnapping plot, and Queen agreed to help. The whole county was anti-Lincoln—in the presidential election of 1860 Abraham Lincoln won 6 votes out of a total of 1,197 cast—and was home to a number of Confederate agents, operatives, and couriers. Queen would have no trouble, he assured Booth, in identifying those sympathetic to his plan. And tomorrow, at church, he would introduce the actor to one of them, Dr. Samuel A. Mudd. In the meantime, Queen had to get word to Dr. Mudd to attend Sunday services at St. Mary's Catholic Church, Dr. Queen's parish, instead of St. Peter's, Mudd's customary place of worship.

The Queen family took Booth to church with them on Sunday morning, November 13, 1864, and John C. Thompson, Dr. Queen's son-in-law, made the fateful introduction, presenting Booth to Dr. Mudd. The next day Booth returned to Washington by stage and checked in at the National.

On December 17, 1864, Booth returned to Charles County to visit his new friends and to meet another one. He spent the night at Dr. Queen's and the next morning attended church with the family. Again, Dr. Mudd appeared at St. Mary's. Booth embellished his cover story. Now, in addition to looking for farmland to purchase, he said he wanted to buy a horse. That part of his story was actually true—Booth did need horses for the kidnapping gang he hoped to assemble. He could easily have purchased mounts in Washington, but shopping for them in Charles County gave him an excuse to travel to Bryantown. Samuel Mudd was happy to offer assistance. After church Booth rode home with the doctor and spent the night of December 18 at his farm. The next day Mudd introduced his guest to one of his neighbors, George Gardiner, who sold him a peculiar, one-eyed horse. At the Bryantown Tavern, Mudd also introduced Booth to a much more important friend—the prominent Confederate operative Thomas Harbin. Harbin's job would be to help Booth after the kidnapper and his prize continued south through Charles County and approached the lower Potomac for a river crossing. Harbin joined the conspiracy, and on December 22, Booth rode the one-eyed horse back to Washington.

Dr. Mudd had served Booth well in Charles County, but now the actor needed the doctor's help in Washington. A Confederate courier named John H. Surratt Jr. operated out of his mother's boardinghouse on H Street and from her country tavern at Surrattsville, Maryland, about twelve miles south of Washington and located at a strategic point along Booth's likely escape route. Booth asked Mudd if he would come to the capital city on December 23 and introduce him to Surratt. Mudd agreed and called on Booth at the National Hotel the next day. Together they walked to Mary Surratt's boardinghouse, but before they got there, Mudd spotted John Surratt and another man walking toward them on Seventh Street. Mudd introduced Booth to Surratt, and the actor invited everyone—Mudd, Surratt, and Louis Weichmann, Surratt's friend and a boarder at the H Street house—back to his room at the National for drinks and private conversation. Booth recruited Surratt into the conspiracy and soon became a frequent H Street visitor, where he befriended Surratt's widowed mother, Mary, and his impressionable young sister, Anna.

His work done, Samuel Mudd returned to his farm just before Christmas 1864 and awaited further word from Booth, which never arrived. Lincoln's second inauguration came and went on March 4, 1865, Richmond fell on April 3, and Lee surrendered on April 9, but Dr. Mudd saw no more of Booth. Yes, Booth had sent liquor and supplies to Mudd's farm for hiding until the day came, but it never did, and Booth never returned to call for them. Given the disastrous events of April 1865, Mudd assumed that Union victory had overtaken Booth, and that the actor surely had abandoned his scheme to kidnap the president.

Now, FOUR MONTHS LATER, BOOTH WAS HERE AGAIN, though the doctor, standing in the pitch black of his front yard, did not know it yet. Once inside, Mudd guided the stranger to the upholstered settee in the front parlor. Booth sat, rotated his fatigued body, and immediately reclined into the soft, welcoming fabric. Mudd struck a match. The tiny flame hinted at no more than the vague outline of a human form lying upon the settee. Mudd lit an oil lamp and dialed the flame up to permit a proper examination of his new patient. Their eyes locked in recognition and in an instant the doctor knew the identity of the man who lay prostrate before him. How could he fail to recognize the stage star's familiar thick, black hair, porcelain pale complexion, trademark moustache, and striking good looks? But what on earth, he wondered, was Booth doing here, in the middle of the night? Booth saw no reason to tell him, at least not yet. So, unlike at Surratt's tavern, where, just four hours ago, the assassin had boasted promiscuously to John Lloyd, this time he held his tongue.

Before Mudd could proceed with examination and treatment, he would have to pry the tall, thigh-high cavalry boot off Booth's left leg. Booth was in no condition to remove it. Mudd stood at one end of the settee, took firm grip of the heel and sole, and tugged. Booth's jaw clamped tight in pain. The boot would not budge. Mudd tried to rock the pliable leather past Booth's ankle but the boot held fast, as though it had been cemented to his foot. In a way, it had. The injury had caused Booth's tissue to swell up and create a skintight seal that could not be broken without inflicting agony upon the patient and possibly augmenting the damage.

Mudd reached for a surgical knife, its shiny steel blade glinting under the lamp's yellow flame. If he could not pull the boot free, then he would cut it off. He sliced a longitudinal, six-inch incision along the top of the boot near the ankle, careful not to cut too deep and open Booth's soft flesh. Mudd set the instrument aside, seized the boot firmly, and pulled slowly. This time it slipped off. He dropped the boot to the floor, removed Booth's sock, pushed his pant leg up his calf, and began the examination.

David Herold interrupted and told Mudd that they were in a hurry. "His friend urged me to attend to his leg as soon as possible, as they were very anxious to get to Washington," Mudd noted. The doctor worked his fingers slowly along Booth's calf, ankle, and foot, feeling for bone beneath muscles, tendons, and tissue. He found it quickly, a broken fibula near the left ankle. The diagnosis was elementary: Mudd informed Booth that he had suffered a "'direct fracture'—one bone broken about two inches above the ankle joint." The doctor did "not regard it as a peculiarly painful or dangerous wound," reassuring Booth that he "did not find the adjoining bone fractured in any way…there was nothing resembling a compound fracture."

And yes, Mudd could treat the injury, but he possessed no splints for broken bones and improvised. He rummaged around for an old bandbox. "I had no proper paste-board for making splints…[so] I…took a piece of the bandbox and split it in half, doubled it at right angles, and took some paste and pasted it into a splint." Dr. Mudd finished his work within three-quarters of an hour.

It was about 5:00 A.M. now. Booth knew he should press on. If federal troops were lucky enough to pick up his scent, they could capture him at Dr. Mudd's by first light. David Herold spoke up again. If Booth could not ride, Davey pondered, perhaps Dr. Mudd could help them find another mode of transportation?: "[Herold] enquired if they could not reach some point on the Potomac, where they could get a boat to Washington." Booth considered his options. Yes, he could ride on, but how much more could he and the horses take, given their present condition, and how far could they run without breaking down? And the morning sun's first light would expose the assassin to great danger on the open road. Satisfied that no one in Mudd's locale—including the doctor himself—knew about the assassination yet, Booth calculated his next move. The assassin knew he was still traveling ahead of the news, but he also knew that soon the news would spread and overtake him, making the daylight hours unsafe for travel.

Booth weighed the risks and chose sanctuary. No one in the world knew he'd gone to Dr. Mudd's this night. He hadn't known that he'd go there himself until after he shot Lincoln and injured his leg. Better to hide out and chance discovery than be caught in open country at sunrise. They would spend what few hours remained of this night at the farm, rest there until the evening of Saturday, April 15, and then, once more, vanish into the night.

Mudd invited Booth and Herold to remain in the house, enticing his guests with visions of soft mattresses and beds, and leading them from the parlor to the front-hall staircase. Booth grasped the railing tightly, supporting himself while Mudd aided his ascent to the second floor. The doctor offered them a room to share, bade them good night, descended the stairs, and returned to his wife. The men will spend the night, he informed her. Unbeknownst to Mudd, he had just extended his hospitality to Lincoln's assassin and his accomplice. Mudd stepped outside, walked around his farmyard giving instructions to his hired hands for the day's work, and returned to bed.

Their secret safe from the Mudds, and their whereabouts a mystery to the manhunters, Davey and Booth collapsed into their beds. As Booth drifted off to sleep, he still did not know whether his master plan had succeeded or failed. Had George Atzerodt and Lewis Powell carried out their missions and assassinated Vice President Johnson and Secretary of State Seward? And what of the president—had Booth killed Abraham Lincoln, or did the tyrant still live?

While Booth slept the first cavalry patrol rode south from Washington, heading for Piscataway, Maryland. Soon this contingent from the Thirteenth New York Cavalry, commanded by Lieutenant David Dana, would ride close to Dr. Mudd's farm. Booth had about seven hours.

Chapter Five

"Find the Murderers"

---························⟡························---

NO MORE DREAMS CAME TO ABRAHAM LINCOLN DURING THE
night of his deep, last sleep at the Petersen house. His brain was
dead and beyond the reach of any nocturnal imaginings. His soul would
soon embark on the journey that he had traveled many times before in
his recurring dream. Soon he would travel farther than he ever had before, finally reaching the indistinct shore that, to him, foretold the coming of great events.

By 4:00 A.M. Edwin Stanton was sure that he was dealing with a conspiracy. The evidence seized in Booth's hotel room included a mysterious letter that seemed to foretell the assassination.

Hookstown, Balto Co.
March 27th, 1865.

Dear John:
    Was business so important that you could not remain in
Balto till I saw you. I came in as soon as I could, but found you
had gone to W____n. I called to see Mike, but learned from his
mother he had gone out with you and had not returned. I
concluded therefore he had gone with you. How inconsiderate
you have been. When I left you, you stated we would not

meet in a month or so. Therefore I made application for
employment, an answer to which I shall receive during the
week. I told my parents I had ceased with you. Can I then
under existing circumstances, come as you request. You
know full well that the G___t. suspicions something is going
on there. Therefore, the undertaking is becoming more
complicated. Why not for the present desist, for various
reasons, which if you look into, you can readily see, without
my making any mention thereof. You, nor any one can censure
me for my present course. You have been its cause, for how can
I now come after telling them I had left you. Suspicion rests
upon me now from my whole family, and even parties in the
country. I will be compelled to leave home nay how, and how
soon I care not. None, no not one, were more in for the
enterprise than myself, and to day would be there, had you
not done as you have—by this I mean, manner of proceeding.
I am, as you well know, in need. I am, you may say, in rags
whereas to day I ought to be well clothed. I do not feel right
stalking about with means, and more from appearances a
beggar. I feel my dependence, but even all this would and was
forgotten, for I was one with you. Time more propitious will
arrive yet. Do not act rashly or in haste. I would prefer you
first query, "go and see how it will be taken at R___d," and ere
long I shall be better prepared to again be with you. I dislike
writing, and would sooner verbally make known my views. Yet
your non writing causes me thus to proceed. Do not in anger
peruse this. Weigh all I have said, and as a rational man and
a FRIEND, you can not censure or upbraid my conduct. I
sincerely trust this nor aught else that shall or may occur, will
ever be an obstacle to obliterate our former friendship and
attachment. Write me to Balto as I expect to be about
Wednesday or Thursday. Or if you can possibly come on,

I will Tuesday meet you in Balto. At B___, Ever I subscribe myself.

Your friend,
Sam.

The recovery of this letter, which Booth had carelessly— or possibly willfully, given his incriminating letter to the *National Intelligencer*— failed to destroy, was a stunning development. Stanton realized that it brimmed with clues: Booth had at least two conspirators named "Sam" and "Mike"; Sam was in Baltimore; the assassination was premeditated, planned before March 27; and the Confederacy might be involved. What else could "see how it will be taken in Richmond" mean?

The *Daily Morning Chronicle,* one of Washington's major papers, described the frantic beginning of the manhunt:

> No sooner had the dreadful event been announced in the street, than Superintendent Richards and his assistants were at work to discover the assassins. In a few moments the tele-graph had aroused the…police force of the city….Every measure of precaution was taken to preserve order in the city, and every street was patrolled. At the request of Mr. Richards General Augur sent horses to mount the police. Every road out of Washington was picketed, and every possible avenue of escape thoroughly guarded. Steamboats about to depart down the Potomac were stopped.
>
> As it is suspected that this conspiracy originated in Mary-land, the telegraph flashed the mournful news to Baltimore, and all the cavalry was immediately put upon active duty. Every road was picketed, and every precaution taken to pre-vent the escape of the assassins.

Stanton sent another telegram to General Dix telling him about the new evidence and updating him on Lincoln's condition:

Washington City,
No. 458 Tenth Street, April 15, 1865—4.10 A.M.

Major-General Dix:
    The President continues insensible and is sinking.
Secretary Seward remains without change. Frederick Seward's
skull is fractured in two places besides a severe cut upon the
head. The attendant is alive, but hopeless. Major Seward's
wounds are not dangerous.
    It is now ascertained with reasonable certainty that two
assassins were engaged in the horrible crime, Wilkes Booth
being the one that shot the President the other a companion of
his whose name is not known but whose description is so clear
that he can hardly escape. It appears from a letter found in
Booth's trunk that the murder was planned before the 4th of
March but fell through then because the accomplice backed
out until Richmond could be heard from. Booth and his
accomplice were at the livery stable at 6 this evening, and left
there with their horse about 10 o'clock, or shortly before that
hour. It would seem that they had for several days been seeking
their chance, but for some unknown reason it was not carried
into effect until last night. One of them has evidently made his
way to Baltimore, the other has not yet been traced.

At the Petersen house Dr. Abbott recorded melancholy statistics in the minutes he kept that night: "5:50 A.M., respiration 28, and regular sleeping."

"6:00 A.M., pulse failing, respiration 28."

At 6:00 A.M., a fainting sickness overcame Secretary of the Navy Welles. He had been cooped up in the claustrophobic Petersen house all night. Welles rose from his bedside chair, where he had sat listening to the sound of Lincoln's breathing. Welles needed fresh air and decided to go for a walk. When he got outside, stood on the top step, and looked down to the street, he witnessed a remarkable scene: thousands of citizens, keeping their all-night vigil for their dying president. Welles descended the turned staircase and walked among them. They recognized Lincoln's bearded "Father Neptune," and individual faces emerged from the crowd and spoke to him: "[They] stepped forward as I passed, to inquire into the condition of the President, and to ask if there was hope. Intense grief was on every countenance when I replied that the President could survive but a short time. The colored people especially—and there were at this time more of them, perhaps than of whites—were overwhelmed with grief." After a while, Welles turned back: "It was a dark and gloomy morning, and rain set in before I returned to the house." He wanted to be there at the end.

"6:30 A.M., still failing and labored breathing."

"7:00 A.M., symptoms of immediate dissolution."

In Maryland, at the same hour, Lieutenant Dana arrived in Piscataway. Dana, although he held junior rank, had senior-level connections in Washington. His brother, Charles, was Lincoln's assistant secretary of war and a confidant of Stanton. David Dana and his patrol from the Thirteenth New York Cavalry had left Washington two hours ago, at 5:00 A.M. As soon as he reached Piscataway, he telegraphed Washington to report the progress of his early-morning expedition. "I arrived at this place at 7 A.M., and at once sent a man to Chapel Point to notify the cavalry at that point of the murder of the President, with description of the parties who committed the deed. With the arrangements which have been made it is impossible for them to get across the river in this direction." Dana had already gotten his first tip, and he relayed it to headquarters: "I have reliable information that the person who murdered Secretary Seward is Boyce or Boyd, the man who killed Captain Watkins in Maryland. I think it without doubt true." Of course it wasn't. Less than nine hours into the manhunt, Dana was pursuing the kind of false lead that would come to bedevil the manhunters in the days ahead.

. . .

$\mathcal{A}$T THE PETERSEN HOUSE, ABRAHAM LINCOLN BEGAN THE death struggle.

The end was coming on fast. Surgeon General Barnes placed his finger on Lincoln's carotid artery; Dr. Leale placed his finger on the president's right radial pulse; and Dr. Taft placed his hand over the heart. The doctors and nearly every man in the room fished out pocket watches on gold chains. It was 7:20 A.M., April 15, 1865. More than once, they thought that Lincoln had passed away. But the strong body resisted death and rallied again, as it had so many times through the long night.

It was 7:21 A.M. Death was imminent.

At 7:21 and 55 seconds, Abraham Lincoln drew his last breath.

His heart stopped beating at 7:22 and 10 seconds. It was over.

"He is gone; he is dead," one of the doctors said. To the Reverend Dr. Gurley, the Lincoln family's minister, it seemed that four or five minutes passed "without the slightest noise or movement" by anyone in the room. "We all stood transfixed in our positions, speechless, around the dead body of that great and good man."

Edwin Stanton spoke first. He turned to his right and looked at Gurley. "Doctor, will you say anything?"

"I will speak to God," replied the minister, "let us pray." He summoned up such a stirring prayer that later no one, not even Gurley, could remember what he said. James Tanner tried to scribble down the words, but at this crucial moment the lead tip of his only pencil snapped and he wasn't able to write any more.

Gurley finished and everyone murmured "Amen." Then, no one dared to speak.

Again Stanton broke the silence. "Now he belongs to the angels."

Edwin Stanton composed himself, reached for pen and paper, and wrote a single sentence. There was nothing else to say. It was the telegram that would, as soon as a messenger ran it over to the War Department for transmission, announce the sad news to the nation.

WASHINGTON CITY, April 15, 1865.

Major General Dix,
New York:
    Abraham Lincoln died this morning at 22 minutes after
7 o'clock.
                                            EDWIN M. STANTON

One by one those who were there at the end quietly filed out of the little back bedroom. Reverend Dr. Gurley and Robert Lincoln told Mary. She would not go to the death chamber; she could not bear it. She never saw her husband's face again. Around 9:00 A.M. she left the Petersen house. As she descended the stairs, coachman Francis Burke, who had waited all night to take the president home, readied to carry the widowed first lady there. Before she got in the carriage, she glared at Ford's Theatre across the street: "That dreadful house…that dreadful house," she moaned.

The room was empty of all visitors now, save one. Edwin Stanton and the president were alone. The morning light streaming through the back windows raked across Lincoln's still face. Stanton closed the blinds and approached the president's body. He took from his pocket a small knife or pair of scissors and bent over Lincoln's head. Gently he cut a generous lock of hair—more than one hundred strands—and sealed it in a plain, white envelope. Stanton signed his name in ink on the upper right corner, and then addressed the envelope: "To Mrs. Welles." The lock was not for him, but a gift for Mary Jane Welles, wife of Secretary of the Navy Gideon Welles and one of Mary Lincoln's few friends in Washington. In 1862, Mrs. Welles had helped nurse Willie Lincoln, ill with typhoid fever, until his death on February 20. Then, in the aftermath, Mary Jane did double duty, continuing to nurse Tad, also ill, while also caring for Mary Lincoln, helpless in her grief. Nine months later, in November 1863, the Welleses' three-year-old son died of diphtheria. With that loss, Mary Jane Welles and Mary Lincoln shared a sadness that brought them even closer. Within an hour of the assassination, Mary Lincoln had dispatched messengers to summon Mary Jane to her side. Stanton knew that if any woman in Washington deserved a sacred lock of the martyr's hair it was Mary Jane Welles. Later, Mrs. Welles framed the cherished relic with dried flowers that had adorned the president's coffin at the White House funeral. Lost in reverie, Lincoln's god of war gazed down at his fallen chief and wept. Abraham Lincoln was gone. "To the angels."

It was time to take him home. Stanton ordered soldiers to go quickly and bring what was necessary to transport the body of the slain president. He ordered another soldier to guard the door to the death room and to allow no one to enter and disturb the president's body. When the soldiers returned from their errand and turned down Tenth Street, the crowd began to wail. The men carried a plain, pine box, the final refutation of their hopes. They knew already, of course, that the president was dead. They had seen the cabinet secretaries leave the house, and then Mary Lincoln. But the sight of the crude, improvised coffin made it too real. It was finished. The box looked like a shipping crate, not a proper coffin for a head of state. Lincoln would not have minded. He was always a man of simple tastes. This was the plain, roughly hewn coffin of a rail-splitter.

The men carried the box up the curving stairs and down the narrow hallway. Stanton supervised them as they rested the box on the floor. They unfurled an American flag and approached the president's naked body. They wrapped him in the cotton bunting, and, if they followed custom, were careful to position the canton's thirty-six, five-pointed stars over his face. These were the national colors of the Union. During the war Lincoln insisted that the flag retain its full complement of stars, refusing to acknowledge that the seceded states had actually left the Union. They lifted the president from the bed, placed him in the box, and screwed down the lid. The only sound in the room was the squeaking of the screws being tightened in their holes.

Stanton nodded in assent. In unison, the men bent down and inched their fingers under the bottom edges of the box; it had no pallbearers' handles. They eased it up from the floor and began shuffling their feet down the narrow hallway to the front door. They carried the president into the street and loaded him onto the back of a simple, horse-drawn wagon. The driver snapped the reins and the modest procession, escorted by a small contingent of bareheaded officers on foot, took Abraham Lincoln home to the White House. There were no bands, drums, or trumpets, just the cadence of horses' hooves and the footsteps of the officers. Lincoln would have liked the simplicity.

After Lincoln's body was removed, Stanton and the other members of the cabinet—save Seward—met in the back parlor of the Petersen house. Andrew Johnson was not present when Lincoln died, so the cabinet sent to him an official, written notification of the president's death and of his succession to the presidency. They urged that the new president be sworn in immediately, and Johnson sent back word that he would be pleased to take the oath of office at 11:00 A.M. in his room at the Kirkwood. In the late morning of April 15, Chief Justice Chase and the officials in attendance found a changed man. Six weeks ago, an intoxicated Johnson had embarrassed himself by giving a foolish, rambling speech on Inauguration Day. Lincoln forgave him and said no more about it. The morning of Lincoln's death found Johnson sober, grave, dignified, and deeply moved. Given the tragic and unprecedented circumstances of his elevation to the presidency, it was decided collectively that it would not be appropriate for him to deliver a formal, public inaugural address.

Between the time Lincoln died and his body was removed from the Petersen house, the first newspaper account of the assassination hit the streets of Washington. The *Daily Morning Chronicle* announced the terrible news with a series of headlines: "MURDER OF President Lincoln. / ATTEMPT TO ASSASSINATE THE SECRETARY OF STATE. / MANNER OF ASSASSINATION / Safety of Other Members of the Cabinet. / Description of the Assassin / THE POLICE INVESTIGATION / THE SURGEONS' LATEST REPORTS."

Suspecting that the president's entire cabinet had been marked for death, and hearing that a would-be assassin had been scared off from Stanton's home, *Chronicle* reporters had rushed to all of their homes to discover whether they had been attacked, too:

It, therefore, is evident, that the aim of the plotters was to paralyze the country by at once striking down the head, the heart, and the arm of the country.

We went in search of the Vice-President, and found he was safe in his apartments at the Kirkwood. We called at Chief Justice Chase's and learned there, that he too was safe. Secretaries Stanton, Welles, and Usher, and…the other members of the Cabinet, were with the President…and we are gratified to be able to announce that all the members of the Cabinet, save Mr. Seward, are unharmed.

This man Booth has played more than once at Ford's theatre, and is, of course, acquainted with its exits and entrances, and the facility with which he escaped behind the scenes is well understood.…[Booth] has long been a man of intemperate habits and subject to temporary fits of great excitement. His capture is certain, but if he is true to his nature he will commit suicide, and thus appropriately end his career.

Over the next few days, newspapers in Washington, Baltimore, New York, Philadelphia, and Chicago published reams of unsubstantiated gossip. They tantalized readers by claiming that particular arrests were only days—even hours—away; readers assumed that high-level leaders of the Confederacy, including President Jefferson Davis, who was still at large, would be named as conspirators. One Washington paper boasted that more than one hundred criminals would face trial, and another wrote that certainly twenty-one and perhaps even twenty-three would hang. The public devoured every word and clamored for more.

The news reached Elmira, New York, on the morning of April 15. John Cass, proprietor of a clothing store on the corner of Walter and Baldwin streets, took his morning paper, the *Elmira Advertiser,* at home, and by 7:30 A.M. he had read that the president had been assassinated but was still alive. He walked to the telegraph office opposite his store but there was no additional news. Then it came, a little after 9:00 A.M.; the president was dead. Cass crossed the street, and told his clerks to close for the day. Then he noticed a man crossing the street, making a beeline for Cass's store. The man, dressed in a fashionable jacket that bespoke foreign tailoring, stepped inside. Cass thought he looked Canadian. The stranger asked for white shirts of a particular style and manufacturer. Cass, having none in stock, tried to interest the customer in other shirts. The man demurred, Cass recalled: "He examined them, but said he would rather have those of the make which he had been accustomed to wearing."

Cass said he had just received some "very bad news."

"What?" the customer asked.

"Of the death of Abraham Lincoln," Cass said.

With that, John Surratt walked out of the store.

THE BACK BEDROOM OF THE PETERSEN HOUSE WAS EMPTY FOR the first time in twelve hours. Stanton left the room unguarded. Unlike Ford's Theatre, the house where Lincoln died was not a crime scene. No one collected the bloody sheets, pillowcases, pillows, and towels as evidence of the great crime. Soon one of the boarders, a photographer named Julius Ulke, set up his camera in the corner of the room, facing the bed. The bloodied linens, bathed in morning light, were still wet. Ulke's haunting photograph of the death chamber, lost for nearly a century, preserved a scene that words cannot adequately describe.

William Clark returned to the Petersen house and found his room in shambles. That night he climbed into Lincoln's deathbed and fell asleep under the same coverlet that warmed the body of the dying pres-

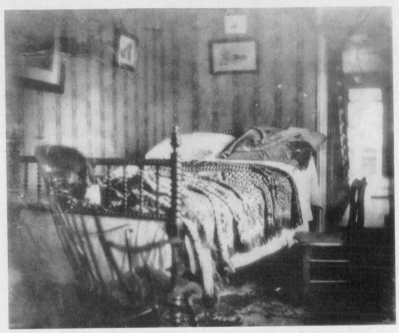

Morning, April 15, 1865. Lincoln's deathbed shortly after his body
was taken home to the White House.

ident. Four days later, the day of Lincoln's funeral, he wrote a letter to
his sister, Ida F. Clark, in Boston:

*Since the death of our President hundreds daily call at the
house to gain admission to my room.*

*I was engaged nearly all of Sunday with one of Frank
Leslie's Special Artists aiding him viz making a correct
drawing of the last moments of Mr. Lincoln, as I knew the
position of every one present he succeeded in executing a fine
sketch, which will appear in their paper the last of this week.
He intends, from this same drawing to have some fine large
steel engravings executed. He also took a sketch of nearly every
article in my room which will appear in their paper. He wished*

*to mention the names of all in particularly of yourself, Clara
and Nannie, but I told him he must not do that, as they were
members of my family and I did not want them to be made so
public. He also urged me to give him my picture or at least
allow him to take my sketch, but I could not see that either.*

*Everybody has a great desire to obtain some memento from
my room so that whoever comes in has to be closely watched
for fear they will steal something.*

*I have a lock of his hair which I have had neatly framed,
also a piece of linen with a portion of his brain, the pillow case
upon which he lay when he died and nearly all his wearing
apparel but the latter I intend to send to Robt Lincoln as soon
as the funeral is over, as I consider him the one most justly
entitled to them.*

*The same matrass is on my bed, and the same coverlit
covers me nightly that covered him while dying.*

*Enclosed you will find a piece of lace that Mrs. Lincoln
wore on her head during the evening and was dropped by her
while entering my room to see her dying husband. It is worth
keeping for its historical value.*

William Petersen, the previous night merely the anonymous owner
of one of several hundred equally anonymous boardinghouses scattered
throughout the nation's capital, had become, by early morning, proprietor of the famous "house where Lincoln died." That unwelcome
honor—and the rabid attention of newspaper reporters and curiosity
seekers—displeased him. In particular Petersen resented the implica-
tion that the president had died dishonorably, not at the Executive Mansion, but in a shabby boardinghouse. Lincoln would not have complained.
Eighteen years ago he began his Washington career in another boardinghouse not much different from the one where it ended. Elected to Congress in 1846, Lincoln came to Washington for the first time in 1847 and
moved into Mrs. Sprigg's boardinghouse across the street from the Cap-

itol, not far from First and East Capitol streets. There was no shame in it then. Lincoln would have felt no shame in dying in one now.

$\mathcal{L}$ITTLE MORE THAN AN HOUR BEFORE LINCOLN DIED, GEORGE Atzerodt arose from his humble quarters at the Pennsylvania House and left the hotel. A servant just back from fetching a carriage to take a woman to the 6:15 A.M. train ran into him outside:

"What brings you out so early this morning?"

"Well," Atzerodt replied, "I have got business."

When Atzerodt walked past Creaser's house on F Street, between Eighth and Ninth streets, opposite the Patent Office, and along Booth's escape route just two blocks from Ford's Theatre, he tossed his knife under a wood carriage step, into the gutter. A few minutes later, an eagle-eyed woman looking out a third-story window in the building next to Creaser's shoe store saw it there and sent a black woman to get it. But the woman did not want the knife in her house so a passerby, William Clendenin, volunteered to take the clue, still in its sheath, to Almarin C. Richards, the chief of police.

The night before, the authorities had done little to pursue Booth during the first hour after the assassination. At Ford's Theatre the immediate concern was the condition of the president, not the whereabouts of Booth. But by early morning, Stanton had summoned the iron will for which he was renowned and planned the manhunt. The government—Vice President Johnson and the cabinet—had survived the night; no more assassinations had occurred; and no invading army stormed the capital. Stanton coordinated—or at least tried to—the efforts of the local police force, detectives, and the army.

From New York City came another offer of help, twelve hours after Stanton had asked its chief of police to send his finest detectives to Washington. On April 15, at 1:40 P.M., Stanton received a telegram from Detective H. S. Olcott, proposing to join the manhunt: "If Lieutenant-Colonel Morgan or I or any of my employees can serve you and the country in any way, no matter what, or anywhere, we are ready." John Wilkes Booth was still at large. He had escaped the first, frantic night of the manhunt. Now it might not be so easy to capture him quickly. Stanton reached for Olcott's helping hand, telegraphing a prompt reply: "I desire your services. Come to Washington at once, and bring your force of detectives with you." Olcott hurried to move that night: "I leave at midnight with such of my men as live in town. The rest will follow forthwith."

That afternoon Stanton also summoned Lieutenant Colonel Lafayette C. Baker, head of the self-styled "National Detective Police," and one of his favorites.

WAR DEPARTMENT
Washington City, April 15, 1865—3:20 P.M.

Col. L. C. BAKER,
New York:
  Come here immediately and see if you can find the murderers of the President.

  EDWIN M. STANTON,
  Secretary of War.

Stanton vowed to apprehend Booth and all those who conspired with him to commit what became known as "the great crime." Southern leaders feared that Stanton might accuse them of complicity in the murder. One of them, Governor F. H. Pierpont of Virginia, sent a message to the War Department pleading that his state was blameless, and condemning Booth for shouting "Sic semper tyrannis" at Ford's Theatre: "Loyal Virginia sends her tribute of mourning for the fall of the Nation's President by the hands of a dastardly agent of treason, who dared to repeat the motto of our State at the moment of the perpetration of his accursed crime."

Soldiers, policemen, and private detectives fanned out over Washington, Maryland, and Virginia in pursuit of the actor and his accomplices. On assassination night John H. Surratt was named as one of Booth's possible accomplices and was the first suspect in the Seward knife attack. But when soldiers had searched for him at his mother's boardinghouse a few hours after Lincoln was shot, he was not there. Stanton declared the search and capture of John Wilkes Booth to be the nation's top priority. Booth and his conspirators had to be caught before they disappeared into the Deep South, where they would find succor in the heart of the stricken Confederacy. On the morning of April 15, the nation held its collective breath and with one voice asked, "Will Booth be taken?"

I͟T WAS A DANGEROUS TIME TO BE A FRIEND OF JOHN Wilkes Booth. On the night of the fourteenth, when the actors huddled backstage at Ford's Theatre a few minutes after Lincoln was shot, John Matthews feared the worst. "There were shouts of 'burn' and 'hang' and 'lynch'" coming from the audience, he recalled, and then Matthews made a discovery that put him in fear for his life.

> When taking off my coat the letter which Booth had given me dropped out of the pocket. I had forgotten about it. I said "Great God! There is the letter that John gave me in the afternoon." It was in an envelope, sealed and stamped for the post office. I opened it, and glanced hastily over the letter. I saw it was a statement of what he was going to do. I read it very hurriedly. It was written in a sort of patriotic strain, and was to this effect; That he had for a long time devoted his money, his time, and his energies to the accomplishment of an end; that a short time ago he had been worth so much money—twenty or thirty thousand dollars, I think—all of which he had spent furthering this enterprise; but that he had been baffled. It then went on: "The moment has come at

last when my plans must be changed. The world may censure me for what I am about to do; but I am sure posterity will justify me." Signed. "Men who love their country more than gold or life: J. W. Booth, Payne, Atzerodt, and Herold."

In the crowded dressing rooms, surrounded by excited actors running amok, Matthews read Booth's letter. No one paid attention to the piece of paper he clutched in his hands. He read it a second time and then asked himself, "What shall I do with this letter?" The audience in the theatre had not stopped shouting. Matthews considered handing the letter over to the authorities. The roar of the mob persuaded him otherwise. "If this paper is found on me," Matthews reasoned, "I will be compromised—no doubt lynched on the spot." Even if he survived the night, he knew that the letter's brush would tar him forever: "I will be associated with the letter, and suspicions will grow out of it that can never be explained away, and I will be ruined." He knew what he had to do to protect himself: "I burned it up."

Matthews was not alone. On the night of April 14, others in Washington attempted to obliterate evidence of their connection to Lincoln's assassin. And the next morning, as news of Lincoln's death spread across the nation, many other letters written in Booth's hand certainly perished in flames. Indeed, fewer than one hundred of Booth's letters and manuscripts survived the tumultuous days that followed the assassination. One of his paramours even sought to destroy herself. Ella Turner, a petite, sensual, redheaded prostitute, placed Booth's photo under her pillow, saturated a piece of cloth with chloroform, pressed the poisonous anesthetic to her delicate face, and tried to fill her lungs with a fatal dose. At 11:00 A.M. on April 15, residents of her house found her in her room, collapsed on her bed, unconscious but alive. Several doctors were summoned. The press got hold of the story, and the Washington *Evening Star* published the lurid details of her rescue: "Proper remedies were immediately applied, when she soon aroused and asked for Booth's picture, which she had concealed under the pillow of her bed, at the same time remarking to the physicians that she 'did not thank them for saving her life.'" Soon she came to her senses and chose to survive her lover's crime.

Booth's female correspondents had more to worry about than the letters he had sent to them. They could dispose of those documents easily enough. But what about the love notes that they had mailed to him, and that were in his possession? Many women—single, engaged, and married—had written incriminating letters to their idol offering to surrender whatever pleasures he chose to take from them. George Alfred Townsend penned an unforgettable vignette of a typical case:

> The beauty of this man and his easy confidentiality, not familiar, but marked by a mild and even dignity, made women impassioned of him. He was licentious as men, and particularly as actors go, but not a seducer, as far as I can learn. I have traced one case in Philadelphia where a young girl who had seen him on stage became enamored of him.
>
> She sent him bouquets, notes, photographs and all the accessories of an intrigue. Booth, to whom such things were common, yielded to the girl's importunities at last and gave her an interview. He was surprised to find that so bold a correspondent was so young, so fresh, and so beautiful. He told her therefore, in pity, the consequences of pursuing him; that he entertained no affection for her, though a sufficient desire, and that he was a man of the world to whom all women grew fulsome in their turn.
>
> "Go home," he said, "and beware of actors. They are to be seen, not to be known."
>
> The girl, yet more infatuated, persisted. Booth, who had no real virtue except by scintillations, became what he had promised, and one more soul went to the isles of Cypress.

On April 14, and for weeks to come, more than one woman prayed that Booth had destroyed her letters before he killed the president. Fortune spared the reputations of the assassin's admirers—not one of their love letters was discovered and published during the manhunt. But when news of the assassination reached Boston, a singular young girl decided to cherish, and not obliterate, her intimate bond to Lincoln's killer.

They had met in Boston the previous year, during Booth's successful, monthlong theatrical engagement at the Boston Museum. It was an astonishing run—between April 25 and May 28, 1864, Booth, onstage almost every night, performed the greatest roles in the Shakespearean canon—Richard III, Hamlet, Romeo, Othello, Shylock, and Macbeth. He met her sometime during that month in Boston. Her name was Isabel Sumner. The daughter of a respectable merchant family, she possessed an intelligent face, a slender frame, and ravishing beauty. She was sixteen years old, and Booth proposed that they become lovers. He was smitten immediately, and pursued Isabel with an ardor uncommon for a man who was used to having women throw themselves at him. "God bless this sweet face before me," he cooed in a letter written as he gazed at the photograph she had given him. "It would move me to do anything."

The stage star courted the teenage beauty in a series of emotionally uninhibited letters that made him sound like a teenager: "I LOVE YOU...in the fountain of my heart a seal is set to keep its waters, pure and bright for thee alone." Booth gave Isabel a signed photograph of himself, a lock of his hair, and a ring. Why did the debauched, worldly actor so crave this innocent, young girl? Booth answered the question himself in a letter: "I will...never, never cease to think of you as something pure and sacred, A bright and happy dream, from which I have been awoke to Sadness."

When Isabel learned that Lincoln's assassin was her lover, she could not bring herself to destroy John's letters and gifts. Instead, she hid them for the next sixty-two years, until her death in 1927. As best as anyone could remember, she never spoke the name John Wilkes Booth again. Fortunately for Isabel Sumner, Booth did not carry her photo in his wallet the night he left the National Hotel to murder Abraham Lincoln. Neither Stanton's detectives nor the newspapers discovered her, and her connection to Booth stayed a secret for the next one hundred and thirty years.

$\mathcal{F}$RANCES MUDD ROSE AT 6:00 A.M. AND CALLED FOR HER SERvants to get breakfast ready. At 7:00 A.M., Mrs. Mudd woke her husband. David Herold, after only two hours of rest, shambled downstairs. John Wilkes Booth, his mind and body still spent from his great day, stayed in bed. He had ridden too far from Washington to hear the ringing bells of the city's churches and firehouses tolling in mourning. Dr. Mudd invited Herold to join his family for breakfast. Frances prepared a plate of food for Booth and told a servant to carry it upstairs and set it on his bedside table.

Herold questioned Mudd about his local contacts, especially those who lived close to the river. Davey's evident knowledge of the area prompted Frances Mudd to inquire if he lived in their county.

"No, ma'am," he replied, "but I have been frolicking around for five or six months."

Amused by his boyish demeanor, Frances teased him: "All play and no work makes Jack a bad boy. Your father ought to make you go to work."

"My father is dead," Herold responded, "and," he added jauntily, "I am ahead of the old lady."

As he bantered at the breakfast table, the good-natured Davey Herold appeared oblivious to the grave peril he faced. He was running for his life, but Frances Mudd observed that "he seemed not to have a care in the world." Before Mudd left the house, Herold asked him for two favors. "After breakfast, when I was about to leave for my farm-work, this young man asked me if I had a razor about the house, that his friend desired to take a shave, as perhaps he would feel better." The doctor provided a straight razor, soap, and water. And, wondered Davey, could

Mudd make a pair of crutches for Booth, nothing fancy, just something simple for him "to hobble along with"? The physician, handy with wood and tools, complied: "I got two arm pieces and whittled them out as best I could." Then Mudd took the pieces to one of his hired men, an old Englishman named John Best, and, using a saw and an auger, "he and I made a rude pair of crutches out of a piece of plank" and sent them to Booth.

When breakfast was finished, Herold went back to bed. Lieutenant Dana and the Thirteenth New York Cavalry patrol left Piscataway and pressed on toward Bryantown. Frances Mudd did not hear a sound from Herold or Booth for the next four hours until around noon, when Davey came down to devour his second meal of the day. While Herold dined, the Thirteenth New York reached Bryantown around noon. David Dana's men were just a few miles from Dr. Mudd's. This was the closest the manhunters had gotten to Booth since the assassination. As before, Booth stayed in bed. The servant who brought him dinner found Saturday morning's breakfast tray, its food untouched, still sitting on the bedside table. Improvidently, Booth skipped the midday meal, too. He must have been famished, and who knew when his next meal might come?

 By 8:00 A.M. GEORGE ATZERODT HAD MADE IT TO GEORGE-town. He showed up at Matthews & Co.'s store at 49 High Street and paid a call on an acquaintance, John Caldwell. Atzerodt said that he was going to the country and asked Caldwell if he wanted to buy his watch. "I told him that I had a watch of my own, and did not want another." Then Atzerodt asked for a loan of $10. Caldwell refused. "I told him that I did not have any money to spare." Atzerodt unbelted his revolver and offered it to Caldwell. "Lend me $10.00, and take this as security, and I will bring the money or send it to you next week." The storekeeper looked the weapon over. "I thought the revolver was good security for the money, and I let him have the money, expecting him to pay it back....I did not inquire of him why it was loaded and capped." Atzerodt left the store and continued on his journey. He had decided to leave Washington. He knew a place where he thought he would be safe.

At the Executive Mansion the soldiers carried the president's temporary coffin to the second-floor guest bedroom for the autopsy. Cutting open Abraham Lincoln's brain and body served little purpose. The surgeons knew what killed him—a single bullet through the brain. They were hiding their voyeurism behind the camouflage of scientific inquiry. Their chosen surgeon reached for his saws and knives while his brother physicians watched. And they wanted the bullet. The nation could hardly bury its martyred Father Abraham with a lead ball lodged in his brain. They cut it out, marked it as evidence, and preserved it for history. When they were finished Mary Lincoln sent a request: Please cut a lock of his hair for her. His blood, according to a newspaper report, was drained from his corpse by the embalmer—the same mortuary artist who preserved the little body of Willie Lincoln in 1862—transferred to glass jars, and "sacredly preserved."

Gideon Welles, at the White House to check on his wife, Mary Jane, while she cared for Mrs. Lincoln, descended the staircase, accompanied by Attorney General James Speed. At the foot of the stairs, they found Tad Lincoln staring out of a window. Welles never forgot the sight of the grieving boy: "'Tad'...seeing us, cried aloud his tears, 'O, Mr. Welles, who killed my father?'" It was more than the navy secretary could bear. All through the previous night, and while he had watched the president die that morning, Welles had suppressed his emotions. Now, standing beside little Tad, he lost all composure and poured forth his tears.

At Dr. Mudd's kitchen table, Davey asked him where he could get his hands on a buggy or carriage to transport Booth. Mudd suggested that Davey ride with him to his father's place and try there first. Thomas Davis, the hired hand in charge of Mudd's horses, saddled their mounts.

Frances Mudd was concerned that Booth had not eaten all day, and just as her husband and David Herold were leaving, she asked if she could visit him. "Yes, certainly you can," Dr. Mudd replied. She arrayed a tray with savory fare—"some cake, a couple of oranges, and some wine"—and carried it upstairs. Placing the tray on the table, she asked Booth how he was feeling.

"My back hurts me dreadfully," he complained. "I must have hurt it when the horse fell and broke my leg."

Booth declined the cake and wine and pleaded for brandy instead. Frances regretted that they had none but offered as a substitute "some good whiskey"—his spirit of choice at the Star Saloon and Surratt's tavern. Strangely, he declined the whiskey, too.

Mrs. Mudd apologized: "I guess you think I have very little hospitality; you have been sick all day and I have not been up to see you." Once more she asked Booth if she could do anything for him. He spoke no more, and she left the room.

When Samuel Mudd and David Herold arrived at Oak Hill, his father's farm a few miles to the east, Dr. George Mudd was not at home. Sam's younger brother, Henry Lowe Mudd Jr., advised them that all the carriages but one were broken down and in need of repair. He could not let them have the good carriage without their father's permission because tomorrow was Easter Sunday, and the elder Mudd might need it. Herold suggested that they ride on to Bryantown and try their luck there. Samuel Mudd agreed, and they spurred their horses on at an unhurried pace. When they got within sight of the edge of town, Davey yanked back hard on the reins and brought his horse to a dead stop. He could not believe what he saw, several hundred yards ahead. Mounted men, wearing dark blue shell jackets trimmed with yellow piping. Yankee cavalry. Manhunters.

Herold had just spotted the vanguard of the Thirteenth New York

Cavalry. Ordered to pursue John Wilkes Booth from Washington, Dana had led his troops into Bryantown, a well-known locale of Confederate intrigue, commandeered the tavern, and occupied the town. Dana intended to establish a command center there, and from Bryantown launch cavalry patrols through the surrounding countryside, in pursuit of the Lincoln and Seward assassins.

Herold made a quick decision. He didn't need that carriage after all, he told Mudd. Booth can still ride a horse. Before the troops could spot them, Davey turned his horse around and galloped immediately back to Mudd's farm to warn Booth. Puzzled by Davey's skedaddling (Booth hadn't told the doctor yet that he was Lincoln's assassin), Mudd continued into Bryantown at a leisurely pace, just as he had done countless times on a quiet Saturday afternoon.

Mudd went about his business, purchasing supplies—calico and pepper from Mr. Beans's store—and iron nails from another establishment. He greeted friends and neighbors he passed in the street, as always. But a strange, wild atmosphere hung over Bryantown. "The town was full of soldiers and people coming and going all the while," noted one of the manhunters, Colonel H. H. Wells. The determined cavalrymen's faces glowered with anger and the seriousness of their purpose. Mudd wondered what had happened.

Then somebody blurted it out. Abraham Lincoln had been assassinated in Washington last night. He died early this morning. The cavalry is here in pursuit of the assassin who escaped. Detectives and soldiers are going to turn over Charles County hunting for the murderer. Did Mudd's mind flash back to the 4:00 A.M. knock on his door? Could it be?

Who killed the president? the citizens demanded of the soldiers. The secret was impossible to keep. It was the actor. Booth. Edwin Booth? voices in the crowd wondered aloud. No, not Edwin, but his brother John, the soldiers told them. Lincoln's assassin was John Wilkes Booth.

Mudd displayed no outward signs of alarm. And no eyes fixed him with accusing stares. He remained calm and did not, by word or deed, betray the terrible secret known, at this moment, to him alone: America's most wanted man was hiding in his house, less than five miles away. The Thirteenth New York could be there in half an hour.

Back at Mudd's farm, David Herold jumped off his horse and scurried to the house. Frances was in the kitchen supervising the servants as they prepared the next day's Easter Sunday dinner. Davey, spying her through a window, tapped on the pane and she opened the front door. She asked Herold if he had found a carriage. "No, ma'am," Davey replied. "We stopped over at the Doctor's father's and asked for his carriage, but tomorrow being Easter Sunday, his family had to go to church, and he could not spare it. I then rode some distance down the road with the Doctor, and then concluded to return and try the horses." Herold was convincing enough that he aroused no suspicion in Mrs. Mudd.

Davey excused himself and hurried upstairs. Booth was still in bed, but he wouldn't be for long. The cavalry is here, Davey warned his master; they are at Bryantown, just down the road. Herold explained how he turned back, and how Dr. Mudd rode into town. Booth sat up immediately. Davey helped him out of bed and Booth propped himself up on the crutches. Frances was alerted by the creaky floorboards above her head—"I heard them moving around the room and in a short time they came down"—and waited for them at the foot of the stairs. As Booth hobbled on his crutches, his right leg encased in his knee-high riding boot and his left foot bare, and a brace of heavy, holstered revolvers belted around his waist, his face presented a "picture of agony" to Frances Mudd. She implored Davey to leave Booth there to rest, but the young man reassured her: "If he suffers much we won't go far. I will take him to my lady-love's, not far from here."

It was around 3:00 P.M., Saturday, April 15, and Booth was in grave danger. Only one man, Samuel Mudd, stood between him and disaster. Over in nearby Bryantown, Mudd had the power to end the manhunt that afternoon. All Dr. Mudd needed to do was tell the soldiers. He could do it with a few well-chosen words: John Wilkes Booth and an accomplice are hiding at my farm; he's in the front bedroom on the second floor; he has a broken leg; he cannot run away; I'll take you there now. All he had to do was speak those words, and Dr. Samuel A. Mudd would become, overnight, a national hero.

Booth faced the most difficult choice of his escape. Should he leave Mudd's farm at once or wait for the doctor to return? Both options presented risks. Mudd's farm was in the land of the great Zekiah swamp, and he and Davey did not know the ground. A wrong turn might trap them in the notorious, fearful morass. Moreover, although Booth knew that rebel operatives lived nearby, including William Burtles, he did not know the way to their homes. If he and Davey fled now, it would put them on the roads in broad daylight without knowing where to go.

Waiting for Dr. Mudd to come home presented great risks, too. If the doctor had betrayed him to the troops in Bryantown, Booth was a dead man. If they did not kill him on the spot at Mudd's farm, then the manhunters would escort their captured prey back to Washington for a hanging. Booth had seen that once before. He had to decide now. Yes, perhaps he should have taken Mudd into his confidence. It would have been better for the doctor to have heard the truth from him rather than from the soldiers in town. Still, Booth concluded, Mudd would not betray him. Instead of fleeing the farm immediately, he waited for the doctor's return.

Booth's assessment of Mudd's character proved true. When the doctor finished his business in Bryantown, he got on his horse and, ignoring the troopers he passed on the way, rode calmly out of town. He decided to protect Booth and said nothing to anyone. But he had some choice words to say to Booth face-to-face.

In Washington, Clara Harris, her father, and Justice Cartter returned during daylight to the scene of the previous night's crime. Together they scrutinized the locks on the doors leading to the president's box, examined the little spot in the wall where Booth had scraped away the plaster, and peered through the hole through which the assassin espied Lincoln. At first they thought it was a bullet hole—evidence that Booth had shot at Lincoln blindly, the ball passing through the door before finding its target. Then they realized it was a peephole. They went into the box. The theatre was eerily quiet now and showed little evidence of the previous night's mayhem—just some overturned chairs, scattered pieces of paper littering the floor, and the bare box, already stripped of its flags and bunting by souvenir hunters. The bloodstains were still there.

Stanton wanted to see the box, too, and so, like one of his detectives prowling for clues, he too retraced Booth's steps to visualize each scene in the assassin's script. He also wanted to see the play. Perhaps a reenactment of *Our American Cousin* would provide a vital, hitherto neglected clue. Stanton rounded up what cast members could be found, commandeered Ford's, and ordered a surreal, private performance in the empty theatre. No one laughed this time at the once silly but forever-more riveting line: *"You sockdologizing old mantrap."* When Stanton and his aides heard the words echo through the house, did their eyes dart involuntarily up to the president's box? The run-through of the play confirmed it—Booth had cleverly timed his attack to coincide with Harry Hawk's funny, solitary moment onstage.

Stanton was determined to preserve the scene of the crime. He ordered that it be surrounded by a twenty-four-hour guard. And he decided that he wanted photographs of the interior, to record exactly how it appeared at the moment of the assassination. He allowed Mathew Brady and his assistant to set up their big, wet-plate camera and make a series of exposures that, together, offered a panorama of the entire stage and its scenery during act 3, scene 2. Then Brady photographed the exterior of the president's box, newly decorated with replacement flags and bunting for this purpose. He also photographed the approach to the box, and the outer door leading to the vestibule. The job challenged Brady's skill. Photographing the vast interior, illuminated only by gaslight, and perhaps by whatever daylight reached the stage from opened doors and windows on the opposite end of the theatre facing Tenth

Street, required long and careful exposures to allow the glass-plate negatives to absorb sufficient light to capture the necessary details.

$\mathscr{B}$ACK AT THE FARM, BOOTH AND HEROLD WAITED PATIENTLY for Dr. Mudd. But there was no sign of him. It was close to 6:00 in the evening and he still had not come home from Bryantown. What was taking him so long? Mudd's tardiness was a good sign, though. If the doctor had betrayed Booth, the cavalry would have galloped to the farm two hours ago.

Finally, sometime between 6:00 and 7:00 P.M., a rider turned from the main road and approached the farm. It was Dr. Mudd. He was alone and brought no cavalry escort. Booth's knowing judgment was correct—the doctor was no Judas. But he was angry.

Mudd rode up to his guests, dropped down from the saddle, and strode toward Booth. His face could not conceal his distress. He ordered Booth and Herold to leave his farm at once, and accused the actor of lying to him. Booth did not tell Mudd what he had done, and had put the doctor and his family in great danger.

Ignoring Mudd's anger, Booth seized upon the priceless news that the doctor brought back from Bryantown. The president was dead, and the fame was his. Twenty hours after the assassination, Dr. Mudd had just given John Wilkes Booth the first official confirmation that he had killed Lincoln. True, the assassin did not see how he could have missed. But it had all happened so fast. Lincoln moved at the last moment, and then Rathbone attacked Booth, leaving the actor no time to pause and admire his handiwork. There was a chance that the wound was not fatal. There had been enough room for doubt that in Surrattsville, Booth had qualified his boast to John Lloyd, saying only that he was "pretty certain" he had assassinated the president.

Dr. Mudd was not as jubilant as his patient about this news. Booth might rejoice at the tyrant's death, but Mudd was angry and afraid. By coming there, Booth had placed Mudd and his entire family in great danger. Yes, Mudd had agreed to facilitate the kidnapping of Abraham Lincoln, but no one had consulted him about murder. But now, by offering Booth his hospitality, he had unwittingly implicated himself in the most shocking crime of the Civil War, indeed, in all of American history—the murder of the president of the United States.

Mudd continued to demand that Booth and Herold leave his farm at once. A patrol from the Thirteenth New York Cavalry might descend upon them without warning within the hour. Were federal troops to discover Lincoln's assassin hiding out in his home, Dr. Mudd feared he would suffer terrible consequences. The only way to avert that disaster was to make Booth and Herold saddle their horses and ride away.

But Mudd was still sympathetic to the assassin's plight. He was no fan of Abraham Lincoln, the Union, or the black man, and he would have rejoiced at the kidnapping of the president. Booth may have abused his hospitality, but not enough to make Mudd betray him. He assured Booth that, as long as he and Herold agreed to leave now, he would still help them.

First, he gave them the names of two trustworthy Maryland Confederate operatives, William Burtles and Captain Samuel Cox. Then Mudd explained the route to the next stop on their underground rebel railroad. They must travel southeast in a wide arc to swing around and below Bryantown to avoid the troops there. Then, turning west, they would find Burtles's place, "Hagen's Folly," about two miles due south of Bryantown. Cox's farm was several miles southwest from Burtles's, and from there the two men would be within striking distance of the Potomac River and, on its western bank, Virginia. Mudd gave Booth the name of a doctor on the Virginia side in case his leg continued to trouble him.

Mudd promised Booth that he would not betray him. He would not ride back to Bryantown this evening and report that Lincoln's assassin came calling in the dead of night. Dr. Mudd would hold his tongue and give Booth a head start. If the soldiers came to question him, he would say only that two strangers in need of medical assistance stopped briefly at his farm. Then he would send the manhunters in the wrong direction.

Davey helped Booth mount his horse, eased him onto the saddle, and handed him the crude but sturdy crutches Samuel Mudd and John Best fashioned for him. The actor balanced the sticks horizontally across his saddle, thrust the toe of his right boot through the stirrup, and then gingerly slipped his other foot, sheathed in an unlaced, loose-fitting brogan, into the left stirrup. The shoe was a parting gift from Dr. Mudd—Booth would never have squeezed his left foot into his other boot. He abandoned the luxurious, expensive piece of footwear, now scarred by Mudd's scalpel, on the bedroom floor. Awkwardly his hands manipulated the crutches and reins at the same time. Herold vaulted into the saddle with ease. Samuel Mudd, relieved by their departure and by his own escape from near disaster, watched them ride off to the southeast until they vanished from sight.

It was around 7:00 P.M., April 15, fifteen hours since David Herold pounded on Mudd's door and just over twenty-one hours since John Wilkes Booth shot the president. As dusk faded to dark, Booth and Herold continued south, careful to watch the western horizon, on their right, for signs of cavalry out of Bryantown. They had a long night's ride ahead of them. But they had survived until the sunset of the first day.

Back at his farm, Dr. Mudd went about his usual end-of-the-day business. In the hours that followed Booth's departure, a peaceful quiet settled over his place. Horses stabled, servants done with their chores, his own work completed, and his family safe behind locked doors, Mudd contemplated his encounter with history, and danger. Bedtime approached, and no soldiers had come. He and Frances turned down the lamps. Tonight no strangers—assassins or manhunters—materialized in the night to awaken him suddenly from his dreams. He, too, had survived this day.

•   •   •

$\mathcal{A}$LTHOUGH DR. MUDD HAD IDENTIFIED THE ROUTE THEY must take, Booth and Herold got lost anyway. Fortunately, they found a local man, Oswell Swann, half black and half Piscataway Indian, wandering about on foot. Swann knew the territory. He had heard about the president's murder, but showed no alarm when two strangers on horseback approached him in the dark, asking if he knew the way to William Burtles's. They offered Swann $2 to serve as their guide, asked if he had any whiskey, and told him to go to his cabin and get his horse. Then, inexplicably, for reasons he never revealed, Booth changed his mind. Forget Burtles, the assassin said, and take us straight to Captain Cox. Booth offered him an extra $5. Swann agreed.

The swamp angel Oswell Swann earned his pay this night. Booth and Herold, free of the muck, snakes, and wild, overgrown vegetation of the infernal Zekiah morass, returned to the civilization of cultivated Maryland fields and familiar farmhouses. Swann had guided them safely to the very doorstep of Captain Samuel Cox, master of Rich Hill. It was between midnight and 1:00 A.M. of the new day, April 16, Easter Sunday, approximately twenty-six hours since the assassination, and seventeen hours since Abraham Lincoln died.

Good Friday 1865 was America's darkest day since the unexpected death of George Washington on December 14, 1799, sixty-six years earlier, a moment that elderly Washingtonians recalled from their youth. The Sunday following Lincoln's death was Easter, and it would be forever known as "Black Easter" to those who lived through it. The Sunday *Morning Chronicle* summed up the mood of the nation when it said the murder transformed "a season of rejoicing to mourning," and there arose "a wail throughout the land." Across the land ministers stayed up late Saturday night and by candle, lamp, or gaslight scratched out the final phrases of fresh sermons they began composing as soon as they heard, on the morning of the fifteenth, the terrible news.

In the early hours of Black Easter, Booth and Herold sought their salvation, not in a church, but at the door of a faithful Confederate. If Cox turned them away, Christ's dying words on Good Friday's cross, "it is finished," would describe their fate. The assassins were still too far north. Booth's broken leg bone and the unplanned medical detour to Dr. Mudd's farm cost them not only fifteen precious hours but took them to the east, out of their way, so that their escape timetable was now almost a day behind schedule.

Booth and Herold approached the Cox house. They decided to use the same strategy they used at the Surrattsville tavern: Booth would hang back in the shadows while Herold did the talking, but with Captain Cox they would not immediately blurt out their secret. If necessary, they were willing to beg for their lives. Cox was their last hope in Maryland, and there was no turning back if he refused them. David Herold dismounted, walked up the front piazza of the finely built, expansive farmhouse, and sounded the knocker. Booth remained on his horse under the cover of a shaggy ailanthus tree in the yard. Cox poked his head out from a second-story window and asked, "Who's there?" Herold refused to give his name, unsure if he could trust the captain. He disclosed only that he accompanied a man who needed help. Cox spotted Booth lurking under the tree's shadow, hiding from the moonlight. Herold asked if they could come in.

Suspicious but intrigued enough to come downstairs, Cox opened the door and appraised the worn-out, crazy-eyed man standing before him. The callow-looking stranger seemed more like a boy than a man. The wily farmer's eyes scanned the vicinity. Perhaps Herold was an outlaw and his plea was a trick to let other desperadoes rush the house. Uneasy, and sensing that the stranger held back his real story, Cox began shutting the door. Desperate, Booth dismounted with some difficulty and hobbled up the porch to the door. In great pain, he pleaded with Cox for aid. According to the captain's son, "it was there by a brilliant moon that Cox saw the initials 'J.W.B.' tattooed on his arm." And it was there that the honey-tongued thespian, as he did with Sergeant Cobb at the Navy Yard Bridge, again used his seductive art to win over a man to his cause. Cox swung open the door and invited the fugitives into his home. To the nation, Black Easter dawned as a day of great mourning; to John Wilkes Booth, it began as a day of salvation.

What Booth said to Cox on the front porch of Rich Hill around 1:00 A.M. on April 16—as well as the conversations and plans that followed during the next few hours that the actor and Herold spent in the house—remain a mystery. Naturally, Cox and his son later denied that the assassin and his scout ever set foot in their home. When Oswell Swann swore that he saw Booth and Herold go inside, a faithful Cox slave, Mary Swann, called him a liar and backed up her captain. But given Booth's state of mind, the precariousness of his position, and the extraordinary thing that the captain and his son were about to do to help their guests, there is little doubt that Booth unburdened himself and confessed all to his hosts. The assassin of the president of the United States was in their midst, injured, desperate, and on the run from a frenzied manhunt. Father and son beheld the murderer, then decided to save him. Cox told Booth that there was only one man, a person of very special skills, who could get them across the Potomac into Virginia.

In the morning, after sunrise, they would summon him. But for now it was much too dangerous for Booth and Herold to remain at Rich Hill. Instead, Cox explained, he would hide them in a nearly impenetrable, heavily wooded pine thicket some distance from his house. No one would search for them there, Cox assured them, and it was extremely unlikely that any of the locals would stumble upon them. They were not to build a fire. Then, in the morning, someone would come for them. That person would signal them with a peculiar whistle as he approached. They were to beware anyone who failed to make that sound. After wolfing down the food that Cox offered, Booth and Herold mounted up for the ride to the pine thicket. Cox ordered his overseer, Franklin Robey, to take them there.

Oswell Swann still waited for them outside, perhaps hoping for an additional fee to guide the strangers to another destination. When Booth and Herold emerged from the house, Davey walked straight to his horse, neglecting the actor's disability. Booth, standing beside his horse, impatient and helpless, chided him in an annoyed voice: "Don't you know I can't get on?" Davey came back and helped his master into the saddle. Booth paid Swann $12 for his services, and then, to throw suspicion off their hosts, he and Herold complained conspicuously about Cox's lack of hospitality. "I thought Cox was a man of Southern feeling," murmured Booth. If Swann took the bait, he went home believing that Cox had rebuffed his unwanted midnight callers. Just to be sure, David Herold threatened him: "Don't you say anything—if you tell that you saw anybody you will not live long." If their luck held, they would cross the river to Virginia sometime after nightfall on April 16, between sixteen and twenty-four hours from now. If, that is, they could survive just one more day in Maryland.

$\mathcal{B}$OOTH AND HEROLD ENTERED THE PINES, DISMOUNTED, and tied off their horses. The animals had served them well, but they were hungry and thirsty and unused to spending the night outdoors and in the open. These were city stable horses that rented by the hour or the day, not expedition horses suited for days in the field. Exhausted, the two men unrolled their blankets on the damp earth, lay down, and gazed up at the immense black sky decorated by countless points of twinkling light. It would be morning in a few hours. If Captain Cox's word was true, it was safe to doze off until then.

The rising sun and chirping birds woke Booth and Herold early in the morning. Now they could do nothing but wait. Back at Rich Hill, Samuel Cox had to find out whether his man would actually help Booth and Herold. Cox instructed his eighteen-year-old son, Samuel Jr., to ride over to "Huckleberry" Farm, about four miles to the southeast, and bring the owner, Thomas A. Jones, to Rich Hill right away. Cox warned the boy to be cautious and told him that if anyone, especially soldiers, stopped and questioned him on the way and asked where he was going, he should tell the truth about his destination. But if asked why he was going there, then the youth must not disclose the reason. Instead, he should lie and say that he was heading to Huckleberry to ask Jones for some seed corn. It was planting season, and no one would suspect such an innocent request from one farmer to another.

Around 8:00 A.M., Samuel Cox Jr. arrived at Huckleberry, just as Confederate agent and river boatman Thomas A. Jones finished his breakfast. The secret service veteran spent his entire life trailblazing through the fields, thickets, and forests of rural Maryland and navigating its streams, marshes, and rivers. During the war he had ferried hundreds of men, and the occasional female spy like the beautiful Sarah Slater, across the Potomac River between Maryland and Virginia. On some nights Jones organized not one but two trips across the Potomac in a small rowboat. In addition, he transported the Confederate mail between the two states and sent south fresh Union newspapers that provided intelligence to Richmond and were scrutinized by the highest leaders of the Confederacy. Jones was an indispensable, mysterious, and laconic secret agent fighting the shadow war along the watery borders between Union and rebel territory. The Union army had never caught him in action—he was a river ghost to the boys in blue. "Not one letter or paper was ever lost," he boasted. And his mastery of the river was so complete that he was even able to calculate the most propitious time, almost down to the minute, to begin a trip across. "I had noticed that a little before sunset, the reflection of the high bluffs near Pope's Creek extended out into the Potomac till it nearly met the shadows cast by the Virginia woods, and therefore, at that time of evening it was very difficult to observe as small an object floating in the river as a rowboat."

Jones's service to the Confederacy had cost him dearly. Suspected of disloyal activity, federal forces arrested and jailed him for months at the Old Capitol prison in Washington. Then his beloved wife died. He had to sell his other farm at Pope's Creek, and when he went to Richmond at the beginning of April 1865 to collect the money owed to him by the Confederate government, he discovered that the army had evacuated the city and Jones went unpaid. He lost $2,300 due for three years' service, and, even worse, upon the collapse of the Confederacy, he lost the

$3,000 he had invested in Confederate bonds at the beginning of the war. All of this meant that Thomas Jones needed as much money as he could lay his hands on.

The Cox boy dutifully mentioned the seed corn, but once he saw that Jones was alone, he whispered the true nature of his mission. His father wanted to see Jones at once. "Some strangers were at our house last night," the boy said. Jones's eyes lit up—could he mean the heroes who assassinated President Lincoln? The report electrified Jones. The day before, on the evening of Saturday, April 15, around the time that Booth and Herold left the sanctuary of Dr. Mudd's and undertook the next leg of their escape, Jones happened to be visiting his former farm at Pope's Creek. Two Union soldiers rode up and asked what appeared to be an innocent question. Who owned that little boat down in the creek? For Jones the war ended when Richmond fell on April 3 and the Army of Northern Virginia surrendered on the ninth. There would be no more secret river crossings, no more thrilling escapes from Union army and navy pursuers, no more mysterious signal lights flashed across the water from one state to another. The war was over, and Jones saw no need for any prolonged cunning. He told the soldiers that the boat was his.

His response prompted a strange but vaguely worded warning from one of the soldiers. "You had better keep an eye to it. There are suspicious characters somewhere in the neighborhood who will be wanting to cross the river, and if you don't look sharp you will lose your boat."

Since when did Union soldiers care whether a Southern farmer in disloyal territory lost his rowboat? There was more to this.

"Indeed," replied Jones. "I will look after it. I would not like to lose it, as it is my fishing boat and the shad are beginning to run."

The soldiers whispered to each other, then seemed to nod in agreement. The one who asked about the boat turned to Jones. "Have you heard the news, friend?"

No, he had not, replied Jones.

"Then I will tell you. Our President was assassinated at 10 o'clock last night."

Jones uttered an ambiguous exclamation. "Is it possible!"

Yes, the soldier answered, "and the men who did it came this way."

Now, a day later, Jones felt it in his bones: Captain Cox wanted to see him about something connected to the assassination.

Jones saddled up and accompanied young Cox to Rich Hill. Although he had questions, Jones spoke little during the ride. His wartime experiences taught him to never talk about dangerous subjects except when absolutely necessary. Once they got to Rich Hill, Captain Cox could do the talking; Jones would do the listening. Until then, the riders trotted northeast quietly, their silence broken only by harmless remarks about the weather or the condition of the roads. When Jones arrived at Rich Hill at about 9:00 A.M., he saw Captain Cox waiting outside at the front gate. Jones dismounted, and Cox led him to an open place where no one could hide and eavesdrop on their conversation. An experienced secret agent, Jones sensed that Cox wanted to tell him something important. But his experience also counseled him to let his friend tell him in his own way, at his own pace. They spoke in pleasantries for several minutes, until Cox could avoid the subject no more. "Tom, I had visitors about four o'clock this morning."

Normally Jones possessed the talent to remain stone silent and let another man talk, but now he could not restrain himself. He blurted out, "Who were they, and what did they want?"

"They want to get across the river," Cox explained. He paused, then spoke in a whisper. "Have you heard that Lincoln was killed Friday night?"

Yes, Jones replied, telling Cox about his encounter with the two soldiers.

For a full minute Cox did not speak. Then he broke the silence: "Tom, we must get those men who were here this morning across the river."

Jones's intuition was right—not only did Cox want to see him about the assassination, the killers were here! With that, Cox opened the flood-gates and told Jones everything about the late-night visit from Booth and Herold. "Tom, you must get him across."

Jones was no coward—four years of loyal, dangerous service to the Confederacy had proved that. But the war was over. Jones mulled the situation over: "I knew that to assist in any way the assassin of Mr. Lincoln would be to put my life in jeopardy. I knew that the whole of southern Maryland would soon be—nay, was even then—swarming with soldiers and bloodhounds on the trail, eager to avenge the murder of their beloved president and reap their reward. I hesitated for a moment as I weighed these matters."

Cox implored him a third time: "Tom, can't you put these men across?"

Jones made up his mind. "I will see what I can do, but the odds are against me. I must see these men; where are they?"

WHERE WAS JOHN WILKES BOOTH? THAT IS EXACTLY WHAT the entire country—Stanton and his men in Washington, soldiers and detectives in the field, sailors on the rivers and at sea, the American people everywhere, and, of course, the newspapers—wanted to know. And when would he be captured? The daily papers were filled with ridiculous predictions. On April 16, the *Chicago Tribune*, several hundred miles away from the center of action in Washington, announced that Lincoln's assassin would be taken momentarily: "The escape of the paracide, Booth, and his confederates can only be for a few days or hours. Millions of eyes are in vigilant search of them, and soon they will be in the hands of justice...no place on this side of perdition can shelter them." Except for a pine thicket, perhaps. Ignorant of the situation, optimistic editors in faraway Chicago predicted Booth's "quick capture and hanging." Then, to hedge their bets, they published an absurd and contradictory headline: "The Assassin Arrested, or Still at Large." Was he still on the run, the *Tribune* asked, or was there any truth to the "unconfirmed report that Booth was arrested at 9:00 A.M. near Fort Hastings on the Bladensburg Road," when the foolish assassin "approached our pickets boldly."

The April 16 edition of the *New York Herald* shared the *Chicago Tribune*'s optimism: "The most expert detectives in the country are engaged in the investigation, and no pains, labor, skill or expense will be spared in its prosecution."

CAPTAIN COX TOLD THOMAS JONES THAT HIS OVERSEER FRANKlin Robey had guided Booth and Herold in the middle of the night to a pine thicket about a mile west of his house. Lincoln's killer was there now, waiting for someone to come and rescue him. Cox gave Jones the whistle code, a trio of varying notes, and cautioned him to approach the fugitives warily. Heavily armed and skittish, they might kill him. "Take care how you approach them. They are fully armed and might shoot you through mistake."

Alone, Jones rode west toward his unsought rendezvous with Lincoln's assassin. The sun was at his back. That would make him a more difficult target.

Soon after he entered the pines, Jones saw movement. It was not the fugitives. Instead, he found an unattended bay mare, with black legs, mane, and tail, and a white star on her forehead. The horse, fitted with a saddle and bridle, wandered around and grazed in a small clearing made some time previously for a tobacco bed. Jones tied the animal to a tree and pressed forward. Quietly, he inched deeper into the woods. The pines were thick now, and Jones could not see more than thirty or forty feet in front of him. He'd better give the signal soon, he thought, before he caught the two men by surprise and they shot him. Jones stopped in his tracks and whistled an odd mix of notes, like an intoxicated bluebird.

David Herold, "scarcely more than a boy," Jones thought, rose from the brush and aimed his Spencer carbine at him. The weapon was cocked and ready to fire. "Who are you, and what do you want," demanded Herold. He brandished the weapon menacingly.

"I come from Cox," Jones replied. "He told me I would find you here. I am a friend; you have nothing to fear from me."

Herold stared at Jones, then, satisfied, relaxed his tense grip on the Spencer and spoke curtly. "Follow me." He guided Jones thirty yards deeper into the pines, through thick undergrowth, to a man partly concealed by the brush. Jones's excitement grew. He was about to discover the answer to the question that, for the past thirty-six hours, possessed an entire nation—where was John Wilkes Booth?

"This friend comes from Captain Cox," said Herold, looking down to a man on the ground.

Nearly overcome by a mixture of thrill and fear, Jones saw John Wilkes Booth for the first time. "He was lying on the ground with his head supported by his hand. His carbine, pistols and knife were close behind him. A blanket was drawn partly over him. His slouch hat and crutch were lying by him. He was dressed in dark—I think black—clothes...travel-stained...though he was exceedingly pale and his features bore the evident trace of suffering, I have seldom, if ever, seen a more strikingly handsome man."

Prior to meeting Booth, Jones had little enthusiasm for this risky scheme. Yes, he had promised Cox that he would help, and he would never go back on his word to his old friend. But he did not relish the duty. Meeting the assassin changed everything.

"His voice was pleasant," noted Jones. "Though he seemed to be suffering intense pain from his broken leg, his manner was courteous and polite," he observed with approval. Booth, even in these dire circumstances, remembered how to please an audience, and Jones was smitten. "But sooner had I seen him in his helpless and suffering condition than I gave my whole mind to the problem of how to get him across the river. Murderer though I knew him to be, his condition so enlisted my sympathy in his behalf that my horror of his deed was almost forgotten in my compassion for the man, and I felt it my bounden duty to do all I

could to aid him; and I made up my mind, be the consequences to me
what they might, from that time forth my every energy should be bent
to the accomplishment of what then seemed to be the well-nigh hopeless task of getting him to Virginia."

Booth confided what Jones already knew—he had killed Lincoln.
The assassin conceded that the odds were against him. "He said he knew
the United States Government would use every means in its power to
secure his capture." But, vowed the actor, his aroused black eyes glowing
with their signature brightness, "John Wilkes Booth will never be taken
alive." Thomas Jones was sure he meant it.

Jones proposed a plan. He would do all he could to get Booth and
Herold across to Virginia, but they must leave it to him to decide when
and how they would make the attempt. Patience was essential. Jones
was willing to assume great personal risk, but not to lead a blatantly
suicidal mission. "You must stay right here, however long, and wait till I
can see some way to get you out; and I do not believe I can get you out
until this hue and cry is somewhat over. Meantime, I will see that you
are fed." Jones hoped that the soldiers and detectives scouring the area
would give up soon and ride on to new territory once they concluded
that Booth was not hiding nearby.

Until then, Booth and Herold must not leave the pine thicket, make
noise, or do anything that might let anyone know they were there. Jones
said they had to wait for exactly the right moment to cross the Potomac.
They needed a dark night, smooth water, deserted riverbanks, and the
departure of many of the soldiers and detectives who had already followed Booth south into Maryland. That might take days. Jones persuaded Booth and Herold to adopt his ingenious, counterintuitive plan.
The best way for them to escape, Jones reasoned, was to stop running
from their pursuers and to go into hiding. Manhunters were already
concentrating south of Washington. Soon federal forces would join David Dana and infest Charles County. It was smarter to try to escape by
standing still, letting the manhunters sweep through the region, before
they moved on to search elsewhere.

With his simple plan, Jones confounded the whole manhunt for John Wilkes Booth. A lone Confederate agent, without resources and nearly penniless, had just checkmated the frantic pursuit by thousands of men being orchestrated from Washington by Secretary of War Stanton.

STANTON MAY HAVE LOST BOOTH'S TRAIL IN THE PINES, BUT he was closing in on the author of the notorious "Sam" letter found in Booth's room at the National the night of the assassination. On the afternoon of April 16, Charles Dana received a telegram from Provost Marshal James McPhail in Baltimore: "I have traced Samuel Arnold to Fortress Monroe. Will send two men for him who know him personally. Send me a telegraph order to make arrest at fortress. Telegraphing for arrest may flush it." Dana replied within fifteen minutes: "Arrest Samuel Arnold, suspected of being concerned in the murder of the President." The hunt for Booth's old school chum was on.

The same day, April 16, Confederate Lieutenant General R. S. Ewell sent a remarkable letter to U. S. Grant, signed by him and also on behalf of sixteen other Confederate generals. They didn't kill Lincoln, Ewell swore. He expressed "unqualified abhorrence and indignation for the assassination of the President of the United States....No language can adequately express the shock produced upon myself, in common with all the other general officers confined here with me, by the occurrence of this appalling crime, and by the seeming tendency in the public mind to connect the South and Southern men with it.... [W]e are not assassins, not the allies of assassins, be they from the North or from the South."

Stanton, along with most government and military officials, as well as the American people, still blamed the Confederacy for Lincoln's murder. Booth, it was widely believed, acted merely as its agent. But if it was not true, perhaps the resources of the Confederacy could be deployed to assist in the manhunt. In a startling move, Stanton considered enlisting the Confederacy's legendary "gray ghost" and cavalry genius, John Singelton Mosby, in the manhunt. On April 16 Stanton telegrammed instructions to General Hancock, soon to parley over surrender terms with Mosby at Winchester, Virginia: "In holding an interview with Mosby it may be needless to caution an old soldier like you to guard against surprise or danger to yourself; but the recent murders show such astounding wickedness that too much precaution cannot be taken. If Mosby is sincere he might do much toward detecting and apprehending the murderers of the President."

Chapter Six

"That Vile Rabble of Human Bloodhounds"

NO ONE EXPECTED BOOTH TO STOP RUNNING. SOON THE manhunters would track Booth to the Surrattsville tavern, and then to Doctor Mudd's. But then the trail went cold. The assassin seemed to simply vanish. Back in Washington, the mood at the War Department turned foul. Had he done it? Had Lincoln's murderer actually escaped?

Booth was a man of impulse and action, not patience and inertia, and he knew the river was tantalizingly close. He was eager to cross it, so that he and Davey could be among friends on the Virginia side this very night. And he was convinced he could be, if only Jones agreed to act decisively. Hiding in a pine thicket for days seemed to increase the danger of capture, not reduce it. Still he deferred to the river ghost's judgment. Booth knew that he still had no choice. Thomas Jones was Booth's only hope. If he and Herold defied Jones, if they left the pines that night and made a desperate run for the river on their own, they would almost certainly be captured or killed. Even if they made it to the riverbank, where would they find a boat? Jones was the only option. Moreover, something about Jones made Booth trust him. The operative's laconic, steely, no-nonsense manner appealed to Booth, who fancied himself an astute judge of other men's hearts. And Jones did know the surrounding terrain and the river as well as Booth knew the streets of Washington and the passageways of Ford's Theatre. If this cunning, rebel nighthawk could not get Booth across, no one could.

Jones had spoken emphatically: "You must stay right here, however long, and wait till I can see some way to get you out." But there would be no doctor. Jones explained that it was too dangerous to bring a local Maryland physician to the pines. Once Booth crossed the river he could seek a rebel doctor in Virginia. Booth and Herold surrendered to Jones's plan and placed themselves in his hands. But the assassin had a few urgent questions. What did the people think? What could Jones tell him about what people were saying about the assassination? Jones assured him that most men of Southern sympathies were gratified by Booth's act.

Booth wanted more. If it was not too much trouble, he asked, could Jones please bring some current Washington newspapers—say, yesterday's *Daily Morning Chronicle,* the *Evening Star,* or the *National Intelligencer*—from Saturday, April 15, the day Lincoln died, or from today, the sixteenth, Black Easter? Incredibly, despite his pain, exhaustion, and dire, life-threatening predicament, the actor was eager to read his reviews. Booth was especially keen to pore over the *Intelligencer* and enjoy a particular article—the contents already quite familiar to him—he expected to find in its pages.

As Jones prepared to leave the thicket, he offered Davey Herold something of more practical use than newspapers—the location of a freshwater spring thirty to forty yards away. The assassins were thirsty, and the spring would sustain them while they waited to cross the river. Jones warned Herold to approach it cautiously because there was a little footpath near it that was used by the locals. Federal troops would never discover it, but better that no one, not even friendly Southerners, lay eyes on the fugitives.

Jones mounted his horse. They would go down to the river as soon as it was safe, he reiterated. Until then, he promised, he would not abandon the assassins. He would come to them every morning, carrying food and newspapers—and hope. Jones spurred his horse, navigated slowly through the pine trees, and vanished from sight. For the next twenty-four hours, until—or if—Jones returned on Monday morning, April 17, Booth and Herold were on their own.

$\mathcal{R}$IDING HOME FROM THE PINE THICKET, THOMAS JONES contemplated the predicament he had just gotten himself into. When he awoke on the morning of April 16, he was just another veteran of Confederate service whose war had come to an end. All Jones wanted to do was lick his wounds, recover as best he could from his financial losses, and work his farm. But now, just a few hours later, he placed himself in greater peril than at any time during his years of secret, wartime exploits. Never had he been entrusted with a more dangerous, and as he would soon learn, valuable secret. An entire nation was demanding with one voice, "Where is John Wilkes Booth?" Thomas Jones was one of four men in the country, including the Coxes and their overseer, who knew the answer. Jones also knew something else. If Union troops caught him harboring the murderer of Abraham Lincoln, the best he could hope for was a long return visit to the Old Capitol prison. The more likely punishment was death. Jones had no illusions about how the North would view him: "I would be looked upon as the vile aider and abettor of a wretch stained with as dark a crime as the recording angel ever wrote down in the eternal book of doom."

Jones's impromptu plan had one overriding theme: do nothing to attract suspicion. That meant following his daily routines and doing nothing out of the ordinary. Getting the newspapers was easy enough. He collected them throughout the war and obtaining them now would not seem unusual. After all, everyone wanted to read the latest news about Lincoln's assassination, and if federal troops caught him with several newspapers in his saddlebags, Jones could plead natural, innocent curiosity. The food would be harder to explain. Why was a local farmer riding around the countryside with a haversack or saddlebags stuffed with provisions? And how could Jones explain the copious bags of feed needed for Booth and Herold's hungry horses? And what about the boat? He had to get it ready to be used at a moment's notice. When the time came to flee to the river, Jones would have to rush to the pine thicket and get Booth and Herold moving fast. The previous day Jones had discovered two Union cavalrymen lurking near his little bateau at Pope's Creek. Perhaps they were staking it out, waiting for Lincoln's assassin to claim it. No, it was too dangerous to take a chance on the bateau. Fortunately for Booth and Herold, Thomas Jones possessed one last boat, an eleven-foot-long, lead-colored, flat-bottomed skiff hidden in marsh grass upstream from the bateau on Pope's Creek. As far as he knew, Union troops hadn't yet found the skiff.

Jones had to secure that second boat immediately: "Booth's only chance for crossing the river depended upon my being able to retain possession and control of one of these two boats." To formulate a plan, Jones summoned up all of his wartime experience in evading Union patrols. As soon as he arrived home Jones instructed his former slave Henry Woodland to take the skiff out every morning and fish for shad with the gill nets. By this time it was not unusual to see a black man fishing with nets on the river in southern Maryland, and Woodland wouldn't attract much attention from Union patrols. Jones instructed Woodland to cast off from Pope's Creek on Monday morning but not to row the boat back to the creek. Instead, he was to land at a place called Dent's Meadow. Then, for the rest of the week, Woodland was to keep up that routine, casting off from Dent's each morning, and landing there in the afternoon with his catch, taking care to conceal the boat from thieves. Jones never told Henry the special significance of Dent's Meadow—the place he had chosen as the perfect location from which to take Booth and Herold across the river.

Jones considered the spot favorable terrain: "Dent's meadow was then a very retired spot back of Huckleberry farm, about one and a half miles north of Pope's Creek, at least a mile from the public road and with no dwelling house in sight. This meadow is a narrow valley opening to the river between high and steep cliffs that were then heavily timbered and covered by an almost impenetrable undergrowth of laurel. A small stream flows through the meadow, widening into a little creek as it approaches the river. It was from this spot I determined to make the attempt of sending Booth across to Virginia." Jones had chosen the place, but now he had to await the right moment.

On Easter Sunday, between 10:00 and 11:00 a.m., George Atzerodt showed up at the home of Hezekiah Metz, about twenty-two miles from Washington, in Montgomery County, Maryland. Atzerodt joined Metz and three of his guests, Somerset Leaman, James E. Leaman, and Nathan Page, for the midday meal. Atzerodt was known to the people in these parts by another name, "Andrew Atwood." Somerset had known him for years, and when Atzerodt arrived at Metz's he teased him:

"Are you the man that killed Abe Lincoln?" The joke must have frozen the German in his tracks.

Atzerodt laughed and said, "Yes."

"Well, Andrew," Leaman continued, "I want to know the truth of it; is it so?" He asked if Lincoln had really been assassinated.

"Yes, it is so; and he died yesterday evening about 3 o'clock."

Leaman asked if it was also true that Seward's throat was cut, and two of his sons were stabbed.

"Yes," Atzerodt replied, "Mr. Seward was stabbed, or rather cut at the throat, but not killed, and two of his sons were stabbed."

Leaman asked if it was also true that General Grant had been murdered.

"No, I don't know whether that is so or not; I don't suppose it is so; if he had been, I should have heard it."

At the dinner table James Leaman also asked about Grant, and Atzerodt replied: "No, I don't suppose he was; if he was killed, he would have been killed probably by a man that got on the same car that Grant got on." Atzerodt did not know it, but with those words he had just sealed his doom. After dinner, oblivious to the danger, he continued on to the home of his cousin, Hartman Richter, arriving there between 2:00 and 3:00 P.M.

$\mathscr{S}$AMUEL MUDD DECIDED THAT HE COULD NOT LET EASTER Sunday, April 16, pass without doing something. By breakfast time, 7:00 A.M., Booth and Herold enjoyed a twelve-hour head start from his farm. If all had gone well, they should have reached William Burtles's place well before sunrise. Although Mudd did not know it, the fugitives made even better progress by bypassing Burtles altogether and riding straight to Captain Cox's.

Mudd considered his predicament. He could choose to do nothing, and wait for federal troops to visit his farm, but perhaps the soldiers might never come. Or they might. Someone might even tip them off. The doctor's servants and former slaves knew he had taken in an injured patient the very night of Lincoln's assassination. Some of them had even seen Booth while he rested in bed or hobbled around on his crutches. Too many people had seen Booth for Mudd to keep the visit a secret forever.

Several of Mudd's neighbors were aware that he knew John Wilkes Booth. Worshippers had spotted them together last winter at St. Mary's on two occasions. And how long would it be before the authorities interviewed George Gardiner, the man who sold Booth the one-eyed horse, or Thomas L. Gardiner, the youth who delivered the animal to the actor? Peter Trotter, the blacksmith, would surely remember the day when Mudd and Booth brought the handicapped mare over for a new set of horseshoes. Moreover, several witnesses had seen Mudd and Booth together in Washington. It was inevitable. At some point, probably soon, the soldiers or detectives would discover two things about Dr. Mudd: he had visitors on assassination night, and, even more damning, he had links to Booth.

Mudd decided to seize the initiative in a way calculated to throw suspicion off himself. Today he would inform on—but not actually betray—Lincoln's assassin. Mudd crafted a simple but clever cover story. He would merely report that two strangers, a man with a broken leg and his youthful companion, had called at his home unexpectedly, in the predawn hours of April 15. He treated the injury, and the strangers did not stay long. He was suspicious of these men, he would say, and thus felt duty bound to report them to the Thirteenth New York Cavalry in Bryantown. Those were the bare bones.

Then Mudd added a clever touch. Instead of riding into Bryantown himself and facing the troops, he would ask his second cousin, Dr. George Mudd, a loyal Unionist, a species rare in these parts, to report the strangers on his behalf. He hoped that having this information come from the lips of a man above suspicion by the federal authorities would allow him to hide beneath his cousin's Unionist coattails if the troops wanted to question him. George Mudd's vague, secondhand report would contain so few details that it would hardly prompt the soldiers to leap into their saddles and gallop off after two strangers. No, the information would be useless until they followed the tip to its source, Samuel Mudd. Lieutenant Dana would have to send a patrol to Sam's farm to press him for details about the strangers. All that would take time, which would give Booth even more time to put miles between himself and his pursuers.

After Easter services on the morning of the sixteenth, Mudd asked his cousin George the favor of passing his story on to the cavalry in Bryantown. Mudd returned home, with an immense feeling of relief. Now, when the soldiers came, it would be at his behest, and not because he had fallen under suspicion. Through the afternoon and into the evening, Mudd anticipated the arrival of the manhunters. But they did not come. Unbeknownst to him, cousin George failed to ride into Bryantown to report the strangers.

By the evening of April 16, Booth enjoyed a twenty-four-hour head start on any pursuers coming from Mudd's farm. And thanks to George Mudd's delay in filing his cousin's report, Union troops, unaware that

Booth had even been at Samuel Mudd's, had not begun their pursuit from that place. From the viewpoint of anxious officials back in Washington—Secretary of War Stanton chief among them—the progress of the manhunt was even worse. John Wilkes Booth had assassinated the president almost forty-eight hours ago but the manhunters had no solid leads. Yes, the police, detectives, and military officers had discovered a number of leads on Booth's cat's-paws and conspirators, but none led to the assassin-in-chief.

Hats, Deringer pistols, abandoned knives, broken revolvers, jackets, one-eyed horses, bankbooks, mysterious letters, plugs of tobacco, hotel registers, notes to vice presidents, theatrical trunks, spurs, bridles, saddles, and eyewitness accounts were all fine clues that made the assassin and his accomplices seem tantalizingly vivid and near. These clues would make good evidence at a criminal trial as proofs of identity and guilt. The evidence collected on April 14 and 15 certainly confirmed that it was Booth who had shot Lincoln, and that he seemed to have not one, but several, coconspirators. And the contents of Atzerodt's room at the Kirkwood—plus Booth's note to Johnson—suggested that the vice president had also been marked for death. But all this evidence spoke to Booth's guilt, not his escape plan. Only the "Sam" letter, which suggested that two accomplices lived in Baltimore, hinted at Booth's possible destination. Booth could be anywhere. Sightings across the country of false Booths did not help the manhunters. With each passing hour Booth's trail grew a little colder. Soon, he would vanish from sight, driving Stanton and his men into a frenzy. Booth's expertise in eluding the manhunters augmented, by the hour, the government's embarrassment over its failure to apprehend him.

On the night of April 16, Stanton had no idea of Booth's whereabouts or destination. Yes, it was probably the assassin who gave the name "Booth" to Sergeant Cobb at the bridge and fled into Maryland. It was fortunate for Stanton that the persistent stable man Fletcher had chased Herold that far and revealed Booth's crossing earlier than the manhunters would have otherwise discovered it. But where did he go after that? At 8:30 P.M. Quartermaster General Meigs telegrammed Colonel Newport, chief quartermaster at Baltimore, with new instructions for the hunt that revealed the manhunters' confusion about Booth's intentions: "The murderers of the President and Secretary of State have, it is believed, gone southeast, and will perhaps attempt to escape by water to the Eastern Shore, or to board some vessel waiting for them, or some vessel going to sea. The Potomac will be patrolled by steamers from Washington.... The object is to catch the murderers. Vigilance and speed." Perhaps, Meigs feared, other conspirators awaited Booth at the shore with an oceangoing vessel, ready to put to sea and sail or steam all the way to France or England for sanctuary. During the war, Confederate blockade-runners had made the dangerous crossing scores of times. Perhaps one was anchored somewhere off the Maryland coast, ready to embark on one last, daring voyage.

On Monday morning, April 17, Thomas Jones appeared to go about his regular business. He tended to chores, ate his usual breakfast at the customary time, and made sure that Henry Woodland continued his daily fishing expeditions. At the pine thicket, Booth and Herold, awake for hours, wondered if their benefactor would return. Jones pulled on his baggy, deep-pocketed overcoat and thrust his arms through the sleeves. He grabbed some bread, butter, and ham, filled a flask with coffee, and stuffed everything into his pockets. He folded the newspapers, printed on soft, thick rag paper, and stashed them in his coat, too. Then, in a clever ruse, he carried a basket of corn on his arm to throw off any Union troops he might encounter. If stopped and questioned, he would claim that he was on his way to feed his hogs that ran free in the woods. A little before 10:00 A.M. Jones mounted his horse and rode toward the pine thicket.

About one hundred yards from Booth's camp, Jones dismounted and led his horse forward on foot, then tied him. Just as he did the previous morning, Jones walked ahead slowly until, within earshot of the assassins, he whistled the secret melody. This time Booth and Herold welcomed him, not with a well-aimed carbine pointed at his heart, but with open arms. They had not eaten in almost thirty hours and eyed the contents of Jones's pockets hungrily as he unloaded them. Booth especially wanted the other treats those pockets yielded—newspapers! At last, three long days after the assassination, he could read about his history-making actions and how they were reported to the nation.

Booth's pleasure could not hide his worsening condition. The leg was bad, and Booth was obviously in more pain than when Jones first saw him twenty-four hours ago. The assassin said he was impatient to continue his escape across the river where he could find shelter indoors and see another doctor. Jones started explaining the situation again but became distracted when he heard a familiar and terrifying noise in the distance—clanking metal and horses' hooves pounding the earth. Instantly Jones recognized the sound— cavalry sabers slapping the saddles of Union troops riding in their direction. It was too late for Herold and Jones to boost Booth up on the bay mare and gallop away, and a fight was out of the question: Booth couldn't walk, Jones was unarmed, and Herold was untested in battle. Plus, with only two revolvers and a Spencer carbine, they couldn't hold off a patrol of Union cavalry for long. The trio hugged the ground and held their breath. The horses, barreling down a road near the pine thicket, closed the distance. They got within two hundred yards. It was Booth's closest brush with manhunters since he galloped down the alley behind Ford's Theatre. Then, instead of veering into the pines, the troops stayed on the road, passed the thicket, and continued on until the sound of hoofbeats dwindled in the distance.

Jones locked eyes with Booth: "You see, my friend, we must wait."

"Yes," Booth conceded, "I leave it all with you."

ON THE MORNING OF THE SEVENTEENTH ANOTHER MAN waited, too. Troops had still not called on Dr. Mudd to pursue his tip—because they did not know about it. It wasn't until Monday afternoon that George Mudd got around to riding to Bryantown. He asked to see the commanding officer and, introduced to Lieutenant Dana, divulged his cousin's vague, one-day-old report about the two suspicious strangers. Then, in an unbelievable stroke of luck for Booth and Herold, Dana dismissed the news as stale and unimportant. He thanked George Mudd and sent him on his way. And, providentially for the assassins, Dana chose not to send troops to Samuel Mudd's farm to investigate. Distracted by other leads, Dana ignored the one tip that placed Lincoln's assassin—if only momentarily—within his reach.

When the soldiers had not come by that evening, Mudd relaxed. Perhaps, by this point, they would not come at all. According to Mudd's calculations, Booth was long gone, probably even across the Potomac River into Virginia by now. With the assassin's trail in Maryland running cold, the manhunters would soon depart Charles County and shift the action to places far from Bryantown and his farm.

According to premature reports in the newspapers, Booth had already moved on. The April 17 *Chicago Tribune* already had him cross the Potomac, reporting "it is now the general impression that the murderer Booth and his accomplices have escaped into Virginia. It is unlikely that a person so well known would attempt to travel through the north." Of course the *Tribune* reported in the same issue: "Booth was captured this morning. The story is that his horse threw him and injured him so severely that he was obliged to seek relief on the Seventh Street road" on the outskirts of Washington. The April 17 *New York Herald* assured its readers, "Detectives are on the hunt. The most expert men in the profession, from New York and other cities are here for this purpose. Colonel L. C. Baker has arrived today, and is engaged in ferreting out the assassins. It is believed they will be caught within twenty-four hours."

THOMAS JONES HAD EXPERIENCED ENOUGH EXCITEMENT FOR one day. He agreed to return to the thicket around the same time next morning, Tuesday the eighteenth, carrying more food and newspapers, but he refused to bring horse feed again. Concealing the feedbags was impossible, and he could not carry enough, anyway, to sate the two ravenous horses. After two days without food, they had ferocious appetites—and they also made a lot of noise. Jones advised the men to get rid of the horses. They wouldn't be needed to get to Dent's Meadow, and they couldn't be ferried across the river in a little rowboat. Better to dispose of them here and now, before the next cavalry patrol came by and they betrayed the site of the camp. Booth agreed: "If we can hear those horses, they can certainly hear the neighing of ours, which are uneasy from want of food and stabling." David Herold reluctantly went along with this. He loved animals, but realized that, with Booth helpless on the ground, the deed fell to him. Jones said good-bye and left for Huckleberry.

The horses had served them well. The white-starred bay that could move like a cat had saved Booth in the alley behind Ford's Theatre. She galloped superbly through downtown Washington, her hooves pounding distance between Booth and any pursuers during the thrilling, moonlit ride. The roan horse had made it possible for Herold to escape from the botched Seward assassination attempt. Now their reward for this faithful service was death. Davey untied both horses and led them by the reins to a quicksand morass about a mile from the pine thicket. Quickly, he shot each one in the head with a pistol or the carbine, and then sank their bodies, still accoutered with saddles, bits, bridles, stirrups, and all. There they rest in an unmarked grave, their skeletons undiscovered to this day.

Killing the horses was the third time since the assassination that David Herold gave up the chance to abandon John Wilkes Booth. On the night of April 14, he kept their rendezvous at Soper's Hill when he could have fled and gone into hiding. On the fifteenth, when he rode from Dr. Mudd's to the vicinity of Bryantown, he could have left Booth behind at the farm and kept riding. Now, in the pine thicket, all he had to do was kill one of the horses, mount the other, and gallop away. Without the lame actor—who, after all, was the main prey of the manhunters—Herold had a better chance of melting into the countryside.

Davey returned to the thicket and sat on the ground beside his master. Never during their escape were they more alone and vulnerable. If Union cavalry descended upon them now, they would not be able to make a run for it. Even two healthy, well-rested men, which Booth and Herold were not, could never outrun a mounted pursuit. And if Thomas Jones decided to abandon them, how would they find a boat to cross the river? They kept low to the ground and waited for nightfall.

Marooned in this desolate place, did Booth reminisce about happier days, when he and his beloved sister, Asia, played as carefree teenagers in the forests of Bel Air, Maryland? Once upon a time, before he became a famous actor and a denizen of America's great cities, Booth loved to commune with nature. Asia's bittersweet memories of their frolics haunted her in the days following the assassination: "In the woods he would throw himself face downward and nestle his nose close into the earth, taking long sniffs of 'the earth's healthy breath'... [h]e declared this process of inhaling wholesome odors and rich scents was delightful... [h]e called it 'burrowing,' and he loved to nibble at sweet roots and twigs, so that I called him rabbit."

As darkness fell for the second night over Booth's lonely, pine thicket encampment, did he remember another night among the pines of another time and place, a magical Halloween eve with Asia that was eerily like this one? "It was a cold, dark night," she reminisced, "with large fiery stars set far up in the black clouds. A perfect starry floor was the heaven that night, and the smell of the earth—which may be the odor of good men's bones rotting, it is so pleasurable and sanctifying—the aroma of the pines, and the rapturous sense of a solemn silence, made us feel happy enough to sing 'Te Deum Laudamus.'"

There would be no joyous song tonight. Instead, Booth and Herold murmured quietly, most likely talking of their crimes and speculating on their fate. What would they do? What would tomorrow bring? When would they cross over the river and find rest on the other side? When Booth smelled the forested scent of the thicket, did its sweet, piney odor take him back to a time of youthful innocence and allow him, briefly, to forget murders and manhunts? In the black safety of the night, Booth and Herold rolled out their coarse, woolen blankets and slumbered, close to the earth.

Ɪɴ Washington that night, the inhabitants of Mary Surratt's boardinghouse prepared for bed, too. The manhunters had been here before. When detectives came to 541 H Street on April 14, just a few hours after the assassination, they left empty-handed. Their quarry, John H. Surratt, was not at home, and John Wilkes Booth was not found hiding there. But tonight the authorities came back, in the evening again, at a time when Mary and Anna Surratt and their boarders were likely to be home. The manhunters were desperate. Three days after the assassination, John Wilkes Booth was still on the run. They had uncovered plenty of clues to prove that he was the assassin, was the head of a conspiracy, and had probably fled south to Maryland, but they had no fresh clues about his present whereabouts. And Seward's assassin remained a mystery man—Stanton did not even know his name. The War Department suspected John Surratt of the Seward attack but had no proof. Someone at that boardinghouse must know something about the assassination, Stanton and his subordinates reasoned. Booth had been a regular caller and was John Surratt's friend. It was time to go back and squeeze harder. It was about 11:00 P.M. on April 17.

Colonel H. H. Wells sent Major H. W. Smith to the boardinghouse to arrest the residents and search the premises. When Smith arrived, he posted a few men outside and told the rest to follow him up the stairs to the front door. He rang the bell, and Mary Surratt came to an open window and asked, "Is that you, Mr. Kirby?" She thought it was a neighbor. Smith said it wasn't Kirby and told her to open the door. When she did, Smith stepped into the hall.

"Are you Mrs. Surratt?"

"I am the widow of John H. Surratt."

And, Smith continued, "the mother of John H. Surratt, Jr.?"

"I am."

"I come to arrest you and all in your house, and take you, for examination, to General Augur's headquarters."

It was odd, Smith recalled later, that Mrs. Surratt "did not ask even for what she was arrested," and that she "expressed no surprise or feeling at all."

While Smith and his men questioned the residents and prepared to transport them by carriage to General Augur's headquarters, another official arrived at about 11:30 P.M. It was R. C. Morgan, under War Department orders from Colonel Olcott to, as Morgan put it, "superintend the seizing of papers and the arrest of the inmates of the house." By the time Morgan got there Smith and his team had already made the arrests, and the boarders were gathered in the parlor, ready to leave.

Morgan called for a carriage to transport the women, went back into the house, and closed the front door. Soon a man walking down H Street stopped at number 541, looked the house over, and walked up the front steps. He didn't notice the men standing nearby in the street. He got to the front door and knocked, then rang the bell. Morgan and Captain Wermerskirch opened the door. Before them stood a large, powerful-looking man, toting a pickax. The man was dressed in a gray coat, black pantaloons, and a fine pair of boots, and he wore atop his head an odd little makeshift hat cut from a shirtsleeve. As soon as the man stepped into the hall Morgan shut the door behind him.

The man sensed that something was wrong.

"I guess I am mistaken."

"Whom do you want to see?"

"Mrs. Surratt."

"You are right: walk in."

Morgan peppered the late-night caller with questions:

"I asked him what he came there at this time of night for. He said he came to dig a gutter: Mrs. Surratt had sent for him. I asked him when.

"In the morning," the man replied.

Morgan asked where he last worked.

"Sometimes on I Street."

Morgan asked where he boarded. "He said he had no boarding house; he was a poor man, who got his living with the pick."

"How much do you make a day?" Morgan asked.

"Sometimes nothing at all, sometimes a dollar, sometimes a dollar and a half."

"Have you any money?"

"Not a cent."

Morgan asked the man why he came at this time of night to work, and he replied that he called just to find out what time he should start work in the morning. The man claimed that he had no previous connection to Mrs. Surratt; she had seen him working in the neighborhood, knew he was a poor man, and offered him work. Morgan asked how old he was.

"About twenty."

Where was he from?

"Fauquier County, Virginia."

The man pulled a piece of paper from his pocket. It was an oath of allegiance to the Union, the type signed by former Confederate soldiers. Powell had signed it "L. Paine." He had just stumbled into the War Department's raid in progress. But Smith, Morgan, Wermerskirch, and the others didn't realize it yet.

The officers noticed that his clothes, while soiled, were much too fine to belong to a day laborer. Their suspicions grew as the man stammered more excuses. William Seward's assassin was a big, young, strong man, too.

Major Smith stepped to the doorway to the front parlor where Mary was sitting and asked her to come into the hall: "Mrs. Surratt, will you step here for a minute?" When she came out, Lewis Powell was standing no more than three paces from her, near a gaslight fixture, and, as Smith remembered, "the gas was turned on at full head."

"Do you know this man? And did you hire him to come and dig a gutter for you?"

It was the man she knew as Reverend Wood! Mary must have shuddered at the sight of him. No, not him, she likely cried silently. Her eyes locked upon the stranger's in recognition. Powell's remarkable face was unforgettable, and he had been to her home at least twice before.

Mary raised her right hand as if swearing an oath. "Before God, sir, I do not know this man; and I have never seen him, and did not hire him to dig a gutter for me."

Powell looked at Mary and said nothing.

Lewis Powell had been caught in a lie. Soon, George Alfred Townsend would make fun of his transparent cover story: "That night he dug a trench deep and broad enough for them to lie in forever." Now Powell was trapped in the house. The soldiers had closed the front door behind him; in moments they would try to seize and arrest him. But unless they all moved at once—took him by surprise, tackled him in unison—they might lose their advantage. Technically, Powell was unarmed. He had abandoned his broken revolver on Seward's floor and his knife, which he had dropped on the street in front of the secretary's house, was in the hands of the government. He carried no more than a workman's tool. But his prodigious strength could turn that tool into a deadly weapon. The pickax's oak butt was a stout club, and its twin, spear-tipped iron points deadly, stabbing prongs. In Powell's hands this humble tool was the equivalent of a primitive, close-combat pole arm from the Middle Ages.

The odds seemed against him; five men against one, confined in a compact foyer. But the tight space favored Powell. The soldiers began to press closer, and the closer they got, the more harm he could do. They were all within his killing range now.

If Powell chose to fight, the clock would start ticking at the first blow.

If he was quick, he could administer a second, skull-smashing strike by the time their hands reached for their holster flaps, and perhaps manage even a third swing of the pick before the survivors could draw, cock, and raise their revolvers. If Powell were lucky, he might deliver a fourth blow before a soldier could jerk the trigger and get off the first panicked, hurried shot. If the bullet went wild, or hit him but failed to kill him instantly, Powell could respond with a fifth, mighty swing of the ax.

He could do all of this in less than ten seconds and when it was over, he could, just as he had at Seward's, step past the broken bodies of men with crushed skulls and gaping wounds and walk out Mrs. Surratt's front door into the night. Powell glared at the soldiers. He could swing that ax quicker than they could draw their pistols. It was his move.

Then the mighty Lewis Powell did something extraordinary. Inexplicably, meekly, without protest, he surrendered without a fight.

The soldiers arrested Powell, Mary Surratt, her daughter Anna, Louis Weichmann, a friend of John Surratt's, and the rest of the boarders, including the terrified little Miss Appolonia Dean, an eleven-year-old schoolgirl who lived alone without her parents at Mary Surratt's.

The soldiers searched the house and uncovered, or so they believed, additional incriminating evidence: photographs of Confederate generals—one of President Jefferson Davis, some stray small-arms ammunition, a bullet mold. And the coup de grâce—a picture of John Wilkes Booth, hidden behind a picture frame.

Powell and Mary Surratt were taken to General Augur's headquarters for questioning. Before leaving the boardinghouse, Mary Surratt begged Colonel Wells to allow her to say a prayer. She fell to her knees and prayed silently.

If Lewis Powell had not blundered into the government's hands this night, he might have escaped Washington and vanished from history. Instead, the government celebrated his capture as the first major break in the manhunt. The capture of Seward's assassin on the third night since Good Friday was a triumph, secondary in importance only to finding the archfiend, John Wilkes Booth. Rival Washington photographers salivated at the prospect of taking the first photos of Lewis Powell and selling copies to a public desperate for news and images of the great crime. But Stanton wasn't quite ready to grant permission. With Booth, Herold, Atzerodt, and John Surratt still at large, forcing Powell to pose for souvenir photos while the manhunt was still under way might come across as an act of premature celebration. There would be time later for photos—of all of them.

Wells tried to question Powell but the laconic assassin refused to co-operate. The colonel noticed bloodstains on his shirt cuffs.

"What do you think of that?" Wells taunted him.

"That's not blood," Powell weakly claimed.

Within hours of Powell's arrest, William Bell, Seward's servant, identified Powell as the knife-wielding maniac. And when Gus Seward came to see him, he was instructed to grab hold of Powell just as he had during the attack. Then Wells ordered Powell to say two words to Gus: "I'm mad." Yes, Seward, affirmed, this was the man.

Henry Wells wanted to interrogate Mary shortly after her arrest so she would have little time to reflect, and to craft well-rehearsed answers to his questions. Perhaps the experienced lawyer and officer was expecting an easily intimidated woman whom he could browbeat into revealing all she knew about her son, about John Wilkes Booth, and about the other conspirators. If so, Wells was wrong. Mary Surratt proved his match, behaved coolly, and divulged no clues to help the manhunters track Booth. At the outset, she admitted freely facts that she was sure Wells already knew from other sources, especially her connection to Booth: "[Booth] has been coming to our house about two months; sometimes he called twice a day; we found him very much a gentleman. I think my son invited him home....My son is a country-bred young gentleman. I was not surprised that he should make the acquaintance of such a man as Mr. Booth because I consider him capable of forming acquaintances in the best society." Wells began the interrogation:

"What was it that brought your son and J. Wilkes Booth together?"

"I don't know."

"Has not the question occurred to you since the murder?"

"Yes, Sir; but I could not account for it, and I think no one could be more surprised than we were that he should be guilty of such an act."

Wells questioned her about John Surratt's connection to Booth's other conspirators.

"Don't you know of his making the acquaintance of a Mr. Atzerodt?"

"He was a German, I think. The name he gave me was 'Port Tobacco.' He remained only part of a week, when I found some liquor in his room; no gentleman can board with me who keeps liquor in his rooms."

Wells shifted the interrogation to the subject of Lewis Powell. The colonel suspected that he had visited the boardinghouse recently posing as a minister named "Wood."

"What was the name of the other young man?"

"I think his name was Wood."

Wells showed her a photograph of David Herold and she denied knowing him. That much was true. Neither Booth nor John Surratt had ever brought Herold to the boardinghouse. Wells continued to play cat and mouse with Mary, inviting her to name other visitors to her home and implying that she might as well tell him because he already knew the answers. "I assure you on the honor of a lady that I would not tell you an untruth." Unimpressed, Wells countered, "I assure you, on the honor of a gentleman, I shall get this information from you." But Wells wasn't getting anywhere. He took a break. "Reflect a moment, and I will send for a glass of water for you," he told Mary. After an aide served her, Wells asked a number of apparently innocuous questions about horses before shifting suddenly to the real subject of his interest—Lewis Powell.

"Did you meet the young man arrested this evening within two or three days and make an arrangement with him to come to your house this evening."

"No, Sir; the ruffian that was in my door when I came away? He was a tremendous hard fellow with a skull cap on, and my daughter commenced crying, and said these gentlemen [Major Smith's raiding party] came to save our lives. I hope they arrested him."

"He tells me now that he met you in the street and you engaged him to come to your house."

"Oh! Oh! It is not so, Sir; for I believe he would have murdered everyone, I assure you."

"When did you see him first?"

"Just as the carriage drew up, he rang the door bell, and my daughter said, 'Oh! There is a murderer.'"

Perhaps Wells appreciated the ironic truth of Mary Surratt's statement. Indeed, she was correct. Powell was a killer, but one who posed no threat to Mary Surratt, her daughter, or the occupants of H Street. During her interview with Colonel Wells, Mary stonewalled the experienced investigator and served Booth well. Yes, she had admitted the Atzerodt connection, but the manhunters had known about that for three days. On the night of the assassination, John Fletcher had identified Atzerodt's bridle and recognized the one-eyed horse, and detectives had also connected him to Booth from their search of the German's room at the Kirkwood House. But Mary Surratt did not tell Henry Wells about Booth's April 14 visit to her, the field glasses, her carriage ride to Surrattsville, the "shooting irons"—or that she had seen Lewis Powell before.

The interrogation over—for now—Wells refused to allow Mary to return home. He told her that she was still under arrest, and that he was sending her to the Old Capitol prison, where she would join the many other suspects and witnesses arrested after the president's murder. Although she did not suspect it this night, Mary Surratt would never see her boardinghouse again.

Monday, April 17, closed as the most successful day in the three-day-old manhunt. Earlier that day government agents arrested Samuel Arnold in Baltimore. On April 14, detectives had ransacked Booth's room at the National, on Sixth and Pennsylvania, a short walk from Ford's Theatre. The "Sam" letter, discovered within hours of the assassination, had, along with a detective's tip, led to Arnold's arrest. Arnold, age thirty-one, a former schoolmate of Booth's and a Confederate army veteran, confessed that he'd participated in Booth's earlier scheme to kidnap the president, but he denied any involvement in or knowledge of the assassination. He argued that the "Sam" letter, rather than proving his guilt, was evidence that he had quit the conspiracy weeks before the assassination.

Michael O'Laughlen, age twenty-eight, another of Booth's boyhood friends and also a former Confederate soldier from Baltimore and participant in the kidnapping plot, was also seized on April 17. Provost Marshal McPhail knew O'Laughlen's family, and Michael turned himself in to "spare his mother." After O'Laughlen's arrest, Charles Dana telegraphed McPhail in Baltimore with instructions on how to transport him to Washington: "Bring [him] here in the train which leaves Baltimore at 6 P.M. Have him in double irons, and use every precaution against escape, but as far as possible avoid everything which can lead to suspicion on the part of the people on the train and give rise to an attempt to lynch the prisoner. A carriage will be in waiting at the depot to convey him to the place of confinement."

Edman Spangler, the thirty-nine-year-old Ford's Theatre stagehand who briefly held the reins of Booth's horse, had been arrested on April 15, and was then released, only to be rearrested on April 17 along with Arnold, O'Laughlen, and Powell. In Spangler's room, detectives made what they thought was an ominous discovery: a long coil of strong rope. Was it for Booth to rappel down from Lincoln's box to the stage? Under any other circumstance, a rope is an innocent stagehand's accessory, but in the aftermath of Lincoln's murder, it led to Spangler's arrest. Poor Spangler had nothing to do with the assassination—or the earlier kidnapping plot. But his long association with Booth, the rope, holding the bay mare's reins, and the allegation by another theatre employee that Spangler said not to tell pursuers which way Booth went down the alley, earned him a cell in the Old Capitol prison. Many other people in the theatre were rounded up, including the Fords. Edwin Stanton declared the theatre a lair to which Lincoln had been lured, and surely those connected to it must have conspired with the assassin. How else could Booth have escaped so smoothly and easily? The theatre building itself was "arrested" by the government—it was ordered closed and was eventually confiscated from the Fords.

These were not the only arrests. The dragnet rounded up more than one hundred suspects: Junius Booth, one of the assassin's brothers; a strange Portuguese sea captain named Celestino; various Confederate sympathizers and agents; and others who expressed disloyal sentiments.

Although the arrest of one suspect after another filled the headlines, Booth and Herold had vanished. The *New York Herald* reported Booth sitting nonchalantly aboard a train to Philadelphia; Washington papers argued Booth was hiding in the capital. One of the most famous and recognizable men in America remained free. The American people demanded vengeance. Across the country, mobs beat suspected Booth sympathizers, and in several cases murdered them. A Union soldier named John F. Madlock, an officer of the U.S. Colored Cavalry in Port Hudson, Louisiana, wrote "a man who rejoiced at Lincoln's death received 16 bullets in his carcass...served him right." Vigilante groups and soldiers forced Booth sympathizers to wear crude, hand-painted wooden signs around their necks reading "assassination sympathizer." According to the *Daily Morning Chronicle*, in nearby Baltimore, an unidentified group of men set upon a photographic studio when rumors spread that the owner sold prints of the infamous actor.

The tumultuous news of the assassination raced the breadth of the nation by telegraph and soon reached U.S. Army posts in California. In San Francisco, General McDowell issued an order to arrest anyone who spoke against Lincoln.

Head Quarters Department of the Pacific
San Francisco, Cal., April 17, 1865.

GENERAL ORDERS,
No. 27
It has come to the knowledge of the Major-General commanding that there have been found within the Department persons so utterly infamous as to exult over the assassination of the President. Such persons become virtually accessories after the fact, and will at once be arrested by any officer or provost marshal or member of the police, having knowledge of the case.
Any paper so offending or expressing any sympathy in any way whatever with the act, will be at once seized and suppressed.
BY COMMAND OF MAJOR GENERAL McDOWELL:
R. C. DRUM,
Assistant Adjutant General

In Grass Valley, California, a minister wrote a letter to a friend back east describing the violence that followed the arrival of the news: "When the news came of the assassination of Lincoln the excitement was tremendous! Several men were shot right down dead by the Copperheads! And others were killed by Republicans in self defense! I loaded my double guns, with four small balls to each barrel and kept it in my study ready for any emergency. I thought I would pray God have mercy on our Country, but I would have a little lead for the Rebels!"

In Illinois, a U.S. Marine wrote a letter to his mother in Lockport, New York, describing the danger to those who spoke against Lincoln.

Mound City, Ill.
April 18th, 1865

Dear Mother,
    We are all in an uproar in this place about the death of the
president and one or two has been shot in this place for using
disloyal sentiments and there will be more shot if they do not
keep their mouths shut. I hope that the president will hang
every one of them now and not leave one just exterminate the
whole race. It is not safe for any one to be out after dark in this
place although I am up all hours of the night ... it will not do to
use any disloyal sentiments where we can hear it or they would
get smacked very quick. I was in hopes that the war was nearly
over but as things look I am afraid it has just begun but I hope
not ... it was hard for Lincoln to die now when he was just on
the eve of seeing this rebellion trodden under foot when every
body was rejoicing in his administration and when every thing
looked bright for him. I would like to have my say with that
Booth. I'll bet he never would want to kill another president. I
would take a pair of shears and cut him in pieces as you would
cut a piece of cloth. Then I would dig out his eyes and then
pour in boiling hot oil. I'd fix him well ... mother give my love
to all the folks and believe me your affectionate son.

Wesley Severs
U.S. Marine Barracks
Mound City, Ill

Booth's escape incensed, but also thrilled, the nation. Photographs
of him became so popular that soon the government banned their sale.
Impossible to enforce, Stanton had the order rescinded. Ads appeared
in *Harper's Weekly, Frank Leslie's,* and other newspapers that shame-
lessly offered Booth photos for sale—alongside mourning ribbons,
badges, and photos of the martyred president. In Boston, a lithography

"The Assassin's Vision." Lincoln's ghost haunts the fleeing Booth.

company commissioned an artist to create a handsome bust portrait of the assassin that it sold in two sizes—small carte-de-visite form for the family album, and as a large print suitable for framing. Other printers rushed out less flattering products—fantasy prints of Satan whispering in Booth's ear moments before he shot Lincoln, and of Booth riding furiously through a swamp infested with alligators and monsters. A carte-de-visite reproduced an allegorical painting titled *The Assassin's Vision*, depicting Booth fleeing Washington, the great dome visible in the distant background, and multiple images of Lincoln's ghost sprouting in the trees above him. A Boston publisher released a piece of sheet music—"The Assassin's Vision Ballad/Words and music by J. W. Turner"—to accompany the eerie artwork. It was the first song written about John Wilkes Booth and the manhunt.

> *The Assassin rode on his fiery steed, His murd'rous work was*
>   *done—*
> *In the darksome night with fleeting speed, Through woods his*
>   *courser run!*

As he hurried away from the scene of death, On his brow were
looks of despair:
Before him! around him! The evening's breath Told him God's
vengeance was there!
The pale moon beamed as onward he fled, The stars looked
down from on high,
The hills and valleys were crimson red As blood to the
murd'rer's eye!
He shuddered! he trembled! And oft looked around, And
dreary seemed each passing breeze,
And lo! the assassin at ev'ry bound Saw a vision appear in the
trees.
Heaven had witnessed! He could not escape! The assassin's fate
was sealed—
"Vengeance is mine!" saith God in his might, As the vision that
night revealed.
The assassin rode on with trembling and fear, And mournfully
murmur'd the breeze;
Before! around him! All vivid and drear, The vision appeared
in the trees.

Edwin Stanton needed help. By the third day it had become obvious that he could not devote his time and brainpower exclusively to the manhunt. He had a lot on his mind. The president's murder was not only a national tragedy, but also a deep personal loss to the secretary. Ever since the wild carriage ride on the night of the fourteenth, and his first sight of his friend in the deathbed, Stanton had used his iron will to suppress his powerful emotions. He had almost broken down at the Petersen house after Lincoln died, but his brain was able to rule his heart. There were other concerns. He had a war to win. Just because Lee had surrendered did not mean that the Civil War was over. Strong Confederate armies remained in the field in North Carolina, Texas, and elsewhere, and their generals had not followed Lee's example. Jefferson

Davis was still at large, the subject of another sensational manhunt. And like the search for Booth, the manhunt for Davis had failed. Soon the conflict might degenerate into a brutal, guerrilla war that might take years to win. And without Lincoln at his side, Stanton had to go on alone. The new president was not ready to assume the role of commander in chief.

There was more. Stanton had to organize Lincoln's majestic funeral and then send the body on an unprecedented national tour, on the way home to Springfield. He had to help plan the reconstruction of the South, manage the entire Union army, conduct the everyday but still vitally essential business of the War Department, decide what to do with Booth's captured conspirators, and organize a military tribunal to try them. He had to investigate the crime, determine the nature and extent of Booth's conspiracy, and send pursuers after the assassin and the rest of his gang. It was more than one mind, even Stanton's brilliant and well-disciplined one, could handle. He had to delegate authority to a small circle of trusted subordinates.

*W*HEN JOHN WILKES BOOTH PLANNED THE ASSASSINATION and his escape he did not prepare for an extended campout under the stars. No, he had focused entirely on the need for speed and movement, not on cowering in the forest like a wounded animal, fearful that every passing sound meant that his hunters were about to grab him. Booth fled Ford's Theatre like a pony express rider, traveling light for speed, unburdened by heavy equipment. Of course, an express rider carried the news: Booth fled from it. He disdained many of the ordinary accoutrements that a cavalryman took with him in the field: pistol belt, cartridge boxes, cap box, ample ammunition, carbine shoulder sling, field glasses, canteen, tin cup, eating utensils, rubberized gum blanket, wool blanket, saddlebags, provisions, and more. Booth had sacrificed necessities to achieve the sprinting speed his horse needed to get from Ford's Theatre to the Eleventh Street Bridge.

This strategy worked superbly and ensured his quick escape from downtown Washington. But it left him ill prepared for the next, unanticipated phase of his journey: outdoor living in open country, the consequence of his broken leg and the dangerous, delaying detour to Dr. Mudd's. Booth fled Ford's Theatre wearing the equivalent of a modern-day business suit. The fabric of his black wool frock coat and trousers was coarser, sturdier, thicker, and a little warmer, but his fine suit remained unsuitable for camping out in the pine thicket. And Booth packed no change of clothing, so his garments soon became soiled. It was one of the first things Thomas Jones noticed about him. Indeed, with each passing day Booth and Herold became less presentable to strangers, ruining a key element of Booth's trademark, winning style—his elegant, beautifully dressed appearance. They could not bathe, change clothes, or even wash the clothes on their backs, and they looked rougher—and smelled worse—every day. They looked like the fugitives they were. Beyond aesthetics, however, their vagabond, ruffian appearance jeopardized the friendly reception they expected to receive at proper Virginia households across the river.

Although Maryland's mid-April spring climate that year was not cold, the nights were chilly and damp, especially for men with no overcoats. The weather wore on the assassins, sapping warmth from their shivering bodies. And the ground was uncomfortable. They had no proper bedding, just a blanket for each man, supplied by either Dr. Mudd or Captain Cox. At least Herold could stand up, walk about, and stretch his legs to relieve his cramped muscles. But Booth's body ached and atrophied as he lay on the ground, shifting positions occasionally to ease his pain. As far as Thomas Jones could tell from his daily visits, Booth never rose from the ground during the time in the thicket.

On the morning of Tuesday, April 18, Jones paid his third call on the fugitives. This visit was briefer and less was said because Jones was in mortal danger. He risked his life every time he ventured into the thicket. Federal cavalrymen and U.S. detectives spread out along the nearby riverbanks and searched day and night for Booth. If soldiers caught Jones with the president's murderer, they might shoot him on the spot or hang him from a pine tree. Soldiers had visited Huckleberry Farm several times, and even searched his home once. Now, Jones handed over the food and more newspapers quickly, then departed. Booth's curiosity about the country's reaction was insatiable, and he beseeched Jones to bring all the papers he could. Jones remembered the scene vividly: "He never tired of the newspapers. And there—surrounded by the sighing pines, he read the world's condemnation of his deed and the price that was offered for his life."

What he read stunned him. Whatever papers Booth held in his hands—the *Daily Morning Chronicle, Evening Star,* or *National Intelligencer* from Washington; the *Sun* from Baltimore; the *Inquirer* from Philadelphia; or the *Herald, Tribune,* or *Times* from New York City— they all reviled him for his loathsome act. Even worse, Booth witnessed the first draft of history transform Abraham Lincoln from a controversial and often unpopular war leader into America's secular saint. Newspapers everywhere condemned the assassin in the most unsparing, unforgiving, vicious language imaginable. The accounts of the Seward attack sent Booth reeling. Had Powell gone insane? The indiscriminate viciousness of his coassassin's assault shocked and revolted Booth. Yes, Seward had to go, and the early, erroneous news accounts reporting the secretary of state's death delighted the actor. But the sons, the nurse, the messenger? At least Powell didn't murder the girl. "Booth then," Herold recalled, "made the remark that he was very sorry for the sons, but he only wished to God that Seward was killed."

Booth wasn't the only one of his coconspirators stunned by news accounts of the attempted murder of Seward. John Surratt, still in Elmira a few days after the assassination, bought, on April 17, several of the New York papers. What he read terrified him. The stories identified him as Seward's assailant. "I could scarcely believe my senses. I gazed upon my name, the letters of which seemed to sometimes grow as large as mountains and then dwindle away to nothing." It was time, Surratt concluded, to flee the country.

Booth searched the papers frantically for the article he wrote—his self-justification for killing the president—for publication in the *Intelligencer*. On the afternoon of the assassination, he had presented it to his actor friend John Matthews in a sealed, addressed envelope for delivery the next day. Incredibly, not one newspaper published or even mentioned his manuscript. So he wrote another one.

Booth drew from his pocket a small datebook for the previous year, 1864. Although obsolete, the book, bound in worn, black covers, contained a number of unused pages. Booth thumbed through it until he reached a blank page, which he annotated "Ti Amo/April 13–14 Friday the Ides." Then, in a cramped, hurried hand, unlike his usual expansive style, he began his manifesto.

"Until today nothing was ever THOUGHT of sacrificing to our country's wrongs. For six months we had worked to capture. But our cause being almost lost, something decisive & great must be done. But its failure was owing to others, who did not strike for their country with a heart. I struck boldly and not as the papers say. I walked with a firm step through a thousand of his friends, was stopped, but pushed on. A Col. was at his side. I shouted Sic semper BEFORE I fired. In jumping broke my leg. I passed all his pickets, rode sixty miles that night, with the bone of my leg tearing the flesh at every jump. I can never repent it, though we hated to kill; Our country owed all her troubles to him, and God simply made me the instrument of his punishment. The country is not what it WAS. This forced Union is not what I have loved. I care not what becomes of me. I have no desire to out-live my country. This night (before the deed), I wrote a long article and left it for one of the Editors of the National Intelligencer, in which I fully set forth our reasons for our proceedings. He or the Govmt…"

At that moment, in midsentence, something—perhaps an interruption by David Herold, an alarming noise in the distance, or the black fall of the night—compelled Booth to stop writing, and his manuscript ends abruptly. Booth was wrong when he accused the newspaper or the government of suppressing his manifesto. He thought that he could

trust John Matthews to deliver it. He didn't consider that his friend, terrified of being connected to Lincoln's assassin, might read the letter and
then destroy it.

When Booth wasn't writing in his little notebook or reading the
newspapers, what did he do while in the pine thicket? There was nothing left but talk. Booth and Herold didn't say much in front of Thomas
Jones, confining their conversations to practical matters like food and
newspapers, Booth's need for medical assistance, and their prospects
for a timely river crossing. That suited Jones fine. He was not a big talker
or the inquisitive type and, prudently, he preferred to spend as little
time as necessary at the fugitives' hiding place. According to Jones,
Booth did not draw him into abstract political discussions, try to im-
press him with exhilarating, firsthand tales of the fatal shot, his dramatic stage leap, or the unforgettable ride out of Washington—nor did
he attempt to justify the assassination. He told Jones that he murdered
Abraham Lincoln, that he didn't regret it, and that was that. Booth and
Herold kept their own counsel about how they intended to escape after
crossing the Potomac, or what their final destination was, if they even
had one.

When alone with Herold, however, Booth could unburden himself.
No doubt he reassured Herold about the very things he most needed to
convince himself—they would cross the Potomac, they would find succor in Virginia, they would survive. And no doubt Booth regaled Davey
with repeated tellings of the assassination drama. And if the newspapers wouldn't let Booth tell the nation his noble motives for his crime,
he could rehearse them over and over before his captive audience of
one. To Herold it did not matter what Booth said. The impressionable
youth had not joined the conspiracy for ideological reasons. He had
been drawn into the actor's orbit by Booth's charisma, not his hatred of
Lincoln. He was simply happy to abide in the presence of his hero, enjoying the actor's private, undivided attention. Although they had
known each other for more than a year, they had never spent this much
time together. After sharing the star with the other conspirators, and

with his many friends and fans, Herold felt privileged to have him to himself. Stranded in the pine thicket, Herold became, by default, the cynosure of Booth's attention. It was like having the great actor stage a marathon performance just for him. The future was unknown. But Booth was certain that David Herold would never abandon him.

Jones sensed Booth's growing impatience and decided to ride over to the town of Port Tobacco on a scouting mission to find out how many Union troops were combing the area. A few weeks after Lincoln's assassination, Civil War journalist George Alfred Townsend damned the town as a rebel cesspool of corruption: "If any place in the world is utterly given over to depravity, it is Port Tobacco....Before the war [it] was the seat of a tobacco aristocracy and a haunt of Negro traders. It passed very naturally into a rebel post for blockade-runners and a rebel post-office general. Gambling, corner fighting, and shooting matches were its lyceum education. Violence and ignorance had every suffrage in the town...five hundred people exist in Port Tobacco; life there reminds me, in connection with the slimy river and the adjacent swamps, of the great reptile period of the world, when iguanadons and pterodactyls and pleosauri ate each other...into this abstract of Gomorrah the few detectives went like angels who visited Lot." Indeed, the town was the stomping ground of the dissolute George Azterodt, Booth's co-conspirator and pathetic failed assassin of Vice President Andrew Johnson. He was so associated with this place that he actually went by the nickname "Port Tobacco."

As Jones rode into Port Tobacco, Union troops finally ventured out from Bryantown to Samuel Mudd's farm. It was noon on Tuesday, April 18, and the manhunt was at a standstill. That morning Lieutenant Alexander Lovett accompanied by detectives William Williams, Simon Gavacan, and Joshua Lloyd, and by nine soldiers from the Provisional Cavalry, had arrived in Bryantown. As David Dana and Alexander Lovett discussed their progress, Dana mentioned Dr. George Mudd's secondhand tale of the two strangers. Intrigued, Lovett decided to follow it up. The last verified sighting of John Wilkes Booth had occurred four days ago, around midnight on Friday, April 14, when Booth and Herold stopped at Surratt's tavern to collect the "shooting irons" and field glasses from John Lloyd. Indeed, it was Lieutenant Lovett who rode to the tavern, questioned Lloyd, and took him into custody. Given the dearth of hot leads, George Mudd's tip, Lovett decided, was worth pursuing. He sent for the doctor.

As soon as George Mudd arrived, soldiers brought him into the inn for questioning. Lovett took him "up into a room in the hotel, and asked him to make a statement of what he heard." It did not take Lovett long to ascertain that the doctor was almost useless. He knew no details, and he had never laid eyes on the two strangers himself. All he knew was what his cousin told him, and that wasn't much: two men called at Dr. Samuel Mudd's late on the night of the assassination, and Sam found them suspicious. He asked George to tell the soldiers.

Lovett decided to pursue the lead to its source, and he ordered his detectives and cavalrymen to mount up. Taking George Mudd with them, they rode to Samuel Mudd's farm. When they arrived at noon, Frances Mudd greeted George and the strangers and explained that her husband was away working in the fields. Lovett asked her to send for him. Until then, the officer suggested, perhaps she could answer a few questions.

ᗩROUND THE TIME THAT LOVETT AND THE DETECTIVES WERE questioning Mrs. Mudd, Thomas Jones put on his best impassive face, sauntered through the door of Port Tobacco's Brawner Hotel, and descended the creaky stairs to the basement. There, noted George Alfred Townsend, "it has a bar in the nethermost cellar, and its patrons, carousing in that imperfect light, look like the denizens of some burglar's crib, talking robbery between their cups." It was market day, and a lot of men and lots of gossip were circulating in town. Jones's simple strategy was to "mingle with the people and listen." An army detective, Captain Williams, eyed Jones and offered him a drink. Somebody in this vice-saturated, ramshackle, rebel town must know something about the as-sassins, Williams persuaded himself. Jones nodded and tightened his fist around the glass. Before he could raise it and wet his lips, Williams faced him, stared him in the eye, and boasted: "I will give one hundred thousand dollars to anyone who will give me the information that will lead to Booth's capture."

"That is a large sum of money and ought to get him," conceded Jones, who then added cryptically, "if money can do it."

Jones needed cash desperately, and he knew what that money could buy him. In 1865, when a Union army private earned thirteen dollars a month and the president of the United States received an annual salary of twenty-five thousand dollars, one hundred thousand dollars was a stupendous fortune. Jones thought about the wife and farm he lost, the time the Union stole from him while he was in the Old Capitol prison, the money owed to him by the Confederacy, and the uncertain econ-omy of the defeated South. And he wasn't getting any younger—soon he would be forty-five years old. He had every reason in the world to divulge Booth's hiding place and seize that reward money. But he didn't say anything. Booth's instincts about Jones's character proved correct. Jones was a man of true Southern feeling who could not be bought. In-deed, his explanation reads like a coda of the antebellum South: "Had I, for MONEY, betrayed the man whose hand I had taken, whose confi-dence I had won, and to whom I promised succor, I would have been, of all traitors, the most abject and despicable. Money won by such vile means would have been accursed and the pale face of the man whose life I had sold, would have haunted me to my grave. True, the hopes of the Confederacy WERE like autumn leaves when the blast has swept by. True, the little I had accumulated through twenty years of unremitting toil WAS irrevocably lost. But, thank God, there was something I still possessed—something I could still call my own, and its name was Honor."

• • •

$\mathscr{S}$UMMONED FROM THE FIELDS, AN ANXIOUS SAMUEL MUDD returned to his farmhouse and found the cavalry patrol waiting for him. It did not look good: nine uniformed soldiers, plus four men wearing civilian clothes. Many of the men, including Lieutenant Lovett, had shed their blue army officers' uniforms and donned civilian clothes as a disguise to blend in with the populace and obtain leads by stealth and guile. Some even assumed false identities, posing as Confederates, or as friends of Booth, in an attempt to persuade assassination sympathizers to let down their guard.

Mudd dismounted his horse, greeted the inquisitors, and quickly rehearsed his cover story one last time. He had had three days to concoct it. If he stuck to the story, behaved naturally, and did nothing to arouse suspicion, all would be well.

Sam told them what happened: two strangers on horseback came near daybreak, one had a broken leg, and he set the bone. The injured man rested on the sofa in the first-floor parlor. He did not mention that Booth went upstairs. The strangers did not stay long, Mudd assured the officer. Pointedly, Lovett asked Mudd if he knew the men. No, the doctor replied, they were complete strangers to him. He "knew nothing of them" and they stayed only a short time, he emphasized. Lovett thought that Mudd looked worried: "He seemed very much excited, and he got as pale as a sheet of paper when he was asked about it, but admitted it,—that there had been two strangers there." Sam's laconic manner— he offered few details—and guilty body language aroused Lovett's suspicion: "He did not seem to care about giving any satisfaction." Mudd volunteered trivial tidbits, including that he had had a pair of crutches made for the injured man. And they left on horseback. Of course they did, Lovett must have thought. Didn't they arrive on horses?

While Lovett continued to question Mudd, Detective Joshua Lloyd began searching the barn and outbuildings for signs of John Wilkes Booth.

Lovett asked Mudd to describe the strangers. The doctor spoke vaguely, providing little more than estimates of height, body weight, and approximate age. The descriptions were similar to those of Booth and Herold, convincing Lovett that the fugitives had been here. Dr. Mudd then said why he'd suspected the strangers—the injured one asked for a razor, soap, and water, and then he shaved off his moustache. Several troopers standing nearby grunted in agreement about the suspicious nature of the shave. Lovett asked Mudd if the man also had a beard: "Oh, yes, a long pair of whiskers!" the doctor exclaimed. Lovett knew that John Wilkes Booth did not have a long beard. No one who saw the assassin at Ford's Theatre mentioned a beard. And Booth could not have grown one in just four short days.

Mudd claimed that the strangers asked for directions to Parson Wilmer's place at Piney Chapel, west of his farm. That was an odd destination for Lincoln's assassin. Wilmer was a loyal Unionist and was considered to be above reproach by federal authorities. Lovett dismissed the tip as a clumsy ruse.

Detective Lloyd returned to the house. The barn and outbuildings were clear, he reported.

After questioning Samuel Mudd for about an hour, Lieutenant Lovett and his patrol left by 1:30 P.M. on Tuesday, April 18. If the doctor thought that he had cleared himself, he was wrong. As the troops and detectives rode away, Alexander Lovett reached the opposite conclusion: "I had my mind made up to arrest him when the proper time should come." Although Lovett thought that Mudd had lied about Booth's alleged destination, he remained duty bound to follow up the doctor's tip: "I went to Mr. Wilmer's and searched his house,—a thing I did not like to do. I was satisfied before I searched that there was nothing there, because I knew the man by reputation. I was satisfied it was only a blind to throw us that way."

In his first encounter with the manhunters, Dr. Mudd had served John Wilkes Booth well. He denied knowing the injured stranger. He lied about the beard. He failed to warn the troops that Booth and Herold were well armed. And he planted a false lead to misdirect the soldiers to search to the west, when Booth rode southeast. But what had this cost him? He had crossed the point of no return—and was on record now. He had given aid and comfort to Abraham Lincoln's killers. At this moment, on the afternoon of April 18, Dr. Samuel A. Mudd was in more peril than Booth and Herold, who were ensconced in the relative safety of the pine thicket.

ON APRIL 18, THOUSANDS OF PEOPLE CONTINUED TO POUR into Washington, D.C., to see Abraham Lincoln's funeral procession, scheduled for the next day. As soon as the War Department announced the events planned for April 19, the Willard Hotel received four hundred telegrams begging for room reservations. Every hotel in the city sold out, compelling thousands of visitors to sleep on the streets and in the parks. By now black crepe and bunting had replaced the ephemeral, patriotic signs and banners that had adorned the city the week before. Gideon Welles noted in his diary the transformation: "Every house, almost, has some drapery, especially the homes of the poor. Profuse exhibition is displayed on the public buildings and the dwellings of the wealthy, but the little black ribbon or strip of cloth from the hovel of the poor negro or the impoverished white is more touching."

On the morning of April 19, the most solemn day in the history of the nation began with the president's funeral in the East Room of the Executive Mansion. Workmen labored through the previous night to construct wood risers to accommodate the six hundred invited guests. Disabled by grief, Mary Lincoln was not among them. She remained secluded in the family quarters, sending her sons, Robert and Tad, downstairs as her representatives. The Reverend Dr. Gurley, who prayed over Lincoln's corpse at the Petersen house, presided this day.

On Pennsylvania Avenue tens of thousands of people jostled for position on both sides of the street to view the funeral catafalque when six magnificent white horses drawing Abraham Lincoln's body made the turn from Fifteenth Street onto the avenue. Nimble children scooted up trees for the best view, and at the hotels, restaurants, stores, and offices lining the avenue every building wept with black crepe, and it seemed that mourners had flung open every single window, poking their heads through to watch the procession below.

The procession rolled slowly forward, the beat of the march measured by muffled bass and tenor drums swathed in crepe. Lincoln's funeral procession was the saddest, most profoundly moving spectacle ever staged in the history of the Republic. There was more. At the U.S. Capitol, in the rotunda beneath the Great Dome, a catafalque waited to receive Lincoln's coffin. Thousands of citizens had already waited hours in line to view Father Abraham. The newspapers said that it would be an open casket. Lincoln had been shot through the head, but the bullet did not disfigure his face, aside from the plum-colored bruising in the vicinity of his right eye socket. The undertaker's artistry had taken care of that. When the funeral was over, the procession done, and the viewing concluded, the president's body would be placed aboard a special train that would carry him home to Springfield.

Only one thing detracted from the sacredness of this day. The murderer, John Wilkes Booth, was still at large. Throughout the solemnities of April 19, no minister or government official mentioned the assassin's name in public. To speak it would desecrate the memory of the honored dead. But the specter of Booth festered, if not on the tongue, then in the mind. It had been five days since Good Friday. Easter had come and gone. And still, Lincoln's killer was free, mocking the manhunters. Something had to be done. Tomorrow, after the president's body left Washington, Edwin Stanton would take an unprecedented step. He planned to issue a dramatic proclamation to the American people that combined an incredible reward with a terrifying threat. But Stanton could not take a break from the hunt. On the morning of the funeral, before the noon service in the East Room, he sent a message to General Hancock at Winchester retracting his flirtation three days ago about enlisting Confederate General Mosby in the manhunt: "There is evidence that Mosby knew of Booth's plan, and was here in this city with him; also that some of the gang are endeavoring to escape by crossing the upper Potomac to get with Mosby or the secesh there. Atzerodt, or Port Tobacco as he is called, is known to have gone to Rockville Saturday to escape in that direction."

In New Orleans, the famous detective Allan Pinkerton did not hear about the assassination until the morning of Lincoln's funeral. News had failed to reach the city until five days after the shooting. Pinkerton loathed being away from the action, and he sent a grandiose and ill-timed telegram to Stanton angling for a starring role in the manhunt:

> This morning's papers contain the deplorable intelligence
> of the assassination of President Lincoln and Secretary
> Seward. Under the providence of God, in February, 1861, I
> was enabled to save him from the fate he has now met. How I
> regret that I had not been near him previous to this fatal act.
> I might have been the means to arrest it. If I can be of any
> service please let me know. The service of my whole force, or
> life itself, is at your disposal, and I trust you will excuse me for
> impressing upon you the necessity of great personal caution on
> your part. At this time the nation cannot spare you.

Pinkerton's self-promotion and obsequious flattery fell flat. And New Orleans was a long way from Washington. Booth had already been on the run for five days, and it would take Pinkerton several days to travel to Washington. Stanton already had a few thousand manhunters in the field. He did not need Pinkerton or his vaunted, all-seeing eye. The detective whose motto was "we never sleep" had managed to sleep five nights before informing himself of the most important news of the war.

WHILE TENS OF THOUSANDS OF MOURNERS VIEWED LINCOLN'S remains in Washington on April 19, manhunters prepared to raid the Philadelphia home of the assassin's sister, Asia Booth Clarke. It was all the fault of her husband, John Sleeper Clarke. On Sunday the sixteenth, Asia remembered that some time ago John Wilkes had entrusted her with some personal papers to safeguard in her vault. When she unlocked the vault and opened her brother's envelopes, she discovered a number of documents, including two amazing letters. One was a tender, intimate letter to their mother that prepared her for his sacrifice to the cause:

> *I have always endeavored to be a good and dutiful son, and*
> *even now would wish to die sooner than give you pain. But,*
> *dearest Mother, though I owe you all, there is another duty, a*
> *noble duty, for the sake of liberty and humanity due to my*
> *country. For four years I have lived (I may say) A slave*
> *in the North (a favored slave it's true, but no less hateful to*
> *me on that account), not daring to express my thoughts or*
> *sentiments . . . but it seems that uncontrollable fate, moving*
> *me for its ends, takes me from you, dear Mother, to do what*
> *work I can for a poor, oppressed, downtrodden people. . . . And*
> *should the last bolt strike your son, dear Mother, bear it*
> *patiently and think at the best life is short.*

Booth's second letter, addressed "To Whom It May Concern," was his political manifesto that described his love for the Confederacy, his hatred of Lincoln, and his scorn for the black man. In the aftermath of the assassination, the text was incriminating, sensational, and even explosive:

> *Right or wrong, God judge me, not man. For be my motive*
> *good or bad, of one thing I am sure, the lasting condemnation*
> *of the North.*
> *I love peace more than life. Have loved the Union beyond*
> *expression. For four years I have waited, hoped and prayed, for*

the dark clouds to break, and for a restoration of our former
sunshine. To wait longer would be a crime. All hope for peace is
dead... God's will be done. I go to see, and share the bitter end.

I have ever held the South were right. The very nomination
of Abraham Lincoln four years ago, spoke plainly, war—
war upon Southern rights and institutions. His election
proved it...

People of the North, to hate tyranny, to love liberty, and
justice, to strike at wrong and oppression, was the teaching of
our fathers...

This country was formed for the white, not for the
black man...

My love... is for the South alone. Nor do I deem it a
dishonor, in attempting to make for her a prisoner of this man
to whom she owes so much misery.

A Confederate, doing duty upon his own responsibility.

J. Wilkes Booth

Improvidently, John Sleeper Clarke brought the documents to John Millward, the U.S. marshal in Philadelphia, and then showed them to an editor at the *Philadelphia Inquirer* newspaper. Clarke, with little concern for the welfare of his pregnant wife or the rest of the Booth family, tried to protect himself by publicizing the manuscripts. Millward forbade publication of the letter to Booth's mother, fearing it might elicit sympathy for the assassin. But he allowed the *Inquirer* to publish the manifesto, which it did on April 19, under a series of excited headlines: "Letter of John Wilkes Booth"; "Proof that he Meditated His Crime Months Ago"; "Confesses That He was Engaged in a Plot to Capture and Carry Off the President"; "A Secession Rhapsody."

Clarke's foolish act provoked the opposite of its intended effect. Like a fire bell in the night, the document summoned swarms of detectives to his door. Asia was furious: "Mr. J. S. Clarke thoughtlessly gave that enclosed letter alluding to a kidnapping scheme to Mr. Stockton, his personal friend and the reporter of a daily paper, and, as every shred of news was voraciously accepted, the letter was published, and arrests followed in quick succession." It was only Clarke's first betrayal. He was ashamed of the Booth name now. Soon he would tell Asia that they must divorce to save his reputation and acting career. John Wilkes Booth had never liked his brother-in-law. Indeed, when Clarke proposed to Asia, Booth warned her that Clarke was an opportunist who sought to exploit their name to further his own stage career. "Always bear in mind that you are a professional stepping-stone," Booth warned her. "Our father's name is a power . . . in the land. It is dower enough for a struggling actor."

John Sleeper Clarke did not deflect suspicion—he excited it. What else, government detectives wondered, might the bowels of that Philadelphia mansion give up in addition to the assassin's stunning declaration? Asia described the frenzied manhunters: "It was like the days of the Bastille in France. Arrests were made suddenly and in dead of night. . . . Detectives, women and men, decoys, and all that vile rabble of human bloodhounds infested the city." John Sleeper Clarke was seized, taken to Washington, and imprisoned in the Old Capitol for a month.

Asia described how detectives swarmed her home: "This unfortunate publication, so useless now when the scheme had failed—and it led to no fresh discoveries—brought a host of miseries, for it not only served for food to newsmongers and enemies, but it directed a free band of male and female detectives to our house. . . . My house, which was an extensive (MYSTERIOUSLY BUILT, it was now called) old mansion, was searched; then, without warning, surprised by a full body of police, surrounded, and searched again. We were under hourly surveillance from outside . . . our letters were few, but they were opened, and no trouble taken to conceal that they had been read first."

Edwin Booth wrote frequently to his sister during the manhunt. "Think no more of him as your brother; he is dead to us now, as soon he must be to all the world, but imagine the boy you loved to be in that better part of his spirit, in another world."

The authorities ransacked the house and confiscated anything connected to John Wilkes Booth, including family books, photographs, and documents that had nothing to do with the assassination. Asia catalogued the violations. "All information contained in his criticisms, letters, playbills and theatrical records, has been lost in the general destruction of papers and effects belonging to Wilkes Booth. All written or printed material found in our possession, everything that bore his name was given up, even the little picture of himself, hung over my babies' beds in the nursery. He had placed it there himself saying, 'Remember me, babies, in your prayers.' Not a vestige remains of aught that belonged to him; his books of music were stolen, seized, or savagely destroyed."

In Maryland, in the early-morning hours of April 20, two separate teams of manhunters were planning another raid and were closing in on George Atzerodt. He had spent the last four nights at Hartman Richter's place, heedless of the great peril he faced. He didn't know that Booth had signed the conspirators' names to an assassins' declaration—luckily for him John Matthews had destroyed it—but he should have suspected by now that detectives would have searched his room at the Kirkwood and discovered his connection to Booth, and thus the others. He should have fled but instead, foolishly, he tarried at his cousin's. Hartman Richter remembered George's casual behavior. "He remained at my house from Sunday till Thursday morning, and occupied himself with walking about, working in the garden a little, and going among the neighbors. He did not attempt to get away, or hide himself."

Nor did he attempt to be discreet. His Easter dinner conversation about the assassination, especially his strange comment about a man following Grant onto the train, seemed too knowing to one of Hezekiah Metz's guests, Nathan Page. Three days later, on Wednesday, April 19, Page mentioned the suspicious story to a local Union informant, James Purdum. Purdum passed the tip to Union forces at Monocacy Junction, and when Captain Solomon Townsend of the First Delaware Cavalry heard it, he took action. Townsend ordered Sergeant Zachariah W. Gemmill to pick up Purdum as a guide, go to the Richters', and arrest Atzerodt.

A second group of manhunters also targeted the Richter place on the morning of April 20: James L. McPhail, the highly effective U.S. Army provost marshal of Maryland, was also in pursuit. McPhail had been active in the manhunt since the night of Lincoln's assassination, when Stanton suspected that Booth might be headed to Baltimore. McPhail had already contributed to the arrests of Samuel Arnold and Michael O'Laughlen on April 17. And unfortunately for George Atzerodt, his brother John, and his brother-in-law, John L. Smith, both served on McPhail's staff. John Atzerodt was a patriot and felt duty bound to help McPhail capture his fugitive brother. He reported that George was known to visit their cousin Hartman Richter in Montgomery County. Perhaps, John suggested, McPhail might find him there. The provost marshal ordered detectives to raid Richter's place.

But Sergeant Gemmill and six cavalrymen under his command got there first, at about 4:00 A.M. Gemmill knocked on the door, and, before Richter would open it, he asked twice who it was. Gemmill was impatient: "I told him to come and see." When Richter came to the door, Gemmill asked him if a man named Atwood—the alias that Atzerodt used at Metz's place—was there. The man had been there, Richter said, but he had left for Frederick, Maryland. When Gemmill said that he would search the house anyway, Richter admitted that Atzerodt was upstairs in bed. Richter's wife chimed in that there were three men up there. Gemmill, holding a candle or lamp, went upstairs with two cavalrymen. They found the hapless Atzerodt in bed. He surrendered meekly, not even asking why he was being taken.

Soon, under questioning by Provost Marshal McPhail, Atzerodt confessed. McPhail didn't even have to squeeze him. Atzerodt had asked for the meeting. George told him about the room at the Kirkwood

House and the coat, the pistol, and the knife. They all belonged to David Herold, Atzerodt claimed. He described how he threw his knife away in the streets of Washington the morning Lincoln died and how he had pawned his pistol in Georgetown. He revealed the kidnapping plot and how it progressed into murder. He described the conspirators' final meeting at the Herndon House. And he implicated Mary Surratt and Dr. Samuel A. Mudd. Atzerodt's capture was a coup. Now the War Department, in addition to seizing Mary Surratt, Samuel Arnold, and Michael O'Laughlen, had in its clutches two of the four men—Powell and Atzerodt—who were actually present at the Herndon House assassination conference.

On the morning of April 20, as Stanton was putting the finishing touches on his proclamation, before sending it to the printer to produce as large broadsides for public posting, and to publish in the newspapers, word reached the War Department that the manhunters had captured George Atzerodt, the vice president's would-be assassin. The foolish German's laundry list of carelessness—abandoning incriminating evidence at the Kirkwood, negligently disposing of his knife, pawning his pistol, and speaking knowingly about the assassination—created a road map of guilt that led Sergeant Gemmill to the slumbering Atzerodt. How characteristic that he was Booth's only conspirator captured unawares in his bed. Newspaper woodcuts gleefully depicted the humiliating circumstances.

The April 20 proclamation offered a $25,000 reward for Atzerodt. Just before it went to press, Edwin Stanton revised it, deleting the just-captured Atzerodt and substituting the name of John Surratt, Mary's missing son. Soon his proclamation hit the streets, offering an unprecedented reward of $100,000 for Lincoln's killers, and threatening with death anyone who gave them aid or comfort. The earlier reward offers of $10,000 on April 15 and $30,000 on April 16 had failed to turn up Booth. Stanton hoped that his new, stupendous offer would motivate Booth's hunters—and his helpers.

War Department, Washington, April 20, 1865

$100,000 REWARD!

THE MURDERER

of our late beloved President, Abraham Lincoln,

IS STILL AT LARGE.

$50,000 REWARD

Will be paid by this Department for his apprehension, in addition to any
reward offered by Municipal Authorities or State Executives.

$25,000 REWARD

Will be paid for the apprehension of JOHN H. SURRATT,
one of Booth's accomplices.

$25,000 REWARD

Will be paid for the apprehension of David C. Harold,
another of Booth's accomplices.

LIBERAL REWARDS will be paid for any information that shall conduce
to the arrest of either of the above-named criminals, or their accomplices.

All persons harboring or secreting the said persons, or either of them, or
aiding or assisting their concealment or escape, will be treated as
accomplices in the murder of the President and the attempted assassination
of the Secretary of State, and shall be subject to trial before a Military
Commission and the punishment of DEATH.

Let the stain of innocent blood be removed from the land by the arrest and punishment of the murderers.

All good citizens are exhorted to aid public justice on this occasion. Every man should consider his own conscience charged with this solemn duty, and rest neither night nor day until it be accomplished.

EDWIN M. STANTON, Secretary of War.

Chapter Seven

"Hunted Like a Dog"

---※---

JOHN WILKES BOOTH AND DAVID HEROLD HAD LANGUISHED IN
the pine thicket for five days and four nights. In the late afternoon of
Thursday, April 20, several hours after his daily morning rendezvous
with the fugitives, Thomas Jones rode over to Allen's Fresh, a little village about three miles west of Huckleberry, where the Zekiah swamp
ends and the Wicomico River begins. He ensconced himself at Colton's
store and employed his favorite intelligence-gathering technique—sit,
watch, listen, and do not speak. He didn't have to wait long. A Union
cavalry patrol, identifiable by its signature sound of brass-hilted, steel-
bladed sabers clanking in their polished, silver-bright iron scabbards,
and guided by a local Maryland scout named John R. Walton, trotted
into town. Some of the troopers walked into Colton's and ordered
drinks. Jones listened keenly to every word they spoke. Then Walton
burst into the room: "We have just got news that those fellows have been
seen down in Mary's County." The announcement roused the cavalrymen as quick as the traditional bugle call of "boots and saddles." They
ran outside, mounted their horses, and galloped away.

Jones suppressed all outward signs of excitement. This was it! This
was the opening he had waited patiently for all week. Several hundred
detectives and soldiers had scoured Charles County, Maryland, for days,
but they had failed to pick up Booth's trail. It was time for them to

continue the search elsewhere. Indeed, there were some reports that Booth had already crossed the Potomac and was in Virginia now. Yes, some manhunters would remain in the region just in case, but it appeared to Jones that the intensity of the search in the immediate area was diminishing. The Union cavalry was riding out of the area, away from the pine thicket. Confident that no other federal troops lurked in the immediate vicinity, Jones resolved "now or never, this is my chance." He wanted to bolt out of Colton's and whip his horse in a wild dash to Booth's hiding place. But he knew better. To avoid suspicion he tarried in the store as though he didn't have a care in the world. Eventually he strolled outside, mounted his horse in a leisurely way, and left Allen's Fresh as slowly as possible. As soon as he reached a safe distance from the village, he laid the whip on hard and galloped frantically for the pines.

It was dusk now, and Jones thought he had perfect weather for a clandestine mission. "It had been cloudy and misty all day," he wrote, "and as night came darkly on, the clouds seemed to grow denser and the dampness more intense. A gray fog, rising from the marsh below the village and floating up the swamp, wrapped in shrouds the trees whose motionless forms were growing dim in the gathering gloom." Darkness fell before Jones reached the thicket. He dismounted and walked deeper into the pines, exercising special caution. He had never been there at night, and Booth and Herold did not expect him. Jones knew that they were impatient and nervous, and he did not want to scare them so much that they cut him down with gunfire on the verge of completing his mission. At a safe distance, he pursed his lips and emitted the secret, three-note whistle code. As before, Herold answered, then emerged from behind the camouflage of black pine trunks and brush and led Jones deeper into the woods, to Booth's earthen sickbed. The assassin and his chamberlain all but salivated with anticipation. This unexpected nighttime call could mean only one thing: Thomas Jones had important news. Was this the night?

"The coast seems to be clear," Jones reported, in the understated, dispassionate manner that was his trademark, "and the darkness favors us. Let us make the attempt." Booth and Herold could hardly believe their ears. Finally, freed from the prison of these damned woods, where the tall, rigid pines loomed over them like the bars of a jail cell, they could push on to Virginia. They gathered their meager belongings, including the precious field glasses, which Booth considered so important to his escape that, on the afternoon of the assassination, he sent Mary Surratt on a special mission to deliver them to her country tavern. But the instrument was useless in the thicket because visibility in the pines could be measured in yards, not miles; its purpose was to peer far into the distance and scout the safety of new ground. Booth grabbed the field glasses for the vistas he must have expected to see in the coming days.

Jones cautioned them to stay alert and not let down their guard. To get to the Potomac, they had to complete a perilous trek of about three and a half miles down a series of hidden paths and public roads. With only one horse for three men, Jones proposed that Booth ride his mare and that Herold, on foot, lead it by the bridle. Jones, also on foot, would lead the way. Jones and Herold struggled to lift Booth from the ground and propped him in the saddle. The actor was in great pain. Indeed, Jones observed, "every movement, in spite of his stoicism, wrung a groan of anguish from his lips." They handed the assassin the Spencer carbine and the two revolvers, rolled the blankets and tied them behind the saddle, and got under way, proceeding down the rough cart track that led to the public road. Jones insisted that no one speak or make a sound. As soon as they set foot on the public road, he warned them, they would be in great danger from travelers and from two houses built close to the road.

Jones walked fifty or sixty yards ahead, like an infantry picket probing in advance of the main body, listening to every sound as he peered through the mist, searching for hostile riders. All was quiet. Jones stopped dead in his tracks, paused a few moments, and whistled for his companions to come up. Every few minutes Jones repeated the process until they reached the segment of their journey he dreaded most—the mile-long stretch of public road between the cart track and his farm. They were so vulnerable on the open road that even Thomas Jones, wily veteran of hundreds of dangerous, Confederate nighttime missions, was on edge: "When I paused to listen, the croaking of a frog, the distant barking of a dog, the whir of the wing of some nightbird as it passed over my head, would cause my heart to beat quicker, and my breath to come faster." Jones whistled for Booth and Herold to enter the public highway and follow him. When they caught up to Jones, he grabbed the bridle and jerked the horse a few yards off to the side of the road and told them to wait. Jones crept past the first house, occupied by Sam Thomas, a black man whose bothersome children were always under-foot. A lamplight, too weak to illuminate the road, glowed dimly through a window. Jones walked well past the house and whistled for his companions to continue. "When I gave the low whistle agreed upon as the signal that the road was clear, it sounded in my ears as loud as the blast of a trumpet, and though the ground was soft and yielding, the tramping of the slowly advancing horse … was like the approaching of a troop." Booth and Herold passed the Thomas dwelling undetected.

Jones feared the next house even more because its owner, John Ware, kept several dogs. Jones walked past Ware's gate and listened. Not hear-ing a sound, he continued past the house and whistled, fearing that he might arouse a pack of barking dogs. Not one hound rose up at the sig-nal. Finally, Jones reached the end of the public road and led Booth and Herold, their nerves seriously frayed, on to the safety of his farm. It was between nine and ten o'clock. By then, "the night had grown inky dark. No rain was falling, but the dampness clung to every thing and fell in drops upon us as we made our way among the trees." Jones halted his party under two pear trees near his stable, about fifty yards from the house.

Booth craved the shelter—even for just a few minutes—of a roof over his head and the warming glow of a fire in the hearth and assumed that Jones would usher them into his home before the last rush to the river. "Wait here," Jones said, "while I go in and get you some supper, which you can eat here while I get something for myself."

Booth's heart sank and he pleaded, "Oh, can't I go in and get some of your hot coffee?"

"My friend, it wouldn't do," answered Jones. "Indeed it would not be safe. There are servants in the house who would be sure to see you and then we would all be lost. Remember, this is your last chance to get away."

Booth knew Jones was right. Soon enough, on the Virginia side, shelter, a fire, and a bed awaited him. Jones, knowing how Booth suffered from his broken leg and from living outdoors, hated to turn him down: "It cut me to the heart when this poor creature, whose head had not been under a roof, who had not tasted warm food, felt the glow of a fire, or seen a cheerful light for nearly a week, there in the dark, wet night at my threshold, made this piteous request."

Jones slipped into his house through the kitchen, where Henry Woodland was at the table eating a late supper. Jones collected his wits and pretended that this was just another typical spring night at Huckleberry, and not the climactic hour of a day that saw him spying on Union troops, galloping to rescue Lincoln's assassin and his companion, leading them on a perilous night ride, and posting them outside his farmhouse, not more than fifty yards from his kitchen table.

"How many shad did you catch?" Jones queried Henry.

The fishing was good, he replied: "I caught about seventy, master."

Then Jones zeroed in with the critical question that would decide everything that night: "Did you bring the boat to Dent's Meadow, and leave it there, Henry?"

The lives of John Wilkes Booth and David Herold depended on the answer. "Yes, master."

Concealing his delight, Jones carried on innocently: "We had better get out another net tomorrow. The fish are running well."

Jones proceeded to his dining room, where his supper waited on the table. In front of several family members, and without exchanging a word with any of them, he scooped up enough food for two men and carried it out of the house: "They knew better than to question me about anything in those days," Jones recalled. On his way out, Jones snatched a candle and slipped it into one of his coat pockets.

After Booth and Herold wolfed down their supper, the first time they had enjoyed more than one meal a day since their confinement in the pine thicket, Herold and Jones got Booth back into the saddle and headed to the river, about one mile distant. Jones walked ahead of them, whistling for them to come up through the open fields. Three hundred yards from the river they came to a wood fence too high for the horse to step over and too well built to dismantle easily. From here the crippled actor would have to struggle to the river on foot. Herold and Jones helped Booth dismount, and he winced in pain as they lifted him over the fence. Leaving the horse behind, Jones and Herold, along with the makeshift crutches provided by Dr. Mudd, supported Booth's weight between them as they stepped carefully down the steep and narrow path that led to the boat. What if it was gone? Jones worried. Unless Union troops had stumbled upon it within the last several hours, it should be just a few yards ahead where Henry Woodland left it. As they inched toward Dent's Meadow, Booth's senses must have come alive—he could hear the river's current lapping its banks. Jones heard it, too: "As we approached we could hear its sullen roar…a mournful sound coming through the darkness."

The trio pressed forward, until they began to see the outline of a dull gray shape emerge from the darkness. At last! Booth's spirits soared at the sight of the humble craft. His broken leg, the scourging newspaper accounts, and the monotony of the pine thicket had worn down his optimism. Seeing the skiff must have aroused an excitement in him that he had not experienced since his triumphant ride across the Navy Yard Bridge, the first key milestone in his escape after fleeing Ford's Theatre. Crossing the Potomac from Maryland to Virginia would be the second. Jones waded into the shallows and brought in the boat.

He and Herold helped Booth struggle into the craft, seating him at the stern. They laid the weapons and crutches on the wood hull planks with a dull thud. They handed him a single oar to steer. Herold climbed aboard, settled into the bow seat to row, and seized the other two oars, locking them into place. Jones hunkered down, produced the candle from his coat, and told Booth to bring out his pocket compass. The actor snapped open the square, velvet-lined case while Jones, concealing the candle under an oilcloth coat, ignited a match and lit the wick. Their faces inches apart, Jones, clenching the dripping candle over the protective glass cover that shielded the magnetized, dancing needle, showed Booth the true course to steer. "Keep to that," he promised, "and it will bring you into the Machodoc Creek." Jones handed Booth the candle, cautioning him to hide its faint glow during the crossing, and then gave Booth his final gift, the name of a contact on the other side: "Mrs. Quesenberry lives near the mouth of this creek. If you tell her you come from me I think she will take care of you."

Jones grabbed the stern firmly and began pushing Booth and Herold gently into the Potomac. Booth turned suddenly and spoke: "Wait a minute, old fellow." The grateful assassin thrust a fistful of Union greenbacks at Jones. Jones rebuffed the gesture, protesting that he had not helped him for money. He agreed to accept just eighteen dollars, the price he paid for the boat a year ago in Baltimore.

Choked with emotion, Booth understood that he would never see Jones again: "God bless you, my dear friend, for all you have done for me. Good-bye, old fellow."

Jones shoved them off, and Herold gripped the oars and stroked toward the Virginia shore, two miles distant. The river was dark as India ink and the boat soon vanished against the black, glass-smooth surface of the powerful current moving under a moonless night. Who can tell, wondered Jones, what thoughts possessed Booth as he entrusted himself "to the mercies of the dark water."

More certain is the significance of the pine-thicket days—John Wilkes Booth's "lost week"—in the twelve-day chase for Lincoln's killer. Booth and Herold spent more than one-third of the entire manhunt in the pine thicket. It was in the pines where Booth confronted the nation's reaction to him and his crime, where news of Powell's mad attack shocked his conscience, where he learned his manifesto would not be published and his voice would be silenced, where he realized that, although he performed the great crime magnificently, he failed to plan properly for the next act, the denouement of a successful, untroubled escape, and where he learned that he had made Abraham Lincoln a martyred hero greater than the living president had ever been in life. The assassin's mysterious disappearance also affected the nation. In vanishing, he drove the manhunters to distraction, shook the people's confidence in their government, attained the reputation of a devious, master criminal, and fueled rumors of a massive conspiracy. How else could one man, the most wanted man in American history, escape justice?

John Wilkes Booth's escape and disappearance unfolded as though scripted not by a master criminal, but by a master dramatist. Each additional day of Booth's absence from the stage intensified the story's dramatic arc. In his absence his bit players, minor characters, supporting cast, and costars built up the drama: actors, stagehands, and theatre owners thrown behind bars; Booth's suicidal lover exposed; his other lovers in hiding; the suspicious widow Mary Surratt seized during a late-night raid, along with her entire household; the maniacal and merciless Lewis Powell taken on her doorstep; Edman Spangler released, then taken again; Sam Arnold and Michael O'Laughlen clapped in irons; detectives in hot pursuit of bungling vice-presidential assassin George Atzerodt, capturing him the morning of the twentieth; Dr. Samuel Mudd under unshakable suspicion. Each day the public expected the morning and evening papers to carry news of yet another astounding arrest or shocking revelation. Events conspired toward an inexorable climax, awaiting only the stage star's return to the action. On the night of April 20, Thomas Jones set him on that course. Although the lost week discouraged Booth, it also gave him hope. Languishing in the pine thicket had prevented his capture. He did not know who the manhunters were, how many of them there were, or what search plan they followed, but he had felt their presence, vague, hovering, and near. Though he never saw them, and heard them but once, the day that a cavalry patrol rode past the thicket, he knew from the newspapers that the War Department was mounting a major effort against him. Jones could do what Booth could not—move among the manhunters, watch their movements, eavesdrop on their conversations, and even speak to them. God—or fate—delivered unto him a guardian angel, a man of Southern honor and the old code who, by risking his own life, saved Booth's. God willing, prayed the assassin, other men like Thomas Jones awaited his arrival on the other side in old Virginia. Such men were better than gold, and he only needed to find a few.

THOMAS JONES NEVER SAW JOHN WILKES BOOTH OR DAVID Herold—or his boat—again. As soon as the wide waters of the Potomac swallowed all sight and sound of the two men, Jones ascended the steep terrain above the launching point, retrieved his horse by the fence, and rode back to the safety of Huckleberry. The roads were deserted, ensuring no one would be able to testify later to his whereabouts that night. When he got home, he unsaddled his horse, climbed into bed, and took quiet satisfaction in the success of his most spectacular mission. One clever man had just thwarted the will and resources of a nation. For five days and four nights, from the morning of Sunday, April 16, through the evening of Thursday, April 20, while a frustrated, avenging nation scoured the country for Lincoln's assassin, Jones had concealed, sheltered, and sustained the most hated, wanted man in America. And on that dark Thursday night, while army cavalry and navy gunboats continued the furious search, intent on preventing Booth and his loyal cat's-paw from crossing the Potomac, Jones launched them on their voyage across the waters to the dark, indistinct shore on the other side. They should be landing in Virginia right about now, thought Jones, as he drifted off to sleep. But while Jones slept more quietly and peacefully

than he had in weeks, John Wilkes Booth and David Herold were rowing in the wrong direction!

*B*y Thursday, April 20, Samuel A. Mudd hadn't been
sleeping very well since he had been questioned by Lieutenant Lovett
three days before. The experience had left him unnerved. The detectives, rather than expressing gratitude, had behaved diffidently, and
seemed to treat him with suspicion. Mudd worried about what he had
told them—and even more about the vital information he withheld.
Maybe he *should* have revealed that he had met John Wilkes Booth before. But he had no opportunity to remedy this because Alexander
Lovett and the detectives did not return. And surely, Dr. Mudd reasoned, John Wilkes Booth and David Herold must have not only crossed
the Potomac by now, but pushed deep into Virginia. The soldiers and
detectives must be concentrating the hunt there now, many miles and a
wide river away from Bryantown.

On the morning of Friday, April 21, Dr. Mudd ate breakfast, went
about his customary farm work, and left for his fields. The manhunt
was now seven days old, and there were no real leads. Without solid
leads, with no prospects for capturing Booth anytime soon, the authorities remembered Samuel Mudd. In Washington, Colonel H. H. Wells
decided to come down to Bryantown to coordinate the search personally. It was time for him to meet this suspicious doctor that Lieutenant
Lovett had told him about.

Although Mudd had been a reluctant witness when interviewed on
April 18, he did provide some useful information. Thanks to the doctor,
the hunters knew that Booth was not traveling alone, but with a younger
man, almost certainly David Herold. And they knew that Booth suffered from a broken leg and impaired mobility. And thanks to Mudd,
they knew that the assassin had shaved his signature moustache. Indeed,
based on Mudd's information, the War Department revised Stanton's
April 20 proclamation to the nation. The first three printings of the re-

ward poster stated that Booth wore "a heavy black moustache." Soon the War Department revised the text and printed a fourth edition, adding the phrase "which he may have shaved off."

Lieutenant Lovett and company set out from Bryantown to question Mudd again and bring him in to see Colonel Wells. When Lovett arrived in the morning, the doctor was out again. Frances sent for her husband. When Mudd arrived, Lovett intercepted him in the yard and escorted him inside. The officer told Mudd to bring him the razor that he lent to the stranger. And the men were strangers, Mudd reminded Lovett. But the doctor started to recall other details. The man with the broken leg was armed: "The injured man had a pair of revolvers." Mudd said he had forgotten to tell them that on Tuesday. Frances Mudd reported that the stranger wore a false beard—she saw it become partly detached from his face when he walked down the stairs.

Pistols? False beards? Lieutenant Lovett said that he and his men would have to search the house. Oh, that's right, Mudd recalled, the injured stranger left one of his boots behind. Mudd explained how he had cut it off the man's swollen leg. The boot—hidden under the stranger's bed in the second-floor front room—was produced for Lovett's inspection. The officer peered down the tube until something caught his eye. He rolled the leather down a little and there it was—handwriting, in black ink. It was the name of a bootmaker in New York. Dr. Mudd interjected at once that he had not noticed the writing before. Next to the manufacturer's mark was more writing, the name of the owner. Lovett read the name. He *knew* it. His heart raced as he stared at the incontrovertible proof—"J. Wilkes."

Lovett took Mudd back to Bryantown to face Colonel Wells. On the ride over, Lovett continued to question Mudd, and the doctor continued to divulge hitherto unmentioned details. Lovett asked whether the strangers "had much money about them." Yes, Mudd confessed, Booth had a thick roll of cash—"considerable greenbacks." Lovett turned and addressed one of his men: Show him the photograph, he ordered. The detective withdrew from his pocket a small carte-de-visite and held up the image of John Wilkes Booth for Mudd's inspection. No, that wasn't the man, Mudd insisted, though it does, he added cryptically, look a little like him across the eyes.

Mudd and Lovett rode along for a few minutes without speaking. Then, the officer noticed that the doctor "seemed to turn very pale, and blue about the lips, like a man that is frightened of something." Samuel Mudd was terrified. The authorities, he feared, would discover his terrible secret very soon. Perhaps Colonel Wells, waiting in Bryantown to confront him, already knew it. Things might go better for him, he convinced himself, if he volunteered the truth—at least a carefully edited portion of it—now. Mudd steered his horse close to Lovett's and spoke as calmly and nonchalantly as a man facing the hangman's noose could muster: he knew John Wilkes Booth. He had met him last fall.

Lovett reeled at the explosive revelation, and at the matter-of-fact manner by which Dr. Mudd conveyed it. Yes, continued the doctor, he had met Booth last year—in November or December—when the actor traveled through the neighborhood looking for real estate. Mudd said he had been introduced to Booth at church and had helped him buy a horse.

At Bryantown, Mudd repeated to Colonel Wells the same story that he told Lieutenant Lovett several times. The men were strangers to him: "I never saw either of the parties before, nor can I conceive of who sent them to my house." The young man said his name was "Henson," and the injured one said his was "Tyson" or "Tyser," Mudd could not remember which. Wells picked up Mudd's furtive scent right off. He asked if the injured stranger looked like Booth. No, replied Mudd. Wells found it odd that Mudd failed to recognize a man especially one so celebrated—that he had met before, and not briefly. After all, Mudd and Booth had met at church in broad daylight, they had shopped for horses together, they had visited the blacksmith, and Booth had slept at Mudd's home.

But Mudd protested that he never got a good look at the stranger: "I did not see his face at all," he said. The man "had a heavy shawl on all the

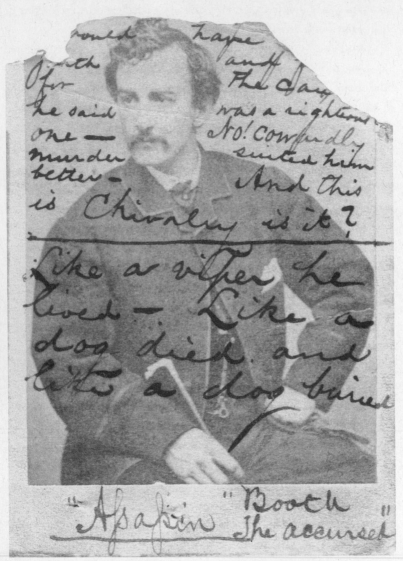

A photograph issued to one of the manhunters,
defaced with sentiments of the moment.

time," and he raised it to conceal the lower half of his face. Even when the man got into bed, "he had very little to say," and he kept "his cloak thrown around him and seemed inclined to sleep."

In that case, wondered Wells, how was Mudd able to provide such an accurate description of the stranger? The doctor's report was re-markably well observed: "He had a pretty full forehead and his skin was fair. He was very pale when I saw him, and appeared as if accustomed to in-door rather than out-door life." Moreover, the man had a moustache and a "long, heavy beard"; it was even longer than Colonel Wells's own substantial one, Mudd asserted. But unfortunately, Mudd apologized, he could not determine whether it was a natural or artificial beard. Fi-nally, Mudd confirmed, the man did shave off the moustache after he was given the razor. The doctor even described the qualities of the stranger's hair. And he saw the eyes. All very interesting details about a face Mudd claimed he never saw.

Yes, Mudd admitted, he had met Booth before, but he swore that the injured man was not Lincoln's assassin. And, he added, not only did the man in the photo not look like the stranger, he did not even look like John Wilkes Booth! "A photograph of Booth was...shown me by a de-tective, but I did not observe any resemblance between the two men, though I must say that I have very often been shown likenesses of inti-mate friends, and failed to recognize them by their pictures."

One of the detectives interrupted the interrogation to give Wells a piece of evidence no one had told him about—John Wilkes Booth's boot, fresh from Mudd's farmhouse. Wells stared at the boot and, frus-trated, feigning concern for the doctor's well-being, issued a warning: "I said it seemed to me that he was concealing the facts, and that I did not know whether he understood that that was the strongest evidence of his guilt that could be produced at that time, and that might endanger his safety."

It was now midafternoon. Wells had been at Mudd for three hours straight and still could not break him. "He did not seem unwilling to answer a direct question that I asked; but I discovered almost immediately, that, unless I did ask the direct question, important facts were omitted." Wells pressed on relentlessly. His strategy was not to threaten the doctor overtly, but to keep him talking for several hours until he wore him down. The doctor offered gossipy, trivial details of no value to the manhunters: "They paid me $25.00 for my services, which they rather pressed me to accept. I told them a small fee would answer." Although the men stayed at his place for fifteen hours, Mudd claimed that he hardly spoke to them at all: "I had very little conversation with these men during the day."

Wells wondered if Mudd had noticed Booth's prominent tattoo, the initials "JWB" inked boldly between the thumb and forefinger of the actor's left hand. Cleverly, the doctor denied seeing the hand at all: "My examination was quite short ... I did not observe his hand to see whether it was small or large." Or, implicitly, whether it was tattooed. Mudd repeated his tale about sending Booth and Herold off in the direction of Piney Chapel: "Before they left they inquired the way to Rev. Mr. Wilmer's ... he is regarded by neighbors as a Union man." In any event Mudd did not see which way they went: "I did not see the parties when they left in the afternoon ... I did not go out." And, by the way, "I have always called myself a Union man, though I have never voted with the administration party."

Mudd cautioned Wells that the pale stranger was well armed, but said nothing about Davey's Spencer carbine: "The injured man had a belt with two revolvers in it concealed under his clothing, which I discovered when he got into bed after having his wound dressed." It was late in the afternoon. Wells had questioned Dr. Mudd—and the doctor had parried him—for close to six hours. The colonel produced another carte-de-visite photograph of Lincoln's assassin and told Mudd to look at it carefully. Do you or do you not recognize him as the stranger? Wells demanded. No, that was not the man. On second thought, Mudd admitted it. He said that he realized it just now. Yes, the stranger was John Wilkes Booth. Lincoln's assassin *had* taken refuge at his farm. And, either intentionally or unwittingly, Dr. Samuel A. Mudd had helped him escape.

As Colonel Wells brought the interview to a close around 6:00 P.M. on Friday, April 21, he mentioned a little formality that he would take care of. To avoid confusion, and to make things clear, he would write out a statement of Mudd's testimony. The doctor was free to go. But would he please return to Bryantown on Saturday to sign it? As Mudd departed, Colonel Henry Wells spoke ominously: "One of the strongest circumstances against you is, that you have failed to give early information, as you might have done, in this matter."

Mudd, exhausted by the morning's questioning by Lieutenant Lovett, followed by six more hours with Colonel Wells, rode home. He had accomplished his mission. Tonight, in a few hours, Booth and Herold would land safely in Virginia, far from the reach of Colonel Wells, Lieutenant Lovett and his detectives, and Lieutenant Dana and the Thirteenth New York Cavalry. They had lost the assassin's scent and would never pick it up again. Unless other manhunters picked up Booth's trail soon and continued the chase, he would escape. Soon, unless somebody stopped him, John Wilkes Booth would vanish into the Deep South. Once that happened, Union forces would never find him. Mudd had played a large role in helping Booth escape Maryland. Soon, however, he would pay a terrible price for his lies.

ONCE JOHN WILKES BOOTH ATTEMPTED TO CROSS THE POtomac on Thursday the twentieth, and finally reached Virginia early on Sunday the twenty-third, the sanctuary of Thomas Jones's Huckleberry did not survive long undisturbed. Union detectives suspected that a man of Jones's reputation must know something about Booth's escape and they arrested him. But they had no evidence, and, true to his character, he volunteered nothing. The troops confined Jones at the Bryantown Tavern, locking him up in a second-floor, back bedroom. Like the

Surratt's tavern, the Bryantown establishment served as a way station for mysterious, wartime Confederate intrigues.

The detectives didn't know it, but they had, in a sense, conveyed Thomas Jones to a scene of the crime. At this very tavern, in a first-floor parlor below the bedroom that served as the river ghost's ersatz jail, John Wilkes Booth met with Samuel Mudd and rebel agent Thomas Harbin when the actor plotted his madcap scheme to kidnap Abraham Lincoln. The detectives also ensnared Captain Cox in their dragnet. Oswell Swann, who guided the fugitives to Rich Hill early on Easter morning, Sunday, April 16, gave information against the captain. Cox insisted that when the two strangers came to his door, he dismissed them and ordered them on their way. But Swann disputed him and swore that Cox invited the criminals into his home, where they spent several hours. The detectives locked up Cox with Jones and posted two guards outside their door. Before they went to sleep on the floor, their heads resting on their saddles, Cox turned to his good friend and experienced secret agent for advice. "What shall I do, Tom?" he whispered in the dark. "Stick to what you have said," counseled Jones, "and admit nothing else."

The detectives, frustrated at their lack of progress, tried to trick Jones into confessing by loitering in the yard below his bedroom window and talking loudly about his forthcoming and imminent hanging. Still Jones would not talk. Even when transferred to the dreaded Old Capitol prison, site of his former, devastating incarceration, and current home to John T. Ford, Junius Brutus Booth, John Sleeper Clarke, and many others ensnared by the manhunt, he refused to provide any information about John Wilkes Booth. During the wagon ride from Bryantown to Washington, an unsubtle government agent had tried, once again, to loosen his captive's tongue with alcohol. Detective Franklin genially offered a bottle of whiskey, which Jones pretended to drink. When the officer saw that his prisoner refused to get drunk, he cursed him all the way to the capital.

The detectives failed to realize it, but when they arrested Jones, they also captured an eyewitness who possessed intimate knowledge of how he helped Booth and Herold. But they could never make her talk. Jones was forced to leave her behind in Bryantown, but he laughed at the detectives' ignorance about their valuable prize—his horse: "This mare was the same one Booth had ridden from the pines to the river that memorable...night. She was a flea-bitten gray, named Kit. Had her complicity been known, what an object of interest she would have been." Instead, Kit lived out the rest of her days in quiet anonymity.

Jones knew he possessed the trump card that he could play to outbluff the detectives: not a single eyewitness could place him in the company of Booth and Herold. Whenever he had traveled to and from the pine thicket, he always rode alone. When he had guided the assassins to the boat at Dent's Meadow, he did it alone, and no one saw him coming or going. As long as Samuel Cox and the captain's son kept faith and did not implicate him, the detectives could not make a case against him. Booth and Herold were the only ones who could betray Jones. But Booth had vowed to die before being taken alive. Eventually, Jones reasoned, the government would have to release him.

And that is exactly what happened. Freed in the aftermath of the manhunt, Thomas A. Jones passed from memory and, eventually, from history as a forgotten footnote, merely one of the hundreds of men and women arrested, never charged, and soon released during the great manhunt of April 1865. Captain Cox, too, won his liberty. Oswell Swann was the only witness against him. Cox's loyal servant girl, Mary, denounced Oswell as a liar and swore that Booth never entered the house. Jones guessed correctly that the two conflicting black witnesses canceled out each other: "Mary's positive and persistent declaration that Booth had not entered the house—unshaken by threats or offered bribes—saved Cox's life when it hung in the balance." When the ever-observant Jones, peering out from a window of the Old Capitol, spotted Swann leaving the prison, heading for the Navy Yard Bridge and Maryland beyond, he knew that Cox was safe. Jones informed his relieved friend, "You have nothing more to fear. The only witness against you has been dismissed and is going home."

• • •

$\mathcal{T}$HOMAS JONES RETURNED TO HUCKLEBERRY AND KEPT JOHN Wilkes Booth's secret for nearly twenty years. Because of his silence, the saga of Booth's missing "lost week" remained a puzzle, indeed, the chief unsolved mystery of the twelve-day chase for Lincoln's killer. Then, in 1883, George Alfred Townsend vowed to solve the mystery. Townsend, friend of Mark Twain, and a leading journalist of the nineteenth century, and one of the best writers who covered the Civil War, reported the Lincoln assassination for a newspaper and also wrote a vivid, luridly entertaining book about John Wilkes Booth. Possessed by the assassination and the manhunt, Townsend could not let go. Beginning in April 1865 and continuing on and off for the next two decades, he haunted the scenes of the crime, tracked down many of the Southerners who helped Booth during the chase, and interviewed a number of the manhunters. Townsend collected obscure names and facts that would have been lost to history without his detective work.

In 1883, during his third attempt to retrace Booth's escape route, Townsend coaxed Judge Frederick Stone, in 1865 a defense counsel at the trial of several of Booth's conspirators, and now a U.S. congressman, to talk about Booth's notorious lost week. Stone confessed that there was a man who hid Booth and Herold and helped them cross the Potomac. This man was still alive. Perhaps, after all these years, he would talk to Townsend. The tip elated the journalist, whose scoop-seeking sensibilities alerted him to the value of breaking the story on the great mystery of the manhunt. But Stone refused to name Booth's savior. In Port Tobacco, the very place where Thomas Jones had refused to betray the assassin for $100,000, Townsend persuaded several young locals, including members of Captain Cox's family, to divulge the elusive name. Townsend wrote a letter to Jones: "I am a writer for the press and, sometimes, of books. It might be of mutual advantage for us to meet."

He courted Jones with letters until, finally, the aging but still quick-witted veteran agreed to meet in Baltimore, Maryland, on December

11, 1883, to reveal his story. There, in room 52 of the Barnum Hotel, Jones broke his lifelong silence and told the story that, eighteen years ago, he refused to confess under threat of death or sell for a reward of $100,000. The times were different now, thought Jones. He could not harm John Wilkes Booth now. And he was an old man. If he did not preserve his memories soon, the story of his great adventure would follow him to the grave. Too many stories of the War of the Rebellion had already died with their tellers. Townsend sat spellbound as Jones regaled him until almost midnight with the thrilling, hitherto-lost tale of the pine thicket and the Potomac crossing. Jones so mesmerized Townsend that the writer beseeched him to meet again the next day to continue the story. Jones agreed. For the interview, and for the coveted, once-priceless knowledge that could have brought Thomas Jones sudden death—or instant riches—George Alfred Townsend paid him the grand sum of sixty dollars.

Later, several years after Townsend wrote about Jones, another journalist staged a dramatic reunion of the river ghost and Captain Williams. Modestly, Jones wondered if the captain would even remember him. Williams recognized him instantly: "Of course I remember you. I can never forget that come-to-the-Lord-and-be-saved expression you wear now and then. But if I had known then what I do now, how different things would have been! Why, you ought to be shot! If you had told me where Booth was you would have been the biggest man in America, and would have had money by the flour barrel full."

Jones demurred, just as he did that day long ago at Brawner's Tavern: "Yes, and a conscience full of purgatory, and the everlasting hatred of the people I loved. No, Captain, I never the first time thought of betraying Booth. After he was placed in my hands I determined to die before I would betray him...how could I give up the life of that poor devil over there in the pine thicket hovering between life and death."

The captain said that Jones didn't fool him then: "Myself and the other officers believed that you knew more than you would tell, but that sanctimonious look of yours saved you." Williams elaborated: "I remember when I made the offer…in the saloon he was standing next to me at the bar and I could not detect the least movement or change of face. There was something which told me he knew where Booth was, or could give us which could lead to his capture, but he couldn't be worked. No amount of money or glory would have tempted him. No human being can read his face and tell what is passing in his mind. It is like a stone."

In April 1894, the twenty-ninth anniversary of Lincoln's assassination, an old man ambled up Tenth Street in Washington, D.C., until he stopped in front of house number 453. The rectangular wood, painted signboard attached to the famous brick house read: "THIS HOUSE IN WHICH ABRAHAM LINCOLN DIED CONTAINS THE OLDROYD LINCOLN MEMORIAL COLLECTION OF OVER 3,000. ARTICLES RELATING TO ABRAHAM LINCOLN. OPEN ALL HOURS DAY & EVENING. ADMISSION 25¢." Osborn H. Oldroyd, Washington eccentric, had become, like George Alfred Townsend, obsessed with the assassination. He occupied the Petersen House and turned it into a tourist attraction nearly three-quarters of a century before Ford's Theatre, a gutted ruin, became the museum it is today. In Petersen's basement, Oldroyd installed his personal museum, a late-nineteenth-century cabinet of curiosities where preposterous relics of dubious provenance lay side by side with priceless historical treasures, all preserved under thick display glass in oak jeweler's floor cases, illuminated unevenly by yellow, incandescent, electric bulbs. Over the years Oldroyd amassed an impressive but indiscriminate hoard of trash and treasure, and for the bargain price of a quarter tourists could ogle his collection and view Abraham Lincoln's death room. Soon Oldroyd, like Townsend, would retrace Booth's escape route and write about his adventures. But today history showed up at his door.

The old man, now seventy-four, gripped the cast-iron railing and ascended the same stairs where, a generation earlier, Dr. Leale and the others carried the dying president up to the little, second-floor back bedroom. He stood silently in the death chamber. The room was quiet now, not like the night twenty-nine years earlier when frantic doctors stripped Lincoln of his clothes, searching his body for wounds, while Mary Lincoln's wailing, unsettling cries echoed through the halls. The old man visualized the bloody scene that unfolded here and recalled his memories of the assassin who scripted that mournful night. Satisfied, he sought out the proprietor of this haunting memorial to sadness and death. "My name is Thomas A. Jones," he informed Oldroyd, "and I am the man who cared for and fed Booth and Herold while they were in hiding, after committing the awful deed."

Within the year, in March 1895, Thomas Jones joined Abraham Lincoln and John Wilkes Booth in death. His estate was valued at a meager $271.70, prior to claims that reduced the balance to $181.60. Obituaries in the Southern papers remarked on his "zeal," "fidelity," "courage," and, of course, above all the other antebellum virtues, his "honor." One newspaper published this benediction: "There is no one who does not believe that Thomas A. Jones acted the part of a hero." His grave at Saint Mary's Church in Newport, Maryland, was marked by a fragrant cedar stob that rotted away a long time ago.

DAVID HEROLD DIPPED THE BLADES DEEP AND PULLED HARD, and the skiff, unburdened of its usual heavy cargo of fish and water logged nets, responded to his experienced touch at the oars. He and Booth could see Thomas Jones standing motionless at the river's edge, watching them glide away. Soon their guardian angel, like the river ghost he was, vanished from sight, followed by all signs of the shoreline, blanketed by the cloaking mist. The gentle, rhythmic rocking of the boat upon the water exhilarated Booth. After the detour to Dr. Mudd's and the interminable delay at the pine thicket, it felt good to be on the move again. Miraculously, these delays, although exposing them to great danger, had not proven fatal to their escape. Now Booth and Herold could say good riddance to Maryland and all their troubles there, leaving behind the stymied detectives and federal troops who pursued them. With each stroke, Herold propelled them a few yards closer to Virginia.

Booth bent down low, huddled over his compass, and checked their bearings. He dared not light the candle again—its reflection on the water could magnify its tiny flame into a shining beacon that would reveal their position to the Union gunboats that patrolled the river. But he had no choice: he couldn't read the dial in the dark. Puzzled, he stared at the needle dancing on its spindle as melting wax dripped over its glass and wood housing. They were supposed to be rowing from Maryland west across the Potomac to Virginia and then south until they reached Machodoc Creek. But the needle indicated that they were heading northwest, in the opposite direction. Was the compass broken? Booth shook and rotated the case, but the needle always returned to the proper position, still tugging north. No, the compass was true.

If only Thomas Jones had piloted them across himself, directing Herold at the oars and Booth at the makeshift rudder while charting the course personally with the compass. David Herold was a competent enough navigator of the Maryland and Virginia coastal marshes, creeks, and rivers, but he was not a professional seaman. And it was one thing to ply the waters during daylight hours while hunting for pleasure, another to run them at night when in danger as the object of the hunt. Herold had never made a trip across the Potomac under conditions like these: under pressure, pursued, and in near total darkness. Thomas Jones, seasoned agent, had done it hundreds of times.

They had been on the water far too long: they should be in Virginia by now. David Herold did not need a watch to tell him that. His chafed palms and fingers and his burning arm and leg muscles made it clear enough. He and Booth heard sounds, but the water played tricks with noises in the night, making it impossible to judge their origin or distance. They spotted a few lights but could not determine whether they were moving or stationary, a boat under way, or a fixed marker onshore. Disoriented, unsure of their location, the fugitives continued rowing north, then turned to the west, passing Mathias Point. Their boat was a tiny speck afloat on an unforgiving river. The water exhaled a cool, damp breath that chilled them to the bone, but at least the battered little gray skiff was holding up. Surrounded by darkness and water, traveling slowly but with far to go, Booth and Herold confronted the obvious: they were losing their race with the manhunters.

They had to land soon. The slightly built Herold was no Lewis Powell, and he did not possess the strength to row all night. Booth observed the strain on Herold's face with each stroke and sensed that the youth was failing. But where to beach the skiff? Herold turned around from his rowing position and searched the horizon ahead for landmarks. Then, off to their right, he spotted the contours of a familiar-looking sight: Blossum Point, beyond which flowed a wide-mouthed inlet, extending north. Herold told Booth that he recognized this place. If they rowed up that inlet, they would come to Nanjemoy Creek, a place Herold knew very well. He had made many hunting trips to this region of Maryland's countryside: "I am passionately fond of partridge shooting and nearly every fall take two or three months for that purpose," he later confessed.

At the mouth of the creek, on the eastern side, they would find, Herold explained, a farm called Indiantown, and two men, Peregrine Davis and John J. Hughes. And Herold assured Booth that he knew these men well: "They are persons I have known for five or six years, and whom I have been in the habit of visiting for a long time." Davis owned the property and his son-in-law, Hughes, farmed it. That was the good news. The bad news was that Indiantown was in Maryland. After a frightening, disorienting, and exhausting night on the Potomac, they were in the wrong place. Indeed, they were back in Maryland where they started, but twice as far from their destination, Machodoc Creek, Virginia, as they were when they embarked upon their crossing. Now, north of the original position where Thomas Jones shoved them off, they were, once again, vulnerable to the roving Union patrols that pursued them. They had labored on the water for more than five hours. Weary, disappointed, another day behind schedule, and again in grave danger, they put in to Nanjemoy Creek early on the morning of Friday, April 21.

Booth and Herold concealed the boat as best they could. The Hughes farmhouse was not far from the creek, and Herold persuaded Booth to cover the distance on foot. Herold wanted to avoid the risk of Booth being discovered alone while he was off visiting Hughes. Taking their weapons, blankets, and other possessions, they proceeded to Indiantown. Herold was confident that Hughes would welcome them. The youth's affable, hail-fellow-well-met manner had won him many friends in southern Maryland during his hunting expeditions over the last several years, and they had watched him grow from an eager teenager to a young adult and experienced outdoorsman. Moreover, Davey knew Perry Davis and John Hughes as men of Southern sympathies and actions. They would not turn him in to Union authorities. There was also a strong chance that the farmer already knew that Davey had been implicated as one of Booth's accomplices in the assassination. Several newspapers had named him, and the day before, on the morning of the twentieth, the War Department had printed huge broadsides offering a $50,000 reward for Booth and $25,000 for Herold.

Hughes was happy to see his old acquaintance but shocked at his raffish appearance. Hughes also immediately knew Booth's identity. The farmer invited them into his home and fed them. What were their plans? Hughes asked. Davey explained their predicament: after rowing all night, taking the wrong course, and failing to reach Virginia, here they were, exhausted and stranded. They would try the river again tonight and make for Virginia. Until then, they must keep out of sight. It was too dangerous to walk around the countryside or launch the boat during daylight. A Union gunboat or shore patrol could spot them easily. May they, Herold asked, hide at Indiantown from morning until nightfall?

Hughes wanted to help, but he did not want to die. It was much too dangerous, he argued, for the fugitives to remain in the house all morning and afternoon. The manhunters increased in number and got better organized every day. Union troops and detectives swarmed over Maryland, salivating at the prospect of the new War Department rewards announced on April 20. Yes, they may take refuge at Indiantown, agreed Hughes, but they must leave the house and hide outdoors. He would sustain them with food and news. Beyond that, there was little he could do for them on the Maryland side of the river. No overland escape was possible from Nanjemoy Creek. The only land route would take the assassins farther north, in the opposite direction from Virginia, and directly into the path of Union forces pouring south. The Potomac River remained their only possible escape, and Booth and Herold already possessed a sturdy boat. Hughes suggested a suitable place for them to hide. The three men agreed that it would be best for all if the fugitives left Indiantown as soon as possible.

Booth's heart sank. He was banished once again to lie on the ground—and wait. Tonight would mark another twenty-four hours that he and Herold had spent outdoors. They had been living outdoors for six days, ever since they left Dr. Mudd's on the evening of April 15. The fugitives could not endure a second, grueling experience like the one they had just suffered at the pine thicket: five days and four nights without shelter, waiting to cross the river. No, they must cross tonight. Until then, they had no choice but to hide near the low-lying wetlands close to Nanjemoy Creek. Disgusted, Booth pulled his 1864 datebook from his coat and stared at the calendar he had drawn for late April, May, and June 1865. He found the day's date, April 21, and scribbled down a one-word notation that summarized his view of the situation: "Swamp."

Datebook in hand, he flipped through the pages until he found the one containing the first entry he wrote after the assassination. He would make another entry now, he decided. Booth put pen to paper and, within a few intense minutes, produced an astonishing document.

> After being hunted like a dog through swamps, woods, and last night being chased by gun boats till I was forced to re-

turn wet cold and starving, with every man's hand against me, I am here in despair. And why; For doing what Brutus was honored for, for what made Tell a Hero. And yet I for striking down a greater tyrant than they ever knew am looked upon as a common cutthroat. My action was purer than either of theirs. One hoped to be great himself. The other had not only his country's but his own wrongs to avenge. I hoped for no gain. I knew no private wrong. I struck for my country and that alone. A country groaned beneath this tyranny and prayed for this end. Yet now behold the cold hand they extend to me. God *cannot* pardon me if I have done wrong. Yet I cannot see any wrong except in serving a degenerate people. The little, the very little I left behind to clear my name, the Govmt will not allow to be printed. So ends all. For my country I have given up all that makes life sweet and Holy, brought misery upon my family, and am sure there is no pardon in the Heaven for me since man condemns me so. I have only *heard* of what has been done (except what I did myself) and it fills me with horror. God try and forgive me, and bless my mother. To night I will once more try the river with the intent to cross; though I have a greater desire and almost a mind to return to Washington and in a measure clear my name, which I feel I can do. I do not repent the blow I struck. I may before God but not to man.

I think I have done well, though I am abandoned, with the curse of Cain upon me, when if the world knew my heart, *that one* blow would have made me great, though I did desire no greatness.

To night I try to escape these blood hounds once more. Who, who can read his fate God's will be done.

I have too great a soul to die like a criminal. O may he, may he spare me that and let me die bravely.

I bless the entire world. Have never hated or wronged anyone. This last was not a wrong, unless God deems it so. And its with him to damn or bless me. And for this brave boy with me who often prays (yes, before and since) with a true and sincere heart, was it a crime in him, if so, why can he pray the same I do not wish to shed a drop of blood, but "I must fight the course." Tis all thats left me.

Booth compared himself to not one but two ancient, persecuted villains, the first biblical, the second Shakespearean. By naming Cain, Booth conjured up the primal curse from the Bible's first book, at Genesis 4:8–14: "[A]nd it came to pass, when they were in the field, that Cain rose up against Abel, his brother, and slew him. And the Lord said unto Cain, Where *is* Abel thy brother? And he said, I know not: *am* I my brother's keeper? And he said, What hast though done? The voice of thy brother's blood crieth unto me from the ground. And now *art* though cursed from the earth, which has opened her mouth to receive thy brother's blood from thy hand; When thou tillest the ground, it shall not thenceforth yield unto thee her strength; a fugitive and a vagabond shalt thou be in the earth. And Cain said unto the Lord, My punishment IS greater than I can bear. Behold, thou hast driven me out this day from the face of the earth; and from thy face shall I be hid; and I shall be a fugitive and a vagabond in the earth; and it shall come to pass, THAT every one that findeth me shall slay me."

The second villain Booth did not identify by name, but quoted: "I must fight the course." With that passage Booth invoked the haunted spirit of Shakespeare's greatest tragic figure, Macbeth. In act 5, scene 7, the last act's penultimate scene, death is near. Macbeth's act of tyrannicide has summoned his own end. Ill omens abound: his enemies have massed for battle, Birnham Wood is on the move, war trumpets sound, the climax is imminent. Trapped, Macbeth vows to fight on: "They have tied me to the stake. I cannot fly, / But bear-like I must fight the course." As in the hideous sport of bearbaiting, where the dangerous but ultimately doomed beast is tied to a stake and vicious dogs are set upon him, Macbeth is fated to struggle, then die.

Booth shut the book and tracked the setting sun, waiting for the darkness. They would have reached Virginia about twenty-six hours ago if they had crossed the Potomac successfully the previous night of Thursday, April 20. Now they were another day behind schedule, for all the good the schedule had done them. Booth shot Lincoln on April 14 and now, seven days later, he was still in Maryland. Washington, D.C., was only forty miles away. The Deep South, far below Maryland and Virginia, where, after four years of civil war, many towns and counties had never seen a Yankee soldier, was beginning to seem an unattainable dream. The heart of Dixieland was a long way away.

As night fell over Indiantown, it was time to push off. They knew the route: south to Blossum Point, east around Mathias Point, then south again, hugging the shoreline until they reached Machodoc Creek where, they prayed, Thomas Jones's memorably named contact, Mrs. Quesenberry, was waiting for them. Then, at this critical moment, when they needed to escape from Maryland as quickly as possible, Booth and Herold did something inexplicable—they did nothing. During the night of Friday, April 21, they did not go down to the mouth of the Nanjemoy, retrieve the skiff, enter the Potomac, and row south to Virginia. Instead, they sat in the dark and did nothing.

Why did they not take to the water that night? Was David Herold too tired and were his muscles too weak for consecutive nights of heavy rowing? Did Booth fear federal gunboats in the vicinity? Were they exploring another option, a new escape route, perhaps a daring and counterintuitive thrust north by land? Or were they just too dejected after their failed crossing on the previous night? Whatever the reason, Booth and Herold chose not to make the attempt. They paid a steep price for their delay. Now they would have to waste another day at Indiantown, concealing themselves through the morning, afternoon, and evening until, once more, the sun set and darkness came.

While Booth and Herold remained in place, their hunters pursued them with renewed vigor. The evidence collected at Dr. Mudd's, plus alleged sightings of the fugitives southwest of his farm, suggested that Lincoln's assassin was making for the Potomac and a river crossing to Virginia. The couriers and the telegraph wires jumped all day with intense traffic. General Augur wrote to General Slough at Alexandria: "Has the Michigan Cavalry yet left for the lower country as we spoke of this morning? If not, hurry it up." W. W. Winship, captain and provost marshal at Alexandria, reported to Colonel Taylor in Washington, "the cavalry will start immediately with instruction to publish to fishermen, negroes, and others a description of the assassins and the reward for their apprehension, and to scout and picket the river to below Dumfried until further orders."

Winship also received an update from General Augur: "When Booth was last heard from he was near Wicomico River, Maryland. It is feared he has crossed into Virginia. He had broken his leg and was on crutches. He had also shaved off his mustache. Let your cavalry know these particulars, and let them go down below Aquia and, if possible, connect with the cavalry I send down by boat to-night into Westmoreland County." Winship's laconic reply promised action: "Your dispatch is received. The cavalry started at 5 P.M."

From Washington, Colonel Taylor, assistant adjutant general for the Twenty-second Army Corps, sent word to N. B. Sweitzer, commander of the Sixteenth New York Cavalry. "The major-general commanding directs that you place a battalion of your regiment on board a steamer...and proceed down the Potomac, debarking on the Virginia shore as nearly opposite the mouth of the Wicomico River, probably at or near Nomini Bay, as practicable. Having landed your people you will use them as you may judge best for the discovery of Booth, the murderer of the President, and any of his accomplices who may have succeeded in crossing the Potomac."

At 9:00 P.M. on Saturday, April 22, Gideon Welles telegraphed Lieutenant Commander Eastman, U.S. steamer *Don*, at Saint Inigoes, Maryland: "Booth was near Bryantown last Saturday, where Doctor Mudd set his ankle, which was broken by a fall from his horse. The utmost vigilance is necessary in the Potomac and Patuxent to prevent his escape. All boats should be searched for and destroyed, and a daily and nightly patrol established on both shores. Inform your people that more than $100,000 is offered for him. Allow none of your boats to leave, except for search elsewhere."

General Augur sent urgent word to Commander Parker, U.S. Navy at Saint Inigoes, Maryland. "There is reason to believe that Booth and an accomplice are in the swamps about Allen's Fresh, emptying into Wicomico River. He is evidently trying to cross into Virginia. Have you the Potomac well guarded there and above? Fearing that he may have already crossed, I wish to send a force of cavalry to Nomini Bay. Can I land horses there or in that vicinity, and with how much water? Please inform me at once."

Augur flashed a second message to Parker: "There is no longer any doubt that Booth and an accomplice were near Bryantown on Saturday last, inquiring for Piney Church. He is very lame, having broken his leg, and was last seen on crutches. He was undoubtedly endeavoring to cross into Virginia. I am desired to request your most vigilant co-operation, by a rigid and active blockade of all the Potomac, to prevent his escape into Virginia."

Chapter Eight

"I Have Some Little Pride"

ON THE NIGHT OF SATURDAY, APRIL 22, JOHN WILKES BOOTH and David Herold gathered themselves and made for their boat. They would have been in Virginia around fifty hours ago if they had crossed on the twentieth, and about twenty-six hours ago if they left Indiantown at the first opportunity, the night of the twenty-first. They compounded their original error by tarrying at Indiantown an extra day. All told, they had lost two days since they left Thomas Jones and had wasted more than thirty-six hours during their Indiantown diversion. If they had any hope of surviving the manhunt, they could not afford to squander any more time and make any more mistakes. They had endured so many setbacks: Booth's debilitating injury; delays at Dr. Mudd's and the pine thicket; the aborted river crossing; the Indiantown folly. These episodes robbed Booth and Herold of time, momentum, and mental fortitude.

When they climbed aboard the skiff and rowed out to the Potomac, they knew their lives depended on navigating a proper course to Machodoc Creek, Virginia. The first sign was not auspicious. Herold nearly rowed into trouble moments after getting under way: "That night, at sundown, we crossed the mouth of Nanjemoy Creek, [and] passed within 300 yards of a gunboat." But the lead-colored skiff melted into the colors of the water, and the sailors failed to spot it. Lucky to escape the U.S. Navy vessel, Herold stuck to the proper course, and, after several hours, spotted the mouth of a creek on the horizon, off his right shoulder. He turned west and rowed in that direction. They landed the skiff and disembarked with their pistols, carbine, and blankets. At last, on the morning of Sunday, April 23, nine days after the assassination, John Wilkes Booth and David Herold set foot on Virginia soil.

They scanned the terrain for enemy soldiers or local, friendly Virginians. The creek looked deserted, and no one had seen them. But something was wrong. In a few seconds Booth and Herold realized their mistake. They had done it again. This was not Machodoc Creek. They were again in the wrong place.

Rowing south along the shore, David Herold had mistaken the mouth of Gambo Creek for Machodoc Creek and landed their boat prematurely. But the error did not approach the catastrophic proportions of their misguided landing at Nanjemoy Creek and Indiantown. From earlier trips to the region, Herold recognized exactly where they were. The Machodoc was just one mile southwest of the Gambo. It wouldn't even be necessary to launch the skiff again. The Machodoc and Mrs. Quesenberry's place were accessible by an overland route. Herold could walk there in less than half an hour. Booth's leg made the brief journey impossible for him, so he waited near the boat while Herold sought out Mrs. Quesenberry. She certainly came well recommended, and Booth expected Davey to return soon with good news, food, and horses.

Herold arrived at the Quesenberry place around 1:00 P.M., Sunday, April 23. Elizabeth Quesenberry, a thirty-nine-year-old widow with three young daughters, was a remarkable woman. A figure of proper breeding and distinguished lineage, she served the Confederate signal agents and couriers who operated in the northern neck of Virginia. Like Sarah Slater, Belle Boyd, Rose Greenhow, and innumerable other Southern women—including possibly the intriguing, alluring Branson sisters of Baltimore, Lewis Powell's special friends—Elizabeth Quesenberry served the cause behind the scenes by aiding the work of the Confederate underground. The names of most of these women have been lost to history and Elizabeth's would have faded from memory long ago had Lincoln's assassin not come calling.

Bizarrely, false reports spread that morning that Booth was dressing as a woman. General James Barnes, commanding at Point Lookout, Maryland, forwarded an odd report to Stanton, explaining that he had just received the following dispatch from a Captain Willauer at Leonardtown: "Sergeant Bagley, of the mounted detachment stationed at Millstone Landing, informs me that J. Wilkes Booth was seen passing through Great Mills on foot about 9 o'clock this morning. He was dressed in woman's attire. The sergeant and his men are in pursuit. I will send all the cavalry I have out immediately. Everything shall be done that can be done to secure him. The citizens recognized him as he was passing through." Barnes informed Stanton, "Great Mills is situated at the head of Saint Mary's River, about ten miles from Saint Inigoes and twenty from here."

General Hancock spread the rumor by sending it to Major General Torbert at Winchester, Major General Emory at Cumberland, and General Stevens at Harper's Ferry. Hancock ordered them to tell all their subordinate commanders along the Baltimore and Ohio Railroad and in West Virginia to the Kanawha that they must not relax their vigilance: "Booth has not yet been arrested, and it is thought that he may attempt to escape in disguise of a woman or otherwise through that portion of the country."

Mrs. Quesenberry was not at home when Herold arrived. Instead, he found her fifteen-year-old daughter. The assassin's emissary asked if her mother was there. No, replied the girl, she was away, but could be sent for. Please do, Herold requested. Booth's young accomplice, in spite of his disheveled, unwashed, and unshaven state that made him unsuitable for polite conversation with proper young ladies, attempted to engage the teenager in social banter: "I suppose that you ladies pleasure a good deal on the river?"

"We have no boat," the girl replied curtly.

In that case, Herold was pleased to inform her, he had a boat nearby at Gambo Creek and, if she liked, she could have it. The girl considered the meaning of the stranger's odd offer.

As soon as Elizabeth Quesenberry returned, David Herold got down to business. Quesenberry maintained her guard: wartime experience taught her to be suspicious of strangers, especially ones who looked like Herold and who offered gifts of boats to teenage girls. Herold announced that Thomas Jones had sent him to her. That recommendation, plus a few choice details, persuaded her that this stranger really knew Jones and was not an undercover Union detective trying to entrap her. If Herold came from Jones, and Jones disclosed her name to him, she felt obligated to offer assistance. But what kind?

Herold revealed there were two of them. The other man, unable to walk, waited at Gambo Creek. Davey asked for food and transportation—either saddled horses or a wagon and team—to ride south. Suspecting or already knowing who Herold's companion was, Quesenberry calculated that this was too big a job to handle alone. By now the news that Lincoln's assassin was on the run had spread throughout the countryside of Virginia's northern neck. Only a fool wouldn't suspect that John Wilkes Booth was heading for the state. If he had not already crossed the Potomac, he would try soon, and his likely landing spot was somewhere nearby. And here, in Mrs. Quesenberry's front yard, stood a suspicious young stranger, offering to give away his boat, and asking for horses. As an experienced Confederate agent, she knew what to do: summon help at once. She sent for Thomas Harbin, a leading Confederate agent in the area with the kind of experience to handle this delicate situation. Moreover, Harbin possessed two other equally important credentials. He was Thomas Jones's brother-in-law. And he knew Booth. In December 1864, Dr. Mudd introduced Harbin to Booth at the Bryantown Tavern when the actor was organizing his plot to kidnap Abraham Lincoln.

Thomas Harbin responded promptly to Elizabeth's summons, bringing along another operative, Joseph Baden. Herold explained the situation and asked for help. Quickly, Harbin decided upon the best strategy: go to Booth around sundown, feed him, and get him moving south as swiftly as possible. It was a race now. There was no more time to hide out in fixed positions, evading the manhunters by camouflage and cunning. Booth must make a run from northern Virginia, through the state's interior, and then into the Deep South. Speed of movement was now the key, just like on the night of April 14 when Booth raced out of Washington.

$\mathcal{M}$RS. QUESENBERRY PREPARED FOOD FOR THE FUGITIVES and turned it over to David Herold. She would not ride to Gambo Creek, and she never laid eyes on Booth. An operative never took unnecessary risks. But she did not need to meet Booth to help him. Herold could carry the food, and Harbin would arrange for the horses. Her work was done. Journeying to Gambo Creek personally might have indulged her personal curiosity, but it was not essential to the mission. Harbin mobilized a third operative, William Bryant, with instructions to saddle two horses and bring them to Gambo Creek. Booth, lame and stranded, could not come to them. Bryant needed to retrieve the assassin, get him in the saddle, and escort him to the next stop down the line. About an hour before sunset, Harbin and Herold called on Bryant's place, north of Machodoc Creek and about three miles below Matthias Point. From here they rode to Booth's hiding place near the Gambo. As they approached, Herold signaled the assassin not to shoot, just as Thomas Jones had signaled them in the pine thicket. Bryant and Herold lifted Booth into the saddle and the party rode to their next destination, the home of Dr. Richard Stuart, about eight miles from William Bryant's place.

They arrived at Stuart's after dark around 8:00 P.M., just as the doctor and his family were finishing supper. When the doctor went to the door, he found two men he knew, William Bryant and a man named Crisman, in the company of two strangers. David Herold was on foot and the rest were on horseback, Booth and Bryant riding a sorrel and a gray. Keeping close to his front door, Stuart spoke to the haggard pair:

"Who are you?"

"We are Marylanders in want of accommodations for the night," Herold replied.

Stuart wasn't interested: "It is impossible; I have no accommodations for anybody."

Davey pleaded their case: his brother had broken his leg, and someone recommended they see Stuart for medical treatment and help on their journey.

Unmoved, Stuart's answer was the same—no.

Well, wasn't he a doctor? Herold demanded.

Stuart possessed a quick riposte for any question. "I am no surgeon. I am only a physician," he begged off, implying that he knew nothing about broken bones, setting fractures, or making splints.

But the recommendation came from Dr. Mudd, Herold boasted.

Unimpressed, Stuart claimed he had never heard of him: "I don't know Dr. Mudd—never saw him. I don't know that I had ever heard of Dr. Mudd." And anyway, "Nobody was authorized to recommend anybody to me."

Booth did not speak, relying on Herold to press the matter: "If you listen to the circumstances of the case, you will be able to do it."

Alarmed by the stranger's persistence, Stuart rebuffed him: "I don't want to know anything about you."

Stuart agreed to give them some food, but that was all. He did not like their appearance or manner and was suspicious of their story: "I did not really believe he had a broken leg; I thought that it was all put on." Their tale did not make sense. Herold claimed that they were Confederate soldiers eager to continue the war after Lee's surrender: "We are Marylanders going to Mosby." But Stuart knew that Mosby's war was over: "Mosby has surrendered, I understand, you will have to get your paroles." Obviously the strangers were lying.

Reluctantly, Stuart told them to come in the house for their meal.

The sooner they ate, the quicker he could get rid of them. Herold walked in, and Booth followed on his crutches. Stuart's three adult daughters and his son-in-law were seated at the table. The fugitives joined them and began their meal. Booth and Herold were an odd spectacle at Stuart's fine table. How out of place these haggard travelers seemed. Or did they? Yes, Herold was obviously a callow, verbose youth of the common class. But Booth's filthy clothes, unshaven face, and malodorous body could not camouflage who he really was. His cultivated manners, educated voice, and physical poise marked him as a gentleman. The dichotomy between Booth's appearance and his status must have puzzled his well-born tablemates.

It also puzzled Dr. Stuart. While the strangers dined, the doctor remained outside, chatting with William Bryant: "It is very strange," mused Stuart. "I know nothing about these men; I cannot accommodate them; you will have to take them somewhere else." Bryant professed that he did not know their names, either, that they emerged from the marshes near his house and asked to be taken to Dr. Stuart's. The doctor entered the house to check on his unwanted guests. When he stepped back outside, Bryant and the horses were gone! He exploited Stuart's brief disappearance into the house to skedaddle and abandon the problem to the doctor. Bryant had done what the strangers asked; his job here was done.

Stuart panicked. His eyes darted up the road and spotted Bryant two or three hundred yards away. Stuart started running and overtook Bryant: "You must take these men away," he pleaded. "I can't accommodate them." Stuart dashed back into the house to roust his guests. They had been inside a quarter of an hour. They had enjoyed their promised meal. They must leave—now: "The old man is waiting for you; he is anxious to be off; it is cold; he is not well, and wants to go home." Obeying, Booth and Herold rose from the table immediately and left the house without protest.

Once outside, they again asked Stuart for help: "It was after they got outside that they were so importunate that I should try to accommodate them." If Stuart wouldn't treat Booth's injury or let them spend the night, wouldn't he at least get them to Fredericksburg? Stuart rebuffed them again, offering only the possibility of help: "I told them that I had a neighbor near there, a colored man who sometimes hired his wagon, and probably he would do it if he was not very busy, and it would be no harm to try."

By now Stuart knew exactly who his visitors were. Obviously, they were not Confederate soldiers. That feeble ruse collapsed under superficial examination. The lame man was a well-spoken gentleman, his garrulous boy companion of humbler origins. Judging by their appearance, they had been living outdoors, without shelter, for a week or two. They had traveled south from Maryland into Virginia. They were desperate. And one had a broken leg. They fit the profiles of two men known to the whole country by now. Who could these men be but John Wilkes Booth and David Herold? Stuart dared not speak their names, but his eagerness to eject them from his land shows that he knew how dangerous they could be to him and his family: "I was suspicious of them. I did not know but they might be some of the characters who had been connected with the vile acts of assassination…which I had heard of a few days before."

Again Booth suffered "the cold hand they extend to me." Bryant and his charges departed Cleydael and rode on to the home of Stuart's "colored man," William Lucas.

$\mathcal{B}$RYANT, BOOTH, AND HEROLD APPROACHED THE HUMBLE Lucas cabin—a world removed from Dr. Stuart's opulent Cleydael estate—around midnight. It was quiet and dark inside. William, his wife, and his son were asleep. Davey leaned in close to the crude, barred plank door. "Lucas!" he called sharply. Herold's summons woke the dogs sleeping nearby, raising a chorus of barks. The hounds woke William Lucas, who, when he heard one of Bryant's horses neighing in the yard, suspected that thieves were after his team. Then again he heard a strange voice: "Lucas." He did not recognize the speaker and refused to unlock the door. "People had been shot that way," he reasoned.

Lucas demanded that the voice identify itself. Instead, the speaker, unwilling to disclose his identity, and communicating as through a secret code, uttered the names of three men and asked if Lucas knew them, implying through attitude of voice that he should. He didn't and became frightened. The strange voice must belong to a robber or a horse thief. There was no way that he would open his door to the mysterious, threatening stranger standing on the other side, inches away. The stranger called out a fourth name, William Bryant. Lucas knew this one, but what difference did that make? The stranger could have picked up the name anywhere. Then a second voice called out: Lucas. It is me, William Bryant. You know me. Relieved, Lucas unlocked the door, swung it open, and stepped outside. Bryant and two strangers stepped forward.

"We want to stay here tonight," the youngest member of the trio declared bluntly, omitting the courtesy of an introduction.

Bewildered by the unexpected request, and put off by Herold's rudeness, Lucas resisted: "You cannot do it. I am a colored man and have no right to take care of white people; I have only one room in the house and my wife is sick."

Herold became belligerent: "We are Confederate soldiers, we have been in service three years; we have been knocking about all night, and don't intend to any longer...we are going to stay."

Before Lucas could object again, Booth hobbled around him on his crutches, forced his way into the cabin, and claimed a chair.

Pursuing the lame man into his home, Lucas chastised them for their rudeness: "Gentlemen, you have treated me very badly."

Booth, seething from Dr. Stuart's rebuff, was in no mood for etiquette lessons from an impudent, free black man who did not know his place. How dare Dr. Stuart, lapsed gentleman, cast him into the night? Stuart had not heard the last from John Wilkes Booth. And how dare Stuart, adding insult to the injury, banish him to some Negro shack, degrading the great tragedian like a man of the lowest class and order, like some filthy beggar or runaway slave. "This country was formed for the *white,* not for the black man," Booth had declared in his secret political manifesto of 1864; "Nigger citizenship," he spewed venomously in response to Lincoln's April 11, 1865, speech. And now, here he sat, begging a black man for accommodations, and suffering insults in reply: Never!

Booth's simmering blood boiled over in a way it had not since the assassination night. Still seated, the actor froze William Lucas with a hateful stare while dropping his hand to his waist, his fingers feeling for the handle of his knife. He had not unsheathed it in anger since he baptized its razor-sharp blade with Major Rathbone's blood, now dried and still caked on the knife, partly obscuring its acid-etched, defiantly patriotic mottos. Booth could easily have cleansed the knife in Dr. Mudd's washbasin, or in the freshwater spring at the pine thicket, but chose not to. Instead, he cherished its stained, mirrored surface like a relic of a martyred saint, a vivid, tangible memento of the assassination. He had lost the ultrasouvenir—his Deringer—when he grappled with Rathbone in the president's box. But he still possessed the knife as a personal reminder that blood had been spilt, and there was no turning back: "I have done the deed," in the words of Macbeth. The bloody keepsake resonated like a symbolic stigmata of wounds not suffered, but inflicted, by the assassin's hand.

Booth's hand rose from his waistband until the quickly moving blade caught William Lucas's eye. "Old man, how do you like that?" Booth growled, waving the knife in the air.

"I do not like it at all!" pleaded Lucas, who was always terrified of knives.

Booth was one provocation away from unwinding another powerful, arcing swing of the blade, but he calmed himself. Murdering a black family in their cabin was sure to attract unwanted attention. And Booth considered himself in a class above the common cutthroat. As he argued in his datebook, his motives were purer than those of Brutus or

William Tell. Booth still burned at a world turned upside down, but reason dictated that he use, and not kill, William Lucas.

The actor sheathed the knife and assumed a less threatening guise. The point had been made, and Booth did not need to brandish the pistols and carbine. In the cabin's dim light, Lucas saw them clearly enough. Booth informed Lucas what they really wanted: "We were sent here, old man; we understand you have good teams." So it *was* the horses, Lucas thought, just as he feared when he heard the strange voice outside his door. Lucas pleaded with Booth to leave his horses alone, explaining that he had hired hands coming Monday to plant corn. Convinced that the strangers would try to steal the horses, Lucas spoke evasively and claimed that the animals were far away, in the pasture. It would be hard searching for them in the dark. Booth turned to Herold and closed the matter: "Well, Dave, we will not go on any further, but stay here and make this old man get us this horse in the morning." William Bryant, his task done, rode away, abandoning Lucas and his family to the strangers he had brought into their cabin.

Lucas was terrified to be alone with them and, fearing Booth's knife slitting his throat while he slept, he surrendered his cabin: "I was afraid to go to sleep and my wife and I went out on the step and stayed there the rest of the night."

In the morning, a little after 6:00, Booth and Herold ordered Lucas to get the horses. They hitched them to his wagon and climbed aboard. For the last time, Lucas beseeched them: were they really going to take his horses and not pay him? Feeling generous, Booth asked what price he charged for a ride to Port Conway, a small town on the Rappahannock River about ten miles away. Ten dollars in gold coins or $20 in greenbacks, quoted Lucas. But Booth and Herold were obviously taking a one-way trip; how would he get his horses and wagon back? He asked them to take his twenty-one-year-old son Charles along for the ride so the boy could bring the team home. Booth said no, but Herold, in rare dissent from his master, yielded: "Yes, he can go, as you have a large family and a crop on hand and you can have your team back again."

It was settled. Within minutes William Lucas would be free of Lincoln's assassins, patiently awaiting, with an extra $20 in his pocket, Charlie's return with the horses in a few hours. Then Lucas, still smarting from the indignity of his midnight eviction, made a mistake. He couldn't keep his mouth shut. He taunted the strangers about the Confederacy's defeat: "I thought you would be done pressing horses in the Northern Neck," he added, "since the fall of Richmond." Lucas's insolence enraged Booth, causing an eruption of his volcanic temper. Richmond? Did this damned black rascal dare mention Richmond? Asia Booth Clarke knew her brother's sensitivity on that subject. She described how their brother Junius, walking with Wilkes "one night...in the streets of Washington...beheld the tears run from his eyes as he turned his face towards Richmond, saying brokenly, 'Virginia—Virginia.' It was like the wail of a Roman father over his slaughtered child. This idealized city of his love had deeper hold upon his heart than any feminine beauty."

Ignorant of Booth's passion, Lucas could not have uttered a more dangerous provocation. Asia, however, recognized that the city's fall the week prior to Lincoln's assassination helped spur her brother to commit his great crime: "[T]he fall of Richmond rang in with maddening, exasperating clang of joy, and that triumphant entry into the fallen city...breathed air afresh upon the fire which consumed him." If Richmond's fall could provoke John Wilkes Booth to murder the president of the United States, how might Lucas's blasphemous slander provoke the assassin to punish *him*?

Booth's pitiless black eyes burned through Lucas like searing coals: "Repeat that again," he dared Lucas. One more insult, and Booth was ready to draw one of his revolvers and shoot the old man on the spot. Lucas knew he had made a terrible mistake. He had pushed Booth too far, and the actor was ready to explode in violence. Wisely, the old man backed off: "I said no more to him." Young Charlie Lucas climbed aboard the wagon and seized the reins, signaling his readiness to serve Booth and Herold by driving them to Port Conway or—at this tense moment—any place they wanted to go. Wordlessly, Booth reached under his coat and pulled out, not a revolver, but a wad of cash. Peeling off $20 in paper currency, he bent low and handed the money to Mrs. Lucas.

As the wagon rolled away around 7:00 A.M., it came to Booth; he knew how to deal with Dr. Stuart.

They reached Port Conway around noon, and Charlie steered the wagon toward the ferry landing, near the home of William Rollins. Booth asked Charlie to wait a few minutes before driving his father's wagon home. The actor wanted to write a letter to Dr. Stuart, and he wanted Charlie to deliver it.

A letter? John Wilkes Booth was running for his life. He didn't know where the manhunters were. The newspapers he read did not reveal their unit designations, their strength of numbers, or their search assignments. In his ignorance, and to ensure his survival, Booth had to assume that he might encounter Union troops and detectives at any moment, anywhere along his route. They might be behind him or lying in wait ahead of him. He was always in danger. Conceivably every minute might count, and even a slight delay might make the difference between freedom and death. Incredibly, foolishly, with his life at stake, Booth took time to indulge his undisciplined, theatrical impulses. He insisted on having the last word and upbraiding Stuart for his appalling, shameful manners. He opened his 1864 datebook to a blank page and began writing feverishly. After finishing the note, he read it over and, dissatisfied, ripped it out and tucked it out of sight inside one of the book's interior flaps. He started over, composed another note, and carefully removed the page.

Dated Monday, April 24, 1865, Booth's caustic rebuke assumed Shakespearean pretensions:

Dear Sir:

> *Forgive me, but I have some little pride. I hate to blame*
> *you for your want of hospitality: you know your own affairs. I*

*was sick and tired, with a broken leg, in need of medical
advice. I would not have turned a dog from my door in such
a condition. However, you were kind enough to give me something to eat, for which I not only thank you, but on account of
the reluctant manner in which it was bestowed, feel bound to
pay for it. It is not the substance, but the manner in which a
kindness is extended, that makes one happy for the acceptance
thereof. The sauce in meat is ceremony; meeting were bare
without it. Be kind enough to accept the enclosed two dollars
and a half (though hard to spare) for what we have received.*

Yours respectfully, STRANGER.

Booth judged Stuart guilty of committing the ultimate sin in gen-
teel Virginia society—inhospitality. It was the sort of accusation that,
leveled at a more leisurely time, might trigger a duel. Indeed, had Booth
more time, he might have tried to soliloquize the doctor in person.
Booth's letter climaxed with an insulting rebuke of offering to pay a
petty sum of *cash* in exchange for Stuart's grudging hospitality. Thespian to the end, Booth invoked Shakespeare to dramatize his point,
drawing his letter's penultimate "ceremony" line from *Macbeth,* act 3,
scene 4. There, Lady Macbeth, speaking at the haunted banquet that
followed her husband's murder of Duncan in his sleep, opined on, of all
things, proper hospitality: "The feast is sold / That is not often vouched,
while 'tis a-making, / 'Tis given with welcome. To feed were best at
home; / From thence, the sauce to meat is ceremony. / Meeting were
bare without it." Booth quoted the obscure phrase from memory nearly
perfectly, committing only the minor error of writing "in" instead of
"to" "meat."

In other words, Booth was saying that a feast seems grudgingly and
mercenarily given unless it is repeatedly graced with assurances of welcome. Plain eating is best done in one's own domestic setting; on more
social occasions, the spice to a feast is ceremony; gatherings are too un-
adorned without it.

Booth's two drafts differed little. The chief differences were in the sums of money Booth offered and the closing salutations. First Booth wrote "$5.00." On second thought he cut the sum in half. And perhaps he intended the smaller amount to augment the greater insult. Booth closed the first draft with "Most respectfully, your obedient servant." The actor judged that salutation too respectful to the unworthy doctor and substituted the less florid "Yours respectfully."

How strange, too, that in Booth's last writings—his journal entries and his final letter—he quoted from his victim's favorite texts. The cadences of the King James Bible resonated in many of Abraham Lincoln's finest writings, and his love of Shakespeare knew no bounds. During private, social evenings at the White House, the president often sat by the fire and read his aloud to his small, intimate circle of friends. In a letter to the celebrated actor James Henry Hackett, Lincoln expounded on his favorites: "Some of Shakespeare's plays I have never read; while others I have gone over perhaps as frequently as any unprofessional reader. Among the latter are *Lear, Richard Third, Henry Eighth, Hamlet,* and especially *Macbeth.* I think nothing equals *Macbeth.* It is wonderful."

It was *Macbeth* that Lincoln chose to read aloud to his guests on a Potomac cruise aboard the *River Queen* on Sunday five days before the assassination. One of the president's companions described that memorable performance:

On Sunday, April 9th, we were steaming up the Potomac. That whole day the conversation dwelt upon literary subjects. Mr. Lincoln read to us for several hours passages taken from Shakespeare. Most of these were from "Macbeth," and, in particular, the verses which follow Duncan's assassination. I cannot recall this reading without being awed at the remembrance, when Macbeth becomes king after the murder of Duncan, he falls prey to the most horrible torments of mind. Either because he was struck by the weird beauty of these verses, or from a vague presentiment coming over him, Mr. Lincoln paused here while reading, and began to explain to us how true a description of the murderer that one was; when, the dark deed achieved, its tortured perpetrator came to envy the sleep of his victim; and he read over again the same scene.

Gleeful at the prospect of taking symbolic revenge against Stuart, Booth folded two and a half dollars into a small, tight square and then wrapped his letter around the money. He called Charlie Lucas over and handed him the insulting ensemble. If only he could see Stuart's face when the old doctor read his rebuke, Booth gloated.

Charlie Lucas braked the wagon to a stop in front of the home of William Rollins, a former Port Conway store owner who made his living by fishing and farming. Booth and Herold did not know him. Rollins was in his backyard preparing his fishing nets and did not see the wagon's approach. When he walked around his house, he recognized William Lucas's horses. Then he saw the two strangers, David Herold standing at the gate, and another man sitting in the wagon. Herold asked an old man sitting nearby for some water, and the fellow filled a tin dipper to the rim and passed it to Herold. As Davey began walking to the wagon, the cup spilled over: "It is too full," he called out to Booth. "I'll drink some of it."

Thirsty, Booth yelled back, "Bring it down here."

Still holding the dipper, Herold turned to Rollins and asked if he knew anybody who could take them to Orange Court House. When Rollins said no, Herold asked if he would take them at least part of the way. Rollins offered to drive them to Bowling Green, about fifteen miles distant, for a fee. Intrigued, Herold invited Rollins to come over to the wagon and meet his friend. "This man says he has a wagon and will take us to Bowling Green for ten dollars," Herold reported, as he climbed aboard Lucas's wagon and surrendered the refreshing cup. Booth asked Rollins to confirm the distance, and the fisherman added, tantalizingly, that the Fredericksburg and Richmond railroad was just two and a half miles from there.

Then, improvidently, Herold asked if there was a hotel nearby where Booth could lay up his injured leg for a couple of days. He should have known there was no time for that. Perpetuating their masquerade as Confederate soldiers, Herold volunteered the familiar story: his companion had been wounded near Petersburg. Rollins told them about a hotel at Bowling Green. Then Booth switched subjects, inquiring whether Rollins would take him and Davey across the Rappahannock, only two or three hundred yards wide at this point, and land them on the other side at Port Royal. Rollins offered to do it for the same price that the ferry operating between Port Conway and Port Royal charged—ten cents one way. He would be happy to transport them in his boat after he went down to the river and put out his fishing nets. The tide was about to rise, and that meant prime fishing time.

Booth wanted to cross at once. As soon as the nets are set, Rollins reiterated. Frustrated, Booth tried to entice him with more money: "I don't want to be lying over here. We'll pay you more than the ferriage." The actor could not persuade him. The tide was rising now, and the fisherman wasn't going to miss out on a good catch. At that moment three mounted figures appeared on the hill just above Port Conway, about fifty yards from the river, and surveyed the town. They were soldiers. And a wagon down by the wharf, parked in front of William Rollins's house, caught their eye.

The men spurred their horses and descended slowly to Port Conway. When they got within twenty yards of the wagon, Herold jumped out and thrust his hand inside the breast of his coat. One of the men noticed Davey's clumsy, obvious move immediately. He had seen men draw pistols before. Another member of the trio took note of the wagon, which was drawn, he thought, "by two very wretched looking horses." Then they looked over to the man sitting in the wagon: "[He] was dressed in a dark suit that looked seamed and ravelly, as if from rough contact with thorny undergrowth. On his head was a seedy looking

black slouch hat, which he kept well pulled down over his forehead...
his beard, of a coal-black hue, was of about two weeks' growth and gave
his face an unclean appearance."

ON MONDAY, APRIL 24, DR. SAMUEL A. MUDD SAW SOLDIERS,
too. There would be no more questions today, no additional searches of
the house and outbuildings, no marathon, cat-and-mouse interrogations at Bryantown. The soldiers came to his farm to arrest him and
take him away to Washington. There he would languish, locked up in
the fearsome Old Capitol prison, across the street from the great dome,
shining symbol of the Union that he, John Wilkes Booth, and all the
others, had tried to topple. Confined incommunicado, Samuel A. Mudd
waited to learn what terrible price the government would seek to exact
from him.

BOOTH AND HEROLD HAD BEEN DREADING THIS MOMENT, IF
not at Port Conway, then somewhere along their escape route. It was
only a matter of time. Their first encounter with soldiers was inevitable.
Fate chose Port Conway. Booth and Herold tensed for action. As the
riders approached, Herold walked toward them, creating distance between them and Booth, and all the while scrutinizing their uniforms
and equipment. Their jackets did not look blue. Davey, adopting his
usual, disarming manner of the friendly sidekick, called out to the men:
"Gentlemen, whose command do you belong to?"

One of them, an officer, responded: "To Mosby's command."

Herold was relieved. They were Confederates!

These men weren't just everyday soldiers. Even though two of them
were eighteen years old and one was nineteen years old, First Lieutenant
Mortimer B. Ruggles, Private Absalom R. Bainbridge, and Private William S. Jett were veterans of one of the Confederacy's most elite, renowned cavalry units, commanded by the legendary John Singleton

Mosby. Herold was elated: "If I am not inquisitive," he asked Ruggles, "can I ask you where you are going?"

William Jett jumped in: "That is a secret. Nobody knows where we are going because I never tell anybody." And who was asking? They decided to turn the tables on the stranger and asked him to what command did *he* belong?

Davey performed well: "We belong to A. P. Hill's Corps; I have my wounded brother a Marylander who was wounded in the fight below Petersburg."

Where is this wound? queried Jett.

"In the leg." Jett pursued the interrogation and requested their names.

"Our name is Boyd; his name is James William Boyd and mine is David E. Boyd." Herold assumed the guise of an enthusiastic Confederate, a militant bitter-ender, zealous to continue the fight, wherever it was. "Come gentlemen I suppose you are all going to the Southern Army," Herold ventured confidentially, adding that "we are also anxious to get over there ourselves and wish you to take us along with you."

Booth struggled out of the wagon, propped himself up on his crutches, and began walking toward them.

Mosby's men thought Herold was odd and overeager and did not reply to him or dismount their horses. Guessing that this was the opportune moment for some social lubrication, Davey played host: "Come gentlemen, get down; we have got something to drink here; we will go and take a drink."

Jett declined curtly: "Thank you Sir, I never drink anything." Jett rode about twenty yards away from Herold, dismounted, and tied his horse to a gate. Ruggles and Bainbridge dismounted and sat on Rollins's steps.

As soon as Jett rejoined the group, Herold tapped him on the shoulder and asked if they could speak privately. They walked to the wharf, and Herold proposed a plan: "I take it for granted that you are raising a command to go south to Mexico and I want you to let us go with you."

Real soldiers did not talk this way, Jett knew: "I was thrown aback that such an idea should have entered any man's head." The verbose "David E. Boyd," if that was his true name, was holding something back. "I cannot go with any man that I do not know anything about," Jett explained. He stared Herold down and asked a simple question: "Who are you?"

"We are," Herold spouted excitedly in a trembling voice, "the assassinators of the president." Herold pointed to where Booth stood some yards off. "Yonder is the assassinator! Yonder is J. Wilkes Booth, the man who killed the president."

Dumbstruck, Private William Jett did not say a word. Interpreting Jett's silence as a sign of disbelief, Herold asked him if he had noticed Booth's indelible proof of identity—the initials "JWB" tattoed on his left hand. Ruggles walked up to Herold and Jett, but Jett found that all he could do was mumble to his friend "here is a strange thing." Then they told Ruggles the stunning news. Booth was just a few feet away, swinging forward on the crutches. Within seconds they were face-to-face with Lincoln's assassin, his marked hand hidden discreetly by a shawl.

"I suppose you have been told who I am?" Booth asked.

Ruggles was transfixed: "Instantly he dropped his weight back upon his crutch, and drawing a revolver said sternly, with the utmost coolness, 'Yes, I am John Wilkes Booth, the slayer of Abraham Lincoln, and I am worth just $175,000 to the man who captures me.'"

"Do you wish to go over the river now, sir?" an approaching voice interrupted. It was William Rollins, back from setting his nets. He had walked to his house, gotten his coat, and called down to Booth at the ferryboat landing where the assassin stood with Herold and the soldiers.

"Yes," Booth shouted back.

"Come on then," Rollins beckoned.

But Booth hesitated and inched closer to Herold and the soldiers.

Rollins shouted out to Booth again: "If you wish to go over the river, come on."

Herold spoke for his master: "If you are in a hurry go on; we are not going over now." Instead, the fugitives huddled with Ruggles, Jett, and Bainbridge, concocting an alternative scheme. They told the trio that they wanted to throw themselves entirely upon their protection. Jett agreed to help, and Ruggles vouchsafed their fidelity: "We were not men to take 'blood money.'" The soldiers promised to accompany the assassins across the river in the ferryboat and help them on the other side.

Booth had won their loyalty not by mesmerizing them with the riveting story of how he had struck down the president, but with his laconic, stoic demeanor. The assassin confided to William Jett that he thought the murder "was nothing to brag about," and the soldier agreed: "I do not either." Ruggles noticed about Booth the same thing his comrades did—the actor was in agony, but he took it like a man: "I noticed that his wounded leg was greatly swollen, inflamed, and dark, as from bruised blood, while it seemed to have been wretchedly dressed, the splints being simply pasteboard rudely tied about it. That he suffered intense pain all the time there was no doubt, though he tried to conceal his agony, both physical and mental."

Booth's confession took them by surprise, and the fact that they were standing in the presence of—and even conversing with—Lincoln's assassin stunned them. But Ruggles could not help admiring him: "[T]he coolness of the man won our admiration; for we saw that he was wounded, desperate, and at bay. His face was haggard, pinched with suffering, his dark eyes sunken, but strangely bright."

Before departing on the ferry, Herold and Jett walked back to Rollins's place, found him outside, and made a curious request: did he have a bottle of ink? Rollins led them into the house, took a small bottle from the mantel, and laid it on the table. Jett sat in a chair, set out a piece of paper, and began writing. Herold told Jett to let him do it, and Jett tore off the part of the paper he had already written on. Herold copied it, writing five or six lines. They had forged an army parole document for Jett in case he encountered Union troops.

The ferryboat had almost reached the Port Conway side of the river.

Time to cross over to Port Royal. Herold picked up his carbine, wound the white, cotton sling around his shoulders, and again told Rollins that he and his friend did not need a ride: "I have met with some friends out here and they say it is not worth while to hire a wagon to go on to Bowling Green, as we can all go along together and ride and tie." As Davey gathered his blanket, Rollins, admiring its luxurious shag finish on one side, made the oddest compliment.

"That's a very nice concern you've got there," he said.

"Yes, a lady in Maryland gave me that," Herold acknowledged proudly.

James Thornton, a free black man who operated the ferry for its owner, Champe Thornton, piloted the craft to the wharf. David Herold dismissed the wagon and Charlie Lucas turned his team around and headed for home. Herold reminded him to deliver Mr. Boyd's letter to Dr. Stuart. Booth explained to Ruggles that he was unable to walk anymore, so the lieutenant lifted him onto his horse and prepared to board. James Thornton opened the gate and ushered the waiting customers— five men and three horses—aboard. To Thornton, the strangers appeared unremarkable—just another band of bedraggled rebels heading home after losing the war.

Herold, Jett, and Bainbridge stepped onto the flat, wood planks of the ferry's bottom, the two Confederates leading their horses by the reins. Ruggles, also on foot, carried Booth's crutches, Herold carried the carbine, and Booth had the pistols and knife. Ruggles noticed that Major Rathbone's blood was still on the blade. Around his neck Booth suspended the field glasses from a leather strap joined by an adjustable metal buckle. Ignoring ferry rules, the assassin, who wanted to avoid the searing pain that accompanied every mount and dismount of the horse, refused to get out of the saddle and he rode Ruggles's horse right onto the barge. Mounted men made the ferry top-heavy, but Thornton let Booth's infraction slide. Later, after it was all over, showman P. T. Barnum offered Ruggles a nice price for the saddle graced by John Wilkes Booth's posterior during the short ferry trip.

With his passengers all aboard, Thornton cut loose from the wharf and eased the slow-moving, awkward craft across the Rappahannock to the old, dilapidated colonial town of Port Royal. During the crossing the men hardly spoke, not wanting the colored man to learn anything about them. Bainbridge became suspicious of Thornton, anyway: "The ferryman eyed us all very closely and we said but very little." Bainbridge unglued his eyes from Thornton and witnessed, as the actor towered over them, a memorable scene: "Booth sat squarely on his horse, looking expectantly towards the opposite shore." As soon at they landed and Thornton opened the gate, Booth spurred Ruggles's horse onto the wharf.

The assassin was in good spirits again, and he laughed as Herold and their new friends gathered around him to celebrate the successful crossing. Broaching the humble Rappahannock was no great feat in itself, but it represented the culmination of this phase of the escape. Booth and Herold had crossed the mighty Potomac, escaped from Maryland, landed in Virginia, found—finally, after suffering bitter disappointments—loyal Confederate comrades, and passed safely south through the state's northern neck. Now, south of the Rappahannock, John Wilkes Booth looked forward to a swift journey through open country, to the interior of the Old Dominion. Overcome with emotion, Booth sang out: "I'm safe in glorious old Virginia, thank God!"

Or was he? There was something about young Willie Jett that Booth did not know. Had he known it, the assassin would have fled from this boy's company faster than he had galloped away from Ford's Theatre. Booth might have even shot him for it. On the surface, the thing seemed innocuous, even innocent. Neither Booth nor Jett knew it yet, but their meeting had set in motion a chain of events that would lead to the actor's downfall.

For now all was well and Jett led the caravan a few blocks to the Port Royal home of Randolph Peyton. Jett knew him and thought he would take them in. Before Jett approached the house, Booth asked him to continue the ruse and introduce him as a wounded Confederate soldier named James Boyd. Peyton's two spinster sisters, Sarah Jane and Lucy, answered the door. Jett asked if they would be kind enough to give shelter for two nights to a wounded Confederate soldier and his brother. The Peytons agreed to take the strangers in, and Jett beckoned Booth to come forward. Booth hobbled inside and reclined on a chaise lounge. It was the first time he had stretched out on a piece of furniture since he napped on the upholstered, black horsehair sofa in Dr. Mudd's front parlor. After a few minutes Sarah Jane called Jett aside. She wanted to speak to him alone in the parlor. On second thought, she explained, this man could not stay here. Her brother Randolph was away at his farm and would not be back tonight. It was not right, without their brother at home, to permit strangers to sleep in the same house with two unmarried women. Regrettably, Sarah Jane informed Jett, she must rescind her premature offer of hospitality. She hated to say no to a wounded Confederate soldier, but in her brother's absence, she had no choice.

Jett accepted the refusal graciously. Making a scene would do no good. He asked if the Peytons' neighbors across the street, the Catlitts, might take in Mr. Boyd. Sarah Jane said she did not know. Jett elected to try but discovered that, like Randolph Peyton, Mr. Catlitt was not home. Sarah Jane made a helpful suggestion: "You can get him in anywhere up the road—Mr. Garrett's or anywhere else." Jett agreed to try. At around 1:00 P.M. he helped Booth rise from the Peytons' chaise lounge and stand up on his crutches. As they walked outside, Jett called to their comrades: "Boys, ride on further up to road." After putting Booth on Ruggles's horse, the men doubled up on the two remaining animals, Herold riding behind Jett, and Ruggles behind Bainbridge.

*T*HREE AND A HALF MILES AWAY, RICHARD H. GARRETT presided over his five-hundred-acre farm, Locust Hill. It was a happy time. His two eldest sons, both in Confederate service, had just come home from the war. The caravan of riders, pacing slowly from Port Royal to the southwest, arrived in the late afternoon. David Herold jumped off Jett's horse as soon as they passed the gate, and loitered near the road with Bainbridge, who dismounted and gave his horse to Booth. Jett, Booth, and Ruggles rode on to the house. As he had with Miss Sarah Jane Peyton, Booth asked Jett to introduce him by his pseudonym. Willie Jett introduced himself to Mr. Garrett from the saddle and then presented James Boyd: "Here is a wounded Confederate soldier that we want you to take care of for a day or so: will you do it?"

Garrett thought of his sons, who had returned safely just a few days ago. He would return that blessing with a kindness: "Yes, certainly I will."

Around three o'clock in the afternoon of Monday, April 24, John Wilkes Booth had found refuge for the night. And he had survived another day.

Booth got down from Ruggles's horse. Their mission accomplished, the Confederates wanted to push on. Jett and Ruggles bade the assassin a quick farewell—"we will see you again"—and trotted away from Locust Hill, leading Bainbridge's riderless horse by the reins. Unbeknownst to Booth, Willie Jett had no intention of returning to Garrett's farm or of ever seeing the assassin again. When Jett and Ruggles reached the gate, they reined their horses to a stop. Bainbridge mounted up and David Herold clambered on, riding double with him. Davey wanted to accompany them to Bowling Green to purchase, of all things, a new pair of shoes. He decided to spend the night with the young Confederates and rejoin Booth tomorrow, April 25, at Garrett's farm.

Almost like a jealous younger brother showing off, Herold boasted to Jett that he, too, had a tattoo, just like Booth. Indeed, Booth had only one, but Davey had two. He rolled up both coat sleeves above the elbow and displayed a heart and anchor on his right arm and his initials, "DEH," on his left. Jett noticed that the "H," although still legible, was blurry: during his idle time in the pine thicket Davy had rubbed it for hours, trying desperately to erase the identifying mark with friction and heat.

The presence of Booth, Jett, and Ruggles in the Garretts' front yard had provoked a dog's bark, and the sound alerted John M. Garrett, one of Richard's sons, who was lying down in an upstairs bedroom. John had joined the Confederate army at the beginning of the war in 1861, serving first in the Fredericksburg Artillery and then in Lightfoot's Battalion. He was active for the duration until Lee's surrender on April 9, when he returned to the family farm. Looking out the window a little after 3:00 P.M., he saw a man with two crutches, who was leaning on only one. The man was wrapped in a gray shawl and was standing near his father, while two men on horseback were talking. In a few minutes, the mounted men rode off, taking the lame man's horse with them. John watched as his father and the stranger walked toward the house. It all seemed normal enough, and John Garrett returned to his bed.

Booth and old man Garrett lounged on the front porch, which extended along the length of the house. In about half an hour, a little after 3:30 P.M., John Garrett came downstairs and walked out the front door to spend the evening with a neighbor. His father introduced him to James Boyd. Neither father nor son suspected that Boyd was anyone other than who he said he was—a simple Confederate veteran, making his way home.

Chapter Nine

"Useless, Useless"

—◆◈◆—

B OOTH HAD BEEN LUCKY. ON APRIL 24, THE MAJORITY OF THE manhunters were still spinning their wheels in Maryland, uncertain whether their quarry had crossed the Potomac. Compared with the level of activity in Maryland, Virginia's northern neck was still lightly patrolled. That was about to change.

That morning, Major James O'Beirne had a telegram sent to the War Department telegraph office in Washington. It was this office that, on the night of the assassination, sent Stanton's telegrams that broke the news to military commanders, and to the nation. It was this office that transmitted Stanton's orders to begin the manhunt. And from this office came the news flash that the president was dead. Now, ten days later, Major Thomas Eckert, head of the telegraph office, received a message from Major O'Beirne that galvanized the manhunt. Two men, reported O'Beirne, had been seen crossing the Potomac on April 16. If those men were Booth and Herold, then Lincoln's assassin had been in Virginia for the past eight days. This report required action.

And Colonel Lafayette C. Baker just happened to be on the scene when the telegraph arrived. The notorious detective and War Department "agent," and a favorite of Stanton's, had been in town since April 16, in response to Stanton's dramatic telegram summoning him from New York to join the manhunt and find the murderers of the president.

Since his arrival his imperious, deceitful, and self-promoting demeanor had rubbed a number of the hunters the wrong way. He tried to steal other detectives' leads and, without prior authorization, he had even issued a $30,000 reward proclamation of his own. He was snooping around the telegraph office when Eckert heard from O'Beirne. Baker read the message:

PORT TOBACCO, MD., April 24, 1865 10 A.M.
(Received 11 A.M.)

Major ECKERT:
Have just met Major O'Beirne, whose force had arrested Doctor Mudd and Thompson. Mudd set Booth's left leg (fractured), furnished crutches, and helped him and Herold off. They have been tracked as far as the swamp near Bryantown, and under one theory it is possible they may be still concealed in swamp which leads from Bryantown to Allen's Fresh, or in neck of land between Wicomico and Potomac Rivers. Other evidence leads to the belief that they crossed from Swan Point to White Point, Va., on Sunday morning, April 16, about 9:30, in a small boat, also captured by Major O'Beirne. John M. Lloyd has been arrested, and virtually acknowledged complicity. I will continue with Major O'Beirne, in whom I have very great confidence. We propose first to thoroughly scour swamp and country to-day, and if unsuccessful and additional evidence will justify it, we then propose to cross with force into Virginia and follow up that trail as long as there is any hope. At all events we will keep moving, and if there is any chance you may rely upon our making most of it. Country here is being thoroughly scoured by infantry and cavalry.

S.H. BECKWITH

Baker seized the telegram, rushed back to his Pennsylvania Avenue headquarters across the street from Willard's, and told his cousin, Detective Luther Byron Baker, the news.

"We have got a sure thing," Lafayette said, "I think Booth has crossed the river, and I want you to go right out."

"There are no men to go with me."

"We will have some soldiers detailed." Lafayette begin writing a request for troops to General Hancock. "Is there no one in the office who can go with you," he asked his cousin.

"No one but Colonel Conger," Luther replied.

"Can he ride?"

"I think so."

There was just one problem with O'Beirne's clue. Yes, two men had been seen crossing the river on April 16. But they were not John Wilkes Booth and David Herold.

AROUND THE SAME TIME THAT BOOTH ARRIVED AT Garrett's farm, an unsuspecting young army officer in Washington, D.C., got swept up in the manhunt's whirlwind. On the afternoon of April 24, capturing Lincoln's killer was the last thing on the mind of Lieutenant Edward P. Doherty, a company commander in the Sixteenth New York Cavalry regiment. While others took up the frenzied pursuit of John Wilkes Booth, Doherty's unit had not received orders to join the chase. Instead, he whiled away the time enjoying the spring afternoon: "I was seated, with another officer ... on a bench in the park opposite the White House."

A messenger tracked him down, interrupting his leisure with an urgent, written message: "HEADQUARTERS, DEPARTMENT OF WASHINGTON / April 24, 1865 / Commanding Officer 16th New York Cavalry / Sir: You will at once detail a reliable and discreet commissioned officer with twenty-five men, well mounted, with three days' rations and forage, to report at once to Colonel L. C. Baker, Agent of the

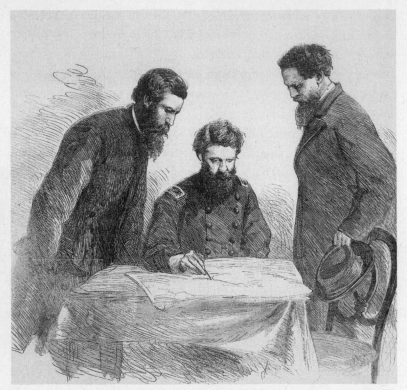

Luther Baker, Lafayette Baker, and Everton Conger
pose as manhunters for *Harper's Weekly*.

War Department, at 211 Pennsylvania Ave. / Command of General C. C. Augur." Doherty's commanding officer, Colonel N. B. Sweitzer, had annotated the order and assigned the mission to Doherty: "In accordance with the foregoing order First Lieutenant E. P. Doherty is hereby detailed for the duty, and will report at once to Colonel Baker."

Doherty rushed back to his barracks, ordered his bugler to blow "boots and saddles," and he took the first twenty-six men who jumped to the call. Doherty wondered what this mission was about, but it was not the business of a lowly lieutenant to ask questions. He would find out soon enough, when he arrived at Baker's headquarters. Within half an hour the lieutenant and his detail reported to Colonel Baker, who handed him freshly printed, paper carte-de-visite photographs of three men. Doherty failed to recognize two of them—they were standing poses and the faces were tiny—but the clearer image of the third man electrified him. It was John Wilkes Booth. He was going after Lincoln's assassin!

But not by himself, Lafayette Baker admonished him. He was to take two detectives with him, Lafayette's cousin, Luther Byron Baker, and Everton J. Conger, a former cavalry colonel from the 1st District of Columbia Cavalry. Colonel Baker decided to stay behind in Washington, where he could continue to intercept telegrams and also safeguard his interest in the reward money. Colonel Baker gave Doherty his destination, and with that the twenty-six-man detachment of the Sixteenth New York Cavalry, accompanied by two detectives, began its pursuit of Lincoln's assassin. Doherty led his men to the Sixth Street wharf, where they boarded the steamer *John S. Ide*—an unusual name that combined the assassin's first name with an insinuation of the ides of March and Julius Caesar's misfortune. The vessel plied the waters of Aquia Creek and landed at the wharf at Belle Plaine, Virginia, where the troops disembarked and traveled overland, south toward Fredericksburg. If they kept moving, the troopers of the Sixteenth New York would reach Port Conway, where Booth and Herold had crossed the Rappahannock, by tomorrow afternoon, April 25.

$\mathcal{N}$o ONE IN WASHINGTON WAS CONFIDENT THAT THE SIXteenth New York Cavalry was on Booth's trail. And Stanton's dramatic—and lucrative—four-day-old proclamation of April 20 had still not resulted in Booth's capture. The War Department issued a new proclamation on April 24. This one offered no additional rewards and appealed not to greed but to the patriotism of the black population of Washington, Maryland, and Virginia.

THE MURDER OF PRESIDENT LINCOLN.
APPEAL TO THE COLORED PEOPLE!
HEADQUARTERS MIDDLE MILITARY DIVISION,
Washington, D.C., April 24, 1865.

To the colored people of the District of Columbia and of Maryland, of Alexandria and the border counties of Virginia:

Your President has been murdered! He has fallen by the assassin and without a moment's warning, simply and solely because he was your friend and the friend of our country. Had he been unfaithful to you and to the great cause of human freedom he might have lived. The pistol from which he met his death, though held by Booth, was fired by the hands of treason and slavery. Think of this and remember how long and how anxiously this good man labored to break your chains and to make you happy. I now appeal to you, by every consideration which can move loyal and grateful hearts, to aid in discovering and arresting his murderer. Concealed by traitors, he is believed to be lurking somewhere within the limits of the District of Columbia, of the State of Maryland, or Virginia. Go forth, then, and watch, and listen, and inquire, and search, and pray, by day and night, until you shall have succeeded in dragging this monstrous and bloody criminal from his hiding place. You can do much; even the humblest and feeblest among you, by patience and unwearied vigilance, may render the most important assistance.

Large rewards have been offered by the Government, and by municipal authorities, and they will be paid for the apprehension of this murderer, or for any information which will aid in his arrest. But I feel that you need no such stimulus as this. You will hunt down this cowardly assassin of your best friend, as you would the murderer of your own father. Do this, and God, whose servant has been slain, and the country which has given you freedom, will bless you for this noble act of duty.

All information which may lead to the arrest of Booth, or Surratt, or Harold, should be communicated to these headquarters, or to General

Holt, Judge Advocate General, at Washington, or, if immediate action is required, then to the nearest military authorities.

All officers and soldiers in this command, and all loyal people, are enjoined to increased vigilance.

W. S. HANCOCK
Major General U.S. Volunteers
Commanding Middle Military Division

Hancock had the text set in type, the crude layout evidence of the haste with which it was produced. Then he had his proclamation printed as one-page, letter-size handbills or broadsides, which were distributed by his men to the black people of Washington, D.C.; Maryland; and Virginia. Hancock's instinct that Booth could not escape without encountering blacks was correct—the assassin had been seen by a number of them—and perhaps, Hancock reasoned, his call to action might inspire someone to hunt down Booth, or at least to inform on him.

On THE EVENING OF APRIL 24, BEFORE IT GOT DARK, RICHARD Garrett invited his guest inside for supper. Booth took pleasure in the old man's genuine hospitality, so different from Dr. Stuart's cold hand. No one at the Garrett table hurried him to wolf down his meal and get out of the house. Instead, Booth savored his leisurely supper and the friendly company and engaged the family in harmless small talk. John Garrett returned home after dark and found that Boyd was still at the table with his entire family—his father, Richard; and stepmother, Fannie; his younger brothers, William and Richard; three sisters; and Miss Lucinda K. B. Holloway, Fannie's unmarried sister and the children's live-in tutor. After supper Booth hobbled outside, sat on the wood front steps, and removed a pipe from one of his coat pockets. Could John

Garrett spare some tobacco and a match? Booth wondered. In no time the assassin ignited a bowl of Virginia tobacco, cured in a local barn— perhaps the Garretts' own, before they stopped drying the leaves there—and enjoyed his first smoke in days. Booth luxuriated in a blissful respite from the manhunt and found a temporary peace on the front porch of this quiet, remote Caroline County farmhouse, a satisfying meal settling in his belly, the sweet aroma of pipe tobacco pleasuring his senses.

John Garrett suggested that they retire and invited Booth to share his room. Booth would sleep in a real bed tonight. Relying on his good, weight-bearing leg, he walked and half jumped up the stairs to the second floor. Booth stripped off his frock coat and unbuttoned his vest, exposing to Garrett a leather belt supporting two revolvers and a Bowie knife. Booth draped his clothes over a chair and unbuckled his pistol belt, which he hung over the headboard of one of the two beds in the room. The Garrett farmhouse might be a peaceful sanctuary, but the assassin wanted his weapons close by and within a quick arm's reach while he slept. Who knew what trouble the night might bring?

$\mathcal{B}$OOTH SAT IN A CHAIR AND ASKED GARRETT TO HELP HIM pull off his tall, knee-high, leather riding boot. Garrett took a good hold and yanked hard until the snugly fitting boot popped off. On his other foot Booth wore a government-issue leather army shoe, slit open at the top to make taking it on and off easier. When Booth slipped out of his trousers, Garrett got a close look at the bad leg and asked how it had happened. Given John Garrett's four years of service, Booth knew he had to talk convincingly to fool a man who had seen real war wounds before. His story worked again: "He told me that he was wounded at the evacuation of Petersburg. He…kept up the impression all along that he had been a Confederate soldier, and he now said that he had belonged to A. P. Hill's corps, and that he had been wounded by a shell fragment at the evacuation of Petersburg. He said his wound was not very painful except when he touched it."

Garrett offered Booth one of the beds, and he and his brother William shared the other. Their guest was exhausted. Booth got into bed, turned over, and spoke just two words: "Good night." John Garrett assumed, correctly, that Mr. Boyd wanted to speak no more that night. The soft mattress and pillow lulled Booth to a quick slumber. It was his first night in a proper bed—not counting one night in the rude Lucas cabin—since April 15, nine days ago. It felt good to rise from the cold earth and sleep like a civilized man again. It was also the first night of the manhunt that Booth and Herold spent apart.

At Belle Plaine the manhunters had divided their forces, too. Two columns, one of five men commanded by Everton Conger, and the other with the rest of the men, led by Edward Doherty, both probed south. The cavalrymen searched farmhouses and barns, questioned inhabitants, and sometimes adopted various ruses to trick the locals. As the Sixteenth New York worked all night toward Port Conway, Booth's hard-won head start from the manhunters began to shrink. It had taken Booth ten days to travel from downtown Washington to the Port Conway ferry. It would take the Sixteenth New York, alerted by telegraph and transported by steamboat, just one day to close the gap between Washington and Port Conway. The same superior technology that the Union had used to defeat the Confederacy was now employed against Booth.

Booth's mind surrendered to fatigue and roamed freely through the landscape of his dreams, where no man could follow him. He did not need his pistols during the night. He slept deeply and undisturbed and did not awaken until late in the morning on Tuesday, April 25. It was the eleventh sunrise since the assassination. John Garrett awoke early. Observing their guest still fast asleep, he dressed quietly and went downstairs. When William Garrett followed his brother down a few minutes later, Booth was still asleep. The actor was unaccustomed to farmers' hours. His body followed the nighttime rhythms of the city and theatre life, not the crack-of-dawn rigors of country living. William told his eleven-year-old brother Richard to watch over Booth until he awoke, then bring their guest his crutches and gun belt and wait on him while he dressed. William left the house to graze the cattle before returning for breakfast.

When Booth failed to answer the breakfast call, John Garrett went upstairs to check on him. Booth, awakened by the summons echoing through the house, had just gotten up. Garrett told him that breakfast was ready, but Booth, still weary, begged off. Please tell the family not to hold the meal for him, he requested. That was fine, replied Garrett: "[I]t was entirely unnecessary as we were not in the habit of waiting meals for soldiers as they were privileged characters and might eat when they got ready." John Garrett walked downstairs, ate, and rode over to Mr. Acres, a neighborhood shoemaker, to have a pair of boots repaired.

Eventually Booth roused himself. Little Richard Garrett fetched his clothes and crutches and helped him dress. Booth sat in the chair, inserted his leg into the tall boot and, unable to use his bad leg for leverage, pulled extra hard with his arm and back muscles. Delicately, he slipped the foot of his broken leg into the low-cut shoe. He eyed his pistol belt, still hanging on the headboard. He decided that he would not need his revolvers or Bowie knife this morning. He left the belt on the bed. He stood up, took the crutches, and, unarmed, proceeded downstairs, careful not to misstep and tumble down the stairs. Booth headed to the front porch, reached into a pocket for his pipe and a pinch of tobacco, and enjoyed a late-morning smoke. After he finished off the bowl, Booth stepped down to the front yard and inspected the property a little, venturing to the barn and back. On the front porch he reclined on a bench and promptly dozed off. His spent body and overtaxed brain craved the rejuvenating sleep.

When Booth woke up, William Garrett joined him on the porch. William asked the same question that his brother posed last night: where had he been wounded? On cue, the actor trotted out the stock story about Petersburg, the exploding artillery shell, the leg wound. Why did William ask? Hadn't his brother already told him this morning what Booth had said the night before? Booth, perhaps suspicious that William was testing him for any discrepancies in his story, spun a convoluted tale to explain how he ended up at Locust Hill.

It all started at Petersburg, began Booth, showing William his injured leg for effect. After the evacuation of that city, he wanted to go to Annapolis, Maryland. He crossed the Potomac but then discovered that the federals were forcing all Confederate soldiers to swear a loyalty oath to the Union, and of course he would never agree to that. Booth claimed that until a few days ago, he had taken refuge in a small, unnamed Maryland town. Then he and his cousin, also named Boyd, went on a "spree," hired two horses, and encountered some Union cavalry troops. Unwisely, they boasted to their former enemies how easily they had crossed the Potomac. This riled the cavalrymen, who informed on them and triggered a subsequent pursuit. Booth laid it on thick for Garrett now. When the cavalry caught up with them, they got into a "fracas" that led to "a little shooting touch" before they escaped by fleeing into a swamp, where they spent the night. The next evening, Booth explained, he and his cousin tied their horses in a pine thicket and walked down to the Potomac River, where they had to spend almost all of their money to buy a boat, to cross back over to Virginia. But it was a stormy eve, and they spent all night on the river without crossing, instead finding themselves opposite Mathias Point. Then, finally, reaching the point, they made their way to Port Royal, and the Garrett farm.

It was a wild, deceitful tale, sprinkled cleverly with sufficient truthful details—Booth was chased by cavalry, he did travel with another man, he did cross a swamp, he did hide in the pines, he did buy a boat, and he did cross the Potomac—that it seemed believable, or at least coherent. Booth told this complex tale to establish in Garrett's mind two vital ideas, one true, the other false: the truth that the Union cavalry was after him, and the lie about why. Booth wanted William Garrett to know, by his own admission, before William discovered it later on his own, that the cavalry might be coming. And he wanted him to believe that it was for a trivial reason. That way, if horse soldiers did arrive in the neighborhood, asking questions about two men, William Garrett would not be surprised, and he would never suspect that his house-guests were Lincoln's assassins. William Garrett did not challenge the saga's authenticity. Booth, satisfied that he had accomplished his purpose, got up from the porch and, with the help of his crutches, went for another solitary walk, again in the direction of the barn. Then Booth returned to the house and sat down on the lawn with the young Garrett children.

IT WAS A BEAUTIFUL DAY, REMEMBERED ELEVEN-YEAR-OLD Richard Baynham Garrett: "That day was bright and warm. It was an unusually early spring that year, and the grass in the yard was like velvet, while the great orchard in front of the house was white with apple blossoms." Booth relaxed by entertaining his little audience. "All the forenoon," recalled Richard Garrett, "our visitor lounged upon the grass under the apple trees and talked or played with the children...he had a pocket compass, which he took pains to explain to the children, and laughed at their puzzled faces when he made the needle move by holding the point of his pocket knife above it." Booth took special delight in three-year-old Cora Lee Garrett. "He called her his little blue-eyed pet," recalled her nine-year-old sister Lillian Florence Garrett, or Lillie. "At the last meal he took with us, she sat by his side in her high chair." At the dinner table, Cora's mother spoke sharply to the girl and, Lillie reported, the child "burst into tears. Booth at once began to soothe her, and said, "'What, is that my little blue eyes crying?'"

Early in the afternoon the Garretts and their guest took their seats at the dinner table. John, back from Acres the shoemaker, sat down next to his brother William, and opposite Booth. He had heard some exciting news while on his errand, John announced. A man told him that a recent issue of a Richmond newspaper reported that the U.S. government was offering a $140,000 reward for Abraham Lincoln's assassin. The Garretts had heard rumors about the murder as early as April 22 or 23, but without confirmation until John heard the story about the reward a couple of hours ago. William boasted that if the reward was that big, the assassin "had better not come this way or he would be gobbled up." Booth smiled wryly. How much was that reward, again? he asked. John restated the figure. "I would sooner suppose more like $500,000," suggested Booth, suppressing mild hurt at what he felt was too modest an amount. Surely the president's assassin, the most wanted man in America, was worth more than $140,000? Had Booth known the true, much lower figure—a mere $50,000—he would have been truly insulted.

The family began a lively discussion of the assassination. "While at dinner the tragic event was commented upon, as to the motive which prompted the deed and its effect upon the public welfare," Lucinda Holloway observed. Booth listened attentively, not speaking a word. Then one of Garrett's daughters suggested that Lincoln's assassin must have been a paid killer.

Booth gazed at the girl, smiled, and broke his silence: "Do you think so, Miss? By whom do you suppose he was paid?"

"Oh," she replied witlessly, "I suppose by both the North and the South."

"It is my opinion," Booth replied knowingly, "he wasn't paid a cent." Instead, he speculated, the assassin "did it for notoriety's sake."

Booth improvised this little bit of theatre flawlessly. The Garretts did not know it, but the actor-assassin had just staged a spontaneous, unscripted performance at their dinner table. "I did not notice any uneasiness about him," admitted John Garrett.

Ingeniously, while masquerading as another man, the assassin commented on his own crime, and analyzed, for the pleasure of his private audience, and also for his personal amusement, the motives of Lincoln's killer.

After dinner Booth went outside and relaxed on the porch bench, by now his favorite place at the house. He was in no hurry to leave Locust

Hill. He needed rest. Considering his ordeal over the last eleven days, he would happily spend a month with the Garretts recuperating from his injury and regaining his strength. Plenty of sleep, good cooking, some pipe tobacco, clean clothes, and leisurely rests in the fields would revive his body and spirit. And perhaps an occasional shot of whiskey or brandy, his favorites. Reluctant to break the spell of this idyll, Booth said nothing to the Garretts all morning or at the afternoon dinner table about leaving Locust Hill.

But it was time. Booth asked John Garrett if he had a map of Virginia. Booth owned one, but his copy of "Perrine's New Topographical War Map of the Southern States," a handy field guide that folded into a pocket-size booklet protected by yellow, paper board covers, was back in Washington, in the hands of U.S. detectives who had discovered it in George Atzerodt's room at the Kirkwood House. Garrett told Booth that he owned no map of the state. Then what about that big map of several Southern states hanging on a wall in the house, suggested Booth. Would John be kind enough to take it down so that Booth could study it? Garrett went inside, unpinned the school map, and spread it on a table.

Booth's eyes ranged over the map and he asked Garrett for a piece of paper. John obliged, asking why Booth wanted the map. He explained that he was plotting the route from Locust Hill to Orange Court House. There he hoped to obtain a horse from one of the many Marylanders who he heard frequented the area. Then Booth told John, just as he had told William Garrett that morning, that he refused to return to Maryland because he would never sign an oath of allegiance to the Union. From Orange Court House, Booth planned to ride for Confederate General Joe Johnston's army, still in the field and, unlike Lee's surrendered Army of Northern Virginia, still a viable fighting force. And from there he would cross the border into his ultimate destination, Mexico. Booth declared that it was better to leave the country than swear loyalty to the Union. Garrett left the room and Booth remained hunched over the table, staring at the map, writing notes on the routes to distant places he hoped to reach. Alone, Booth tore a piece out of the map and stuffed Virginia in his pocket.

This was no time for a geography lesson. Booth should have departed Locust Hill at first light, and certainly no later than several hours ago, when he awoke in late morning. He was still too far north, and Garrett's farm sat within striking distance of Union troops. In truth, as the afternoon lengthened, Booth shouldn't be there at all. The man-hunters could appear at any moment without warning. He *should* leave at once; he dare not remain there any longer than one more night. Finished with the map, Booth came out onto the porch and sat on the bench. John Garrett saw him remove from his pocket "a small memorandum book" and begin writing. From his position, sitting below Booth on the front steps, John could not see what he wrote.

Distracted by noise from the road, Garrett looked up and saw a few riders moving past their front gate. "There goes some of your party now," John said, guessing the riders were the same men who had dropped Booth at Locust Hill yesterday afternoon. Booth looked up from his book. He asked John to go into the house, walk up to the bedroom, and get his pistol belt. Confused, Garrett asked why Booth wanted his revolvers. "You go and get my pistols!" the assassin commanded without explanation. Garrett obeyed, but when he got to the bedroom and looked out the window, the men were gone. They had ridden past the gate, in the direction of Port Royal, without turning into the farm. He left the gun belt hanging on the headboard, returned to the front porch without the pistols, and told Booth that the men were gone. The assassin and Garrett took their seats.

Five minutes later John Garrett noticed a stranger, on foot, walking from the gate toward the house. Booth rose from the bench and shouted for eleven-year-old Richard Garrett to run upstairs and bring down his pistols right away. In a flash, the child was back on the porch carrying the heavy gun belt. Quickly, Booth swung the belt under his coat and wrapped it around his waist, cinching the buckle tight. Then he stepped off the porch and began walking toward the approaching stranger. John and little Richard Garrett watched transfixed, expecting a gun battle to break out in their yard at any moment. Booth and the stranger, who had a carbine slung around his shoulder, met midway between the road's inner gate and the farmhouse. Booth did not draw his pistols and the stranger did not level his long arm. It was David Herold, who was back from his overnight stay a few miles southeast of Bowling Green at the home of Joseph Clarke, a friend of Bainbridge. After waiting for Davey all day, Booth had begun to wonder if he was coming back.

Booth and Herold stood in place about fifty yards from the house and talked for several minutes. "What do you intend to do?" asked Davey.

"Well, I intend to stay here all night," Booth announced.

Herold did not like the sound of that plan. Lingering in one place too long increased their risk of capture. And he was losing heart for life on the run: "I would like to go home. I am sick and tired of this way of living."

Then, together, they walked to the house. Booth introduced Davey as his cousin, David E. Boyd. Booth asked John Garrett if cousin Boyd could spend the night, too. Naturally, after the regal treatment the Garretts had accorded Booth, the assassin assumed that Garrett would offer his cousin similar hospitality.

John's reply shocked him: "I told him that father was the proprietor of the house and that I could not take him in." John adopted a sudden, brusque manner and cold tone of voice to convey an additional message, "intending by what I said to let him see that I did not want to take him."

Booth's panic at the sight of the riders and of the stranger walking up the road had made Garrett suspicious. To discourage the Boyds, John added that his father was away and he had no idea when he would return to approve or veto Booth's request. Unperturbed, Herold offered to sit on the porch steps and wait as long as it took for old man Garrett to come home. After eleven days of hiding out, he was used to waiting.

• • •

*A*ND AFTER ELEVEN DAYS OF SEARCHING, SOME OF THE MAN-
hunters were getting frustrated. Captain William Cross Hazelton of the
Eighth Illinois Cavalry, one of the units pursuing Booth in Maryland,
wrote a letter to his mother that typified the exasperation felt by many
of the soldiers and detectives in the field:

> I have been endeavoring to get an opportunity to write you
> but have been so constantly on the move for the last two weeks
> that I've had no chance to write.
> We were first ordered to Washington to form part of the
> military escort at President Lincoln's funeral, immediately
> after which we were sent here into Maryland in pursuit of
> Booth and some of his accomplices who were known to have
> come here. We traced Booth to the house of a Dr. Mudd where
> he went to have his leg set, a bone which had been broken by a
> fall off his horse. At this Doctor's he arrived on the morning
> after the murder. He had with him a man by the name of
> Harrold, one of his accomplices and a desperado well known
> in these parts. Here he remained until 2:00 o'clock in the
> afternoon of the same day. From here we were unable to trace
> him farther for some days. In vain we scoured the country in
> all directions. I was out with my Company night and day.
> With us were some of the most expert detectives of the United
> States, but all our efforts to trace him further failed until at
> length a free negro came in and reported that he acted as a
> guide for them to the house of a Captain Cox some fifteen
> miles from here. At that time I happened to be the only officer
> off duty, and at 12:00 o'clock at night started with thirty men,
> two detectives and this same negro guide for the home of
> Captain Cox.

We reached there just at daylight, saw Captain Cox (a
notorious "secesh!") but he denied all knowledge of the parties.

We obtained evidence, however, that Booth and Harrold
remained at his house some four hours in private conversation
with him. They then mounted their horse, Booth being lifted
on the horse by the negro guide whom they dismissed, and
again we lost all trace of them. Cox we arrested and he is now
in the Old Capitol prison.

The great difficulty is the people here are all traitors, and
we can get no information from them. A report reached us
the day before yesterday that they had been seen not far from
where I am now writing. They came to the edge of a woods and
called for this colored woman (our informant) to bring them
some food. She describes the men and said one of them had
crutches. We immediately surrounded and one hundred of our
men searched it through and through, but found nothing. The
country here is heavily wooded, making it next to impossible to
find one who makes any effort to escape. I hope, however, we
will yet find him if he is not across the Potomac.

Captain Hazelton's hope was in vain. Booth had crossed the Potomac days ago, leaving behind him and the hundreds of other troops,
detectives, and policemen who still, clueless, hunted for him in Maryland. Unbeknownst to them the theatre of action had shifted across the
river, to Virginia.

𝒯HE SIXTEENTH NEW YORK CAVALRY RODE INTO PORT CON-
way, Virginia, on Tuesday, April 25, between 3:00 and 4:00 P.M. William
Rollins, sitting on his front steps, watched their arrival. Luther Baker
spotted him and walked over to his house. Had Rollins seen any strangers cross the river at this spot in the last couple days? Baker asked. The
detective was not interested in any parties crossing from Port Royal to

Port Conway, just those that crossed over from the Port Conway side. Of course he had, said Rollins: "There were a good many people crossing there." How about a man with a broken leg? Baker continued. Yes, he crossed yesterday around noon, the fisherman revealed. The report jolted Baker. It must be Booth. Finally, eleven days after the assassination, and more than a week after Booth seemed to fall off the face of the earth for several days during his pine-thicket encampment, the manhunters picked up a fresh scent of their prey. If it was Booth, then Lincoln's assassin was only a little more than a day's ride ahead of them.

Rollins offered additional details: "[T]wo men came…in a wagon the day before…and…crossed the river…I had some conversation with them." Only yesterday, Booth and Herold had stood on this spot, in front of these same steps, conversing with Rollins just as Baker spoke to him now. The detective devoured every morsel of intelligence that Rollins could recall. These men wanted to go to Bowling Green, said Rollins, and they offered to pay him to take them there in his wagon. But, impatiently, they refused to wait for him to set his fishing nets. Instead, the lame man and his young companion made other plans as soon as they fell in with three Confederate soldiers, each mounted on horseback. They all crossed over the Rappahannock together on Thornton's ferry.

Baker was intrigued by these Confederate soldiers. Earlier intelligence—reports from Surratt's tavern and Dr. Mudd's farm—indicated that Booth and Herold were traveling alone. This was the first time anyone heard that they had linked up with rebel troops. If Rollins was telling the truth, it might mean that the assassins had come under the protection of the Confederate army and were being escorted south on horseback. That would make it tougher to catch them now. Rebels with knowledge of the country could move fast and would be able to outrace the Sixteenth New York. Furthermore, the three soldiers at the ferry could be part of a larger Confederate force, superior in numbers to the Union patrol. The deeper Baker, Conger, and Doherty probed into rebel territory with their small, lightly armed unit, the greater their risk of being ambushed by Confederate forces, guerrillas, or bushwhackers.

Luther Baker decided to worry about those things later. Yesterday, John Wilkes Booth was in Port Conway. Today Baker had no choice but to pick up the chase from that spot. Baker reached into his pocket and withdrew three small, sepia-toned, carte-de-visite paper photographs, fresh from the photography lab at the U.S. Army Medical Museum. He showed the first carte to Rollins: is this one of the strangers who crossed the river yesterday? The image was of a tall, lean man without facial hair. No, replied the helpful fisherman. He had never seen that man. Rollins, without realizing it, had just given Baker a valuable piece of intelligence. John Surratt, Confederate operative, son of Mary Surratt, and wanted man, was not traveling with Booth.

Baker held out the second photograph, a full-length image of a younger man—he looked like a teenager—posing with his hand resting on a tabletop. What about this man? Yes, Rollins responded, that is the man who arrived in Port Conway on the wagon with the lame man. They were together and he did most of the talking for the fellow with the broken leg. Rollins had just identified David Herold. Baker's excitement grew as he handed Rollins the final photograph—a bust portrait of a handsome, black-haired man with a black moustache, clothed in a black frock coat. The details in this photo were sharper than in the other two and appeared to be more professional.

Baker didn't say a word while William Rollins studied the photograph. Baker read the hesitation on Rollins's face and grew concerned. Rollins looked puzzled. "I was not sure whether he had a moustache," the fisherman admitted. Baker relaxed. Rollins had now confirmed what the manhunters suspected—that Dr. Mudd had told the truth about the razor and the shave. And, indeed, the latest edition of the April 20 reward broadside was correct when it proclaimed: "Booth…wears a heavy black moustache…which there is some reason to believe has been shaved off."

Rollins added another qualification: "And when I saw him his cap was pulled down over his forehead." At that Baker was unsure if Rollins had seen the lame man's face or not. "But," continued Rollins, "I thought there was a likeness across the eyes." Booth's piercing eyes were hard to forget. Yes, said Rollins, this is "the likeness of the other man with the broken leg." Baker rejoiced. Rollins had identified John Wilkes Booth. They were on the right track. Although the assassin enjoyed a full day's head start over the manhunters, he would have to stop somewhere to rest. Baker believed that hard riding by the Sixteenth New York could close the gap.

In addition to providing positive identifications of Booth and Herold, and confirming that they had crossed to Port Royal, Rollins had more information that made him an invaluable resource to the manhunters. He could also identify one of the three Confederate soldiers who had escorted the men across the river. His name was Willie Jett, and Rollins had a pretty good idea of where that rebel was headed. He lived in Westmoreland County, and Rollins guessed that after landing in Port Royal, he rode straight for Bowling Green: "[He] was in the habit of staying there a good deal of his time." The strangers had asked Rollins to take them to Bowling Green; wasn't it plausible that they requested the same of Jett, and that the rebel escorted them there? They might still be in Bowling Green: the lame man's companion told Rollins that they needed to rest for a couple days.

Mrs. Rollins had even more to tell before they shoved off. In addition to Jett, she named the other two Confederate soldiers—Bainbridge and Ruggles—who had crossed with Booth and Herold. Then she offered up a true gold nugget of gossip: Jett, according to local rumor, "was courting a young lady by the name of Gouldman, whose father kept a hotel at Bowling Green." She was Izora Gouldman, the innkeeper's sixteen-year-old daughter. Jett and Ruggles stayed there on the twenty-fourth. Bainbridge had a friend, Joseph Clarke, whose widowed mother, Virginia Clarke, owned a thousand-acre farm southwest of

Bowling Green. Herold and Bainbridge spent the night there, then retrieved Ruggles from Star Hotel, stopped at Trappe, then dropped Davey at the Garretts' farm.

The Sixteenth New York's mission was obvious: boots and saddles at once, and immediate pursuit. But first, before they could gallop to Bowling Green—or anywhere else—they had to float across the Rappahannock on the slow ferry. The crossing would consume valuable time, but they had no choice. The ferry could not hold more than nine men and nine horses per trip. It would take three crossings—requiring six one-way trips by the ferryboat—and almost two hours, to transport the entire command to Port Royal. Baker ordered a black man to go out on the dock and hail the ferry to come over right away from the Port Royal side. In the meantime, Lieutenant Doherty, followed shortly by Detective Conger, came over and spoke to Rollins. While they waited for the ferryboat, Conger had time to take down a statement in writing from Rollins.

Luther Baker, pleased with Rollins's cooperation and the quality of information he provided, decided to press him into temporary service. The fisherman should accompany the cavalry across the river and lead the pursuit of Booth to Bowling Green. Will he, Baker asked, "Go of [his] own accord or under arrest?" Rollins considered his options. He did not object to joining the troops, but he and his wife, Betsy, worried what their neighbors might think. Cooperating with the Yankees might not go over well with the locals, and the family might suffer repercussions later. Rollins asked Baker to go through the ritual of placing him under mock arrest to avoid the appearance of impropriety. The detective agreed to the charade if it meant securing Rollins's assistance.

Rollins got his horse and led the animal onto the ferry. On the other side a corporal whom Baker let in on the ruse took charge of Rollins and paraded him through Port Royal like a prisoner. By 4:30 P.M. on April 25, the entire patrol was across. With his reputation as a good Southerner secure, Rollins guided the Union cavalry toward Bowling Green. En route, about three miles out from Port Royal, they encountered a black man riding toward them from the direction of Bowling Green.

Not wanting to stop the cavalry's progress to the Star Hotel, Doherty spurred forward to intercept the rider: "Not wishing to lose time, I rode ahead of the column and directed the negro to turn back and ride beside myself." Brief questioning suggested that Jett was still in Bowling Green. Farther down the road, the patrol stopped at a halfway house between Port Royal and Bowling Green, the notorious den called "The Trappe." Rollins stayed outside while Conger and Baker went inside for between half an hour and forty-five minutes to question the occupants.

Never was a Civil War roadside tavern more aptly named. Widow Martha Carter and her four or five unmarried daughters kept what Luther Baker described discreetly as "a house of entertainment." The cavalry found no men at the log house, but, noticed Baker, "when we were searching the premises the ladies seemed very much excited." The women disclosed that four men had passed through on April 24, but only three of them passed back on the twenty-fifth. It did not sound to Baker like Booth was among them: "From their description, we could not ascertain that the lame man was along."

$\mathscr{I}$T WAS 4:00 P.M. ON TUESDAY, APRIL 25. THE SUN WOULD set in a few hours, and John Garrett could tell that the Boyd cousins were not planning to go anywhere that night. Ten minutes later, as Garrett fretted about what to do with his now unwanted guests, an even more disturbing incident occurred. Two horsemen, riding rapidly from the direction of Port Royal, burst through the Garretts' outer gate and galloped toward the house at top speed. Booth and Herold left the porch to meet them. Garrett recognized Ruggles, one of the two Confederates he'd spied from his bedroom window yesterday afternoon when they delivered Booth into his father's care. Bainbridge was at his side.

Like Paul Revere, Ruggles and Bainbridge carried electrifying news—the cavalry was coming! "Marylanders you had better watch out," one of them shouted. "There are forty Yankee cavalry coming up the hill!" Even as they spoke, the patrol was crossing the Rappahannock River on the ferry between Port Conway and Port Royal. The Confederates had seen them with their own eyes from a hillcrest overlooking the ferry landing. And the soldiers had spotted them on the crest, watching their movements from across the river. Soon the whole troop would be across the river and riding southwest, following the identical route that Ruggles and Bainbridge had just raced down. Without even reining their animals to a complete halt, the riders warned Booth and Herold to hide themselves. Then they turned their horses around and galloped to the southwest, away from Port Royal and toward Bowling Green.

$\mathcal{B}$OOTH AND HEROLD LOOKED AT EACH OTHER AND, WITH-out exchanging a word, made for the woods behind Garrett's barn. They waited for a time, but no cavalry came. Was it a false alarm? After a while Herold emerged from the forest and walked back to the farmhouse, where John Garrett stood in the front yard. Amiably, seemingly unworried, Herold asked Garrett what he thought about the news of Union cavalry at Port Royal. Was it credible? Garrett did not think so; he could not imagine how the cavalry would have gotten to Port Conway. As they spoke Garrett spotted a "black boy" named Jim coming down the road from Port Royal. Jim had belonged to J. H. Pendleton, and Garrett knew him. Leaving Herold in the yard, Garrett hailed Jim and questioned him about cavalry crossing on the ferry. It was true all right, confirmed Jim. The Union troops were already over the river and in Port Royal when he left there.

Garrett reported the news to Herold, who acted unconcerned. If the pistol incident worried Garrett, Booth's flight into the woods with Davey frightened him even more. Garrett complained vociferously: "I told him…that since he had come here my suspicions were aroused that all was not right with him and [Booth], and I would be very glad if they would leave our house for we are peaceable citizens and did not want to get into any difficulty."

Herold laughed off John Garrett's concern: "There is no danger. Don't make yourself alarmed about it; we will not get you into any trouble." Davey asked for something to eat but Garrett refused him: "I told him we had nothing cooked and that he could not get anything to eat…until supper unless he promised that he would leave."

While Garrett and Herold stood in the front yard bickering, a thunderous sound coming from the direction of Port Royal shook the earth and caught them off guard. "There goes the cavalry now!" Garrett exclaimed. Incredibly, the soldiers, racing for Bowling Green, rode right past Locust Hill and the front gate that led to the Garrett farmhouse. Oblivious to their surroundings, the soldiers—either failing to notice or taking no interest in the two men standing in the front yard—galloped on by. Even their local guide, William Rollins, did not spot David Herold, owner of that beautiful blanket. "Well, that is all," Davey observed nonchalantly.

John Garrett, certain that Davey knew the patrol's purpose, asked him again to leave Locust Hill.

The cavalry out of sight, obscured by a trailing dust cloud, Herold turned to Garrett and asked if he knew where he could buy a horse. John said not likely: "Both armies had stripped the country pretty well of horses." If horses can't be bought at any price, then what about hiring a team and a wagon, Davey proposed. John told him about a colored man named Freeman who lived nearby and sometimes hired out a conveyance. And what did Garrett estimate it might cost to engage transport to Orange Court House? Freeman, John confided, had a weakness for specie—coin money—and he might drive as far as Guineau's Station for $6. Herold possessed no coins, but dug his hand into a pocket and pulled out a piece of paper currency: "Here's a Secretary Chase note; I'll give this to get there." Would that be enough? The former druggist's clerk picked up a twig, sat on the ground, and drew the mathematics of the value conversion in the dirt, calculating that the $10 note was worth $7.30 in coin, more than enough to pay the price of a wagon ride.

*H*EROLD HANDED GARRETT THE CASH AND ASKED HIM TO arrange the ride. Leaving Davey on the front porch, Garrett rushed to Freeman's place as fast as he could. If he could find him at home, and induce him with the $10 note to transport the Boyds, the Garretts could be free of the suspicious strangers within the hour, well before sundown. When Garrett returned home, Herold and Booth were waiting for him in the yard. "What luck?" Herold asked. Garrett told them that Freeman was not home, but he would nonetheless find a way to send them on their way, even if he had to take them himself. Garrett said he knew Booth could not walk, and he didn't expect them to leave Locust Hill on foot.

But John Garrett did not tell the Boyd cousins what else he had learned from Freeman's wife. After confirming to John that the horsemen were Union cavalry, she revealed what they were after: "They asked [me] if there were any white men there." Mrs. Freeman was sure that the soldiers were hunting for someone. She confirmed Garrett's every suspicion about the strangers. Yes, he must make them leave now, this very afternoon, as soon as he returned home from the Freeman place. He would give them the ride himself. When would they like to go? asked Garrett, implying that he was prepared to get under way at once. He didn't get the answer he wanted. Unhurried, Booth and Herold said they did not want to leave until tomorrow morning. They would go on the morning of April 26. But it was suppertime now, and the "Boyds" were hungry.

This night's table did not sustain yesterday's convivial banter. Although Richard Garrett was back at his farm, his son John spoke for the family now. In the presence of their guests, they talked no more of the Lincoln assassination. After supper Booth brought up his departure and asked John Garrett how he planned to send them to Orange Court

House. There were only two options: wagon team or horseback. Garrett spoke vaguely, claiming that he had not decided yet, but said it would probably be the latter.

Booth responded enthusiastically: "Well that's the very thing, send us horseback."

The assassin's eagerness exacerbated John's suspicions about them: "I thought at once they wanted to go on horseback, so as to make way with the horses." And why was Booth always hobbling around the place, especially near the barn? Was he staking out the stable for some horse stealing? Garrett could imagine how the scene might unfold the next morning: alone on an isolated road, outnumbered two to one by the heavily armed Boyd cousins, they would steal the horses—maybe even kill him—and he would be powerless to stop them. "Never mind," Garrett reassured his guests, before morning's light he would decide what to do with them.

Booth and Herold excused themselves from the table and adjourned to their favorite spot, the bench on the front porch, where they sat side by side for a long time. John Garrett joined them. Then Davey started behaving oddly. Always chatty, he started to babble a fantastic tale to Garrett: "Herold [was] running on and on and talking a great deal of nonsense so that I thought he was the worse for liquor." Davey boasted that he, too, like his cousin James Boyd and the Garrett boys, had served in the Confederate army. Recklessly, Davey claimed affiliation with the Thirtieth Virginia Infantry regiment. He even specified his small unit, Company "C," and named his commander, Captain Robinson. All lies. Garrett confronted Davey and revealed his personal knowledge of that regiment; he said he knew that "Captain Robinson" did not exist. Booth's voluble companion backed down and qualified his tale: "To tell you the truth I was there only one week. I was then on picket and the first night I was wounded." Eagerly, Herold rolled up a sleeve again to show off not one of his juvenile tattoos, but a scar that he claimed had resulted from a battle wound. Davey's foolish monologue convinced John Garrett even more that he shouldn't trust them.

It was dark now. Booth and Herold remained on the bench, watching the evening sky's last clouds and colors fade to black. The fragrant scent of the spring night filled their nostrils until the sweetly burning smoke rising from Booth's pipe flavored the air. It was more pleasurable to experience nature's beauty from the comfort of a front porch than from the cold ground of their pine thicket, Indiantown, and Gambo Creek encampments. Those painful days were behind them now. They could tell that the Garrett family had turned against them, just like Dr. Stuart, but that did not matter now. The Locust Hill oasis had sustained and revived Booth. Tomorrow morning, Wednesday, April 26, he would continue his journey south toward his final destination, yet unknown. It would be the twelfth day.

IN THE MEANTIME, BOOTH AND HEROLD NEEDED TO REST for the morning's work. Booth signaled his man that it was time to retire, and they proposed to John Garrett that they turn in. Davey helped his master stand up, the actor tucked his crutches under his arms, and they walked to the front door. They planned to share Booth's bed, just as John and William Garrett shared a bed to accommodate Booth. Two in a soft bed in close quarters was better than two on the unyielding ground in a pine forest with room enough to spare. John Garrett stood between them and the door and barked a stunning question:

"I asked them where they thought of sleeping."

Why, "in the house," of course, Booth replied.

"No, gentleman, you can't sleep in my house."

Booth was incredulous. Was John Garrett denying him the bed that, only a night before, was his? Booth sensed the weight hanging from his hips. He was still wearing the pistol belt. He had never unbuckled it since the cavalry rode past that afternoon. And Davey's carbine was close by. With his revolvers and knife within easy reach, Booth considered Garrett's poor manners. Doctor Stuart's crime was bad enough— he refused shelter to a wounded, desperate man. But John Garrett's offense was worse—his father had kindly offered Booth shelter one day, and John cruelly robbed it from him the next. The prospect of another night sleeping on the ground was hateful to Booth. He could always threaten the Garretts, just like when he had menaced the cowering William Lucas. His weapons would certainly get him back upstairs, onto that restful mattress and soft pillow.

John Garrett still did not know the true identity of the man he was throwing out of his house. He was pretty sure that the Boyd cousins were in some kind of trouble, but he failed to imagine its magnitude, and that Lincoln's killer was a guest at his family's dinner table. This was the man who put a bullet in the brain of the president of the United States, who ordered the murders of the vice president and secretary of state, and who threatened to cut the throat of a harmless, black freeman who dared refuse Booth the accommodations of his humble cabin. John Wilkes Booth fancied himself a paternalistic, courtly man, and in truth he often was. But when pressed he could also become a ruthless, vicious one. What, then, was Booth to do with the young, rude Mr. John Garrett?

David Herold intervened: "We'll sleep under the house then." Davey hoped to defuse the situation, but the obstinate Garrett would not budge an inch.

Impossible, he retorted. The dogs sleep under there and would bite them, perhaps even attacking them in their sleep.

Gamely, Herold tried again: "Well, what's in the barn then?"

Hay and fodder, John Garrett replied.

"We'll sleep in the barn then," Herold announced in a voice indicating that the matter was closed. Garrett relented. He could not eject them from Locust Hill by force. There were children in the house. The Boyds were better armed, and any violence might endanger not just him, but the whole family.

Booth and Herold headed toward their new quarters, a modest-sized tobacco barn, forty-eight by fifty feet, with a pitched roof that stood one hundred fifty to two hundred feet from the main house. In addition to the hay and fodder that Garrett mentioned, the fugitives discovered several pieces of furniture. Neighbors from colonial Port Royal who wanted to protect their Early American furniture from vandalism or theft by Yankee raiders had stored some valuable pieces in the barn. The Garretts did not offer Booth and Herold mattresses, blankets, lanterns, candles, or other comforts. Booth wrapped himself in his shawl and plain wool blanket, while Herold unrolled his big, fancy blanket, "smooth on one side and with a heavy shag on the other, about the color of a buffalo robe." It was an impressive piece of craftsmanship that had attracted not only William Rollins at Port Conway but also John Garrett. By 9:00 P.M. Booth and Herold had lain down on the plank floor and settled in for the night. Unbeknownst to them, the Garretts, already guilty of inhospitality, were at that moment conspiring to commit a worse crime, treachery. Lincoln's assassin had just walked into a trap.

John and William Garrett swung the barn door shut behind the fugitives. Neither Booth nor Herold paid heed to the black, iron lock. Perhaps, blinded by the dark, they failed to see the sturdy piece of hardware as they passed through the doorway. As soon as the door closed, John Garrett whispered to his brother, "We had better lock those men up." John was sure that the Boyds were scheming to steal their horses in the middle of the night. What better way to foil the theft than by imprisoning the strangers in the tobacco shed until tomorrow morning? John crept around the perimeter of the building until he found a crevice between the boards, close to the ground. Dropping to his belly, he pressed his ear to the crevice and eavesdropped on Booth and Herold. John wanted to "see if I could find out anything about them. I thought that maybe they would be talking together and I might learn what their intentions were." But the strangers frustrated Garrett's primitive effort at intelligence gathering: "They were talking to each other in a low tone [and] I could not distinguish a word they said."

While his brother John eavesdropped, William Garrett tiptoed to the front door and, as quietly as he could, inserted the key into the lock. To avoid alerting the barn's occupants he turned the key slowly, so the locking mechanism would softly grind, and not loudly snap, into place. It worked. Booth and Herold did not hear the sliding bolt; they did not know that they were prisoners. The brothers returned to the house in time for nightly family worship conducted by their father. After evening prayers they retired to their room, each with a bed to himself again, now that they had thrown Booth out of the house. Still, John Garrett remained uneasy. What if the Boyds broke out of the barn? Then they would, in their anger, steal the horses for sure. John suggested to William that they spend the night outside and keep the barn under surveillance. Both Garretts grabbed the blankets from their beds, William seized his pistol, and they hustled outside. They chose one of the two corn houses as their guard post: "We unlocked the corn house between the barn, or tobacco house, and the stables and spread out the blankets and lay down there." There they watched and waited, observing the barn and listening keenly for suspicious sounds in the night.

$\mathcal{T}$HE CAVALRY PATROL APPROACHED BOWLING GREEN AT around 11:00 P.M., April 25. About half a mile out, Doherty ordered ten of his men to dismount, and, by stealth, to follow Detective Baker into the town. Doherty, Conger, and Rollins rode quietly with the main body into the town and, by midnight, found the Star Hotel. They immediately commanded their men to surround the hotel and allow no one to leave. But their mission was thwarted, albeit temporarily, by an embarrassing incident. Lincoln's assassin might be sleeping inside, but, comically, they could not get in. "We knocked about fifteen minutes at each door without receiving any reply," according to Doherty. When no one answered the front door, they tried the side door, but no one answered there, either. Eventually they saw a black man walking down the street, and they dragooned him for assistance. He took Conger and Doherty around to the back and showed them the entrance to the "Negro house" at the rear of the Star. Baker was already lurking at the front door. They crept into the building and almost immediately encountered another black man. Where is Willie Jett? Doherty asked. In bed, the servant replied. Conger demanded to know where the room was.

Mrs. Julia Gouldman, now awake, opened the door between the hotel and the Negro house. Doherty and Conger pushed through without an introduction and asked her a single question: where was her son, Jesse? She led them upstairs to a second-floor bedroom. Prepared for anything, the officer and detectives rushed in and discovered Jesse Gouldman and Willie Jett sharing a mattress. Already awakened by the commotion, Jett tried to get out of bed. "Is your name Jett?" Conger demanded. "Yes, sir," came the meek reply. "Get up: I want you!" the detective thundered. Jett stood up and yanked on his pants. Then they seized him, hustled him downstairs roughly, and confined him in the parlor. The trio did everything possible to frighten Jett: "We...informed him of our business," said Doherty, "telling him if he did not forthwith inform us where the men were, he should suffer."

Conger reclined in a chair and studied their captive: "Where are the two men who came with you across the river at Port Royal?"

Jett, eyeing Baker and Doherty nervously, approached Conger and whispered a plea: "Can I see you alone?" "Yes, sir: you can," Conger replied magnanimously. Conger asked his counterparts to leave the parlor. The moment they departed, Jett extended his hand to the detective in supplication and betrayed John Wilkes Booth: "I know who you want; and I will tell you where they can be found."

"That's what I want to know," Conger encouraged him.

All that this Confederate Judas begged in return was privacy: Willie wanted no audience to witness his shame.

"They are on the road to Port Royal," Jett confided, "about three miles this side of that."

But where, exactly, queried Conger: "At whose house are they?"

"Mr. Garrett's," Jett said, adding, "I will go there with you, and show where they are now; and you can get them." Willie Jett proved not only a Judas, but an enthusiastic one: "I told them everything from beginning to end. I said I would pilot them to the house where Booth was."

Conger realized that Jett would be an invaluable guide. Without him it might be difficult, if not impossible, to locate the Garrett farmhouse in the middle of the night.

"Have you a horse?" Conger asked.

"Yes, sir."

"Get it, and get ready to go!"

Conger sped Jett upstairs under guard to finish dressing. Quickly he put on his shirt and coat and pulled on his boots. By the time he returned to the parlor, the detectives had already sent a black servant to get his horse.

"You say they are on the road to Port Royal?" Conger asked.

"Yes, sir," Jett verified.

Conger could not believe it: "I have just come from there."

That news surprised the young Confederate: "I thought you came from Richmond: If you have come that way, you have come right past them. I cannot tell you whether they are there now or not."

Perhaps, when the cavalry thundered past Garrett's farm several hours ago on its way to Bowling Green, it had spooked Booth and Herold and prompted them to flee elsewhere. That was beyond Jett's control, he made clear to Detective Baker. It was not his fault if the cavalry had scared off the assassins. The news stunned Baker. A few hours ago, he and the Sixteenth New York had ridden through Port Royal, and then past the farm. The fugitives, Baker guessed, must have heard the pounding hooves of their horses. Booth and Herold had been within his grasp and he had ridden right past them! At around midnight, Conger, Baker, and Doherty, hoping they were not too late, turned the troops around and galloped back to the farm.

Conger, Baker, Doherty, and Jett hurried out of the Star Hotel and mounted their horses. At about 12:30 A.M., Wednesday, April 26, the Sixteenth New York Cavalry headed for Garrett's farm and, they hoped, a rendezvous with Lincoln's assassin. Baker warned Jett not to try any tricks: "He shook hands with the Colonel, and promised on his honor as an officer and a gentleman that he would be true to us. We told him that if he deceived us, it would be death to him—we thinking that perhaps it might be his design to lead us into an ambuscade."

After two hours in the saddle, Jett told Conger that he should slow the column: "We are very near there now to where we go through: let us stop here, and look around." In the dark, Jett had trouble finding the gate to the road that led to Garrett's house. Conger ordered the patrol to halt. He and Jett rode on alone. It is just a little way up, Willie reassured him. Conger trotted ahead of Jett. His eyes scanned the dark roadside but detected no opening. All Conger could see was a bushy, unbroken fence line skirting the road. He turned his horse around and retreated. There is no gate, he complained to Jett.

Then it is just a little farther up the road, Booth's Judas promised. It is hard to judge these distances in the dark. They rode on three hundred yards more, and Baker spurred ahead from the main body to help Conger search for the gate. This time they found it. After unlatching it, Conger sent Baker ahead to find and open the second gate; Jett had told them that it would block their way. Baker vanished into the black night while Conger backtracked to fetch the cavalry. The detective asked Jett a final question: when the cavalry charges down that road, where should they look for the house?

As before, Jett obliged: "I took them to Garrett's gate and directed them how to go into the house and they went in, leaving me at the gate."

Conger ordered Jett and Rollins to remain at the gate, guarded by only one trooper. Soon Baker located the last roadside obstacle that separated them from Booth: "We found a gate, fastened by a latch, dismounted, opened the gate, and the command came through, and a charge was ordered." The Sixteenth New York Cavalry raced up the dirt road and toward the farmhouse.

As the Sixteenth New York closed in on Booth and Herold, the nation did not hold its collective breath, awaiting the exciting climax of the manhunt. Nobody—not Stanton, his officers, the other pursuers, or the press—knew that Conger, Baker, and Doherty had tracked Lincoln's assassin to Port Royal, and to the Garrett farm. Elsewhere, all over Virginia and Maryland, other manhunters, ignorant of what was happening at Garrett's farm, continued the chase. In Maryland, S. H. Beckwith, the man whose tip had set in motion the sequence of events that led the Sixteenth New York to Booth's hiding place, sent, at 1:30 A.M., April 26, another telegram to Major Eckert. The major did not receive it until 8:00 A.M. And Booth had escaped Maryland days ago.

> *Immediately after reporting to you to-day I proceeded with Major O'Beirne to Bryantown, thence to Turner's house, where Booth and Herold were seen by two servants to inquire about food, then enter pine thicket about twenty rods distant from house and two miles north from Bryantown. Parties on the ground had been through, losing the track and accomplishing nothing. We at once penetrated the thicket and deployed. After following probable routes I struck the crutch track, and we followed it in a direction circling around toward the piece of timber from which they first issued far enough to justify the belief they are still in same vicinity from which they started, and that while the troops were searching the thicket where they were last seen, they, by taking course above described, gained time to temporarily conceal themselves again. It appears to us from all we can learn that troops have not been pushed through with much system. The colored troops, while deployed and advancing, upon hearing shout on one part line, made rush in that direction, leaving considerable space uncovered. Cavalry has been operating, and tonight has strong line of pickets around timber. I made map to-day for immediate use, but it would have assisted much if we had a county survey map and a compass. I left Major O'Beirne at Bryantown, where he was preparing to co-operate with others and make an early and systematic scouring.*

The Sixteenth New York did not need compasses or survey maps. Only a few hundred yards separated them from Booth now.

𝒯HE DOGS HEARD IT FIRST. RISING FROM THE SOUTHWEST. Distant sounds, yet inaudible to human ears, of metal touching metal; of a hundred hooves sending vibrations through the earth; of deep, labored breathing from tired horses; of faint human voices. These early warning signs alerted the dogs sleeping under the Garretts' front porch. At the farm John Garrett, corn-house sentinel, was already awake and became the first one there to hear their approach. William Garrett, lying on a blanket a few feet from his brother, heard them, too.

It was dark and still inside the farmhouse. Old Richard Garrett and the rest of his family had gone to bed hours ago.

All was quiet, too, in the tobacco barn. It was well past midnight, and the Garretts' unwitting prisoners were asleep. As far as John and William could observe from their hiding place, neither Booth nor Herold stirred during the night, realized their predicament, and tried to escape their rustic jail. The horses were safe, and the suspicious Boyd cousins were trapped. The barking dogs and the clanking, rumbling sound finally woke up Booth. Recognizing the unique music of cavalry on the move, the assassin knew he had only a minute or two to react before it was too late.

Booth woke up Davey fast. The cavalry is here, Booth hissed in a low whisper. The assassin's groggy companion snapped to attention. They snatched up their weapons and rushed to the front of the barn. "We went right up to the barn door and tried to get out," recalled Davey, "but found it was locked." The Garretts had imprisoned them! Booth wasted no time and began trying to pry the lock from its mountings. Every second was precious: they had to flee the barn before Union troops surrounded it. Booth guessed that the riders would move on the farmhouse first. He and Herold had to clear out of the tobacco barn before the cavalrymen turned their attention to the outbuildings. No doubt the treacherous Garrett boys would guide the Yankees to the right one.

Booth wheeled around one hundred and eighty degrees. "Come on!" he called to Davey. The assassin scampered fifty feet to the back wall. "[W]e went directly to the back end of the barn, and we tried to kick a board off so we could crawl out," witnessed Herold. Booth, impaired by his injury, and hobbled by his crutches, could not leverage his full weight on his left foot to swing a powerful kick with the right. He struck weakly. The board did not give. Davey fared no better. "Let's kick together!" Booth proposed. They aimed their kicks to strike one board together. Still the iron nails held tight as though cemented into the framing. David Herold was getting worried: "Although we did, our kicks did not do the work."

THE UNION COLUMN RACED UP THE ROAD AND THREW A COR-don around the Garrett farmhouse. Edward Doherty, Luther Baker, and Everton Conger dropped from their saddles, leapt up the porch, and pounded on the door. Awakened by the commotion, Richard Garrett climbed from his bed and walked downstairs in his nightclothes.

DAVID HEROLD PANICKED: "YOU HAD BETTER GIVE UP," HE urged Booth.

No, no, the actor declared, "I will suffer death first."

DOHERTY, BAKER, AND CONGER WAITED IMPATIENTLY ON THE front porch, and the trio pounced as soon as old man Garrett opened the door.

Conger barked first: "Where are the two men who stopped here at your house?"

Startled, Richard Garrett replied vaguely: "They have gone."

"Gone where?" Conger demanded.

"Gone to the woods," explained Garrett.

"What!" Luther Baker interrupted mockingly, "a lame man gone into the woods?"

Well, he had crutches, old Garrett pointed out.

"Will you show me where they are?" Baker continued.

"I will," Garrett promised, "but I will want my pants and boots."

Garrett's interrogators refused to let him back into the house to dress, so his family passed his clothes and boots to him through the door. There on the front porch, in full view of the soldiers, he dressed himself.

Conger decided to play the old man's game, at least momentarily: "Well, sir, whereabouts in the woods have they gone?"

Garrett began a long-winded story of how the men came there without his consent, that he did not want them to stay, and that . . .

Enough, Conger interrupted: "I do not want any long story out of you: I just want to know where these men have gone."

Richard Garrett was afraid, and he babbled his defensive monologue all over again. Conger had heard enough. He turned from the door and spoke gravely to one of his men: "Bring in a lariat rope here, and I will put that man up to the top of one of those locust trees." Even under the threat of hanging, marveled Conger, Garrett "did not seem inclined to tell." A soldier went to get the hemp persuader.

John Garrett emerged from the corn house, walked up to the nearest cavalryman, and asked whom they were pursuing. "That I cannot tell you," the trooper answered mysteriously, telling another soldier to take John to the house. When they got near the house, John saw Doherty, Conger, and Baker on the front porch talking to his father. Spotting John Garrett, Conger bellowed to his soldier escort, "Where did you get this man from?" John Garrett spoke up and came to the rescue of his tongue-tied father.

"Don't hurt the old man: He is scared. I will tell you where the men are you want to find," he said.

"That is what I want to know," said an exasperated Conger. "Where are they?"

Before John had time to answer, Doherty seized him by the collar, pushed him down the steps, put a revolver to his head, and ordered him to tell him where the assassins were.

"In the barn," John Garrett cried out. The two men are in the barn.

Not good enough, warned Conger: "There are three rooms around here, the tobacco-house and two corn houses; if you don't tell me the exact house he is in, your life will pay the forfeit."

They are in the tobacco barn, divulged Garrett.

"Show me the barn," Doherty commanded.

$\mathscr{B}$OOTH AND HEROLD HEARD THE SOLDIERS RUSH AND SUR-round the barn. Maybe stealth could save them just once more, like it had served them in the pine thicket. Booth hushed Herold to remain silent and motionless: "Don't make any noise," he whispered, "maybe they will go off thinking we are not here." Conger, close to the barn now, heard someone moving around inside, rustling the hay. It was David Herold walking about, failing to heed Booth's orders to take cover and, stupidly, revealing that they were in the barn.

$\mathscr{T}$HE LEADERS OF THE SIXTEENTH NEW YORK EXPEDITION WERE not done with John Garrett. They had a special mission for him. Luther Baker summoned John to his side and pointed to the tobacco house: "You must go in to the barn, and get the arms from those men." Garrett objected to the suicidal plan. Ignoring his reaction, Baker went on: "They know you, and you can go in." Yes, Booth and Herold *did* know John Garrett—as the man who ordered them out of his house, refused them the comfort of a bed, and locked them in the barn. That is precisely why he refused Baker's request. He had seen Booth's weapons and knew he would not hesitate to exact vengeance for Garrett's inhospitality and betrayal. No, he would not be the assassin's last victim.

Perhaps Garrett did not understand, Baker explained to him, that this mission was not optional: "I want you to go into that barn and demand the surrender of the arms that man has and bring them out to me. Unless you do it, I will burn your property." Baker didn't mean just the tobacco barn. He meant it all—house, barn, corn houses, and stables. Either John went in, or Baker would "end this affair with a bonfire and shooting match."

By now William Garrett had also emerged from the cover of the corn house and joined his brother near the tobacco barn. William, who had imprisoned the fugitives, pulled the key from his pocket and surrendered it to Baker.

Baker stepped forward and shouted to John Wilkes Booth: "We are going to send this man, on whose premises you are, in to get your arms; and you must come out, and deliver yourselves up." Booth said nothing. It might be a trick, he considered. He readied himself for a dismounted charge by more than twenty cavalrymen the moment the door opened. Baker, key in hand, strode right up to the barn door. He stood within close range of Booth's pistols now. Baker inserted the key, turned the lock, and, slowly, opened the door a little. Booth remained invisible, hiding just several yards away in the black, inner recesses of the barn. He saw movement. He held his pistols tightly, fingers in the trigger guards, thumbs ready to cock the hammers of the single-action Colts. But he held his fire. Baker seized John Garrett and half guided, half pushed him through the door and closed it behind him.

John Garrett stood alone, in the dark, at the mercy of Lincoln's killer. He spoke timidly to the unseen fugitives, reporting that "the barn was surrounded, that resistance was useless, and that [you] had better come out and deliver [yourself] up."

A growling, tenor voice, dripping with malice, echoed from the darkness in reply: "You have implicated me."

Garrett tried to reason with them: "Gentlemen, the cavalry are after you. You are the ones. You had better give yourselves up."

Then, like a ghostly apparition, John Wilkes Booth's pale, haunting visage emerged from the void, like a luminous portrait floating on a black canvas. Then he exploded: "Damn you! You have betrayed me! If you don't get out of here I will shoot you! Get out of this barn at once!" Garrett glimpsed Booth's right hand in motion. The assassin, while cursing Garrett, slowly reached behind his back for one of his revolvers.

Like Harry Hawk had done on the stage of Ford's Theatre after Booth jumped from the president's box, a terrified John Garrett turned and ran, escaped the barn, and nearly leapt into Conger's arms. Booth was going to kill him, Garrett pleaded.

Conger was skeptical: "How do you know he was going to shoot you?"

Because, Garrett claimed in a tremulous voice, "he reached down to the hay behind him to get his revolver." He had come out of the barn just in time, he insisted.

Finally, at the climax of a twelve-day manhunt that had gripped the nation, a heavily armed patrol of Sixteenth New York Cavalry had actually cornered Lincoln's assassin. The situation demanded decisive action, but, at the critical moment, Conger and the others hesitated. Instead of ordering their men to rush the barn and take Booth, they decided to talk him out, and then they delegated the job to a solitary, unarmed man, a civilian—and an ex-rebel soldier, no less—to negotiate Booth's surrender. It was a clear abdication of command responsibility. Twenty-six cavalrymen, each armed with a six-shot revolver, not counting other weapons, could pour a fusillade of 156 conical lead pistol bullets into the barn before having to reload. In response, Booth could fire a mere 12 rounds from the revolvers and 7 from the Spencer carbine. He wouldn't have time to reload. Or the troops could, without warning, before they fired a shot, charge the barn and try to take Booth by surprise. In the dark, and in the few seconds before they seized him, Booth could not pick off more than a few of them before he was subdued. Stanton wanted Booth alive for questioning.

Why did they hesitate? If brave Union men could charge Marye's Heights at Fredericksburg in December 1862 and suffer several thousand casualties, and if the valiant regiments of the Army of Northern Virginia could make the disastrous, suicidal Pickett's charge on the third day at Gettysburg, why couldn't twenty-six soldiers, under the cloak of darkness, charge two civilians hiding in a barn? Surely the honor of capturing Lincoln's assassin was worth the risk of a few casualties.

Even after John Garrett's ill-advised, failed mission, Doherty, Conger, and Baker dithered, pursuing a strategy of talk, not action. The trio deputized Baker as their spokesman. Baker shouted an ultimatum to the occupants: "I want you to surrender. If you don't, I will burn this barn down in fifteen minutes." If the fugitives refused to come out voluntarily, he resolved, then the flames would drive them out. Baker, Conger, and Doherty awaited an answer. It was 2:30 A.M., Wednesday, April 26. From the time the Sixteenth New York arrived at Garrett's farm until this moment, the fugitives had not spoken one word to their pursuers. Then came the first contact.

A voice speaking from inside the barn bellowed three pointed questions: "Who are you?" "What do you want?" "Whom do you want?"

It was John Wilkes Booth. The assassin stepped to the front of the tobacco barn and peered through a space between two boards, eyeballing his counterpart, whom he took, mistakenly, as an army captain.

"We want you," Baker replied, "and we know who you are. Give up your arms and come out!"

Booth stalled to preserve his options: "Let us have a little time to consider it."

Surprisingly, Baker agreed to the delay: "Very well."

Ten or fifteen minutes elapsed without communication between the parties. But the manhunters maintained a keen vigil on all four of the barn walls to ensure that their prey did not slip out unnoticed through a crevice between the boards.

In the meantime, Booth and David Herold got into a heated argument. Davey had no more fight left in him. "I am sick and tired of this way of living," he had complained to his idol on the afternoon of the twenty-fifth, less than twelve hours ago. Herold had convinced himself, naively, that once he talked his way out of trouble the soldiers would send him home. After all, in his mind, he wasn't guilty of anything. Booth killed Lincoln, and Powell stabbed Seward. Davey just came along for the ride. Booth could roast alive in the tobacco barn if he chose, but not him. "You don't choose to give yourself up, let me go out and give myself up," Herold proposed.

"No, you shall not do it," Booth growled in a low voice, so that the soldiers hovering on the other side of the boards could not hear him.

Herold implored Booth to release him from the assassin's service, speaking so loudly that some of the soldiers heard his begging.

Herold started for the door, but Booth menaced him: "[H]e threatened to shoot me and blow his brains out," Herold complained. Furious, the actor denounced his hitherto faithful companion: "You damned coward! Will you leave me now? Go, go! I would not have you stay with me."

Baker, counting down the minutes on his pocket watch, shouted to Booth that he was running out of time. Only five minutes more, and he would torch the barn.

*A*GAIN, BOOTH ASKED: "WHO ARE YOU? AND WHAT DO YOU want?"

Before Baker could reply, Conger took him aside, out of earshot, and suggested how to continue the negotiations: "Do not by any remark made to him allow him to know who we are: you need not tell him who we are. If he thinks we are rebels, or thinks we are his friends, we will take advantage of it. We will not lie to him about it; but we need not answer any question that has any reference to that subject, but simply insist on his coming out, if he will."

Baker agreed with Conger, telling Booth: "It doesn't make any difference who we are: we know who you are, and we want you. We want to take you prisoners."

Booth corrected him. There was no more than one prisoner available for the taking: "I am alone, there is no one with me."

Baker rebuked the assassin: "We know that two men were in there and two must come out." Conger worked his way around the barn's perimeter to select the best place to light the fire.

"This is a hard case," Booth confided to Baker, "it may be I am to be taken by my friends." That assassin held the forlorn hope that soldiers surrounding the barn were Confederate, not Union.

"I am going," insisted Davey. "I don't intend to be burned alive."

Booth relented. Forcing Davey to share his fate would serve no purpose. And it would be wrong. Herold had had several chances to abandon Booth during the manhunt—in Washington on assassination night, in the pine thicket, or during the night the assassin slept alone at Garrett's farm. But on every occasion, the loyal Herold returned to share Booth's fate. Almost certainly, Booth must have concluded that it would be ungrateful, even ungallant, to deny his young follower the chance to live. When others had betrayed Booth, Herold had stuck by him. It was harsh to call him "coward" now. This was the last act. It was time to claim center stage alone. The actor called out to Baker: "Oh Captain— there is a man here who wants to surrender awful bad."

Too excited to remain silent, Lieutenant Doherty blurted out: "Hand out your arms." Yes, chimed Baker almost simultaneously, "Let him hand out his arms."

Their demands perplexed Herold. Would they refuse his surrender until he first handed over Booth's firearms? His master might let him go, but Davey knew that Booth would never give up his guns. "I have none," Herold pleaded.

Doherty did not believe him: "Hand out your arms, and you can come out."

"I have no arms," Herold whimpered, "let me out."

Luther Baker scoffed at Herold's stubborn denials: "We know exactly what you have got." The Garretts, helpfully, had provided Baker and the other officers with a complete inventory of the fugitives' arms and equipment: two revolvers, one Spencer repeating carbine, one Bowie knife, a pistol belt, a couple of blankets, and the clothes on their backs. "You carried a carbine," Baker insisted, "and you must hand it out."

This back-and-forth bickering over the arms devolved into comedy, with one officer and two detectives proving themselves too incompetent to consummate the peaceful, willing surrender of Lincoln's assassin and his guide. Booth spoke up to end the impasse: "The arms are mine; and I have got them."

Baker disputed the assassin: "This man carried a carbine, and he must hand it out."

Booth argued back: "Upon the word and honor of a gentleman, he has no arms: the arms are mine, and I have got them." And he would not give them up. "I own all the arms and intend to use them on you gentlemen." As this wore on, Booth reminded the nitpicking officers that "There is a man in here who wants to come out."

Yes, Herold affirmed: "Let me out, quick; I do not know anything about this man, he is a desperate character, and he is going to shoot me."

Booth supported Herold's charade: "Let him out; that young man is innocent."

Enough, reasoned Lieutenant Doherty. If they can persuade one of the fugitives to come out of the barn without a fight, why not forget the arms, wait no more, and take the man? The lieutenant turned to Baker: "We had better let him out."

"No," the detective countered, "wait until Mr. Conger comes here."

Well, where is he? Doherty demanded. Out of sight, at the back of the barn, preparing to set it on fire. Then they wouldn't wait, Doherty decided.

But Baker resisted his logic: "I ought not to let this man out without consulting him."

"No: Open that door!" Doherty commanded one of his troopers. "I will take that man out myself."

The lieutenant positioned himself to the side, not in front of, the door. If he stayed out of the line of fire, Booth could not see—or shoot—him when he opened the door for Herold's exit. Inches apart, separated only by the width of the barn wall, Doherty and Herold could hear each other's breathing. They caught glimpses of each other through the spaces that divided the boards.

Then, in the last seconds before David Herold left the barn, Booth whispered the last words exchanged between them: "When you go out, don't tell them the arms I have."

"Whoever you are, come out with your hands up," a voice outside the barn shouted.

Davey turned away from Booth and faced the door, now ajar and ready for his passage from fugitive to captive. Doherty ordered Herold not to walk through the door just yet. First he wanted to see his hands to confirm that he was unarmed. The lieutenant told Davey to thrust only one hand through the doorframe. The frightened youth complied, and in a moment Doherty saw a spot of open-palmed, white flesh protruding through the entryway. The lieutenant signaled Davey to send through the other hand. It, too, was empty.

Doherty sprung to the door, seized Herold by the wrists, and yanked hard, pulling him forward through the doorway, and throwing him off balance. Davey's captor tucked his revolver under his armpit, ran both his hands down Herold's body to see if he had any hidden arms, and found none. Then he asked Herold, "Have you got any weapons at all about you?"

"Nothing at all but this," swore Davey, pulling out a piece of paper, a torn fragment of a map, which Doherty put in his pocket. The lieuten-

ant grabbed Herold by the collar and, like a schoolmaster taking an er-
rant pupil by the scruff, marched him away from the barn.

So far the operation at Garrett's farm was no model of a small unit
action. One army officer and two military detectives vying for the command of twenty-six enlisted men had barely accomplished the surrender of the assassin's harmless cat's-paw. Herold had managed to
surrender in spite of the disagreements and competition for authority
among the hunters. Now Doherty, Baker, and Conger faced a bigger
problem. John Wilkes Booth remained in that barn, heavily armed and
waiting for their next move. Yes, they possessed certain advantages. The
assassin was at bay, surrounded, and outnumbered twenty-six to one.
Escape from the tobacco barn seemed impossible. But then, so did escape from an audience of more than one thousand people at Ford's
Theatre. Like Macbeth, Booth could not fly away from Garrett's farm
but, like the doomed, baited bear, he remained lethal.

Booth had died onstage dozens of times in *Richard III, Hamlet,* and
Shakespeare's other great tragedies, but tonight he was not playacting.
He wanted to go down fighting, not hang like a petty thief. "I have too
great a soul to die like a criminal," he wrote in his diary a few nights before. "Oh may he, may he spare me that and let me die bravely." For
Booth, this was his final and greatest performance, not just for the small
audience of soldiers at the improvised theatre of Garrett's farm, but also
for history.

He had already perpetrated the most flamboyant public murder in
American history. Indeed, Booth had not only committed murder, he
had performed it, fully staged before a packed house. At Ford's Theatre,
Booth broke the fourth wall between artist and audience by creating
a new, dark art—performance assassination. Tonight he would script
his own end with a performance that equaled his triumph at Ford's
Theatre.

Their negotiations with the assassin had not gone well. They demanded Booth's immediate surrender, but he persuaded them to give
him more time. They demanded that Herold turn over at least one of

the weapons, but Booth claimed property rights over the arms and released Davey to them empty-handed. Now he had all the guns, and, in
addition, like Jim Bowie at the Alamo twenty-nine years before, a deadly
knife for the close combat of last resort. Booth—not Doherty, Baker, or
Conger—was setting the agenda at Garrett's farm.

In certain respects, Booth enjoyed three significant tactical advantages over the Sixteenth New York Cavalry: he occupied a fortified position, but they had to come in and get him; they were deployed in the
open around the barn and could not see him, but he remained hidden
and could see them; they wanted Booth alive and did not want to be
killed by him, but he was ready to die, and to take some of them with
him. Moreover, the ticking clock favored the assassin. In a few hours,
morning's first light would illuminate the manhunters and render them
perfect targets. At this close range, the Spencer carbine was an outstanding sniper's weapon. Booth could hardly miss.

Frustrated, Doherty wanted to wait until morning, but Baker and
Conger argued forcefully against that. As soon as the sun rose, they reasoned, Booth could see the whole troop and open fire. Sunrise would
transform this pastoral setting into a killing field. One of Doherty's sergeants, Boston Corbett, volunteered for a suicide mission: he would slip
into the barn alone and fight Booth man-to-man: "I offered to Mr. Conger, the detective officer, and to Lieut. Doherty, separately, to go into the
barn and take him or fight him—saying if he killed me his weapons
would then be empty, and they could easily take him alive." Three times
Corbett volunteered to charge in alone; and each time Doherty vetoed
that harebrained scheme and ordered Corbett back to his position.
Corbett was, no doubt, the most eccentric character under Doherty's
command.

A quirky English immigrant who adopted the name "Boston" to
honor the city in which he found Christ, thirty-two-year-old Thomas
Corbett proved to be a hard fighter and a reliable noncommissioned officer. A hatter before the Civil War, he had performed a bizarre, horrific
act of self-mutilation when tempted by fallen women. The records of

Massachusetts General Hospital chronicled the gruesome event: "[Corbett] is a Methodist, and having perused the eighteenth and nineteenth chapters of Matthew, he took a pair of scissors and made an opening one inch long in the lower part of the scrotum. He then drew the testes down and cut them off. He then went to a prayer meeting, walked about some, and ate a hearty dinner. There was not much external hemorrhage, but a clot had filled the opening so that the blood was confined to the scrotum, which was swelled enormously and was black. He called on Dr. Hodges…who laid it open and removed the blood; he tied the cord and sent him here."

Conger and Baker wanted to burn the barn. The searing flames and choking smoke would do the job for them, at no risk to the men. Indeed, the only danger would be to the men who had to get close enough to the barn to lay the kindling against the timbers. Booth might be able to shove his pistol into the four inches of space between each board and shoot them through the head at point-blank range. They thought about the risk involved and concluded that it didn't have to fall to their own men.

Conger sent for the Garrett sons. He had one more job for them, he explained: collect a few armfuls of straw and pile them against the side of the barn. John Garrett roamed the grounds but could not find any fresh straw. It was all in the tobacco barn with Booth, he told Conger. Then find something else that will burn, the detective ordered. John Garrett gathered pine twigs and set them next to the barn. He returned with a second armful and bent low to arrange the pile. The rustling sound alerted Booth, who rushed to the site of the noise. Garrett jumped when he heard that familiar, menacing voice address him from the other side, just a foot or two away: "Young man, I advise you for your own good not to come here again." It was Booth's second warning to him that night. There would not be a third, the assassin promised: "If you do not leave at once I will shoot you." Quickly, John Garrett dropped the pine kindling and retreated out of pistol range.

If they were gathering kindling, Booth realized, the manhunters did not plan on waiting until sunrise. They were going to burn the barn, and soon, probably. Booth decided to retake the initiative and stall the fire. He challenged his pursuers to honorable combat on open ground.

"Captain," he called out to Baker, "I know you to be a brave man, and I believe you to be honorable: I am a cripple." Booth's tantalizing admission thrilled every man who heard it. They had suspected, but were not absolutely sure, that the man in the barn was John Wilkes Booth. They had received reports that Lincoln's assassin was lame, and the Garretts told them that Mr. Boyd had a broken leg. Now the man in the barn confirmed it. "I have got but one leg," Booth continued. "If you will withdraw your men in 'line' one hundred yards from the door, I will come out and fight you."

As a sign of good faith Booth revealed that he had chosen, at least up to now, to spare Baker's life: "Captain, I consider you to be a brave and honorable man; I have had half a dozen opportunities to shoot you, but I did not."

Baker's eyes darted to the burning candle he held improvidently in his hand. The assassin told the truth! Conger suggested that Baker relieve himself of the inviting target immediately: "When Conger said it was presumptuous in me to hold the candle, as Booth might shoot me, I set the candle down about twenty feet from the door."

This was *better* than Shakespeare. Lincoln's assassin had just challenged twenty-six men, a lieutenant, and two detectives to a duel. Or was it, in Booth's mind, a knightly trial by combat, with victory the reward to the just? Baker declined the glove: "We did not come here to fight you, we simply came to make you a prisoner. We do not want any fight with you." Neither did Secretary of War Edwin Stanton, who, back in Washington, awaited news from the manhunters. He wanted the assassin alive to interrogate him and expose fully the secrets of his grand conspiracy. Stanton, convinced that officials at the highest levels of the government of the Confederate States of America had participated in the assassination, wanted Booth to name his coplotters. If Booth was dead, that would satisfy the nation's lust for vengeance, but not Stanton's curiosity. It was far better, the secretary of war believed, to take Booth alive. There would be plenty of time to hang him later, after the trial.

Booth repeated his challenge but reduced the distance to offer more generous odds to his opponents: "If you'll take your men fifty yards from the door, I'll come out and fight you. Give me a chance for my life."

Again Baker declined.

"Well, my brave boys, prepare a stretcher for me!" Booth jauntily replied.

Conger made up his mind and turned to Baker: "We will fire the barn."

"Yes," his fellow detective agreed, "the quicker the better."

Conger bent over and lit the kindling. The pine twigs and needles, mixed with a little hay and highly combustible, burst into flames that licked the dry, weathered boards. Soon the barn's boards and timbers caught fire, and within minutes an entire corner of the barn blazed brightly. The fire illuminated the yard with a yellow-orange glow that flickered eerily across the faces of the men of the Sixteenth. Booth could see them clearly now, but held his fire.

As the fire gathered momentum, it also lit the inside of the barn so that now, for the first time, the soldiers could see their quarry in the gaps between the slats. Booth made a halfhearted attempt to suppress the flames by overturning a table upon them, but that only fueled the rapidly advancing inferno. The assassin was trapped. He had three choices: stay in the barn and burn alive; raise a pistol barrel—probably the .44 caliber with its heavier round to do the job right—to his head and blow out his brains; or script his own blaze of glory by hobbling out the front door and doing battle with the manhunters, welcoming death but risking capture. When Booth was a boy, he prophesied to his sister, Asia, the manner of his death: "I am not to drown, hang, or burn." He had been right so far. He had crossed the Potomac River safely. He would not stay in the barn and die by fire. Nor would he allow himself to be taken and strangle from the rope. Suicide? Never that shameful end, Booth vowed to himself. Richard III did not commit suicide, Macbeth did not die by his own hand, not Brutus, nor Tell. Neither would he. No, no, he must fight the course. And if he must perish, he would die in full struggle against his enemies.

Booth had decided it was better to die than be taken back to Washington to face justice. He had seen a man hanged before. In 1859, he caught the train to Charlestown, Virginia, to witness the execution of abolitionist John Brown, condemned for his ill-fated raid on Harper's Ferry. He had seen Brown driven to the scaffold in a horse-drawn cart, like a piece of meat carried off to market. He watched as Brown ascended the stairs to the platform, was bound, and had the sack pulled over his head. He saw the hangman loop the noose around Brown's neck, and then leave the old man standing in suspense for several minutes until the drop fell. Brown twitched a little, and then it was over. When they cut him down his face was purple.

No, Booth vowed, the prophecy was true. He must not be captured and hanged. The spectacle of a trial would put him on public display for the amusement of the gentlemen of the press and the idle curiosity seekers sure to flock to the proceedings. But he would not command the courtroom as his stage. He would be allowed no press interviews; no dramatic courtroom declarations about his beloved South, Lincoln the tyrant, his dreams, or his motives; and, under prevailing legal customs of the time, no opportunity to speak at all. In the theatre of Booth's trial, the main character would be mute. Lincoln's assassin would be a silent star, seen, but never heard. It would be hard for the voluble, loquacious thespian to bear.

Nor did Booth wish to endure the rituals of the scaffold: the indignity of being bound and trussed, of walking past his own coffin and the open grave, of being stripped of his shoes so that they did not rocket off his feet when his body jerked at the end of the rope. The bodily humiliations were even worse: the swollen tongue, burst blood vessels in the

"I have too great a soul to die like a criminal." Garrett's Farm. April 26, 1865.

eyeballs, unloosed kidneys and bowels, and a blackened, blood-bruised, rope-burned neck. This shameful death of a common criminal was not for him.

And he would have to share the scaffold-stage with his supporting cast of coconspirators. It was far better, Booth decided, to perish here— if he must die tonight. He was dictating the action, and his pursuers responding to his improvised performance.

Booth moved to the center of the barn, where he stood awkwardly balancing the carbine in one hand, a pistol in the other, and a crutch under one arm. He swiveled his head in every direction, measuring how quickly the flames were engulfing him and hoping for a miracle. He glanced toward the door and hopped forward, a crutch under his left arm and in his right hand the Spencer carbine, the butt plate balanced against his hip. "One more stain on the old banner," Booth cried out, conjuring up the Stars and Bars Confederate battle flag, perhaps imagining his own patriotic blood mingling with the vast ocean spilled by the South's quarter million dead.

Unseen by Booth, Sergeant Boston Corbett watched the assassin's every move inside the barn: "Immediately when the fire was lit...I could see him, but he could not see me." Corbett had, by stealth, without Booth seeing him, walked up to one side of the barn and peeked between one of the four-inch gaps that separated each of the barn wall's vertical boards. As the flames grew brighter, Corbett could see Booth clearly: the assassin "turn[ed] towards the fire, either to put the fire out, or else to shoot the one who started it, I do not know which; but he was then coming right towards me...a little to my right,—a full breast view." Now Booth was within easy range of Corbett's pistol. But the sergeant held his fire: "I could have shot him...but as long as he was there, making no demonstration to hurt any one, I did not shoot him, but kept my eye upon him steadily." He saw Booth reach the middle of the barn and face the door.

Outside the barn, Conger, Baker, and Doherty, and the cavalrymen posted near the door tensed for action. No man could endure those hot flames and choking smoke for long, and they expected the door to swing open at any moment and see Booth emerge, either with his hands up or his pistols blazing.

Corbett's eyes followed their prey as Booth got closer to the door. By now the sergeant had drawn his pistol. Booth moved again and leveled the carbine against his hip, as though he was preparing to bring it into firing position. Corbett poked the barrel of his revolver through the slit in the wall and aimed it at Booth. The sergeant described what happened next:

"Finding the fire gaining upon him, he turned to the other side of the barn and got towards where the door was; and, as he got there, I saw him make a movement towards the floor. I supposed he was going to fight his way out. One of the men who was watching told me that [Booth] aimed his carbine at him. He was taking aim with the carbine, but at whom I could not say. My mind was upon him attentively to see that he did no harm; and, when I became impressed that it was time, I shot him. I took steady aim on my arm, and shot him through a large crack in the barn."

The soldiers surrounding the barn heard one shot. Instantly Booth dropped the carbine and crumpled to his knees. His brain commanded movement but his body disobeyed. He could not rise. He could not lift his arms. He could not move at all.

Like sprinters cued by a starting gun, Baker rushed into the barn with Conger at his heels. Baker caught Booth before he toppled over and Conger seized the assassin's pistol, which the actor grasped so tightly that the detective had to twist it to pry it out of his hand.

"It is Booth, certainly," Conger cried jubilantly.

Baker glared disapprovingly: "What on earth did you shoot him for?"

"I did not shoot him," Conger protested, "he has shot himself." Conger stared at the assassin: "Is he dead? Did he shoot himself?"

"No, he did not, either," said Baker.

Conger raised Booth up and asked, "Where is he shot?" Conger searched for the wound: "Where-about is he shot?—in the head or neck?" Conger examined Booth's neck and found a hole where blood was running out. "Yes sir," Conger deduced, "he shot himself."

"No he did not," Baker insisted.

As soon as Lieutenant Doherty heard the shot he ran for the barn, dragging David Herold with him. By the time they entered, the two detectives and several soldiers were hovering over Booth in the middle of a burning barn, and carrying on an animated argument about the origin of the wound. There were better places to continue the debate, suggested Conger: "Let us carry him out of here: this place will soon be burning." They lifted Booth from the floor, carried him under the locust trees a few yards from the door, and laid him on the grass.

Doherty took Herold with him out of the barn. The sight of his master on the ground, apparently dead, threw Davey into a panic of irrational babbling: "Let me go away; let me go around here," he pleaded.

"I will not leave; I will not go away." Herold's whining would not have surprised Lewis Powell, who called him a "little blab." "I was never satisfied with him myself," Powell told Major Eckert, "and so expressed myself to Booth."

"No sir," responded the lieutenant.

Feigning ignorance, Davey asked him, "Who is that that has been shot in the barn?"

Incredulous, Doherty cut him off: "Why, you know well who it is!"

Herold elaborated his alibi: "No, I do not. He told me his name was Boyd."

Doherty had heard enough: "It is Booth; and you know it."

Davey persisted in his denials: "No; I did not know it; I did not know that it was Booth." In captivity, the assassin's disciple denied him thrice.

From under the locust trees, Conger looked back at the barn. If they could save it, perhaps they might preserve vital evidence of the crime: "I went back into the barn immediately to see if the fire could be put down, and tried somewhat myself to put it down; but I could not, it was burning so fast; and there was no water, and nothing to help with." John Garrett ran into the barn and joined the effort, rallying several troopers by yelling, "Boys, let us extinguish the fire." Like Conger, he surrendered to the inevitable: "The soldiers ran and threw furniture and stuff on the fire, but it was too late."

Conger left the barn and went back to the locust trees. Gazing down on Booth's broken body, "I supposed him to be dead. He had all the appearance of a dead man." But, like the stricken William Seward, who looked to his doctor like "an exsanguinated corpse," John Wilkes Booth's life force rallied. He opened his eyes and moved his lips.

Conger called for water, and a soldier offered the contents of his tin, government-issue canteen. Baker produced a crude tin cup, an indispensable utensil common to the baggage of nearly every soldier, North and South, in the war. They splashed some of the cool, reviving water on Booth's face, and he tried to speak. They poured a little into his mouth, and he spit it out. The assassin could not swallow the liquid: he was almost completely paralyzed. Again he moved his lips and tried to speak. With great concentration and labored effort, Booth's vocal cords emitted a barely audible whisper. For the first time in his life, the great thespian and raconteur was at a loss for words, his great stage voice silenced by the bullet that had passed through his neck and spinal column.

Conger and Baker bent down close to Booth's reclining body, tilted their heads, and jutted their ears close to his mouth. Booth formed words with his lips but produced no sounds. Finally, after several attempts, Lincoln's assassin spoke: "Tell mother, I die for my country." It was hard to hear his faint voice above the roar of the crackling fire, the shouts of the men, and the neighing, snorting horses. Conger wanted desperately to confirm the accuracy of what Booth had said. These might be the assassin's historic last words, and they must be reported to the nation exactly as Booth said them. Moreover, Secretary of War Stanton would demand a full accounting of the events at Garrett's barn, including Booth's every word.

Enunciating each syllable slowly and clearly so that Booth could understand him, Conger repeated the phrase verbatim: "Is that what you say?" the detective asked.

"Yes," faintly whispered the assassin.

The tobacco barn was now fully ablaze, and the inferno radiated an intense, searing heat that threatened to combust the locust trees where Booth and his captors reposed. The horses, even though the soldiers had picketed or tied them a good distance away before firing the barn, were growing increasingly restive as the flames intensified. The detectives shouted for everyone to retreat to the Garrett house. Several men seized Booth by the arms, shoulders, and legs, raised his limp body from the ground, and marched in quick time to the farmhouse. They climbed up the stairs and laid Booth flat on the wood-planked piazza, near the bench where, over the past two days, he had sat, smoked, napped, conversed, and planned the next leg of his escape. Blood, seeping from the entry and exit wounds in his neck, pooled under his head and stained several of the floorboards. To relieve Booth's suffering, the Garrett girls carried an old straw mattress from the house and laid it on the porch. Conger and the others folded the soft, pliable bedding in half and laid Booth's head and shoulders on it. Lucinda Holloway carried out a pillow and, gently, placed it under his head.

Doherty brought David Herold to the porch and gave him an order: "Come stand by the house." The officer did not have any wrist or leg irons to shackle Davey, so he improvised with a material that every cavalry unit rode with in ample supply: rope. Doherty bound Herold's hands with a picket rope and tied him to a locust tree about two yards from where Booth's body lay. Doherty kept Davey tied there until they were ready to return to Washington. This position, only six feet from Booth's body, gave Herold a front-row seat for the climax of the chase for Lincoln's killer.

ONCE BOOTH WAS ON THE PORCH, CONGER OBSERVED, HE "revived considerably. He could then talk so as to be intelligibly understood, in a whisper; [but] he could not speak above a whisper." The great, theatrical, tenor voice that once projected beyond the proscenium arch and filled the halls of Washington, Philadelphia, New York, Boston, Chicago, St. Louis, Baltimore, and Richmond had been hushed and could no longer be heard past the first row.

Booth whispered for water and Conger and Baker gave it to him. He asked them to roll him over and turn him facedown. Booth was in agony and wanted to shift positions but was helpless to move himself. Conger thought it a bad idea to roll him over: "You cannot lie on your face." Then at least turn him on his side, the assassin pleaded. They did, but Conger saw that the move did not relieve Booth's suffering: "We turned him upon his side three times.... He could not lie with any comfort, and wanted to be turned immediately back." Baker noticed it, too: "He seemed to suffer extreme pain whenever he was moved, and would scowl, and would several times repeat 'Kill me.'"

Booth wanted to cough but the bullet had severed the communication between his brain and his throat. He asked Conger to put his hand upon his throat, and press down. The detective complied, but nothing happened.

"Harder," Booth instructed Conger.

"I pressed down as hard as I thought necessary, and he made very strong exertions to cough, but was unable to do so—no muscular exertion could be made."

Conger, guessing that Booth feared some asphyxiating obstruction was stuck in his throat, told Booth to let him inspect it: "Open your mouth, and put out your tongue, and I will see if it bleeds." Conger reassured Booth: "There is no blood in your throat; it has not gone through any part of it there."

"Kill me," Booth implored the soldiers. "Kill me, kill me!"

"We don't want to kill you," Conger comforted him, "we want you to get well."

Conger spoke sincerely. They wanted Booth alive so they could bring him back to Washington as a prize for Edwin Stanton. Stanton and others were certain that Booth was merely the agent of a Confederate conspiracy. Indeed, President Andrew Johnson would soon issue another reward proclamation, this one for Jefferson Davis and other Confederate officials, naming them as assassination conspirators. Davis, currently the object of another manhunt, had fled Richmond for the Confederate interior as part of a desperate attempt to continue the war using Southern armies that had not yet surrendered to Union forces. Sam Arnold and Mike O'Laughlen had already confessed everything they knew about the plot. If Booth talked, too, he might give invaluable testimony that implicated the highest officials of the Confederacy.

But thanks to somebody under his command, it was obvious to Conger that John Wilkes Booth was not going back to Washington alive. Who fired that shot? Conger demanded to know. Baker asked him if he knew who did it.

"No, but I will," vowed Conger.

Conger walked away in search of the trigger-happy trooper. He returned soon but, it appeared to Baker, empty-handed.

"Where is the man?"

Conger laughed aloud and replied, "I guess we had better let Providence and the Secretary of War take care of him."

Conger explained to the puzzled Baker what had happened. When he went off to find Booth's killer, Boston Corbett came forward, snapped to attention, saluted Conger, and proclaimed, "Colonel, Providence directed me."

Corbett made the same confession to his commanding officer, Lieutenant Doherty. "Providence directed my hand." Corbett claimed that he had not shot Booth for vengeance, but because he believed the assassin was about to open fire on the soldiers. He did it to protect the lives of his fellow troopers, he insisted. And, Corbett continued, he did not intend to kill Booth. He only wanted to inflict a disabling wound to render the assassin helpless, for capture. And he did not violate any orders from his superiors. The men of the Sixteenth New York had not been ordered to hold their fire. Indeed, Conger, Baker, and Doherty had failed to give them any orders at all on the subject. Corbett exercised his own discretion as a noncommissioned officer and shot Booth: "It was not through fear at all that I shot him, but because it was my impression that it was time the man was shot; for I thought he would do harm to our men in trying to fight his way out of that den if I did not."

Dr. Charles Urquhart, a local physician summoned by Doherty and Baker, arrived on the scene and examined Booth for ten or fifteen minutes. His new patient lapsed in and out of consciousness during the examination. Distracted and confused by the surreal scenes, the befuddled Urquhart said that the wound was nonfatal, then reversed his diagnosis: the wound was mortal; it was impossible for Booth to recover.

Several soldiers compared the location of Booth's fatal wound with the location of Lincoln's wound. Perhaps, they marveled, God's justice directed Corbett's bullet to the back of the assassin's head. Corbett, too, wondered at the coincidence: "[W]hile Booth's body lay before me, yet alive, but wounded, and when I saw that the bullet had struck him just back of the ear, about the same spot that his bullet hit Mr. Lincoln, I said within myself, 'what a fearful God we serve.'" Later, Corbett recalled a prayer he had led at a chapel in Washington before he joined the manhunt: "O Lord, lay not innocent blood to our charge, but bring the guilty speedily to punishment."

Booth noticed Willie Jett standing nearby. After Booth had been shot, the trooper guarding him near the roadside gate brought him up to the house. The sight of the unfaithful young Confederate agitated Booth.

"Did that man betray me?" Booth asked Conger.

Conger evaded the question: "We have taken him prisoner."

"Did Jett betray me?" Booth asked Baker.

"Oh," answered Baker, "never mind anything about Jett."

Conger began rifling Booth's pockets, turning them inside out. "[H]e looked up," admitted Conger, "and knew what was being done." Conger unfolded a handkerchief and laid it neatly next to Booth. On it he placed the contents of the assassin's pockets. "I took his diary, these bills of exchange, money, keys, compass, shavings, tobacco, and a little knife." From Booth's undershirt he yanked a special prize: a handsome stickpin, "a stone set in jet and gold," Conger described it, engraved "Dan Bryant to J.W. Booth." Two years earlier the famous blackface comedian and Booth had exchanged gifts: Booth gave Bryant a flask, and Bryant gave Booth this pin.

Kneeling at Booth's side, Lucinda Holloway ministered to the dying star. As she gazed upon his face—"luminous" is how she remembered it for the rest of her life—Booth stuck out his tongue. He was thirsty. As strangers at Golgotha did for Christ on Good Friday's cross, Lucinda answered his plea: "I took my handkerchief and dipped it in water and moistened his lips. I again moistened his lips and he repeated his message to his mother. Soon he gasped, and I again moistened his lips and tongue a third time."

Booth rallied and opened his eyes.

"The damn rebel is still living!" a soldier cursed.

"My hands," Booth whispered. Baker clasped them, bathed the clammy flesh in cool water, and raised them up for Booth to see. For the last time John Wilkes Booth beheld the hands, now helpless, that had slain a president. Tenderly, Lucinda Holloway massaged his temples and forehead. Her fingertips felt the life draining out of him: "The pulsations in his temples grew weaker and weaker."

Mustering all his remaining strength, waning rapidly now, Booth looked at his hands and spoke again: "Useless, useless."

His breathing turned sporadic and labored, and he gasped for breath every few minutes. "His heart would almost die out; and then it would commence, and, by a few rapid beats, would make a slight motion again," Baker observed.

Booth's lips turned purple and his throat swelled.

He gasped.

The rising sun nudged above the horizon and colored the eastern sky. In Albany, New York, mourners who had waited in line all night filed past Abraham Lincoln's remains, displayed magnificently in the state Capitol's Assembly Chamber. "During the still hours of the morning," said one who witnessed the scene, "a sad procession moved through our streets to and from the Capitol. Aside from the slow tread of this procession, not a sound was to be heard." That afternoon the funeral train would pull out of the station, heading west to the prairies. Lincoln would be home soon.

Booth gasped again.

His vision blurred.

He could not breathe. He gasped a third time.

The sun broke free from the horizon and flooded Garrett's farm with light, which shone on Booth's face. The soldiers tried to shield his eyes by draping clothes over the back of a chair that they set up on the porch between Booth and the sun.

No, do not hide him from the light, Booth might have said, if he could still speak. When he was a boy, his bedroom at Bel Air faced the east and he told his dearest sister, Asia: "No setting sun view for me, it is too melancholy for me; let me see him rise."

The stage grew dark. His body shuddered. Then, no more. John Wilkes Booth was dead. The twelve-day chase for Abraham Lincoln's assassin was over.

Chapter Ten

"So Runs the World Away"

Lucinda Holloway, caressing Booth's hair, had watched him die: "[G]asping three times and crossing his hands upon his breasts, he died just as the day was breaking." She twisted a curl of his hair between her fingers and caught Dr. Urquhart's eye. She did not need to ask. The doctor looked up, watching for his chance when Doherty, Baker, and Conger, distracted, glanced momentarily away from the assassin's corpse. Quicker than their eyes could detect, Urquhart's hand, grasping a pair of razor-sharp surgical scissors, reached down for Booth's head. In an instant he snipped a lock of the rich, black hair and pressed it into Lucinda Holloway's palm. As quickly, she clenched her fingers around the black curl into a tight fist to conceal the precious memento. She was not a craven relic hunter who lusted morbidly, like so many others, for bloody souvenirs of the great crime. No, to her the lock was a private, romantic keepsake of the luminous, dying star. If the soldiers saw what she had done, they would have overpowered her, prying open her balled fist and confiscating her treasure.

Later, when the soldiers were gone, Lucinda entered the house and walked straight to the bookcase that held another prized relic—Booth's field glasses. When no one was looking, she scratched her initials on the buckle of the shoulder strap, and then took the glasses to her mother's house, a safe distance of several miles from Garrett's farm.

. . .

*T*HE GARRETT MEN STOOD BY AS MUTE WITNESSES TO THE drama they had helped author. By locking Booth and Herold in their barn, they made it impossible for the assassin to make a run for it when the Sixteenth New York arrived. Had they captured a notorious murderer or betrayed an injured, helpless man? Even more, a man who had come under their hospitality. Did they deserve honor or opprobrium? The Garretts feared judgment under the old Southern code. Soon, they tried to rewrite the events of this night to cast their actions in a positive light. Ignoring the fact that they evicted Booth from their home on the night of April 25, the Garretts claimed that he had declined the bed on his last night, and that it was Booth who insisted on sleeping under the porch with the sharp-toothed dogs, or in the barn on the hard, wood planks. Conveniently, they overlooked the part of the story about just who locked Booth inside that barn.

In the years ahead, they even invoked Edwin Booth's name in defense of their family's reputation. Edwin, a loyal Unionist, hated John's deeds, but could not bring himself to hate his brother. Touched that the Garrett family took John in, and under the mistaken impression that they offered his misguided brother nothing but kindness and hospitality during the last two days of his life, Edwin wrote the Garretts a grateful letter: "Your family will always have our warmest thanks for your kindness to him whose madness wrought so much ill to us." If Edwin Booth had known the truth, that the Garretts had locked his brother in a barn like an animal, and helped prepare the funeral pyre, then Edwin, rather than lauding their kindness, might instead have wanted to come down to Port Royal and burn the rest of their farm down to the ground.

Edwin Booth might not have been the only one. The newspapers and the public demonized the Garrett farmhouse and gave it human characteristics, just as they had done to Ford's Theatre. George Alfred Townsend's lurid characterization spoke for many: "In the pale moonlight...a plain old farmhouse looked grayly through its environing lo-

Price Twenty-Five Cents.

THE LIFE, CRIME, AND CAPTURE

OF

John Wilkes Booth

AND THE PURSUIT, TRIAL AND EXECUTION OF HIS ACCOMPLICES.

NEW YORK:
DICK & FITZGERALD, PUBLISHERS.

Copies of this work mailed to any address free of Postage.

Journalist George Alfred Townsend's
thrilling account of the manhunt.

custs. It was worn and whitewashed, and two-storied, and its half-human windows glowered down upon the silent cavalrymen like watching owls which stood as sentries over some horrible secret asleep within…in this house, so peaceful by moonlight, murder had washed its spotted hands, and ministered to its satiated appetite."

Conger, Baker, and Doherty wanted to be absolutely certain, before they took the body back to Washington, that they had gotten their man, so they fished from their pockets carte-de-visite photos of Booth. Young Richard Garrett, mesmerized, watched the proceedings:

"I saw it done…our whole family saw it done. [H]e was a strikingly handsome man with a face one could scarcely forget. The detectives had a printed description of him which they proceeded to verify after his death. It agreed in every particular, height, color of hair, eyes, size of hand…I saw the initials J.W.B. just where they were said to be. I saw the detectives place…the photograph of John Wilkes Booth…beside the face of the dead man we had known for two days, and [nothing] in the world could not persuade me that God ever made two men so exactly alike."

Lieutenant Doherty unrolled his scratchy, wool, regulation army blanket and ordered his men to lay Booth's body upon it. He told the Garrett girls to go inside and bring him a thick sewing needle. Then he stitched the blanket around the assassin's corpse, leaving one end open, like a sleeping bag, from which Booth's feet protruded. They needed a wagon. Doherty's men rustled up a local man and hired him to drive the corpse to Port Royal. The man brought the wagon to the Garretts' front porch, where several soldiers heaved Booth in like a sack of corn. David Herold, whimpering, crying, pleading excuses that no one cared to hear, took it all in.

George Alfred Townsend offered his readers an unforgettable picture of Booth's ersatz hearse:

> A venerable old negro living in the vicinity had the misfortune to possess a horse. This horse was a relic of former generations, and showed by his protruding ribs the general leanness of the land. He moved in an eccentric amble, and when put upon his speed was generally run backward. To this old negro's horse was harnessed a very shaky and absurd wagon, which rattled like approaching dissolution, and each part of it ran without any connection or correspondence with any other part. It had no tail-board, and its shafts were sharp as famine; and into this mimicry of a vehicle the murderer was to be sent to the Potomac river.... The old negro geared up his wagon by means of a fossil harness, and when it was backed to the Garrett's porch, they laid within it the discolored corpse. The corpse was tied with ropes around the legs and made fast to the wagon sides.... So moved the cavalcade of retribution, with death in its midst, along the road to Port Royal.... All the way the blood dribbled from the corpse in a slow, incessant, sanguine exudation.

Booth's funeral procession retraced the very route that he, David Herold, and their three young Confederate companions had followed from Port Royal to Garrett's farm two days ago. No sobbing mourners watched this parade. The soldiers forced Herold to walk, but he complained mightily that his feet were killing him. They put him on a horse, tying his feet into the stirrups and his hands to the saddle. On the ride one of the soldiers chatted up Herold and scored a superb souvenir—he persuaded Booth's companion to trade vests with him.

The jostling wagon disturbed Booth's clotted wound, noted Townsend. "When the wagon started, Booth's wound till now scarcely dribbling, began to run anew. It fell through the crack of the wagon, dripping upon the axle, and spotting the road with terrible wafers." It was an eerie re-creation of the street scene in front of Ford's Theatre the night of April 14, when drops of Abraham Lincoln's blood and brains drizzled onto the mud underfoot. Townsend relished the phenomenon of Booth's flowing blood as the stigmata of a cursed corpse: "It stained the planks and soaked the blankets; and the old negro, at a stoppage, dabbled his hand in it by mistake, he drew back instantly, with a shudder and stifled expletive, 'Gor-r-r, dat'll never come off in de world; it's murderer's blood.' He wrung his hands, and looked imploringly at the officers, and shuddered again: 'Gor-r-r, I wouldn't have dat on me fur thousand, thousand dollars.'"

After Luther Baker and Ned Freeman crossed the Rappahannock, they drove Booth's body from Port Conway toward Belle Plaine. Three miles north of that location, Baker haled the *John S. Ide,* which had transported the Sixteenth New York Cavalry to Belle Plaine on the twenty-fourth. There was no wharf above Belle Plaine, so Baker unloaded Booth's corpse from Freeman's wagon, put it in a small boat, and rowed to the *Ide.*

𝒯HOUSANDS AND THOUSANDS OF DOLLARS WERE EXACTLY what Conger, Baker, Doherty, and the men of the Sixteenth New York had in mind. Indeed, as news of the assassin's death spread, manhunters across Virginia, Maryland,. and the District of Columbia fantasized about the same thing: That War Department broadside dated April 20, 1865, and its astounding proclamation—"$100,000.00 REWARD! The murderer of our late, beloved President Is Still At Large." Booth was dead. Mary Surratt, Lewis Powell, George Atzerodt, Sam Arnold, Michael O'Laughlen, Dr. Samuel A. Mudd, Ned Spangler, and David Herold had all been arrested. It was only a matter of time before the U.S. government began writing checks—to someone.

Conger's plan worked. He had arrived in Washington before Booth's body, and now he could claim the credit of being the first to tell Edwin Stanton the news. He rushed from the wharf to Colonel Baker's office, where he broke the news. "He came into the back office," Baker stated, "and said to me that he had got Booth." Conger told the story of Garrett's farm, unfolded his handkerchief, and showed Baker what he had—the effects taken from Booth's body. The two detectives jumped in a buggy and, about 5:00 P.M., drove to the War Department to tell Stanton the news. But the secretary had left his office for the day. They drove on to Stanton's home, leaped out of the buggy, and ran to the front door. They found Stanton in the parlor reclining on a lounge resting, but not asleep. "We have got Booth," Baker told him. Stanton covered his eyes with his hands, paused, and stood up. Conger and Baker laid out Booth's effects on a table. Stanton picked up the diary and, Baker recalled, "after looking at it for some time, he handed it back to me." "Then," continued Baker, Stanton picked up the "little pocket compass." In the quiet of his parlor, Stanton had received the news—Booth had been taken, he was dead, and the manhunt for Lincoln's assassin was over. The secretary of war wasn't ready to celebrate yet. He wanted to be sure that the body being brought to Washington was really John Wilkes Booth. Conger unrolled the handkerchief containing the treasures he had stripped from Booth's still living body and shared his booty with Stanton. Persuasive evidence, Stanton must have concurred, but he had to be absolutely certain. He decided to convene an inquest aboard the *Montauk* as soon as Booth's body arrived in Washington. Witnesses would give notarized statements. An autopsy would be performed. Then Stanton could be sure.

In Washington, the steamer *John S. Ide* rendezvoused off the U.S. Navy Yard with an ironclad gunboat—the *Montauk*—the same vessel that Abraham and Mary Lincoln visited during their carriage ride on the afternoon of the assassination. Stanton took immediate steps to confirm the identity of the man killed at Garrett's farm. At first glance, Booth was barely recognizable. He had shaved off his moustache, and his injury, the psychological stress of the manhunt, and twelve hard days of living mostly outdoors had taken their toll, reported Townsend, on his hitherto magnificent appearance. "It was fairly preserved, though on one side the face distorted, and looking blue-like death, and wildly bandit-like, as if bearen by avenging angels." The War Department wanted to quash the birth of any Booth survival myths. Edwin Stanton had already scrutinized all of the personal effects collected at Garrett's farm: the photos of the girlfriends; the pocket compass that pointed Booth south to imagined safety; the leather-bound pocket calendar. As Stanton turned the pages, he made a startling discovery—Booth had used the calendar as an impromptu diary, and in it he recorded his motive for killing Lincoln, and the turmoil of the manhunt. Only one man, Stanton knew, could have authored these fevered words: Abraham Lincoln's assassin. Stanton announced the news to the nation:

WAR DEPARTMENT
Washington, D.C., April 27, 1865

> *Major General Dix, New York:*
> *J. Wilkes Booth and Harrold were chased from the swamp in St. Mary's county, Maryland, and pursued yesterday morning to Garrett's farm, near Port Royal, on the Rappahannock, by Colonel Baker's forces.*
> *The barn in which they took refuge was fired. Booth, in*

making his escape, was shot through the head and killed,
lingering about three hours, and Harrold taken alive.
    Booth's body and Harrold are now here.

                        EDWIN M. STANTON
                            Secretary of War

News of the arrival of Booth's body spread quickly through the capital, and hundreds of spectators rushed to the river for a glimpse of the dead assassin. "At Washington," George Alfred Townsend reported, "high and low turned out to look on Booth. Only a few were permitted to see his corpse for purposes of recognition." A *Chicago Tribune* correspondent confirmed, with palpable disappointment, that "it seems that the authorities are not inclined to give the wretched carcass the honor of meeting the public gaze."

News of Booth's death traveled across the nation by telegraph, and newspapers everywhere rushed to print with excited stories filled with the details of the manhunt's climax at Garrett's farm. As soon as the news reached Philadelphia, T. J. Hemphill of the Walnut Theatre knew what had to be done. When he called at Asia Booth Clarke's home, she received him at once. Asia knew from the very sight of him what must have happened. "The old man stood steadying himself by the center table; he did not raise his eyes, his face was very pale and working nervously. The attitude and pallor told the news he had been deputed to convey." Asia spoke first.

"Is it over?"

"Yes, madam."

"Taken?"

"Yes."

"Dead?"

"Yes, madam."

Asia, pregnant with twins, collapsed onto a sofa. If one of her new babies was a boy, she had planned to name him John. "My heart beat like strong machinery, powerful and loud it seemed. I lay down with my face to the wall, thanking God solemnly, and heard the old man's sobs choking him, heard him go out, and close the street door after him."

On the *Montauk,* several men who knew Booth in life, including his doctor and dentist, were summoned aboard the ironclad to witness him in death. It was all very official. The War Department even issued an elaborate receipt to the notary who witnessed the testimony. During a careful autopsy, surgeons noted a distinctive old scar on his neck and the tattoo—"JWB"—that Booth had marked on his hand when he was a boy. The cause of death was easy to prove: gunshot via a single bullet through the neck. As proof the surgeons excised the vertebrae it had passed through and also removed part of Booth's thorax and pickled the bone and tissue in a neatly labeled glass specimen jar. Booth's vertebrae repose today in a little-known medical museum, one attraction among thousands in a hideous collection devoted to documenting the wounds of the American Civil War. The surgeon general's handwritten autopsy report was clinical and brief, but betrayed the emotion of the hour. In his letter to Edwin Stanton, Dr. Barnes assured the secretary of war that John Wilkes Booth had suffered:

> *I have the honor to report that in compliance with your orders, assisted by Dr. Woodward, USA, I made at 2 P.M. this day, a postmortem examination of the body of J. Wilkes Booth, lying on board the Monitor Montauk off the Navy Yard.*
>
> *The left leg and foot were encased in an appliance of splints and bandages, upon the removal of which, a fracture of the fibula (small bone of the leg) 3 inches above the ankle joint, accompanied by considerable ecchymosis, was discovered.*
>
> *The cause of death was a gun shot wound in the neck— the ball entering just behind the sterno-cleido muscle—2½ inches above the clavicle—passing through the bony bridge of the fourth and fifth cervical vertebrae—severing the spinal*

chord [sic] and passing out through the body of the sterno-
cleido of right side, 3 inches above the clavicle.

Paralysis of the entire body was immediate, and all the
horrors of consciousness of suffering and death must have been
present to the assassin during the two hours he lingered.

Stanton had decided that a written record of the autopsy was insuf-
ficient. He summoned the celebrated photographer Alexander Gardner,
Mathew Brady's rival and a favorite of President Lincoln's, to photograph Booth's corpse as it lay naked, stretched out on a board on the
deck of the ironclad. Stanton also allowed Gardner to photograph the
conspirators imprisoned on the ironclads *Montauk* and *Saugus.* Gardner took multiple images of Arnold, O'Laughlen, Spangler, Atzerodt,
and Herold, each wearing an unusual type of handcuff called "Lilley
irons," joined by a solid bar that prevented the prisoners from bringing
their hands together. They would see Gardner again soon, when he took
their final portraits. Gardner took special interest in Lewis Powell, pic-
turing him in a number of poses that he soon reproduced as cartes-de-
visite for public sale. But, on Stanton's orders, there would be no public
viewing of the autopsy images. *Harper's Weekly* based a single, discreet
woodcut on one of the horrific images, but the original glass plates and
paper prints of Stanton's trophy photographs vanished 140 years ago,
almost as soon as they were taken, and have never been seen again.

The prominent sculptor Clark Mills, who had recently fashioned a
plaster life mask of Lincoln in March 1865, sought permission to make
a death mask of his assassin. He wanted to come aboard the *Montauk,*
slather Booth's face with wet plaster and, once it dried, pry the mask
from the assassin's countenance. Mills went too far for the secretary of
war. According to a newspaper account, "Mr. Stanton, not deeming him
over loyal, replied: 'You had better take care of your own head.'" Death
masks, Stanton perhaps reasoned, were best suited for honoring great
men, not their murderers.

Stanton certainly hoped that, like the autopsy photographs, Booth's body would vanish. Scoop-seeking reporters lusted to unearth the last great episode of the twelve-day manhunt, the disposal of the assassin's remains.

"What," Townsend probed Lafayette C. Baker, "have you done with the body?"

Colonel Baker uttered a typically portentous, self-dramatizing reply: "That is known to only one man living besides myself. It is gone. I will not tell you where. The only man who knows is sworn to silence. Never till the great trumpet comes shall the grave of Booth be discovered."

"And," Townsend confidentially advised his readers, "this is true."

In the days following the close of the manhunt, all the major American newspapers damned John Wilkes Booth with parting epithets. The most vivid among them was penned by George Alfred Townsend:

Last night, the 27th of April, a small row boat received the carcass of the murderer; two men were in it, they carried the body off into the darkness, and out of that darkness it will never return....In the darkness, like his great crime, may it remain forever, impalpable, invisible, nondescript, condemned to that worse than damnation,—annihilation. The river-bottom may ooze about it laden with great shot and drowning manacles. The earth may have opened to give it that silence and forgiveness which man will never give its memory. The fishes may swim around it, or the daisies grow white above it; but we shall never know. Mysterious, incomprehensible, unattainable, like the dim times through which we live and think upon as if we only dreamed them in perturbed fever, the assassin of a nation's head rests somewhere in the elements, and that is all; but if the indignant seas or the profaned turf shall ever vomit his corpse from their recesses, and it receive humane or Christian burial from some who do not recognize it, let the last words those decaying lips ever uttered be carved above them with a dagger, to tell the history of a young and once promising life—USELESS! USELESS!

But Lafayette Baker had lied to Townsend. The second manhunt for John Wilkes Booth—the one for his corpse—had only begun. To prevent Booth's grave from becoming a shrine, and his body a holy relic of the Lost Cause, sailors from the *Montauk*, accompanied by the Bakers, had pretended to row his body out to deep water and bury it at sea, so weighted down that it could never rise. The press swallowed the bait, and one newspaper, *Frank Leslie's Illustrated News*, even published a front-page woodcut illustrating the faux, watery burial. What really happened was far less dramatic. Lafayette Baker, Luther Baker, and two sailors from the *Montauk* took Booth's body from the gunboat and laid it on the floor of a rowboat. The sailors shoved off from the ironclad's low-riding deck, and rowed away from the Navy Yard, down the Potomac's eastern branch. Booth was on the river again, seven days after Thomas Jones led him to its banks. The sailors made for an army post at Greenleaf's Point called the Old Arsenal, or the Old Penitentiary, a complex of substantial brick buildings and a courtyard surrounded by a high brick wall. They pulled in to a little wood wharf attached to the arsenal. Lafayette Baker stepped onto the wharf and, leaving his cousin in charge of the corpse, walked to the fort to find Major Benton, the ordnance officer Stanton had chosen to put Booth in the grave. Benton and Baker returned to the wharf, looked at the body, and, Luther Baker recalled, "talked the matter over." Benton knew just the place to bury him.

Benton ordered some of his men to carry Booth's body into the fort. They dropped it in a rectangular, wood musket crate, and screwed down the lid. Somebody wrote Booth's name on top. Then they buried the assassin in a secret, unmarked grave at the Old Arsenal penitentiary, the site chosen by Edwin Stanton as the unconsecrated burial ground for John Wilkes Booth, and for several of his conspirators who would soon join him in the grave. Stanton kept the only key. "I gave directions that he should be interred in that place, and that the place should be kept under lock and key," Stanton said. He wanted to be sure that "the body might not be made the subject of glorification by disloyal persons and those sympathizing with the rebellion," or "...the instrument of rejoicing at the sacrifice of Mr. Lincoln." Stanton wanted to keep the worshipers and relic hunters at bay: "The only object was to place his body where it could not be made an improper use of until the excitement had passed away." Booth had escaped once before on assassination night, but he would not escape Stanton again.

Booth's death did not end the manhunt for those who had come in contact with the assassin during his escape. If they thought Boston Corbett had saved them, they were wrong. Stanton wasn't finished with them. His April 20 proclamation had made that clear: "All persons harboring or secreting the said persons...or aiding or assisting their concealment or escape, will be treated as accomplices in the murder of the President...and shall be subject to...the punishment of DEATH." Stanton sent more patrols into Maryland and Virginia to track down everyone who he knew, or suspected, had seen or helped Booth during his twelve days on the run. Thomas Jones, Captain Cox, the Garrett sons, and many more were seized and taken to the Old Capitol prison. Then, curiously, within weeks, Stanton freed them all. He decided to put only eight defendants on trial—Mary Surratt, Lewis Powell, David Herold, George Atzerodt, Samuel Arnold, Michael O'Laughlen, Edman Spangler, and Samuel Mudd. Not one person who helped Booth and Herold in Maryland or Virginia, aside from Dr. Mudd, was punished for aiding Lincoln's assassin. They returned to their homes and families and, for years to come, whispered secret tales of their deeds during the great manhunt.

Several days after Booth's burial, Luther Baker, in a coda to the manhunt, journeyed again to Garrett's farm. It was after sunset. The charred remnants of the cedar posts, boards, and planks that had burned so brightly on the early morning of April 26 had cooled. Baker walked amidst the ruins: "Just before dark I went out to where the barn was burned, thinking I might find some remains…I poked around in the ashes and found some melted lead (it seemed he had some cartridges with him) and pieces of the blanket Herold had."

Another hunt—the one for the reward money—began before Booth's body cooled in the grave. With Booth dead, and his chief accomplices under arrest, awaiting trial for the murder of the president and the attempted assassination of William Seward, it was time to cash in. Hundreds of manhunters rushed to claim a portion of the $100,000 reward. Tipsters with the slightest—or no—connection to the events of April 14 to 26, 1865, angled for their rewards. Among the rival detectives, army officers, enlisted men, policemen, and citizens, the competition was brutal. Applicants exaggerated their roles, downplayed their rivals, and concocted fabulous lies to enhance their stake. In a long affidavit supporting his claim, Lafayette Baker boasted that he was the first to distribute photos of Booth, Herold, and Surratt. Lieutenant Doherty asked soldiers under his command to write affidavits to support his version of the events at Garrett's farm.

At first, Lafayette Baker's intrigues paid off handsomely—$17,500, an impressive sum considering that the salary of the president of the United States was $25,000. Colonel Conger got the same as Baker; Luther Baker got $5,000; and Lieutenant Doherty, commander of the Sixteenth New York Garrett's farm patrol, got only $2,500. Together, the Baker cousins outmaneuvered their rivals and monopolized $22,500, nearly one-quarter of the entire $100,000 reward. Loud, indignant complaints forced Congress to investigate the matter. Claims were reevaluated, reports were published by the Government Printing Office, and all the while, the manhunters lobbied greedily for their money. Booth would have likely enjoyed the grotesque spectacle of this bickering for blood money over the bodies of a dead president and his assassin.

Congress adjusted the figures and finally, more than one year after the manhunt, the U.S. Treasury issued warrants to disburse the reward.

Congress cut Conger's share from $17,500 to $15,000 and raised Doherty to a more generous $5,250. But the Bakers suffered badly. Lafayette Baker, who was not present at Garrett's farm, saw his share reduced from $17,500 to $3,750, while Luther Byron Baker's share was cut from $5,000 to $3,000. God may have guided Boston Corbett's hand at Garrett's farm, but the Almighty did not intervene to line the eccentric sergeant's pocket. He received the same payout as every enlisted man and noncommissioned officer there—$1,653.84.

Conger, Doherty, the Bakers, and the twenty-six men—two sergeants, seven corporals, and seventeen privates—from the Sixteenth New York Cavalry were not the only ones to enjoy a payday for Booth's capture and Herold's arrest. James O'Beirne, H. H. Wells, George Cottingham, and Alexander Lovett were awarded $1,000 each for their roles in the manhunt.

And then there were the other rewards. Nine men received bounties for the capture of George Atzerodt. Sergeant Zachariah Gemmill got the most—$3,598.54—and seven others won subordinate rewards of $2,878.78 each. James W. Purdum, the citizen whose tip contributed to the German's arrest, was paid the same. Major E. R. Artman, 213th Pennsylvania Volunteers, received $1,250.

Ten claimants split the reward money set aside for the arrest of Lewis Powell. Compared with what some other manhunters received for less hazardous work, the bounty for capturing the dangerous Seward assassin was not generous. Major H. W. Smith got the most, $1,000, and the other participants—Detective Richard Morgan, Eli Devore, Charles H. Rosch, Thomas Sampson, and William Wermerskirch—were paid $500 each. Citizens John H. Kimball and P. W. Clark also received $500 each, and two women, Mary Ann Griffin and Susan Jackson—"colored"—received the smallest rewards paid to anyone who shared in the bounty, just $250 each.

The reward payments totaled $104,999.60, and the Treasury Department issued warrants "in satisfaction of all claims," to the dissatisfaction of the many claimants—officers, soldiers, detectives, government

officials, citizens, and crackpots—who dreamed of cashing in on Stanton's April 20 proclamation, but who got nothing.

Richard Garrett also made a claim against the government, not for
helping capture Booth and Herold, but for the damage that the manhunters did to his property. His inventory was extensive. Two thousand
dollars for one "tobacco house...framed on heavy cedar posts, plank
floor throughout...furnished with all the fixtures for curing tobacco,
including prize-press and sticks for hanging tobacco." Then there were
the contents, for which Garrett demanded $2,670: "One wheat-thresh-
ing machine (150); two stoves (25); one set large dining room tables
(mahogany or walnut) (50); ten walnut chairs, cushioned seats (40);
one feather bed (15); one shovel (1); two axes (3); five bushels sugar-
corn seed (7.50); five hundred pounds hay (10)."

In addition, Garrett wanted $21.00 for the fifteen bushels of corn
and 300 pounds of hay consumed by the horses of the Sixteenth New
York. The government actually considered his claim, issued an official
report, and refused to pay him a cent, reasoning that he had, after all,
been disloyal to the Union.

Boston Corbett did enjoy additional compensation—fame. The
public celebrated him as "Lincoln's Avenger." Citizens deluged him with
fan mail, and he faithfully answered their letters, sometimes offering
biographical tidbits, religious counsel, or occasionally a coveted, firsthand account of the events at Garrett's farm. To the delight of autograph seekers, Corbett made a point of signing these letters with his full
name, rank, and unit. The following letters are typical.

> *Clarendon Hotel/Washington, D.C./May 6 1865 My dear*
> *young friend I must give you an answer for you ask so pretty.*
> *May God Bless And Protect You and keep you from the snares*
> *of the Wicked One Who so prevailed with him who took the*
> *life of Our President. The Scripture says, Resist the Devil And*
> *he will flee from you...Boston Corbett/Sergt. Co. L. 16th*
> *N.Y. Cav.*

> Lincoln Barracks/Washington D.C./May 11th 1865 Dear
> Sir, In answer to Your request I would say that Booth was Shot
> on the Morning of the 26th of April 1865 Near Port Royal,
> Virginia at which place we Crossed the Rappahannock in
> Pursuit. He lived but a short time after he was Shot,
> Perhaps 3 hours, and at about Seven O'clock that Morning
> he died. Yours Truly/Boston Corbett/Sergt. Co. L. 16th
> N.Y. Cavalry.

Incredibly, Corbett also corresponded with the assassin's family. Corbett's letter, long lost, its contents unknown, exists only as a shadow in Asia Booth Clarke's memoir of her brother: "We regard Boston Corbett as our deliverer, for by his shot he saved our brother from an ignominious death.... I returned Boston Corbett's letter to him; he did not request it exactly, but I thought it honorable to do so and safer at the time not to retain it.... He is still living, but I know he is not happy.... May he have no regret."

Photographer Mathew Brady scored a coup over his rival Alexander Gardner. Although Gardner had won the right to photograph the conspirators in irons on the navy ironclads, and also Booth's autopsy, Brady secured an exclusive sitting with the man of the hour. Always alert to the commercial possibilities of his art, Brady arranged Corbett in a variety of poses: seated and standing, reading a book and looking at the camera, armed and unarmed. Brady even persuaded Lieutenant Doherty to join the session for a standing, double portrait with Corbett, each man decked out in full cavalry regalia. The greater the number of poses Brady could induce Corbett to assume, the more cartes-de-visite he could sell to a besotted public. Some lucky fans even got Corbett to autograph his photo for their albums. When he appeared in public, reported one newspaper, "he has been greatly lionized, and on the streets was repeatedly surrounded by citizens, who occasionally manifested their appreciation by loud cheers."

A few dissenting voices, including the editors of the *Chicago Tri-*

The man of the hour, Booth's killer, Boston Corbett (top).
Blood money—Corbett's share of the $100,000 reward (bottom).

bune, wondered why the men of the Sixteenth New York had to kill the assassin: "The general regret is that Booth was not taken alive, and the general disposition to complain that he might have been if a combined rush of twenty-eight men surrounding them had been made."

Beyond the reward money, Corbett profited little from his fame. Relic hunters offered fantastic sums for his Colt revolver, up to $1,000, but he refused to part with it. It wasn't his to sell: the weapon had been purchased by the War Department and issued to the sergeant along with his uniform, saber, and other equipment. Then, not long after he shot Booth, somebody stole it from him, and it hasn't been seen since.

Boston Corbett was never punished for shooting Booth. He had violated no orders, and no one could prove that his true motive was anything other than protecting his men. He had the reputation of a good soldier. Luther Baker remembered that "he attended to his duties as a soldier very strictly, and seemed to have a good deal of dignity among the men." But Baker also recalled something else about the eccentric, self-castrating, hard-fighting sergeant: "I noticed from the first that he had an odd expression."

$\mathcal{T}$WO AND A HALF MONTHS AFTER THE DEATH OF JOHN WILKES Booth at Garrett's farm, at around 11:00 A.M. on July 6, 1865, the clock began ticking down on one of the most dramatic events in the history of Washington, the epilogue of the manhunt for Lincoln's killers. It began when Major General Winfield Scott Hancock rode to the Old Arsenal Penitentiary, now Fort Leslie McNair, carrying four sealed envelopes from the War Department. They were addressed neatly in a clerk's hand to four prisoners who had languished in solitary confinement at the arsenal.

Hancock handed the envelopes to Major General John F. Hartranft, commandant of the prison. Hartranft accepted the mail grimly. He suspected, without even breaking the seals, what the envelopes contained, and the unpleasant duty that awaited him. Together, Hartranft and Hancock marched to the prison building and, walking down a long corridor from cell to cell, delivered the envelopes to their recipients—Lewis Powell, Mary Surratt, David Herold, and George Atzerodt.

Torn open in fearful haste, the envelopes contained death warrants. Having been found guilty by a military commission of conspiring with John Wilkes Booth in the assassination of Abraham Lincoln and the attempted assassination of Secretary of State William Seward, the letters informed Powell, Surratt, Herold, and Atzerodt that they were to be put to death by hanging.

For the defendants, that news was bad enough, but the rest was equally shocking. By order of President Andrew Johnson, they would be hanged the next day, on July 7. Hartranft left the stunned prisoners, who had less than a day to live, to contemplate their fates. He had work to do. Did anyone at the fort know how to build a scaffold? Or how to tie a noose?

The rapid conviction, sentencing, and execution of the Lincoln assassination conspirators ended a trial that had meandered through May and June. The archfiend Booth was dead, but eight members of his supporting cast took center stage in his absence.

Johnson, under pressure by Edwin Stanton, had ordered that eight members of Booth's supporting cast be tried by a military tribunal, a controversial move that provoked objections from Secretary of the Navy Gideon Welles and Lincoln's first attorney general, Edward Bates. The trial proceeded anyway and became the great focus for that spring and summer. By the time it was over, the commission had been in session for seven weeks, had taken the testimony of 366 witnesses and had produced a transcript of 4,900 pages.

On June 29, the commission went into secret session. After such a long and complicated trial, observers thought that it might take weeks to reach verdicts. But the end came more quickly. After deliberating just a few days, the tribunal presented the verdicts and sentences to Johnson on July 5. He approved them at once, and the next day Hancock carried the execution orders to the prison.

The residents of Washington did not know until the *Evening Star* came off the press on the afternoon of July 6 that four conspirators would hang the next day. Indeed, it was from the newspapers that Surratt's attorneys learned their client would die. Newsboys rushed onto Pennsylvania Avenue, hawking the issue to eager readers: "Extra. Mrs. Surratt, Payne, Herold and Atzerodt to be Hung!! The Sentences to be Executed Tomorrow!! Mudd, Arnold, and O'Laughlin to be Imprisoned for Life! Spangler to be Imprisoned for Six Years!"

As evening passed and night fell, the news caused a flurry of activity throughout Washington. Reporters converged on the Old Arsenal, but Hartranft barred them from interviewing the condemned. Frustrated but refusing to be outwitted, the gentlemen of the press spied on the prisoners through cell windows, and recorded in their notebooks the last visits of family members and how the condemned behaved. In the courtyard, soldiers labored through the night building a scaffold while the hangman prepared four nooses from thirty-one-strand, two-thirds-inch Boston hemp, supplied by the Navy Yard.

Mrs. Surratt's supporters, including her daughter, rushed to the Executive Mansion to beg Johnson for mercy. He would not see them or be swayed. In a daring, last-minute legal maneuver, the Surratt attorneys got a civil court judge to issue a writ of habeas corpus ordering the army to release her into civilian custody. Johnson ended her last hope by suspending the writ the next morning.

Elsewhere in Washington that night, others reveled at the news of the impending hangings. A pass to the execution—fewer than two hundred were printed—was the hottest ticket in town. Crowds besieged Hancock in the streets and at his hotel, the Metropolitan. According to the *Evening Star,* "his letterbox was filled with letters and cards that projected like a fan, and for a time the entrances to the hotel were completely blockaded." Curiosity seekers needed no pass to surround Surratt's boardinghouse on H Street. The house where the conspirators held their meetings became, in the words of one reporter, "the cynosure of hundreds of curious eyes."

By order of President Johnson, the execution was scheduled to take place between 10:00 A.M. and 2:00 P.M., July 7. At exactly 1:02 P.M., the prisoners, with Surratt at their head, were paraded single file into the courtyard, past four pine boxes and four freshly dug graves, and up the scaffold steps. Terrified, and wearing a black alpaca dress and black veil that completely concealed her face, Mary Surratt could barely walk and needed soldiers and her priests to support her.

Lewis Powell strutted jauntily without fear, "like a king about to be crowned," according to a reporter. David Herold and George Atzerodt shuffled along fretfully. It was a bright, blazing hot Washington summer day. Courteous officers shielded Surratt with parasols and placed a white handkerchief atop Atzerodt's head to protect him from the sun.

The condemned were bound with strips of linen, had nooses looped around their necks and white hoods drawn over their heads. The hangman, who had come to admire Powell's stoicism, whispered into his ear as he tightened the noose: "I want you to die quick."

The giant who had nearly stabbed the secretary of state to death replied, "You know best."

Surratt pleaded to those near her, "Please don't let me fall." When she complained that her wrists had been bound too tightly, a soldier retorted, "Well, it won't hurt long."

Moments before the drop, Atzerodt cried out, "God help me now! Oh! Oh! Oh!" His last word was still on his lips when, at 1:26 P.M., he and the others dropped to their deaths, a moment preserved forever by photographer Alexander Gardner, whose execution series remains the most shocking set of American historical photos ever made.

That night, a mob celebrated the execution by attacking Surratt's boardinghouse to strip it of souvenirs, until the police drove them off. John Surratt, still hiding in Canada, read about his mother's execution in the newspapers. He had fled the United States, arriving in Montreal on April 17. From there he traveled about thirty miles east to St. Liboire. A parish priest, Father Charles Boucher, gave sanctuary to the former Catholic seminarian, and Surratt remained there in hiding from mid-April through the trial, conviction, sentencing, and hanging of his mother. He followed the trial by reading the papers, and through secret correspondence with friends in Washington. In all that time, from the end of April to the first week of July, Surratt made no effort to save his mother from the gallows. Later, he blamed his friends for failing to inform him about the true peril that Mary Surratt faced.

Just hours after the hanging, as the bodies of the conspirators rested in the pine ammunition crates that served as coffins, the editors of the *Evening Star* pronounced their satisfaction with the day's work: "The last act of the tragedy of the 19th century is ended, and the curtain dropped forever upon the lives of its actors. Payne, Herold, Atzerodt and Mrs. Surratt have paid the penalty of their awful crime.... In the bright sunlight of this summer day...the wretched criminals have been hurried into eternity; and tonight, will be hidden in despised graves, loaded with the execrations of mankind."

Lewis Powell, David Herold, and George Azterodt, reunited in the grave with John Wilkes Booth, together again, just as they were that terrible Good Friday evening of April 1865, the night that the chase for Abraham Lincoln's killer began.

𝓑UT LINCOLN'S ASSASSIN HAD NOT REACHED HIS FINAL RESTing place. There remained one, final manhunt for him. February 1869 was the last month of Andrew Johnson's troubled presidency. On March 4, the great hero of the Civil War, General Ulysses S. Grant, would take the oath of office. Soon Johnson's name would be eclipsed, an ephemeral interlude between the old administration of the martyred Lincoln and the new one of the hero Grant. Whatever his reputation, Johnson still possessed the full executive authority of the presidency—including the pardon power—until his final day in office.

It had been almost four years since the assassination of Abraham Lincoln and the great conspiracy trial. The raw wounds of April 1865 had, at least in part, healed. Indeed, when John Surratt Jr., who had fled America after Lincoln's murder, was captured in Europe in 1866 and brought back to the United States for trial in 1867, he was tried, not by the military tribunal that condemned his mother, but by a civil court. And, after a proceeding that produced a voluminous, two-volume transcript of 1,383 printed pages, he was freed. The passions of 1865 had subsided, and President Johnson's thoughts turned to three of the convicted conspirators who had escaped hanging in July 1865—Dr. Samuel Mudd, Samuel Arnold, and Edman Spangler. The fourth, Michael O'Laughlen, had died in prison. Mudd and Arnold, serving life sentences, and Spangler, sentenced to six years, all languished in the American Devil's Island, the faraway military prison at Dry Tortugas, Florida.

On February 8, 1869, President Johnson pardoned Mudd, and soon thereafter Arnold and Spangler. They had survived the manhunt, and now they were free. And, freed from the grave by an order of the president transmitted the same day, was the body of Mary Surratt. Her daughter, Anna, had her remains disinterred from the Old Arsenal and buried the next day at Washington's Mount Olivet Cemetery.

In New York City, one man followed the news with keen interest. He had waited patiently for this day, for he, too, sought to redeem a loved one. He sat at his desk and began writing a letter to the president.

N.Y. Febry 10th, 1869

> *PRIVATE.*
> *Dear Sir—*
> *May I not now ask your kind consideration of my poor Mother's request in relation to her son's remains?*
> *The bearer of this (Mr. John Weaver) is sexton of CHRIST CHURCH, Baltimore, who will observe the strictest secrecy in this matter—and you may rest assured that none in my family desire its publicity.*
> *Unable to visit Washington I have deputed Mr. Weaver—in whom I Have the fullest Confidence, and I beg that you will not delay in ordering the body to be given to his care.*
> *He will retain it (placing it in his vault) until such time as we can remove other members of our family to the BALTIMORE CEMETERY, and thus prevent any special notice of it.*
> *There is also (I am told) a trunk of his at the National Hotel—which I once applied for but was refused—it being under the seal of the War Dept., it may contain relics of the poor misguided boy—which would be dear to his sorrowing mother, and of no use to anyone. Your Excellency would*

greatly lessen the crushing weight of grief that is hurrying
my Mother to the grave by giving immediate orders for the
safe delivery of the remains of John Wilkes Booth to
Mr. Weaver.

Edwin Booth

Five days later, Andrew Johnson ordered the War Department, no longer the domain of the once all-powerful Edwin Stanton, to surrender the body of Lincoln's assassin to his family. A Washington, D.C., undertaker, Harvey and Marr, picked up the body in a wagon and drove into town, and down a familiar alley to a shed behind the funeral establishment. The sturdy wood crate was unloaded and brought inside. John Wilkes Booth would have recognized the little shed. Once it was a stable, fitted out for him by a man named Ned Spangler. Booth had returned to Baptist Alley, behind Ford's Theatre, where the manhunt began.

The *Washington Evening Star* remarked on the delicious irony: "It is a strange coincidence that the remains of J. Wilkes Booth should yesterday have been temporarily deposited in the stable, in the rear of Ford's Theatre, in which he kept his horse, and fronting on the alley through which he made his escape on the night he assassinated President Lincoln. The remains were deposited in the stable by the undertakers…in order to baffle the crowd who had besieged their establishment, on F Street, to satisfy their curiosity by a sight of the body."

From there, Edwin Booth had his brother whisked away to Baltimore, where the remains rested for the next four months in a vault at Green Mount Cemetery. On June 26, 1869, John Wilkes Booth was buried quietly in the family plot at Green Mount. No headstone marks his grave. He lies there still, his epitaph carved not on cold stone or marble, but in his sister's forgiving heart. Asia Booth's loving memoir to her brother closes with a graveside elegy:

"But, granting that he died in vain, yet he gave his all on earth, youth, beauty, manhood, a great human love, the certainty of excellence in his profession, a powerful brain, the strength of an athlete, health and great wealth, for '*his cause.*' This man was noble in life, he periled his immortal soul, and he was brave in death. Already his hidden remains are given Christian burial, and strangers have piled his grave with flowers.

"'So runs the world away.'"

Epilogue

A SIA BOOTH GAVE BIRTH TO TWINS IN AUGUST 1865. ONE WAS a boy, but she dared not name him John. When he grew older, many remarked that he resembled his notorious uncle. Asia stayed married to John Sleeper Clarke, who prospered in England as a celebrated comedian, but who denied her a happy life. "He lives in mystery and silence as far as I am concerned," Asia complained. "He lives a free going bachelor life and does what he likes." In 1879 she wrote to her brother Edwin, "I am so tired of his dukelike haughtiness—his icy indifference, and so disgusted with the many false things he tells me." She remembered her brother John's prophetic warning before her marriage—she would only be Clarke's stepping-stone. Now Clarke was famous in his own right, and Asia and her blackened name were no longer of any use to him. "It is marvelous how he hates me—the mother of nine babies— but I am a *Booth*—that is sufficient."

Asia could keep a secret, too. Unbeknownst to John Sleeper Clarke, in 1874 she began writing a memoir to honor her dead brother. Fearing that her husband would burn the manuscript if he ever found it, she entrusted it to confidantes. It was not published until 1938, fifty years after her death, and sixty-four years after she wrote it. Her brother John had assassinated Abraham Lincoln seventy-four years ago. Asia Booth Clarke died in England on May 16, 1888, at the age of fifty-two. She had wanted to come home and rejoin her family in America. On June 1, she was buried in Green Mount Cemetery in Baltimore. She rests in the Booth family plot, near her brother John.

 $\mathcal{C}$ LARA HARRIS AND HENRY RATHBONE MARRIED IN 1867, HAD three children, and moved to Hanover, Germany. No one ever blamed Rathbone for the night at Ford's Theatre. He was a social guest, not Lincoln's bodyguard. He wasn't assigned the duty of protecting the president. And he didn't see Booth until after the actor fired his pistol. Still, he was an army officer. And he *was* in the box. Fortunately for Rathbone, it did not become widely known that he had asked Dr. Leale to treat his wound before treating Lincoln's. Nor did anyone suggest that he didn't seem to fight quite as hard as Sergeant Robinson or the Seward boys. George Robinson had submitted himself repeatedly to the punishment of Powell's knife, and the sergeant would not have abandoned his patient until Powell stabbed him to death. Rathbone, in contrast, had flinched upon first contact with Booth's avenging blade. Perhaps he should have made Booth cut him again.

Clara would have been better off if John Wilkes Booth had stabbed her fiancé again and slain him at Ford's Theatre on April 14, 1865. If Booth had served her that night, then she would have survived the night eighteen years later when, on December 23, 1883, Henry, after behaving oddly and menacing the children, murdered Clara in their home. In a bizarre, chilling reminder of Booth's crime, Henry selected the assassin's weapons of choice—the pistol and the knife. Rathbone shot his wife and then stabbed her to death. Then he tried to commit suicide with the same blade. It was a brutal, bloody crime that harkened back to the horrific scene in the president's box. But this time Clara's dress was drenched not with Henry's blood, but her own. Henry never returned to America and lived out his remaining days in a German asylum.

• • •

$\mathcal{B}$OSTON CORBETT'S LIFE UNFOLDED AS ODDLY AS ONE MIGHT have guessed. His fame lasted a season, climaxing with his appearance in a front-page woodcut in *Frank Leslie's,* and his May 17 appearance as a witness at the conspiracy trial. Soon the fan letters dwindled to a trickle, then ceased. Photographers no longer begged to take his picture. On September 9, 1865, he wrote to Edward Doherty about his share of the reward, seeking advice on how best to pursue his claim: should he hire Doherty's lawyer or find one of his own. On August 9, 1866, the U.S. Treasury issued him a warrant in the amount of $1,653.84. Corbett left the army, moved west, and got a job as assistant doorkeeper of the Kansas House of Representatives. That sinecure ended on the day in 1887 when he drew a revolver and held the legislature hostage at gunpoint. Confined to the Topeka asylum, he escaped in 1888, and then vanished from history. Nobody knows for sure what happened to him. Perhaps he ended his days still preaching warnings against "the snares of the evil one."

$\mathcal{T}$HOMAS A. JONES KEPT THE SECRET OF THE PINE THICKET and Booth's river crossing for eighteen years, until, in 1883, he divulged the tale to George Alfred Townsend. Later, Jones wrote a book about his adventures: *"J. Wilkes Booth. An Account of His Sojourn in Southern Maryland after the Assassination of Abraham Lincoln, his Passage Across the Potomac, and his death in Virginia. By Thomas A. Jones. The only living man who can tell the story."* In 1893, he traveled north to Chicago to have his manuscript published there by a local printer, and he set up a stand to sell books at the World's Columbian Exposition. According to legend, outraged Union veterans attacked the display and destroyed his stock of books. Today the slim volume, now a rare book, remains a priceless, firsthand account from the manhunt.

In an odd twist, Jones became an amateur dealer in Lincoln assassination memorabilia, scouting Washington and its environs for coveted objects he supplied to collectors. Twenty-five years after the assassination, he advised a customer that reward posters were impossible to find, and that an original April 14 Ford's Theatre playbill for *Our American Cousin* could not be had for less than one hundred dollars. Jones trafficked in photos of the Petersen House and of Mary Surratt's boarding-house, and he offered to locate photos of Boston Corbett. "I have had a good deal of work to do to get said pictures," Jones advised one of his collectors. "You might have looked Washington over for six months and I doubt whether you could have found the pictures you will get through me." Jones even tried to track down his battered old skiff, the one that carried Booth and Herold across the Potomac. That relic would make a sensational collector's prize. The search turned up more rare photos. "When I had been looking around the City to see if I could find out any thing about the Boat that Booth went across the River in," Jones explained, he found a soldier who told him that if he went to a "certain house" at the old arsenal, he would make an interesting discovery—four of Gardner's photos of the hanging. "The house that the President died in is just the same as when the President died," Jones informed a customer, except for Oldroyd's sign out front. Thomas Jones died in March 1895. He was seventy-four years old.

OTHER SURVIVORS OF THE MANHUNT TRADED ON THEIR MEM-ories, too. In 1867, Colonel Lafayette C. Baker published a now forgotten and shabby book, *History of the United States Secret Service,* that was anything but a true history. Baker exaggerated not only his importance in the chase for Booth, but in the entire Civil War. He died in 1868.

His cousin Luther Byron Baker survived him and, by the late 1880s, went on the lecture circuit and became the most successful of the post-assassination entrepreneurs. Armed with a professional manager, a variety of posters, and a four-page promotional brochure crammed with testimonials from satisfied customers, Baker delivered dozens of paid lectures over the next eight years until his death in May 1896, at age sixty-six.

At his lectures Baker sold a substantial souvenir: a large-format, seven-and-five-eighths-by-nine-inch, cardboard-backed, so-called combination picture that depicted Baker riding his horse "Buckskin," the duo surrounded by images of Booth, Corbett, and Lincoln. A descriptive label pasted on the reverse, and written in the purported voice of Buckskin, described the horse's participation in the manhunt. A concluding note, autographed by Baker, verified the animal's story. It was one of the most fetching Lincoln assassination trinkets ever concocted. Death did not end Buckskin's role as Baker's lecture companion. A taxidermy student at the Michigan State Agricultural College stuffed him, and the venerable manhunter stood proudly—albeit mutely—onstage with Baker as an unforgettable prop.

JOHN H. SURRATT JR. ENJOYED LESS SUCCESS AS A LECTURER. In 1870, five years after the assassination—and his mother's hanging—and just three years after his own trial, Surratt tried to exploit his story on the lecture circuit.

He certainly had an amazing story to tell. After his mother's hanging, John Surratt decided that fleeing to Europe offered him the best chance of survival. In September he traveled from St. Liboire to Montreal, moved on to Quebec, sailed to Liverpool, and continued to Rome, where, under the name "John Watson," he joined the Papal Zouaves, the colorfully uniformed army of the Papal States. Surratt blended in with this Catholic milieu, and he felt safely beyond the reach of the manhunters. But in April 1866, around the first anniversary of Lincoln's assassination, a fellow Zouave who recognized Surratt informed on him. Booth's coconspirator was arrested at Verdi on November 7. He escaped from Velletri prison the next day. While walking under guard near the edge of an overlook, Surratt glanced over the precipice. He saw jagged rocks twenty or thirty feet below, and, beyond them, a steep drop down a cliff. Before his guards could restrain him, Surratt, in an escape worthy of John Wilkes Booth, grabbed the balustrade, leaped over it, and tumbled to the rocks. Fortunately for Surratt, he landed uninjured. The rocks where he fell were the prison's waste dump, and a voluminous, filthy pile of human excrement and garbage cushioned his fall.

Surratt fled the Papal States and crossed into the Kingdom of Italy. Proceeding to Naples, and impersonating a Canadian citizen, he tricked the British consul into gaining him passage on a steamer headed for Alexandria, Egypt. But when Surratt disembarked on November 23, 1866, American officials were waiting for him. He was seized and shipped back to America on a U.S. Navy warship. John Surratt landed at the Washington Navy Yard on February 19, 1867, and was imprisoned immediately. His trial before a civil court, and not the military tribunal that condemned his mother, lasted from June through August 1867. The jury was unable to reach a verdict, and he was released. He was charged again in June 1868, but in November the charges were dismissed. John Surratt was a free man. His mother was dead, he had been exposed as a leader in a plot to kidnap President Lincoln, and he had earned the reputation of a coward who had abandoned his mother to die. But at least he was alive. If he had been captured in 1865 and tried by military tribunal, he certainly would have been convicted, and would likely have been executed.

Surratt got up a talk, went to Rockville, Maryland, and on December 6, 1870, made his first public appearance trading on his friendship with John Wilkes Booth and his involvement in the kidnapping plot. Surratt had the audacity to lecture in New York City at The Cooper Union, the site of Abraham Lincoln's triumphant February 1860 address that propelled him to the presidency. Emboldened, he decided to return to the scene of the crime, Washington. He had large, attractively designed posters printed to advertise his appearance at the Odd Fellows Hall on Seventh Street, above D, on December 30, 1870. His mother's boardinghouse and Ford's Theatre were just a few blocks away. But it was too soon. Citizens complained and, despite Surratt's boast in his poster that, "all reports to the contrary notwithstanding," he would "most positively" deliver his lecture, the event was canceled. A reporter found him hiding in a hotel room. John Surratt never lectured again. The last survivor of Booth's conspirators, he died in April 1916.

The aftermath of Powell's knife.

$\mathcal{S}$ECRETARY OF STATE WILLIAM SEWARD AND HIS sons survived their wounds. For the rest of his life, until his death in 1872, William Seward preferred to turn the scarred half of his face away from the camera and pose in profile. A rare frontal portrait reveals how he carried Lewis Powell's terrible, disfiguring mark. Frederick recovered his senses after his grievous head wound, and he lived another fifty years. But, in a family tragedy, death soon claimed the Seward women. In June 1865, Frances died at age fifty-nine. Her weak constitution had succumbed to the stressful assassination attempt. But at least William Seward had been prepared for the possibility of his wife's death. The next year he endured a staggering loss. His brave daughter, Fanny, who had fearlessly challenged Lewis Powell that awful, bloody night, left the world on October 29, 1866. Seward called her death his "great unspeakable sorrow." Her passing, he wrote, left his dreams for the future "broken and destroyed forever." Fanny was twenty-one years old. She would have been a wonderful writer.

• • •

$\mathscr{S}$AMUEL ARNOLD LIVED LONG ENOUGH TO WRITE HIS MEM-
oirs, and the *Baltimore American* newspaper serialized the manuscript
in 1902. By then he was the sole surviving defendant from the Lincoln
assassination conspiracy trial of 1865, and the only one who had ever
written a full account of Booth's kidnapping plot. He was also the only
one who lived long enough to see the new century. He died on September 1, 1906. Arnold joined John Wilkes Booth and Michael O'Laughlen
at Green Mount Cemetery.

$\mathscr{D}$R. MUDD RETURNED TO HIS FARM IN 1869, HAPPY TO BE FREE
of the black prison guards he despised. Soon Ned Spangler journeyed
there, and Mudd took him in until Ned's death on February 7, 1875.
Samuel Mudd passed on in 1883. Before he died, he confessed privately
to Samuel Cox Jr. the truth about the night of April 14, 1865: Mudd admitted that he had known all along that the injured stranger at his door
was John Wilkes Booth. After the doctor's death, one of his lawyers confirmed it. In 1906, Samuel Mudd's daughter published a collection of
his letters, and in 1936, a Hollywood motion picture, *The Prisoner of
Shark Island,* portrayed Mudd as an innocent country doctor obeying
his Hippocratic oath, deceived by Lincoln's assassin. That false image
took hold in the popular mind, and, to this day, many Americans still
believe the myth that Dr. Mudd and his descendants have toiled assidu-
ously for more than a century to perpetuate.

$\mathscr{E}$DWIN M. STANTON DIED IN 1869, THE SAME YEAR THAT JOHN
Wilkes Booth escaped the secret grave to which Lincoln's secretary of
war had condemned him. After the manhunt and conspiracy trial, Stanton's career went into eclipse under the controversial, impeachment-
tainted Johnson presidency. When Johnson tried to fire him, Stanton

refused to surrender his War Department office. General Grant assumed the presidency in 1869, and in December he nominated Stanton to be an associate justice on the U.S. Supreme Court. But Lincoln's right hand died later that month before he could join the court.

Stanton lived long enough to see much of the work of the manhunt undone. Public sympathy for Mary Surratt bloomed; he was accused of suppressing and tampering with Booth's diary, and Congress investigated; he saw Booth, Surratt, Powell, Herold, Atzerodt, and O'Laughlen emerge from their graves; saw the three survivors Mudd, Arnold, and Spangler pardoned; and saw the fugitive John Surratt Jr., who had escaped him in April of 1865, captured, tried, and freed. Perhaps it was best that Stanton did not live to see Surratt dare to boast of his role in the great crime and attempt to profit from the murder of Stanton's commander in chief—and friend.

Stanton's sudden death—he was only fifty-five—troubled Robert Lincoln and took him back four years, to the rear bedroom of the Petersen House. As soon as Robert heard the sad news, he sent a letter to Stanton's son: "I know that it is useless to say anything...and yet when I recall the kindness of your father to me, when my father was lying dead and I felt utterly desperate, hardly able to realize the truth, I am as little able to keep my eyes from filling with tears as he was then." Edwin Stanton was buried at Oak Hill Cemetery in Georgetown, not far from the stone chapel where Abraham Lincoln held a small funeral service for his son Willie. Few people visit his grave. If you drive down R Street, you can see it from your car: the weathered, white obelisk just a few yards behind the formidable, spike-topped iron fence, standing sentinel over his rest.

A CENTURY LATER, AT ANOTHER CEMETERY, MISGUIDED ANTIquarians buried Lewis Powell's remains with honors. His body had vanished long ago. Disinterred from the old arsenal in 1869, Powell was reburied in Holmead Cemetery in Washington. Soon that burial ground went defunct, and Powell's corpse, or so it was thought, became lost. In fact, his body, or at least a portion of it, went temporarily to the Army Medical Museum, and then ended up in the anthropological collections of the Smithsonian Institution. In 1993, somebody discovered his head, still neatly labeled, at the national museum. Powell sympathizers gained possession of the skull, transported it to his native Florida, sealed it in a miniature, hatbox-size coffin, and buried it on November 11—Veterans Day—1994. Powell's headless skeleton was never found, and his bones lie moldering in some unknown grave—or perhaps in the labyrinthine storage vaults of the Smithsonian. And so Seward's violent assassin rests, if not in peace, then in pieces.

ToDAY YOU CAN DRIVE THERE FROM WASHINGTON, D.C., IN A couple of hours. Several landmarks point the way: an antebellum brick row house in the middle of Washington's Chinatown; a Civil War era roadside tavern in Clinton, Maryland; a modest farmhouse hidden nearly from view in the Maryland countryside; an old hotel in Bryantown, Maryland; several nondescript homes in Virginia, their century-and-a-half-old clapboards covered by cheap aluminum siding. When you arrive at Garrett's farm, there isn't much to see. A few scattered trees survive from the dark forest that once grew there. The farmhouse overlooking the tobacco barn where it happened perished from rot and neglect long ago. Relic hunters, like locusts in a wheat field, carried off every last fragment of board and timber that time hadn't ravaged. Some of them have even driven shovels into the site of the burning barn, in hopes of excavating charred embers from the earth.

If you go in summer when the grass is tall, it's hard to spot the iron pipe and homemade tag that somebody pounded into the ground to mark the spot where the farmhouse once stood. But if you go in the spring, perhaps on April 26, the anniversary, you'll see it—the place where, in the middle of the night, the chase for Lincoln's killer came to an end.

The place where it began still stands in Washington, looming over Tenth Street. After the assassination, Ford's Theatre survived arson, abandonment, and disaster. Stanton vowed that the site of Lincoln's murder must never again serve as a house of laughter and public entertainment. He surrounded the theatre with guards, ordered it closed, and confined John T. Ford in the Old Capitol prison for thirty-nine days. Some cabinet members objected to the confiscation, but Stanton was adamant: that "dreadful house" would never open again. Others agreed—there were at least two attempts to burn it down. And the *Army and Navy Journal* spoke for many in applauding Stanton's decisiveness. If Ford "did not know enough, of himself, to close its career as a playhouse, it is fortunate that there is a man in Washington competent and spirited enough to give the instruction." Then the government relented and, on July 7, 1865—the day that Powell, Surratt, Herold, and Atzerodt went to the gallows—gave the theatre back to John Ford. When he announced his intention to reopen it, the public was outraged, and Ford received a number of threats. "You must not think of opening tomorrow night," warned one letter. "I can assure you that it will not be tolerated. You must dispose of the property in some other way. Take even fifty thousand for it and build another and you will be generously supported. But do not attempt to open it again." The anonymous threat was signed by "One of many determined to prevent it."

It was too much for Stanton. He seized Ford's Theatre again in the name of public safety. The government sentenced the building to death as a playhouse, and paid a contractor $28,500 to gut the interior. All evidence of its appearance on the night of April 14, 1865—the gaslights, the decorations, the furniture, the stage, and the president's box—vanished, either destroyed or carted away. By late November 1865, a little more than seven months after the assassination, the once beautiful theatre had been defaced beyond recognition and relegated to a drab, three-floor office building. The Record and Pension Bureau of Stanton's War Department moved in and crammed the space with government clerks and tens of thousands of pounds of files. In 1866, the government bought Ford's Theatre from John Ford for $100,000. In 1867, the top floor became the new home of the Army Medical Museum for the next twenty years, as if this place had not already seen enough horror and death. One day, on June 9, 1893, somebody filed one piece of paper too many, and the excessive load of tons of documents and office equipment caused all the floors to collapse, crushing twenty-two clerks to death, and crippling or injuring sixty-eight more.

Restored in the 1960s to its former glory, Ford's Theatre lives again as both a museum and a working playhouse. Presidents come here again for annual galas, though none sits in the president's box. The restoration was intended as a tribute to Abraham Lincoln, but Ford's has also, inevitably, become a memorial to his assassin. The theatre is dressed to appear just as it did on the night of April 14, 1865. The state box is festooned with flags, and the framed engraving of George Washington that hangs from the front of the box is the actual one that witnessed Booth's leap to the stage. You can follow Booth's steps up the curving staircase, retrace his path to the box, enter the vestibule, and re-create his view of Lincoln's rocking chair. You can sit in the audience and, while listening to a National Park Service historian lecture on the assassination, you can stare up at the box and imagine Booth suspended momentarily in midair, at the apex of his leap.

John Wilkes Booth would have loved it: An entire museum—one of the most popular in America—devoted to his crime. "I must have fame," he once exhorted himself, "fame." He has it at Ford's Theatre, his enduring monument where he is always onstage, forever famous. His fame is of a peculiar kind. Booth was reviled as a fiend during the manhunt. The newspaper editorials, letters from private citizens, mob violence, and the treatment of his body are proof enough of that. Yes, in some quarters there were those who hated Lincoln and admired Booth, but the devotees of the cult of "Our Brutus" dared not express public sympathy for the assassin. Then, over time, something changed. Booth became part of American folklore and his image morphed from evil murderer of a president into fascinating antihero—the brooding, misguided, romantic, and tragic assassin. Booth is not celebrated for the murder, but he has in some way been forgiven for it. What else can explain the presence of large street banners, decorated with the assassin's photo, hanging from lampposts along his F Street escape route, directing tourists to Ford's Theatre? In comparison, the display of Lee Harvey Oswald banners in Dallas, or James Earl Ray banners in Memphis, would be obscene.

Asia Booth foresaw the trajectory of her brother's fame, and she tried to help set it in motion in her secret book. To Asia, Abraham Lincoln and John Wilkes Booth were paired, tragic figures destined to die and bring about a transcendent healing between North and South. Her brother "'saved his country from a king,' but he created for her a martyr....He set the stamp of greatness on an epoch of history, and gave all he had to build this enduring monument to his foe...[t]he South avenged the wrongs inflicted by the North. A life inexpressibly dear was sacrificed wildly for what its possessor deemed best. The life best beloved by the North was dashed madly out when most triumphant. Let the blood of both cement the indissoluble union of our country."

The legend of John Wilkes Booth began within weeks of the manhunt and his death at Garrett's farm. A minister in Texas wrote a poem honoring Booth. In New York City, on May 24, 1865, less than a month after Booth's death, a publisher announced the release of Dion Haco's novel *The Assassinator,* the first fictional account of the murder and manhunt. A clever blending of facts drawn from newspaper accounts, invented dialogue, and fantasy scenes, Haco sensationalized Booth's life and implicated the sad, suicidal Ella Turner in the plot against Lincoln. Ella, "an impetuous and wilful creature," wrote Haco, pursued Booth as her lover: "My determination is fixed to have that man." She sensed that the actor was a man of destiny: "Ella saw that his piercing black eyes were lit up almost with a supernatural light. He seemed to be peering through the dim vista of the future and reading from its pages his name." Haco's purple prose led Booth inexorably to the manhunt's climax at Garrett's barn: "before him a sea of flame, ready to engulf him; beyond the grave a greater sea of flame awaiting him." The novel closed with lurid details of the assassin's autopsy, titillating its readers with fantastic images of the corpse's mutilation: "the head and heart taken from it to be deposited in the Medical Museum," with the headless and heartless trunk "consigned to the care of the secret agents." The novel leaves poor Ella, alone and bereft, clutching her assassin-lover's photo, "covering it with kisses."

Before the year was out, artists had memorialized Lincoln's assassin in wax and in heroically sized oil paintings. A poster for "Terry's Panorama of the War!" advertised "a stupendous work of art" that depicted "startling, terrible and bloody scenes" fresh from the "carnival of treason" by the celebrated artist H. L. Tyng of Boston. The ad promised the viewer a series of paintings, each one seven feet wide and fifteen to twenty feet tall. "Assassination of Lincoln! And Secretary Seward! Life-Size Portrait of Booth, The Assassin!"—all for the modest admission fee of 25 cents for adults and 15 cents for children.

Another art exhibition, "Col. Orr's Grand Museum," outdid even Terry's Panorama. "The Assassination!" screamed the headline of a poster advertising a traveling wax museum of murder. The sculptor, "Sig. Vanodi the greatest living worker in wax," boasted the broadside, had created life-size figures of "President Lincoln, Mrs. Lincoln, Secretary Seward and Booth and Payne, the Assassins!" The exhibitor gave potential customers fair warning: "The figures have now been completed—under the magic touch of the Artist, they spring into an existence almost real…so natural, perfect and life like, that as we gaze upon the assassins we shudder, lest again some fiendish deed be enacted." Orr constructed a replica of the president's box, seated the wax Lincolns in it, and positioned the assassin behind them: "Booth," the poster promised, "is made to preserve the precise attitude in which he leveled his weapon at the head of the president and fired the murderous shot." Additional wax tableaux depicted the capture of Herold and the shooting of Booth.

The mythologizing of Lincoln's assassin continued in the years ahead. In 1868, Dunbar Hylton published a 108-page poem about him, "The Præsidicide." The same year, in New Orleans, a publisher released a sympathetic piece of sheet music—"Our Brutus"—emblazoned with a handsome, full-page lithograph of the assassin. Soon a myth arose that the man killed at Garrett's farm was not John Wilkes Booth, and that the actor had escaped and fled to the American West, where he lived under a false name. The truth that Booth had died near Port Royal, Virginia, on April 26, 1865, could not suppress the bizarre stories. By the close of the nineteenth century, several men had claimed to be Booth. A lawyer named Finis Bates claimed that the assassin was his client, and in 1903 he published a wildly popular book titled *The Escape and Suicide of John Wilkes Booth*. When this false Booth died, allegedly by his own hand, his mummy was exhibited for years at traveling carnivals. It survives to this day, hidden in a private collection. In 1937, a woman wrote a preposterous book claiming that Booth had survived the night at Garrett's farm, lived a secret life, and fathered a child. The proof? Why, the author was the assassin's granddaughter, of course.

The survival myth of John Wilkes Booth, roaming across the land, evokes the traditional fate of the damned, of a cursed spirit who can find no rest. There is no doubt that Booth was the man who died at Garrett's farm. But America's first assassin, who took Father Abraham in his prime, who left a nation bereft, and who robbed us of the rest of the story, haunts us still.

John Wilkes Booth did not get what he wanted. Yes, he did enjoy a singular success: he killed Abraham Lincoln. But in every other way, Booth was a failure. He did not prolong the Civil War, inspire the South to fight on, or overturn the verdict of the battlefield, or of free elections. Nor did he confound emancipation, resuscitate slavery, or save the dying antebellum civilization of the Old South. Booth failed to overthrow the federal government by assassinating its highest officials. Indeed, he failed to murder two of the three men he had marked for death on that "moody, tearful night." He did not become an American hero, but he

THE ASSASSINATION!

The Manager takes pleasure in announcing to the public that he has at great expense succeeded
in engaging

SIG. VANODI

THE GREATEST LIVING WORKER IN WAX,

TO TAKE THE CASTS OF

PRESIDENT LINCOLN,
MRS. LINCOLN,
SECRETARY SEWARD
—AND—
Booth and Payne, the Assassins!

The Statues are now completed—under the magic touch of the Artist, they sprung into an existence almost real. Every lineal feature and lineament are so natural, perfect and life-like, that as we gaze upon the assassins we shudder, lest again some fiendish deed be enacted. In order that the public may form a more perfect conception of the atrocious scene, a box has been constructed in imitation of that in which the Presidential group was gathered on the evening of the assassination.

THE MANAGEMENT IS SUCH THAT THE

PRESIDENT & WIFE

occupy identically the same position which they did on the fatal night; while

BOOTH

is made to preserve the precise attitude in which he leveled his weapon at the head of the president and fired the murderous shot.

THE PRESIDENT LYING-STATE
ON A BEAUTIFULLY DECORATED

CATAFALCO

Built in imitation of the one on which he first reposed at the

Presidential Mansion.

This figure of the President is so just and exact in its representation, that those who saw him, while he lay in solemn state, declare the resemblance as thus so great it is with difficulty that they can reconcile the fact, that it is simply an imitation. Opportunity is now given to the thousands who failed to gaze upon him to see and feel upon so exact counterpart of the Martyr we loved to honor.

A LIFE SIZE FIGURE OF JEFFERSON DAVIS!

As he appeared in the United States Senate, is also to be seen, together with Panoramic Views of the thrilling incidents connected with the Assassination Plot.

CAPTURE OF HARROLD, SHOOTING OF BOOTH, ETC.

A LETTER FROM VANODI, THE ARTIST.

New York, July 1st, 1865.

MR. W. C. COUP—DEAR SIR

Parties are here from Chicago who saw your collection there, and wish to engage for a figure of Lincoln, but as I am about selling my Museum, cannot wish to sell for less, besides, I could think it possible to get up a more another so perfect. think you can only let I'd better than the rest. Hoping for your success believe me yours,
SIG. VANODI

LETTER FROM P. T. BARNUM.

New York, July 1st, 1865.

SIG. VANODI—#3

I regard as your finest masterpiece, see the work made for MR COUP, and have a likeness in representing the features greater of workmanship I ever saw. I'm warrant if the Couple is a perfect.
P. T. BARNUM

WILL BE EXHIBITED

At   On

BOUNDS & JAMES, PRINTERS, 46 STATE STREET, CHICAGO.

History in wax tableaux of assassination.

elevated Lincoln to the American pantheon. And, in his greatest failure, Booth did not survive the manhunt. His was not a suicide mission. He wanted desperately to live, to escape, to bask in the fame and glory he was sure would be his. He got his fame, but at the price of his life. But he lived long enough to recognize his failures, and endure the public condemnation of his act. When he leaped to the stage and shouted "Sic Semper Tyrannis," he must have thought that his immortality as a Southern patriot was sealed. But his last words survive as his true epitaph: "Useless, useless."

Booth may have died at Garrett's farm, but from that burning barn the assassin's malevolent spirit arose to linger over the land for more than a century. When marauding night riders wearing masks and white robes rose up against Reconstruction, Booth rode with them, murmuring "this country was formed for the *white,* not the black man." When men with burning crosses and rope nooses terrorized generations, the spirit of Booth stood by, scorning "nigger citizenship." And when an eloquent man stepped onto the balcony of the Lorraine Motel the day after he gave one of the greatest speeches of his life, a vengeful Booth was there, muttering, "that is the last speech he will ever give."

If Booth could return today to the scene of his crime and visit, as almost one million Americans do every year, the basement museum at Ford's Theatre, he might conclude, from what he found there, that it was, once again, April 14, 1865. Here he would find, preserved in a condition as immaculate as the day he last touched them, protected in climate-controlled, shatterproof glass display cases, the prized relics of the assassination: The original door to the president's box, its peephole still luring curious eyes; the wood music stand he used to bar the door; his revolvers and knives; the Spencer carbine that he and David Herold picked up during their midnight run to Surratt's tavern; his whistle and keys; the photos of his sweethearts; and his notorious pocket calendar diary, its pages still open, as if awaiting a final entry.

When the tourists who come here marvel at Booth's implements of violence and death—none more popular than the Deringer pistol that killed President Lincoln—they usually neglect a less thrilling relic. Few visitors bend down, peer through the glass case at a little shelf set near the ground, and scrutinize a small, everyday object resting in its velvet-lined box. It is Booth's pocket compass, more evocative of his desperate, twelve-day flight from the manhunt than any relic that survived him.

This is the compass that guided him during his dangerous days on the run; that he and Thomas Jones cradled by candlelight as they plotted Booth's course across the wide and black waters of the Potomac; that each day gave him hope as it pointed the way South to his final destination; that he played with on the Garrett lawn to the children's delight; and that the detectives plundered from his pocket as he lay dying at Garrett's farm. Today, almost a century and a half since the great chase for Lincoln's killer began, its blued steel needle still dances on its spindle, still pointing the way South.

Acknowledgments

———— ❧✦❧ ————

I THANK THE PIONEERS, GEORGE ALFRED TOWNSEND (1841 TO 1914), Osborn H. Oldroyd (1842 to 1930), and James O. Hall, who, in his nineties, remains an inspiration. All other scholars of the Lincoln assassination must stand on their shoulders. Townsend, Oldroyd, and Hall followed Booth's path, asked the questions, collected the documents, and pursued the unknown. The rest of us walk in their footsteps, and those tracks span several generations leading in an unbroken line back to the night when Abraham Lincoln was shot. I owe special thanks to Mr. Hall for a memorable day at his home, when he shared some of the knowledge that he has devoted a lifetime to acquiring.

With fond memories, I thank the late Michael Maione, National Park Service historian at Ford's Theatre, who, as far as I know, never appeared anywhere out of uniform, for memorable conversations and good counsel. Mike was the model of a public historian, and those who saw him in action at Ford's, pacing in front of the stage, delivering his famous lecture on the assassination in a bellowing voice, saw him at his best. Once, I cautioned Mike that his enthusiasm was frightening the schoolchildren who flocked in droves to Ford's every summer. "Yes," he said, beaming, "and they will remember me!" They certainly did. And Michael, so shall we. It was "altogether fitting and proper," to borrow Lincoln's phrase from his remarks honoring the dead at Gettysburg, that Mike's memorial service was held at the place he loved—Ford's Theatre.

I thank Library of Congress specialist Clark Evans for quiet days in the rare-book room at the Jefferson Building, when he brought out one delightful Lincoln treasure after another. I also thank John R. Sellers, Historical Specialist at the Library of Congress manuscripts division, for assassination tips, helpful publishing advice, and making available some of the Lincoln treasures from his domain. At the National Archives, Michael Musick was an indispensable guide to the complicated records of the Lincoln assassination.

Two good friends in the Lincoln community, Edward Steers Jr., the premiere contemporary historian of the assassination, and Michael F. Bishop, executive director of the Abraham Lincoln Bicentennial Commission, graciously read and improved the manuscript. Michael Burlingame, Lincoln scholar, editor, and author nonpareil, is unfailingly eager to share his research with colleagues, and he generously answered my questions. At the University of Chicago, David Bevington offered insights into Booth's use of Shakespeare.

Andrea E. Mays, an astute critic of historical nonfiction, read and commented on the manuscript from her unique perspective. She reviewed several incarnations of the book and saved me from making a number of embarrassing errors and omissions.

I also thank Lisa Bertagnoli, journalist, linguist, and student of Southern culture, for reading the manuscript, offering many valuable comments, and for her other contributions.

Mara Mills suggested that I do something useful with the Lincoln library that's been curing on my shelves for years—like write a book.

James Nash, a careful reader of the literature of the war of the rebellion, brought important issues to my attention. Thanks also to James for a macabre summer night in downtown Washington, D.C., when we went to Mary Surratt's boardinghouse to watch, on the 140th anniversary of her hanging, a play about her trial and execution.

I am indebted to Joan Chaconas and Laurie Verge for encouragement, generosity, and friendship. Their research and writing, and their role in preserving Mary Surratt's country house, have materially advanced the scholarship of the Lincoln assassination. Sandra Walia at the Surratt Society's James O. Hall Research Library unlocked the treasure trove of files held there. I was aghast when, years ago, I learned of a group called the Surratt Society. I had assumed, incorrectly, that it was a club of amateur assassination apologists. On the contrary, its staff and members are passionate scholars in pursuit of objective history.

At William H. Seward's magnificent home in Auburn, New York, executive director Peter Wisbey provided haunting photographs and valuable information about Fanny and her father.

David Lovett, an extraordinary historian and bibliographer of the Lincoln and Kennedy assassinations, provided virtually unobtainable books and pamphlets that were essential to my research.

Karen Needles of Documents on Wheels uncovered the hitherto unpublished reward check issued to Booth's killer, Boston Corbett. Karen is an indefatigable researcher who has made numerous contributions to the Lincoln field by ferreting out many exciting and little-known documents at the National Archives, the Library of Congress, and elsewhere.

I thank my friends at the Heritage Foundation, Edwin Meese III, Todd Gaziano, and Paul Rosenzweig, for giving me a home during much of the time I wrote the book. And thanks also to Molly Stark for helping with the manuscript and for solving never-ending computer mysteries.

Thanks to Carol Cohen and Elizabeth Kreul-Starr for typing drafts of the manuscript.

Theodore L. Jones and George A. Didden III handed me the keys to a beautiful but haunted nineteenth-century townhouse big enough to hold a few thousand books, documents, and Civil War newspapers.

I must thank Harold Holzer, vice president of the Metropolitan Museum of Art and co-chairman of the Abraham Lincoln Bicentennial Commission, for expert insights and his hospitality in New York City, and Frank Williams, Chief Justice of Rhode Island and also a member of the Bicentennial Commission, for sharing his great knowledge and wonderful Lincoln library.

Valuable advice on how to think about and tell this story came from Douglas H. Ginsburg, Chief Judge of the United States Court of Appeals for the District of Columbia Circuit, and from Judge J. Harvie Wilkinson III of the United States Court of Appeals for the Fourth Circuit.

Thanks also to the friends who have indulged me by joining my annual nighttime tours of downtown Washington on the anniversary of Lincoln's assassination.

Special thanks to a Southern friend who, after insisting on anonymity, disclosed her family's secret custom: ever since April 15, 1866—the first anniversary of the murder—they have held their annual cotillion on that day to celebrate the assassination of Abraham Lincoln and to honor their Brutus. Their ritual provided a remarkable immediacy about how some Southerners reacted to the events of April 1865—and how some still remember them.

Henry Ferris is a patient and discerning editor who improved the manuscript in countless ways with a fine dramatic sensibility and an unerring instinct for suggesting key scenes that advanced the narrative. I am convinced that the fact he is a Booth descendant influenced the course of this book.

I also thank Michael Morrison at HarperCollins and Lisa Gallagher at William Morrow for their strong support of the book and the personal interest they took in me.

Richard Abate, my literary agent at International Creative Management, gave me his enthusiasm, insights, and friendship. Richard read several drafts of the manuscript, made himself an expert on the subject, and even came down to Washington to explore the assassination sites with me. He made this a better book. Thanks also to my other representatives at ICM, Ron Bernstein and Kate Lee.

My own hunt for John Wilkes Booth began when my grandmother, Elizabeth, a veteran of Chicago's legendary and now extinct tabloid newspaper scene, gave a ten-year-old boy the unusual gift of a framed engraving of Booth's Deringer pistol, along with an April 15, 1865, *Chicago Tribune* clipping, thus triggering the obsession that led to this book. This is in memory of her.

My sister Denise's animated spirit and taste for bizarre historical tales encouraged me from the start. From an early age, she aided and abetted my literary pursuits.

Finally, I thank my parents, Dianne and Lennart Swanson. Without their love and generous support over many years, I never could have written *Manhunt,* or anything else.

James L. Swanson
Washington, D.C.
October 10, 2005

Bibliography

---•❧❦❧•---

A NOTE ON SOURCES

THE LITERATURE OF THE LINCOLN ASSASSINATION IS VAST and I do not pretend to catalog it here. The complete bibliography, which no scholar has ever compiled, contains several thousand books and articles. Any attempt to cite them all, when I could never read them all, seemed pointless, and of little use to a reader who wanted to learn more. The bibliography that follows is hardly comprehensive and is, with a few exceptions, little more than a selective shelf list of books from my own library, and those which I consulted while researching and writing *Manhunt*. I used my best judgment to choose, and cite, the best sources. These are the few hundred books that I either liked the most, found the most helpful, or believed would be most interesting to readers who might use *Manhunt* as the starting point for their own pursuit of John Wilkes Booth. To begin that pursuit, I suggest a handful of titles.

The best modern book on the Lincoln assassination is *Blood on the Moon: The Assassination of Abraham Lincoln,* by Edward Steers Jr. In 1865, three different book publishers printed transcripts of the testimony from the conspiracy trial. Today, the only version that remains in print can be found in *The Trial: The Assassination of President Lincoln*

394   BIBLIOGRAPHY

and the Trial of the Conspirators, edited by Edward Steers Jr. In addition to printing a facsimile of Pitman's one-volume transcript of the proceedings, Steers included essays on the conspirators and the military tribunal by himself and by Lincoln assassination specialists Joan Chaconas, Laurie Verge, Percy E. Martin, Terry Alford, and Burrus Carnahan. From these two books alone, one can gain a comprehensive understanding of the plots against Lincoln, the events of April 1865, the military tribunal, and the execution of the conspirators.

Another essential reference is *Trial of John H. Surratt in the Criminal Court for the District of Columbia,* published in two volumes in 1867. This important and fascinating transcript includes material available nowhere else. Unfortunately, the Surratt volumes have never been reprinted, and are available only in the scarce and costly original edition. The most complete published transcript from the 1865 tribunal is Benjamin Perley Poore's three-volume *The Conspiracy Trial for the Murder of the President.* This set was reprinted some years ago, but the facsimile edition, like the original, is scarce.

The best illustrated histories of the assassination are *Twenty Days* by Dorothy Meserve Kunhardt and Philip B. Kunhardt Jr., and *Lincoln's Assassins: Their Trial and Execution* by James L. Swanson and Daniel R. Weinberg. *Twenty Days* contains more than three hundred black-and-white photos of the people and places connected to the assassination and Lincoln's funeral. *Lincoln's Assassins* contains more than two hundred and fifty color plates of rare period prints, photographs, paintings, books, relics, newspapers, autographs, and documents related to the assassination, manhunt, trial, and execution.

Classic works that have held up well include *The Death of Lincoln* by Clara Laughlin, *Myths After Lincoln* by Lloyd Lewis, and *The Great American Myth* by George Bryan. William Hanchett's *The Lincoln Murder Conspiracies* is a splendid historiography of a century's worth of alternative conspiracy theories. Thomas Reed Turner's *Beware the People Weeping: Public Opinion and the Assassination of Abraham Lincoln* is an outstanding account of how the American people mourned their fallen president.

Essential—and my favorite—period accounts include George Alfred Townsend's *The Life, Crime, and Capture of John Wilkes Booth*, published in 1865 just a few weeks after the manhunt was over; Thomas A. Jones's 1893 memoir, *J. Wilkes Booth*, in which he described how he hid Booth and Herold in the pine thicket and then sent them across the Potomac; and, of course, Asia Booth Clarke's incomparable remembrance of her brother, *The Unlocked Book: A Memoir of John Wilkes Booth by His Sister*, written in secret and not published until 1938. All are scarce in their original editions, but they have been reprinted and are not difficult to obtain, and enjoy. The collected works of John Wilkes Booth, brief as they may be given the destruction of many of his letters and personal papers during the frenzied days of the manhunt, remained unavailable for more than a century until their 1997 publication in *"Right or Wrong, God Judge Me": The Writings of John Wilkes Booth*, edited by John Rhodehamel and Louise Taper.

The various publications of the Surratt Society, an organization of serious researchers, and not assassination apologists, are invaluable to students of Booth's crime, and they include *From War Department Files: Statements Made by the Alleged Lincoln Conspirators Under Examination, 1865; In Pursuit of...: Continuing Research in the Field of the Lincoln Assassination; The Lincoln Assassination: From the Pages of the Surratt Courier (1986–1999)*, published in two volumes; *On the Way to Garrett's Barn;* and *Abraham Lincoln Assassination Bibliography: A Compendium of Reference Materials*, compiled by Blaine V. Houmes. This bibliography, a substantial book in itself, is the most complete guide ever published on the literature of the Lincoln assassination.

The Surratt Courier, the monthly publication of the Surratt Society, and the *Journal of the Lincoln Assassination,* published three times a year by Frederick Hatch, contain valuable articles, book reviews, and news.

Finally, two recent books on Lincoln's assassination, *American Brutus: The Lincoln Assassination Conspiracies* by Michael Kauffman and *The Darkest Dawn: Lincoln, Booth, and the Great American Tragedy* by Thomas Goodrich are wonderfully exhaustive compilations of assassination information.

In addition to the printed sources collected in this essay, and in the bibliography that follows, the original War Department and other government papers connected to the investigation of the Lincoln assassination, the manhunt, the trial of the conspirators, and the distribution of the rewards make up an essential archive. Unfortunately, this collection, which reposes at the National Archives, has never been published. Many of the documents are available in microfilm. The most important sources—the records of the Office of the Judge Advocate General, are in Record Group 153, and bear the name "Investigation and Trial Papers Relating to the Assassination of President Lincoln." Among historians, they are more commonly known as the "Lincoln Assassination Suspects File." They are available on sixteen reels of microfilm called Microcopy-599, or M-599. Another important collection of documents, related chiefly to the various applications for shares of the reward money, are held in Record Group 94, records of the Adjutant General's Office. These materials are available on four reels of microfilm called Microcopy-619, or M-619, on reels 455 through 458. For the convenience of readers who do not own microfilm readers or do not wish to spend hundreds of dollars on twenty or more rolls of microfilm, I have, throughout the chapter notes, cited works where the microfilmed documents have been reprinted for easy reference.

Abott, A. Abott. *The Assassination and Death of Abraham Lincoln, President of the United States of America, at Washington, on the 14th of April, 1865.* New York: American News Company, 1865.

Archer, Mrs. M.A. *Echoes: Volume First.* Hartford: Press of Case, Lockwood & Co., 1867.

Arnold, Isaac N. *Sketch of the Life of Abraham Lincoln.* New York: John B. Bachelder, 1869.

Arnold, Samuel Bland. *Defense and Prison Experiences of a Lincoln Conspirator.* Hattiesburg, Mississippi: The Book Farm, 1940.

Baker, Jean H. *Mary Todd Lincoln: A Biography.* New York: W. W. Norton, 1987.

Baker, Lafayette C. *The Secret Service in the Late War.* Philadelphia: 1867.

Basler, Roy P. *The Lincoln Legend: A Study in Changing Conceptions.* Boston: Houghton Mifflin, 1935.

Basler, Roy P., ed. *The Collected Works of Abraham Lincoln.* New Brunswick, New Jersey: Rutgers University Press, 1953. Eight volumes plus index and supplements.

Bates, David Homer. *Lincoln in the Telegraph Office.* New York: The Century Co., 1907.

Bates, Finis L. *Escape and Suicide of John Wilkes Booth.* Memphis, Tennessee: Finis L. Bates, 1907.

Beale, Howard K., ed. *The Diary of Edward Bates, 1859–1866,* vol. 4 of the *Annual Report of the American Historical Association.* Washington, D.C.: Government Printing Office, 1933.

———. *Diary of Gideon Welles.* New York: W. W. Norton, 1960. 3 volumes.

Beall, John. *Trial of John Y. Beall, as a Spy and Guerreillero, by Military Commission.* New York: D. Appleton and Co., 1865.

Benham, William Burton. *Life of Osborn H. Oldroyd: Founder and Collector of Lincoln Mementos.* Washington, D.C.: privately printed, 1927.

Bernstein, Iver. *The New York City Draft Riots.* New York: Oxford University Press, 1990.

Bingham, John Armor. *Trial of the Conspirators for the Assassination of President Lincoln, s.c. Argument of John A. Bingham, Special Judge Advocate.* Washington, D.C.: Government Printing Office, 1865.

Bishop, Jim. *The Day Lincoln Was Shot.* New York: Harper & Brothers, 1955.

Blake, Mortimer. *Human Depravity John Wilkes Booth: A Sermon Occassioned by the Assassination of President Lincoln, and Delivered in the Winslow Congregational Church, Taunton, Massachusetts on Sunday Evening, April 23, 1865, by the Pastor.* Champlain: privately printed at the Moorsfield Press, 1925.

Blue, Frederick J. *Salmon P. Chase: A Life in Politics.* Kent, Ohio: Kent State University Press, 1987.

Bohn, Casimir. *Bohn's Hand-Book of Washington.* Washington, D.C.: Casimir Bohn, [1856].

Booth, John Wilkes. *Wilkes Booth's Private Confession of the Murder of President Lincoln and His Terrible Oath of Vengeance: Furnished by an Escaped Confederate.* London: Newsagents' Publishing Company, 1865.

Borreson, Ralph. *When Lincoln Died.* New York: Appleton-Century, 1965.

Boyd, Andrew. *Abraham Lincoln, Foully Assassinated April 14, 1865.* Albany, New York: Joel Munsell, Printer, 1868.

————. *Boyd's Washington and Georgetown Directory: 1864.* Washington, D.C.: Hudson Taylor, 1863.

————. *A Memorial Lincoln Bibliography: Being an Account of Books, Eulogies, Sermons, Portraits, Engravings, Medals, etc., Published upon Abraham Lincoln, Sixteenth President of the United States, Assassinated Good Friday, April 14, 1865.* Albany, New York: Andrew Boyd, Directory Publisher, 1870.

Boyd, Belle. *Belle Boyd in Camp and Prison.* New York: Blelock & Company, 1865.

Braver, Adam. *Mr. Lincoln's Wars: A Novel in Thirteen Stories.* New York: William Morrow, 2003.

Brenner, Walter C. *The Ford Theatre Lincoln Assassination Playbills.* Philadelphia: privately printed, 1937.

Brooks, Noah. *Washington in Lincoln's Time.* New York: The Century Co., 1895.

Brooks, Stewart M. *Our Murdered Presidents: The Medical Story.* New York: Frederick Fell, Inc., 1966.

Brown, George William. *Baltimore and the 19th of April, 1861.* Baltimore: N. Murray, 1887.

Browning, Orville Hickman. *The Diary of Orville Hickman Browning. Edited with Introduction and Notes by Theodore Calvin Pease and James G. Randall.* Springfield, Illinois: Illinois State Historical Library, 1925–[33]. 2 vols.

Bryan, George S. *The Great American Myth: The True Story of Lincoln's Murder.* New York: Carrick & Evans, 1940.

Bryan, Vernanne. *Laura Keene: A British Actress on the American Stage, 1826–1873.* Jefferson, North Carolina: McFarland & Co., 1997.

Buckeridge, J. O. *Lincoln's Choice: The Repeating Rifle Which Cut Short the Civil War.* Harrisburg, Pennsylvania: The Stackpole Company, 1956.

Buckingham, J. E. *Reminiscences and Souvenirs of the Assassination of Abraham Lincoln.* Washington, D.C.: Press of Rufus H. Darby, 1894.

Cable, Mary. *The Avenue of the Presidents.* Boston: Houghton Mifflin, 1969.

Cain, Marvin R. *Lincoln's Attorney General: Edward Bates of Missouri.* Columbia, Missouri: University of Missouri Press, 1965.

Campbell, W. P. *The Escape and Wanderings of J. Wilkes Booth Until Ending of the Trail by Suicide in Oklahoma.* Oklahoma City, Oklahoma: privately printed, 1922.

Carpenter, Francis B. *Six Months at the White House with Abraham Lincoln.* New York: Hurd & Houghton, 1866.

Chamlee, Roy Z. *Lincoln's Assassins: A Complete Account of Their Capture, Trial, and Punishment.* Jefferson, North Carolina: McFarland, 1990.

Chase, Salmon P. *Inside Lincoln's Cabinet: The Civil War Diaries of Salmon P. Chase.* Edited by David Donald. New York: Longmans, Green, 1954.

Clark, Allen C. *Abraham Lincoln in the National Capital.* Washington, D.C.: Press of W. F. Roberts Co., 1925.

Clarke, Asia Booth. *The Unlocked Book: A Memoir of John Wilkes Booth by His Sister.* New York: G. P. Putnam's Sons, 1938.

Clarke, Champ. *The Assassination: Death of the President.* Alexandria, Virginia: Time-Life Books, 1987.

Coggeshall, William T. *Lincoln Memorial: The Journeys of Abraham Lincoln: From Springfield to Washington, 1861, as President Elect; and From Washington to Springfield, 1865, as President Martyred.* Columbus, Ohio: Ohio State Journal, 1865.

Cole, Donald B., and John J. McDonough, eds. *Benjamin Brown French: Witness to the Young Republic.* Hanover, New Hampshire: University Press of New England, 1989.

Collyer, William H. *The Death of Booth: Affidavit Dec. 1, 1904 in Pension Claim of Wm. H. Collyer, a Blowhard.* New York: privately printed by D. H. Newhall, 1934.

Cooling, Benjamin Franklin. *Symbol, Sword and Shield: Defending Washington During the Civil War.* Shippensburg, Pennsylvania: White Mane Publishing Company, 1991.

Creahan, John. *The Life of Laura Keene.* Philadelphia: The Rodgers Publishing Co., 1897.

Davis, William C. *An Honorable Defeat: The Last Days of the Confederate Government.* New York: Harcourt, 2001.

———. *Look Away: A History of the Confederate States of America.* New York: The Free Press, 2002.

De Chambrun, Marquis Adolphe. *Impressions of Lincoln and the Civil War: A Foreigner's Account*. New York: Random House, 1952.

Dewitt, David Miller. *The Assassination of Abraham Lincoln and Its Expiation*. New York: Macmillan, 1909.

———. *The Impeachment and Trial of Andrew Johnson*. New York: Macmillan, 1903.

———. *The Judicial Murder of Mary E. Surratt*. Baltimore: J. Murphy, 1895.

Donald, David H. *Lincoln at Home: Two Glimpses of Abraham Lincoln's Family Life*. New York: Simon & Schuster, 2000.

Donald, David Herbert. *Lincoln*. New York: Simon & Schuster, 1995.

Doster, William E. *Lincoln and Episodes of the Civil War*. New York: 1915.

Downes, Alan S. *The Autobiography of Joseph Jefferson*. Cambride: Belknap Press, 1964.

Eisenschiml, Otto. *The Case of A. L____, Aged 56*. Chicago: Abraham Lincoln Book Shop, 1943.

———. *In the Shadow of Lincoln's Death*. New York: Wilfred Funk, Inc., 1940.

———. *Why Was Lincoln Murdered?* Boston: Little, Brown, 1937.

Epperson, James F., ed. *The Positive Identification of the Body of John Wilkes Booth, Civil War Naval Chronology*. Washington, D.C.: Government Printing Office, 1971.

Epstein, Daniel Mark. *Lincoln and Whitman: Parallel Lives in Civil War Washington*. New York: Ballantine Books, 2004.

Eskew, Garnett Laidlaw. *Willard's of Washington: The Epic of a Capital Caravansary*. New York: Coward-McCann, 1954.

Fehrenbacher, Don E., and Virginia Fehrenbacher. *Recollected Words of Abraham Lincoln*. Stanford, California: Stanford University Press, 1996.

Ferguson, W. J. *I Saw Booth Shoot Lincoln*. Boston: Houghton Mifflin, 1930.

Field, Maunsell B. *Memories of Many Men and of Some Women*. New York: Harper & Brothers, 1874.

Fleischner, Jennifer. *Mrs. Lincoln and Mrs. Keckly*. New York: Broadway Books, 2003.

Flower, Frank A. *Edwin McMasters Stanton*. Akron, Ohio: Saalfield Publishing Co., 1905.

Forrester, Izola. *This One Mad Act: The Unknown Story of John Wilkes Booth and His Family, by His Granddaughter*. Boston: Hale, Cushman & Flint, 1937.

Fowler, Robert H. *Album of the Lincoln Murder: Illustrating How It Was Planned, Committed and Avenged*. Harrisburg, Pennsylvania: Stackpole Books, 1965.

Furgurson, Ernest B. *Freedom Rising: Washington in the Civil War*. New York: Knopf, 2004.

Furtwangler, Albert. *Assassin on Stage: Brutus, Hamlet, and the Death of Lincoln*. Urbana: University of Illinois Press, 1991.

Gammans, Harold. *Lincoln Names and Epithets*. Boston: Bruce Humphries, 1955.

Garner, Stanton. *The Civil War World of Herman Melville*. Lawrence: University Press of Kansas, 1993.

Garrett, R. B. *An Interesting Letter About the Death of John Wilkes Booth*. Peoria, Illinois: privately printed for the Oakwood Lincoln Club, 1934.

Garrison, Webb. *The Encyclopedia of Civil War Usage*. Nashville: Cumberland House, 2001.

Gerry, Margarita Spalding, ed. *Through Five Administrations: Reminiscences of Colonel William H. Crook, Body-Guard to President Lincoln*. New York: Harper & Brothers, 1910.

Good, Timothy S. *We Saw Lincoln Shot: One Hundred Eyewitness Accounts*. Jackson: University Press of Mississippi, 1995.

Goodale, Katherine. *Behind the Scenes with Edwin Booth*. Boston: Houghton Mifflin, 1931.

Goodrich, Thomas. *The Darkest Dawn: Lincoln, Booth, and the Great American Tragedy*. Bloomington: Indiana University Press, 2005.

Gray, Clayton. *Conspiracy in Canada*. Montreal: L'Atelier Press, 1957.

Greenhow, Rose. *Mrs. Greenhow: My Imprisonment and the First Year of Abolition Rule at Washington*. London: Richard Bentley, 1863.

Grieve, Victoria. *Ford's Theatre and the Lincoln Assassination*. Alexandria, Virginia: Parks & History Association, 2001.

Gurley, Phineas Densmore. *The Voice of the Rod: A Sermon Preached on Thursday, June 1, 1865, in the New York Avenue Presbyterian Church, Washington, D.C., by the Rev. P. D. Gurley, D.D., Pastor of the Church*. Washington: William Ballantyne Bookseller, 1865.

Gurley, Rev. Phineas D. *Faith in God: Dr. Gurley's Sermon at the Funeral of Abraham Lincoln*. Philadelphia: privately printed, 1940.

Haco, Dion. *J. Wilkes Booth, the Assassinator of President Lincoln*. New York: T. R. Dawley, 1865.

Haley, William D., ed. *Philp's Washington Described*. New York: Rudd & Carleton, 1861.

Hall, Charles H. *A Mournful Easter: A Discourse Delivered in the Church of the Epiphany, Washington, D.C., on Easter Day, April 19* [sic], *1865, by the Rector, Rev. Charles H. Hall, D.D., Being the Second Day after the Assassination of the President of the United States, and a Similar Attempt upon the Secretary of State, on the Night of Good Friday*. Washington, D.C.: Gideon & Pearson, Printers, 1865.

Hall, James O. and Michael Maione, *To Make a Fortune. John Wilkes Booth: Following the Money Trail*. Clinton, Maryland: The Surratt Society, 2003.

Hanchett, William. *The Lincoln Murder Conspiracies*. Urbana: University of Illinois Press, 1983.

Harrell, Carolyn L. *When the Bells Tolled for Lincoln: Southern Reaction to the Assassination*. Macon, Georgia: Mercer University Press, 1997.

Harris, William C. *Lincoln's Last Months*. Cambridge, Massachusetts: Belknap Press, 2004.

Helwig, Rev. J. B. *The Assassination of President Lincoln: What Was the Religious Faith of Those Engaged in the Conspiracy That Resulted in the Assassination of President Lincoln at Washington, D.C., on Friday Evening, April 14, 1865*. Springfield, Ohio: A. D. Hosterman & Co., Printers, n.d.

Henneke, Ben Graf. *Laura Keene: A Biography*. Tulsa, Oklahoma: Council Oak Books, 1990.

Holzer, Harold, Gabor S. Boritt, and Mark E. Neely Jr. *The Lincoln Image: Abraham Lincoln and the Popular Print*. New York: Scribner's, 1984.

Hughes, Glenn. *A History of the American Theatre, 1700 to 1950*. New York: Samuel French, 1951.

Hylton, J. Dunbar, M.D. *The Præsidicide: A Poem*. Philadelphia: Meichel & Plumly, Printers, 1868.

Isacsson, Alfred. *The Travels, Arrest and Trial of John H. Surratt*. Middletown, New York: Vestigium Press, 2003.

Jefferson, Joseph. *The Autobiography of Joseph Jefferson*. New York: The Century Co., 1897.

Johnson, Andrew. *Impeachment and Trial of Andrew Johnson*. Philadelphia: Barclay & Co., 1868.

Johnson, Byron Berkeley. *Abraham Lincoln and Boston Corbett, with Personal Recollections of Each; John Wilkes Booth and Jefferson Davis, a True Story of Their Capture*. Waltham, Massachusetts: 1914.

Jones, Thomas A. *J. Wilkes Booth: An Account of His Sojourn in Southern Maryland After the Assassination of Abraham Lincoln, His Passage Across the Potomac, and His Death in Virginia*. Chicago: Laird & Lee, 1893.

Judson, Edward Zane Carroll. *The Parricides; or, the Doom of the Assassins, the Authors of the Nation's Loss, by Ned Buntline*. New York: Hilton & Co., Publishers, 1865.

Kauffman, Michael. *American Brutus: John Wilkes Booth and the Lincoln Conspiracies*. New York: Random House, 2004.

Keckley, Elizabeth. *Behind the Scenes, or, Thirty Years a Slave, and Four Years in the White House*. New York: G.W. Carleton & Co., 1868.

Kendall, John S. *The Golden Age of the New Orleans Theater*. Baton Rouge: Louisiana State University Press, 1952.

Kimmel, Stanley. *The Mad Booths of Maryland*. Indianapolis: Bobbs-Merrill, 1940.

————. *Mr. Lincoln's Washington*. New York: Bramhall House, 1957.

Kunhardt, Dorothy Meserve, and Philip B. Kunhardt Jr. *Twenty Days*. New York: Harper & Row, 1965.

Lamon, Dorothy, ed. *Recollections of Abraham Lincoln, 1847–1865, by Ward Hill Lamon*. Chicago: A. C. McClurg and Company, 1895.

Lamon, Ward Hill. *Recollections of Abraham Lincoln 1847–1865, edited by Dorothy Lamon Teillard*. Washington, D.C.: published by the editor, 1911.

Lattimer, Dr. John K. *Kennedy and Lincoln: Medical and Ballistic Comparisons of Their Assassinations*. New York: Harcourt Brace Jovanovich, 1980.

Laughlin, Clara E. *The Death of Lincoln: The Story of Booth's Plot, His Deed and the Penalty*. New York: Doubleday, Page & Co., 1909.

Leale, Charles. *Lincoln's Last Hours*. Privately printed, 1909.

Lee, Richard M. *Mr. Lincoln's City*. McLean, Virginia: EPM Publications, 1981.

Leech, Margaret. *Reveille in Washington, 1860–1865*. New York: Harper & Brothers, 1941.

Leonard, Elizabeth D. *Lincoln's Avengers: Justice, Revenge, and Reunion after the Civil War*. New York: W. W. Norton & Company, 2004.

Leonardi, Dell. *The Reincarnation of John Wilkes Booth: A Study in Hypnotic Regression*. Old Greenwich, Connecticut: Devin-Adair, 1975.

Lewis, Lloyd. *Myths After Lincoln*. New York: Harcourt, Brace and Company, 1920.

Lincoln, Abraham. *Abraham Lincoln: An Exhibition at the Library of Congress in Honor of the 150th Anniversary of His Birth.* Washington, D.C.: Library of Congress, 1959.

———. *In Memoriam.* New York: Trent, Filmer & Co., [1865].

———. *The Lincoln Memorial: A Record of the Life, Assassination, and Obsequies of the Martyred President.* New York: Bunce & Huntington, 1865.

———. *The Terrible Tragedy at Washington: Assassination of President Lincoln.* Philadelphia: Barclay & Co., 1865.

Loux, Arthur F. *John Wilkes Booth: Day by Day.* Privately printed, 1989.

Lowenfels, Walter, ed. *Walt Whitman's Civil War.* New York: Knopf, 1960.

Mahoney, Ella V. *Sketches of Tudor Hall and the Booth Family.* Bel Air, Maryland: privately printed, 1925.

Mallon, Thomas. *Henry and Clara.* New York: Ticknor & Fields, 1994.

McClure, Stanley W. *The Lincoln Museum and the House Where Lincoln Died.* Washington, D.C.: Government Printing Office, 1949.

———. *Ford's Theatre and the House Where Lincoln Died.* Washington, D.C.: Government Printing Office, 1969.

McPherson, James M. *Battle Cry of Freedom: The Civil War Era.* New York: Oxford University Press, 1988.

Meredith, Roy. *Mr. Lincoln's Contemporaries: An Album of Portraits by Mathew B. Brady.* New York: Charles Scribner's Sons, 1951.

Miers, Earl Schenk, ed. *When the World Ended: The Diary of Emma Le Conte.* New York: Oxford University Press, 1957.

Miller, Ernest C. *John Wilkes Booth: Oilman.* New York: Exposition Press, 1947.

Mogelever, Jacob. *Death to Traitors: The Story of General Lafayette C. Baker, Lincoln's Forgotten Secret Service Chief.* Garden City, New York: Doubleday & Company, 1960.

Monaghan, Jay. *Lincoln Bibliography, 1839–1939.* Springfield, Illinois: Illinois State Historical Library, 1943–45. 2 volumes.

Morris, B. F., comp. *Memorial Record of the Nation's Tribute to Abraham Lincoln.* Washington, D.C.: W. H. & O. H. Morrison, 1865.

Morris, Clara. *Life on the Stage: My Personal Experiences and Recollections.* New York: McClure, Phillips & Co., 1901.

Mudd, Nettie, ed. *The Life of Dr. Samuel A. Mudd, Containing His Letters from Fort Jefferson, Dry Tortugas Island, Where He Was Imprisoned Four Years for Alleged Complicity in the Assassination of Abraham Lincoln.* New York: Neale Publishing Company, 1906.

Neely, Mark E., Jr. *The Abraham Lincoln Encyclopedia.* New York: McGraw-Hill, 1982.

———. *The Fate of Liberty: Abraham Lincoln and Civil Liberties.* New York: Oxford University Press, 1991.

Nevins, Allan, ed. *Diary of the Civil War: George Templeton Strong.* New York: Macmillan, 1962.

Newman, Ralph G. *"In This Sad World of Ours, Sorrow Comes to All": A Timetable for the Lincoln Funeral Train.* Springfield, Illinois: Civil War Centennial Commission of Illinois, 1965.

Nicolay, John G. *A Short Life of Abraham Lincoln.* New York: The Century Co., 1904.

Nicolay, John G., and John Hay. *Abraham Lincoln.* New York: The Century Co., 1890. 10 volumes.

Niven, John. *Gideon Welles: Lincoln's Secretary of the Navy.* New York: Oxford University Press, 1973.

———. *Salmon P. Chase: A Biography.* New York: Oxford University Press, 1995.

Oates, Stephen B. *With Malice Toward None: The Life of Abraham Lincoln.* New York: Harper & Row, 1977.

Oldroyd, Osborn H. *The Assassination of Abraham Lincoln.* Washington, D.C.: Osborn H. Oldroyd, 1901.

———. *The Oldroyd Lincoln Memorial Collection: Located in the House in Which Lincoln Died.* Washington, D.C.: privately printed by Judd and Detweiler, 1903.

Olszewski, George J. *Restoration of Ford's Theatre.* Washington, D.C.: Government Printing Office, 1963.

Ostendorf, Lloyd. *Lincoln's Photographs: A Complete Album.* Dayton, Ohio: Rockywood Press, 1998.

Ownsbey, Betty J. *Alias "Paine": Lewis Thornton Powell, the Mystery Man of the Lincoln Conspiracy.* Jefferson, North Carolina: McFarland, 1993.

Paludan, Phillip Shaw. *The Presidency of Abraham Lincoln.* Lawrence: University Press of Kansas, 1994.

Parsons, John E. *Henry Deringer's Pocket Pistol.* New York: William Morrow, 1952.

Patrick, Rembert W. *The Fall of Richmond.* Baton Rouge: Louisiana State University Press, 1960.

Peterson, T. B. *The Trial of the Alleged Assassins and Conspirators at Washington*

City, D.C., in May and June, 1865. Philadelphia: T. B. Peterson & Brothers, 1865.

Pinsker, Matthew. *Lincoln's Sanctuary: Abraham Lincoln and the Soldiers' Home.* New York: Oxford University Press, 2003.

Pitman, Benn. *The Assassination of President Lincoln and the Trial of the Conspirators.* Cincinnati: Moore, Wilstach & Baldwin, 1865.

Poetical Tributes to the Memory of Abraham Lincoln. Philadelphia: J. B. Lippincott & Co., 1865.

Poore, Ben Perley, ed. *The Conspiracy Trial for the Murder of the President.* Boston: J. E. Tilton and Company, 1865–1866. 3 volumes.

———. *Perley's Reminiscences of Sixty Years in the National Metropolis.* Philadelphia: Hubbard Brothers, 1886. 2 volumes.

Power, John Carroll. *Abraham Lincoln: His Life, Public Services and Great Funeral Cortege.* Springfield, Illinois: Edwin A. Wilson, 1875.

———. *History of an Attempt to Steal the Body of Abraham Lincoln.* Springfield, Illinois: H. W. Rokker, 1890.

Randall, Ruth Painter. *Lincoln's Sons.* Boston: Little, Brown and Company, 1955.

Reck, W. Emerson. *A. Lincoln: His Last 24 Hours.* Jefferson, North Carolina: McFarland, 1987.

Reynolds, David S. *John Brown, Abolitionist.* New York: Knopf, 2005.

Rhodehamel, John, and Louise Taper, eds. *"Right or Wrong, God Judge Me": The Writings of John Wilkes Booth.* Urbana: University of Illinois Press, 1997.

Risvold, Floyd E., ed. *A True History of the Assassination of Abraham Lincoln and of the Conspiracy of 1865, by Louis J. Weichmann, Chief Witness for the Government of the United States in the Prosecution of the Conspirators.* New York: Knopf, 1975.

Robertson, David. *Booth: A Novel.* New York: Anchor Books, 1998.

Roscoe, Theodore. *The Web of Conspiracy: The Complete Story of the Men Who Murdered Abraham Lincoln.* Englewood Cliffs, New Jersey: Prentice-Hall, 1959.

Ruggles, Eleanor. *Prince of Players: Edwin Booth.* New York: Norton, 1953.

Russell, Pamela Redford. *The Woman Who Loved John Wilkes Booth.* New York: G. P. Putnam's Sons, 1978.

Samples, Gordon. *Lust for Fame: The Stage Career of John Wilkes Booth.* Jefferson, North Carolina: McFarland and Co., 1982.

Sandburg, Carl. *Abraham Lincoln: The War Years.* New York: Harcourt Brace & Company, 1939. 4 volumes.

Searcher, Victor. *The Farewell to Lincoln.* New York: Abingdon Press, 1965.

Sermons Preached in Boston on the Death of Abraham Lincoln, together with the Funeral Services in the East Room of the Executive Mansion at Washington. Boston: J. E. Tilton & Co., 1865.

Seward, Frederick W. *Reminiscences of a War-Time Statesman and Diplomat, 1830–1915.* New York: G. P. Putnam's Sons, 1916.

Seward, William H. *William H. Seward: An Autobiography from 1801 to 1834, with a Memoir of His Life, and Selections from His Letters, 1831–1872, by Frederick W. Seward.* New York: Derby and Miller, 1891. 3 volumes.

Seymour, Mark Wilson, ed. *The Pursuit of John H. Surratt: Despatches from the Official Record of the Assassination of Abraham Lincoln.* Austin, Texas: Civil War Library, 2000.

Shea, John Gilmary, ed. *The Lincoln Memorial: A Record of the Life, Assassination and Obsequies of the Martyred President.* New York: Bunce & Huntington, 1865.

Shelton, Vaughn. *Mask for Treason: The Lincoln Murder Trial.* Harrisburg, Pennsylvania: The Stackpole Company, 1965.

Sherman, Edwin A. *Lincoln's Death Warrant: Or the Peril of Our Country.* Milwaukee: The Wisconsin Patriot, ca. 1892.

Shutes, Milton H. *Lincoln and the Doctors: A Medical Narrative of the Life of Abraham Lincoln.* New York: The Pioneer Press, 1933.

Skinner, Otis. *The Last Tragedian: Booth Tells His Own Story.* New York: Dodd, Mead, 1939.

Smith, Jean Edward. *Grant.* New York: Simon & Schuster, 2001.

Smoot, Richard Mitchell. *The Unwritten History of the Assassination of Abraham Lincoln.* Clinton, Massachusetts: Press of W. J. Coulter, 1908.

Spencer, William V. *Lincolniana: In Memoriam.* Boston: William V. Spencer, 1865.

Starr, John W., Jr. *Further Light on Lincoln's Last Day.* [Harrisburg, Pennsylvania]: privately printed, 1930.

———. *Lincoln's Last Day.* New York: Frederick A. Stokes Co., 1922.

———. *New Light on Lincoln's Last Day.* Privately printed, 1926.

Steers, Edward, Jr. *Blood on the Moon: The Assassination of Abraham Lincoln.* Lexington: University Press of Kentucky, 2001.

———. *The Escape & Capture of John Wilkes Booth.* Gettysburg: Thomas Publications, 1992.

———. *His Name Is Still Mudd: The Case Against Doctor Samuel Alexander Mudd.* Gettysburg, Pennsylvania: Thomas Publications, 1997.

———, ed. *The Trial: The Assassination of President Lincoln and the Trial of the Conspirators.* Lexington: University Press of Kentucky, 2003.

Stern, Philip van Doren. *The Man Who Killed Lincoln: The Story of John Wilkes Booth and His Part in the Assassination.* New York: Random House, 1939.

Stevens, L. L. *Lives, Crimes, and Confessions of the Assassins.* Troy, New York: Daily Times Steam Printing Establishment, 1865.

Surratt, John H. *Life, Trial, and Extraordinary Adventures of John H. Surratt, the Conspirator.* Philadelphia: Barclay & Co., 1867.

———. *Trial of John H. Surratt in the Criminal Court for the District Of Columbia.* Washington, D.C.: Government Printing Office, 1867. 2 volumes.

Swanson, James L., and Daniel R. Weinberg. *Lincoln's Assassins: Their Trial and Execution.* Santa Fe, New Mexico: Arena Editions, 2001.

Taft, Charles Sabin. *Abraham Lincoln's Last Hours: From the Notebook of Charles Sabin Taft, M.D., an Army Surgeon Present at the Assassination, Death and Autopsy.* Chicago: privately printed, 1934.

Taylor, John M. *William Henry Seward: Lincoln's Right Hand.* New York: HarperCollins, 1991.

Taylor, Welford Dunaway. *Our American Cousin: The Play That Changed History.* Washington, D.C.: Beacham Publishing, 1990.

The Terrible Tragedy at Washington: Assassination of President Lincoln. Philadelphia: Barclay & Co., 1865.

Thomas, Benjamin P. *Abraham Lincoln.* New York: Knopf, 1952.

Thomas, Benjamin, and Harold M. Hyman. *Stanton: The Life and Times of Lincoln's Secretary of War.* New York: Knopf, 1962.

Tidwell, William A. *April '65: Confederate Covert Action in the American Civil War.* Kent, Ohio: Kent State University Press, 1995.

Tidwell, William A., with James O. Hall and David Winfred Gaddy. *Come Retribution: The Confederate Secret Service and the Assassination of Lincoln.* Jackson: University Press of Mississippi, 1988.

Townsend, E. D. *Anecdotes of the Civil War.* New York: D. Appleton-Century Company, 1884.

Townsend, George Alfred. *The Life, Crime, and Capture of John Wilkes Booth.* New York: Dick & Fitzgerald, 1865.

————. *Rustics in Rebellion: A Yankee Reporter on the Road to Richmond.* Chapel Hill: University of North Carolina Press, 1950.

Trindal, Elizabeth Steger. *Mary Surratt: An American Tragedy.* Gretna, Louisiana: Pelican Publishing Company, 1996.

Turner, Justin G., and Linda Levitt Turner, eds. *Mary Todd Lincoln: Her Life and Letters.* New York: Knopf, 1972.

Turner, Thomas Reed. *The Assassination of Abraham Lincoln.* Malabar, Florida: Krieger Publishing Company, 1999.

————. *Beware the People Weeping: Public Opinion and the Assassination of Abraham Lincoln.* Baton Rouge: Louisiana State University Press, 1982.

Valentine, David T. *Obsequies of Abraham Lincoln, in the City of New York.* New York: Edmund Jones & Co., 1866.

Van Deusen, Glyndon G. *William Henry Seward.* New York: Oxford University Press, 1967.

Vowell, Sarah. *Assassination Vacation.* New York: Simon & Schuster, 2005.

The War of the Rebellion: A Compilation of the Official Records of the Union and Confederate Armies. 128 volumes. Washington, D.C.: Government Printing Office, 1880–1901.

Wearmouth, John M., and Roberta J. Wearmouth. *Thomas A. Jones: Chief Agent of the Confederate Secret Service in Maryland.* Port Tobacco, Maryland: Stones Throw Publishing, 2000.

Welles, Gideon. *Diary of Gideon Welles: Secretary of the Navy under Lincoln and Johnson.* Boston: Houghton Mifflin, 1911. 3 volumes.

West, Richard S. *Gideon Welles: Lincoln's Navy Department.* Indianapolis: Bobbs-Merrill, 1943.

White, Ronald C., Jr. *The Eloquent President: A Portrait of Lincoln through His Words.* New York: Random House, 2005.

————. *Lincoln's Greatest Speech: The Second Inaugural.* New York: Simon & Schuster, 2002.

Whiteman, Maxwell. *While Lincoln Lay Dying: A Facsimile Reproduction of the First Testimony Taken in Connection with the Assassination of Abraham Lincoln as Recorded by Corporal James Tanner.* Philadelphia: Union League of Philadelphia, 1968.

Williamson, David Brainerd. *Illustrated Life, Services, Martyrdom, and Funeral of Abraham Lincoln.* Philadelphia: T. B. Peterson & Brothers, 1865.

Wilson, Francis. *John Wilkes Booth: Fact and Fiction of Lincoln's Assassination.* Boston: Houghton Mifflin, 1929.

————. *Joseph Jefferson: Reminiscences of a Fellow Player.* New York: Scribner's, 1906.

Wilson, Rufus Rockwell. *Lincoln among His Friends: A Sheaf of Intimate Memories.* Caldwell, Idaho: Caxton Printers, 1942.

Winik, Jay. *April 1865: The Month That Saved America.* New York: HarperCollins, 2001.

Winter, William. *Life and Art of Edwin Booth.* New York: Moffat, 1893.

Woods, Rufus. *The Weirdest Story in American History: The Escape of John Wilkes Booth.* Privately printed, 1944.

PROLOGUE

The best account of Inauguration Day, 1865, is Ronald C. White Jr.'s *Lincoln's Greatest Speech: The Second Inaugural* (New York: Simon & Schuster, 2002). Highly descriptive accounts of the day's events appeared in the Washington newspapers, including those I consider the best "papers of record"—the *Evening Star, Daily Morning Chronicle,* and *National Intelligencer.* The four best Lincoln biographies also cover the event briefly. See David Donald, *Lincoln* (New York: Simon & Schuster, 1995), pages 565–568; Stephen B. Oates, *With Malice Toward None: The Life of Abraham Lincoln* (New York: Harper & Row, 1977), pages 410–412; Benjamin P. Thomas, *Abraham Lincoln* (New York: Knopf, 1952), pages 503–504; and Carl Sandburg, *Abraham Lincoln: The War Years* (New York: Harcourt Brace & Co., 1939), volume 4, pages 85–99. Some critics might question the inclusion of Sandburg's six-volume Lincoln magnum opus, *The Prairie Years* (in two volumes) and *The War Years* (in four volumes) on any list of the "best" biographies. Indeed, Gore Vidal once wrote that Sandburg's biography was the worst thing to happen to Lincoln since his assassination. Sandburg has also come into disfavor among professional historians. Despite certain faults of interpretation, and some inevitable errors, no book about Lincoln has ever been better written, or is more evocative of the spirit of Lincoln's age. Sandburg's treatment on pages 246 through 413 in volume four of *The War Years,* covering Lincoln's last days, the assassination, the tumultuous response, and the funeral is still worth reading.

William Smith's photograph was lost for almost a century until the discovery

in 1962 of a single print, on its original mounting, bearing a letterpress identification of the artist and event. Smith took the photograph for Alexander
Gardner who, working closer to the East Front with another camera, could
not be in two places at once. This specimen was believed to be a unique survival until the discovery of a second example in the late 1990s. A full-page
reproduction of Smith's magnificent image can be found in Lloyd Ostendorf's *Lincoln's Photographs: A Complete Album* (Dayton, Ohio: Rockywood
Press, 1998), at page 206.

Gardner's photographs appear in Ostendorf on pages 208–212.

Noah Brooks's description of the bursting sun appears in his memoir *Washington, D.C., in Lincoln's Time* (New York: The Century Company, 1895). I used
the best edition, the 1971 Georgia University Press reprint, edited by the in-
sightful journalist and Civil War historian Herbert Mitgang. The sunburst
appears at page 213, and Brooks's vision of the shadow of death at 215.

The complete text of Lincoln's Second Inaugural can be read in a number of
books, including *Lincoln's Greatest Speech* by White, at pages 17–19 (White
also illustrates Lincoln's rarely seen handwritten draft); *This Fiery Trial: The
Speeches and Writings of Abraham Lincoln* (New York: Oxford University
Press, 2002), pages 220–221, edited by William E. Gienapp; and *The Collected Works of Abraham Lincoln,* volume 8, pages 332–333 (New Brunswick:
Rutgers University Press, 1952), edited by Roy P. Basler.

The observations of Elizabeth Keckley, dressmaker and confidante to Mary
Lincoln, appear on pages 176–177 of her memoir, *Behind the Scenes. Or,
Thirty Years a Slave, and Four Years in the White House* (New York: G.W. Carleton & Co., 1868). For more on this fascinating and tumultuous relationship, see Jennifer Fleischner, *Mrs. Lincoln and Mrs. Keckly* (New York:
Broadway Books, 2003). Fleischner explains the variant spellings of Elizabeth's last name.

Samuel Knapp Chester's account of the House of Lords episode appears in Ben
Perley Poore, *The Conspiracy Trial for the Murder of the President* (Boston:
J. E. Tilton and Company, 1865), 3 volumes, volume 1, page 49; and in Benn
Pitman's *The Assassination of President Lincoln and the Trial of the Conspira-
tors* (Cincinnati: Moore, Wilstach & Baldwin, 1865), at page 45.

Arthur F. Loux has chronicled Booth's lifetime schedule, as far as it can be as-
certained, in *John Wilkes Booth: Day by Day* (privately printed, 1989).

Booth's lament about "the blues" was taken from Henry B. Phillips at the Petersen house on the night of the assassination. See Maxwell Whiteman,

While Lincoln Lay Dying: A Facsimile Reproduction of the First Testimony Taken in Connection with the Assassination of Abraham Lincoln as Recorded by Corporal James Tanner (Philadelphia: Union League of Philadelphia, 1968), in "Statement of Mr. Henry B. Philips." The book is unpaginated.

Lincoln's April 10, 1865, remarks to the citizen-serenaders are published in Basler, *Collected Works,* volume 8, pages 393–394.

Brooks's description of April 11 and the circumstances of Lincoln's last speech appear on pages 225–227 of *Washington, D.C., in Lincoln's Time.* Keckley's account—including the Tad Lincoln quotation—appears on pages 176 and 177 of *Behind the Scenes.*

Lincoln's last speech is published in Basler, *Collected Works,* volume 8, pages 399–405.

Keckley preserved her fears of assassination in *Behind the Scenes* at page 178.

Booth's angry statement about black voting rights is discussed in Michael Kauffman, *American Brutus: John Wilkes Booth and the Lincoln Conspiracies* (New York: Random House, 2004), at page 209; John Rhodehamel and Louise Taper, *"Right or Wrong, God Judge Me": The Writings of John Wilkes Booth* (Urbana: University of Illinois Press, 1997), at page 15; and William Hanchett, *The Lincoln Murder Conspiracies* (Urbana: University of Illinois Press, 1983), at page 37. Booth's statement about the "last speech" was reported by Lewis Powell to Major Thomas Eckert of the War Department telegraph office. See Eckert's testimony in *House Report* 40, at page 674.

Booth's letter to his mother appears in John Rhodehamel and Louise Taper, *"Right or Wrong,"* at page 144.

CHAPTER ONE

April 1865 was a month like no other in our history. According to one account, "looking back on this rapid succession of events, it is clear that the American people had, in less than a month, lived through the most intensely dramatic series of events in the history of the United States." See James L. Swanson and Daniel R. Weinberg, *Lincoln's Assassins: Their Trial and Execution* (Santa Fe, New Mexico: Arena Editions, 2001), pages 9–11. The best account of those weeks is Jay Winik's *April 1865: The Month That Saved America* (New York: HarperCollins, 2001), a splendid synthesis of matters civil, military, and political. James M. McPherson's *Battle Cry of Freedom: The Civil War* (New York: Oxford University Press, 1988) remains the essential one-volume history of the war, and offers valuable insights on its end.

Ernest B. Furgurson's *Freedom Rising: Washington in the Civil War* (New York: Knopf, 2004) evokes the capital city that Lincoln and Booth knew, as does Margaret Leech's incomparable classic, *Reveille in Washington, 1860–1865* (New York: Harper & Bros., 1941). Any student of the Lincoln assassination should read Winik, McPherson, Furgurson, and Leech in order to understand the context of Booth's crime. To see the streets and architecture of the wartime capital as Lincoln, Booth, the conspirators, and the manhunters saw them, there are no better time machines than two photographic histories, Richard M. Lee's *Mr. Lincoln's City* (McLean, Virginia: EPM Publications, 1981) and Stanley Kimmel's *Mr. Lincoln's Washington* (New York: Bramhall House, 1957).

The description of Booth as Adonis is from the actor Sir Charles Wyndham, and appears in Swanson and Weinberg, *Lincoln's Assassins,* page 147.

My account of the events of April 14, 1865—and of most of the events in the book—is based largely on contemporary newspaper accounts; testimony from the conspiracy trial of 1865; testimony from the John H. Surratt trial of 1867; letters and memoirs of the participants; original photographs, broadsides, and relics; various government documents; and the best books published on the assassination between 1865 and 2005. Although I attribute direct quotations, I do not cite sources for each and every fact in the book. That approach would have resulted in an exceedingly voluminous section of notes that would overburden most readers. *Manhunt* is meant to be not an encyclopedia of the assassination, but a dramatic account of the events of April 14 through 26 that unfolds, as much as possible, in real time. Where Lincoln scholars are in general agreement about certain facts (for example, that Booth had been drinking heavily, or that he usually stayed at the National Hotel, or that women were attracted to him), I refer the reader to the standard references listed in the introduction to the bibliography. In the notes that follow I do call attention to obscure or unusual facts, and I also discuss controversial events when scholars have disagreed about the facts, or their interpretation.

For a history of the play, and its script, see Welford Dunaway Taylor, *Our American Cousin: The Play That Changed History* (Washington, D.C.: Beacham Publishing, 1990).

Secretary of the Navy Gideon Welles recorded Lincoln's dream in his diary. Howard K. Beale, ed., *Diary of Gideon Welles* (New York: W.W. Norton, 1960), volume 2, pages 282–283.

For more on Lincoln's last cabinet meeting, see Doris Kearns Goodwin, *Team of Rivals: The Political Genius of Abraham Lincoln* (New York: Simon & Schuster, 2005), pages 731–732; Donald, *Lincoln,* at pages 590–592; and Oates, *With Malice Toward None,* at pages 427–428.

Lincoln's telegram of June 9, 1863, appears in Basler, *Collected Works,* volume 6, at page 256; and the April 1848 letter in *Collected Works,* volume 1, at pages 465–466.

Henry Clay Ford's suggestion to James Ferguson, and Ferguson's response, appear in Poore, *The Conspiracy Trial,* volume 1, page 190. Also see Pitman, *The Assassination of President Lincoln,* at page 76.

Henry Clay Ford witnessed Booth's laughter at noon, April 14: "He sat on the steps while reading his letter, every now and then looking up and laughing." Pitman, *The Assassination of President Lincoln,* at page 101.

No one admitted to telling Booth that the president was coming to the theatre. Henry Clay Ford, testifying at the conspiracy trial, tried to blur the issue by saying he did not know, and that it could have been anyone: "It was while Booth was there I suppose he learned of the President's visit to the Theatre that evening. There were several around Booth, talking to him." Pitman, *The Assassination of Abraham Lincoln,* at page 100.

All quotations attributed to Dr. Charles Leale come from one source, his firsthand account of the night of April 14 and the morning of April 15, 1865, not published until many years after the assassination. See Charles A. Leale, *Address Delivered Before the Commandery of the State of N.Y. Military Order of the Loyal Legion of the U.S.,* February, 1909.

Ferguson's account of how Booth boasted about his rented horse, and the presence of Maddox, comes from Poore, *The Conspiracy Trial,* volume 1, page 190. Also see Pitman, *The Assassination of President Lincoln,* page 76.

Booth's conversation with Henry Merrick at the National Hotel, published in the April 17, 1865, *New York Tribune,* is reproduced in Rhodehamel and Taper, *"Right or Wrong,"* page 150.

Booth's comment about "splendid acting" is reprinted in Kauffman, *American Brutus,* page 222.

John Matthews left behind at least two accounts of his conversation with Booth. See Rhodehamel and Taper, *"Right or Wrong,"* pages 151–153.

For an account of Julia Dent Grant's sighting of Booth, see Steers, *Blood on the Moon,* page 112.

Booth's note to Vice President Johnson appears in Rhodehamel and Taper,

"Right or Wrong," page 146. There is some disagreement about whether Booth intended this note to be placed in Johnson's mailbox, or in the one next to it, which belonged to Johnson's private secretary, William A. Browning. For further discussion, see footnotes 1 and 2 on page 146 of Rhodehamel and Taper, *"Right or Wrong."*

Spangler described his occupation as "stage carpenter" during his interrogation by the authorities after the assassination. He also recounted his conversation with Booth.

For more on Booth's pistol, see John E. Parsons, *Henry Deringer's Pocket Pistol* (New York: William Morrow, 1952).

Mary Surratt's comments about the "shooting irons" appear in Lloyd's testimony in Poore, *The Conspiracy Trial,* volume 1, pages 117, 118, 121, 122, 123, and 125. Also see Pitman, *The Assassination of President Lincoln,* pages 85–87. Lloyd's account of his intoxication appears in Poore, volume 1, at page 132. Also see Pitman, page 87.

For background on the kidnapping conspiracy, see Edward Steers Jr., *Blood on the Moon: The Assassination of Abraham Lincoln* (Lexington: University Press of Kentucky, 2001), pages 71–78.

The alleged content of Booth's letter to the *National Intelligencer* is highly controversial. Years after the assassination, Matthews claimed to have reconstructed the text from memory. It is more likely that he based his so-called recollections upon the text of Booth's political manifesto discovered in the safe of the assassin's sister. Despite the confusion about what Booth's letter to the newspaper actually said, I am confident that Matthews was correct in remembering that Booth signed his coconspirators' names to the incriminating document. For more on this, see Rhodehamel and Taper, *"Right or Wrong,"* pages 147–153.

Lincoln's note to General Grant appears in Basler, *Collected Works,* volume 8, page 411.

For more on Booth's conspirators, see the following essays collected in Edward Steers Jr., ed., *The Trial: The Assassination of President Lincoln and the Trial of the Conspirators:* Laurie Verge, "Mary Elizabeth Surratt," at pages lii–lix; Joan L. Chaconas, "John H. Surratt Jr.," at pages lx–lxv; Edward Steers Jr., "George Atzerodt," at pages lxvi–lxxi; Betty Ownsbey, "Lewis Thornton Powell, alias Payne," at pages lxxi–lxxvii; Edward Steers Jr., "Samuel Alexander Mudd," pages lxxxvi–lxxxix; Percy E. Martin, "Samuel Arnold and Michael O'Laughlen," pages lxxxviii–xcvi.

For more on Lewis Powell, see Betty J. Ownsbey, *Alias "Paine": Lewis Thornton Powell, the Mystery Man of the Lincoln Conspiracy* (Jefferson, North Carolina: McFarland, 1993). For more on John Harrison Surratt Jr., see Alfred Isacsson, *The Travels, Arrest and Trial of John H. Surratt* (Middletown, New York: Vestigium Press, 2003); and Mark Wilson Seymour, *The Pursuit & Arrest of John H. Surratt* (Austin, Texas: Civil War Library, 2000).

For more on the kidnapping plot, see Steers, *Blood on the Moon,* at pages 71–78.

Mary Lincoln's account of the carriage ride comes from her November 15, 1865, letter to the artist Francis Bicknell Carpenter, published in Justin G. Turner and Linda Levitt Turner, *Mary Todd Lincoln: Her Life and Letters* (New York: Knopf, 1972), at page 283. Carpenter's heroic oil painting of Lincoln reading the Emancipation Proclamation to his cabinet was the source for Ritchie's famous engraving, one of the most beloved images in the Lincoln iconography. For the most recent use of Carpenter's tableaux, see the dust jacket of Goodwin's *Team of Rivals.* An account of the carriage ride also appeared in Francis B. Carpenter, *Six Months at the White House with Abraham Lincoln* (New York: Hurd & Houghton, 1866), at pages 292–293.

Clara Harris's memory of the carriage ride, and her comment on the arrival at Ford's Theatre, come from her letter of April 29, 1865, describing the assassination. It can be found in Timothy S. Good, *We Saw Lincoln Shot: One Hundred Eyewitness Accounts* (Jackson: University Press of Mississippi, 1995), at pages 69–71.

Ferguson's comments appear in Poore, *The Conspiracy Trial,* volume 1, pages 189–194. Also see Pitman, *The Assassination of Abraham Lincoln,* at page 76.

CHAPTER TWO

Clara Harris's letter appears in Good, *We Saw Lincoln Shot,* at pages 69–71.

For Booth's Baptist Alley conversation with Ned Spangler, see Spangler's statement after he was taken into custody. See John Debonay's testimony in Pitman, *The Assassination of President Lincoln,* pages 105–106, and the statement of John Burroughs in Poore, *The Conspiracy Trial,* volume 1, pages 225–228. Also see Pitman, page 75. There is some confusion about the proper spelling of Burroughs's last name, and whether his nickname was "Peanut John" or "John Peanut." Burroughs used the latter in his April 1865 statement to the authorities. Later, at the conspiracy trial, he said on May 16 that his nickname was "John Peanuts." Poore, *The Conspiracy Trial,* volume 1, page 230.

Booth's visit to the Star Saloon, and his choice of beverage, appear in the testimony of Peter Taltavul in Poore, *The Conspiracy Trial,* volume 1, at pages 179–180. Also see Pitman, *Assassination of the President,* at page 72, and *Trial of John H. Surratt,* volume 1, pages 157–158.

Ferguson's statement about Booth's approach to the president's box appears in Poore, *The Conspiracy Trial,* volume 1, page 190. Also see Pitman, *The Assassination of President Lincoln,* pages 76–77.

Mary Jane Anderson's "right wishful" alley sighting of Booth on the afternoon of April 14 is in Poore, *The Conspiracy Trial,* volume 1, page 236. Also see Pitman, *The Assassination of the President,* page 75.

Assassination buffs will have surely noticed by now that, while I mention Lincoln's valet or messenger Charles Forbes, I have omitted from the narrative one John Parker, the president's so-called bodyguard. For three reasons, Parker does not appear in the narrative. First, he was not a "bodyguard" in the modern sense of the word. He was a police officer detailed to guard the Executive Mansion, as the White House was known during Lincoln's administration, from theft and vandalism. Second, the Parker controversy detracts from the immediacy of the story. Many books on the assassination have concocted moments of high—and I argue false—drama by suggesting that if only Parker, who was at Ford's Theatre, had not "abandoned" his post to get a drink, Booth would not have gained entry to the state box, and Lincoln would not have been murdered. Finally, the Parker issue is a red herring. Parker or no Parker, John Wilkes Booth would have been admitted to the box. Forbes admitted at least two people to Lincoln's box that night, a messenger bearing military documents, and Booth. Had Parker been sitting near the entry to the box with Forbes, Parker would have done the same. For more on the Parker controversy, see Steers, *Blood on the Moon,* pages 103, 104, 116.

Ferguson's observation of Booth entering the box appears in Poore, *The Conspiracy Trial,* volume 1, pages 190–191. Also see Pitman, *The Assassination of President Lincoln,* page 76.

The last words that passed between Mary and Abraham Lincoln were preserved by Dr. Anson Henry, in a letter to his wife dated April 19, 1865, the same day as Lincoln's White House funeral. The Henrys were old Illinois friends of the Lincolns living in Washington, and Mary Lincoln confided in a private conversation with the doctor the last words spoken by the president. Henry's letter appears in Milton H. Shutes, *Lincoln and the Doctors* (New York: The Pioneer Press, 1933), page 132.

For the complete dialogue from act 3, scene 2, see Taylor, *Our American Cousin*, pages 80–85.

The exact time of Booth's shot cannot be fixed, in part because no one knows the precise time that the performance began. Ford's, like many theatres at the time, was somewhat casual about curtain time. Witnesses could not agree, and surviving testimony, letters, and oral history support multiple conclusions. Booth may have shot Lincoln as early as 10:13 or as late as 10:30 P.M. I suspect that the time was close to 10:15 P.M., but as late as 10:20 P.M. For a fuller discussion of this, and for a number of recollections from those at Ford's Theatre, see Timothy S. Good, *We Saw Lincoln Shot: One Hundred Eyewitness Accounts* (Jackson: University Press of Mississippi, 1995). Good believes that Booth fired close to 10:30 P.M.

David Donald describes the tough, Clary's Grove boys in *Lincoln*, at pages 40–41, and Donald confirms, on page 568, that in the spring of 1865 Lincoln "continued to be a physically powerful man."

Ferguson's description of Lincoln's position at the moment he was shot appears in Poore, *The Conspiracy Trial*, volume 1, pages 190–191.

Major Rathbone reported that Booth shouted "Freedom." Rathbone's account of the assassination and knife attack appears in Poore, *The Conspiracy Trial*, volume 1, pages 195–198. Also see Pitman, *The Assassination of the President*, at pages 78–79. Clara Harris also described the stabbing in her April 29, 1865, letter. See Good, *We Saw Lincoln Shot*, at pages 69–71.

Witnesses disagreed about what Booth said, and where he said it. Booth later claimed that he cried "Sic semper" while standing in the box before he shot Lincoln, but Rathbone remembered only the word "Freedom." During the manhunt Booth wrote in his makeshift diary: "I shouted Sic semper *before* I fired." See Rhodehamel and Taper, *"Right or Wrong,"* at page 154. Based on the available evidence, I believe that Booth said in the box and onstage the words I attribute to him in the narrative. For an extensive discussion, see Good, *We Saw Lincoln Shot*.

Rathbone's testimony on the barred door is in Poore, *The Conspiracy Trial*, volume 1, at page 195.

Ferguson described Booth's exultation to Stanton at the Petersen house on the night of the assassination, and James Tanner recorded his statement that Booth said "I have done it." See Good, *We Saw Lincoln Shot,* at page 32. Later, at the trial, Ferguson neglected to mention "I have done it" in his testimony as published in Poore, *The Conspiracy Trial,* volume 1, page 197.

The first words of Rathbone appear in Poore, *The Conspiracy Trial,* volume 1, page 197.

Booth's broken bone has become the subject of minor controversy. A handful of assassination buffs insist that Booth was not injured when he fell to the stage at Ford's Theatre. Instead, they argue, not long after he crossed the Navy Yard Bridge, his horse slipped and fell on the roads outside Washington, breaking a bone in the actor's left leg. Although a fascinating diversion, the issue of where Booth was injured, onstage at Ford's between 10:15 and 10:30 P.M., or on the roads between the Navy Yard Bridge and Surrattsville sometime before midnight, is a tempest in a teapot in the story of the manhunt. However it happened, Booth's broken leg made a visit to Dr. Mudd essential. I agree with Edward Steers that in this matter we should accept, along with other evidence, Booth's own account of his injury, when he wrote: "In jumping broke my leg." Rhodehamel and Taper, *"Right or Wrong,"* at page 154.

Seward's carriage accident is covered in Glyndon G. Van Deusen, *William Henry Seward* (New York: Oxford University Press, 1967), at page 411.

A number of accounts describe the events at the home of Secretary of State Seward. See Glyndon G. Van Deusen, *William Henry Seward* (New York: Oxford University Press, 1967), pages 412–415; and Benjamin Thomas and Harold M. Hyman, *Stanton: The Life and Times of Lincoln's Secretary of War* (New York: Knopf, 1962), pages 396, 397. For Fanny Seward's account of the attempted assassination of her father, I relied primarily upon her diary as featured in Patricia Carley Johnson, "I Have Supped Full of Horrors," *American Heritage,* October 1959, volume 10, number 6, pages 59–65 and 96–101. An account by Sergeant Robinson appears in Poore, *The Conspiracy Trial,* volume 1, pages 479–480. Also see Pitman, *The Assassination of the President,* pages 155–156. William Bell's testimony appears in Poore, volume 2, page 130, and in Pitman, pages 154–155; Augustus Seward's testimony is in Poore, volume 2, page 5, and in Pitman, pages 156–157; Dr. Tullio S. Verdi's testimony appears in Poore, volume 2, page 100, and in Pitman, pages 157–158; and the testimony of Surgeon General Joseph K. Barnes appears in Poore, volume 2, at pages 21 and 60, and in Pitman at page 157.

Other valuable sources for the Seward attack include Dr. Tullio S. Verdi's article, "The Assassination of the Sewards," published in *Republic* magazine in
July 1873 and reprinted in Frederick Hatch, ed., *Journal of the Lincoln Assassination*, volume 16, number 3, December 2003, page 46; Frederick Hatch,
"I'm Mad! I'm Mad," *Journal of the Lincoln Assassination*, volume 3, number
3, December 1989, pages 34–38; and Dr. John K. Lattimer, "The Stabbing of
Lincoln's Secretary of State on the Night the President Was Shot," *Journal of
the American Medical Association*, volume 192, number 2, April 12, 1965,
pages 99–106. Dr. Lattimer also covers the Seward attack in his book, *Kennedy and Lincoln: Medical and Ballistic Comparisons of Their Assassinations*
(New York: Harcourt Brace Jovanovich, 1980).

CHAPTER THREE

Joseph B. Stewart's account appears in *Trial of John H. Surratt* (Washington,
D.C.: Government Printing Office, 1867), volume 1, pages 125–127, and in
volume 2, pages 984–987.

Mary Anderson's description of the knife appears in Poore, *The Conspiracy
Trial*, volume 1, page 237; and her account of Booth galloping away is on
page 239. Mary Ann Turner's account of the hoofbeats is in Poore, volume 1,
at page 234.

Booth's command to John Peanut comes from Peanut's statement, as does the
description of the assassin's blow to the head and kick.

Sergeant Cobb's account of his encounter with Booth at the bridge appears in
Poore, *The Conspiracy Trial*, volume 1, pages 251–252. Also see Pitman, *The
Assassination of President Lincoln*, pages 84–85. That Booth disclosed his real
name, and his destination, the vicinity of Beantown, remains inexplicable.

For this continuation of the events at the Seward house, see the Seward source
notes in chapter 2.

Sergeant Robinson's letter requesting Powell's knife is illustrated in Swanson
and Weinberg, *Lincoln's Assassins*, page 44. A period bronze casting of Robinson's medal appears on the same page.

Clara Harris's description of the stabbing is in Good, *We Saw Lincoln Shot*.

Dr. Leale's account appeared in *Harper's Weekly* in 1909.

The description of Laura Keene claiming center stage and beseeching the audience appears in John Creahan, *The Life of Laura Keene* (Philadelphia: The
Rodgers Publishing Company, 1897), at page 27.

Fletcher's testimony about Atzerodt's promise of a present is in Poore, *The

Conspiracy Trial, volume 1, at pages 328, 331. Also see *Trial of John H. Surratt,* volume 1, at page 229. Fletcher's pursuit of Herold and the horse is in Poore, volume 1, at pages 328–334. Also see Pitman, pages 83–84, and *Trial of John H. Surratt,* pages 227–229. The exchange between Fletcher and Sergeant Cobb appears in Poore, volume 1, at page 329. Also see Pitman, page 84. Fletcher's description of the horse is in Poore, volume 1, at page 332. Also see Pitman, at page 84.

The Mrs. Ord episode is discussed in Donald, *Lincoln,* at pages 572–573.

For more on Laura Keene, see Creahan, *The Life of Laura Keene;* Vernanne Bryan, *Laura Keene: A British Actress on the American Stage, 1826–1873* (Jefferson, North Carolina: McFarland & Company, 1997); and Ben Graf Henneke, *Laura Keene: A Biography* (Tulsa: Council Oaks, 1990).

George Alfred Townsend's description of Lincoln on the floor of the president's box appears in his book *The Life, Crime, and Capture of John Wilkes Booth* (New York: Dick & Fitzgerald, 1865), at page 10.

Asia Booth Clarke's derogatory comments about Lincoln's choice of Good Friday entertainment appear in her memoirs, at page 99.

John Lee's testimony about the search of Atzerodt's hotel room is in Poore, volume 1, at pages 63–66. Also see Pitman, *Assassination of the President,* page 144.

Seaton Munroe's comments appear in Creahan, *The Life of Laura Keene,* at page 28, and in Seaton Munroe, "Recollections of Lincoln's Assassination," *North American Review,* April 1896, pages 424–434.

Bersch did paint his scene of Lincoln being carried across Tenth Street to the Petersen house. It is now in the collection of the National Park Service, and is illustrated in Victoria Grieve, *Ford's Theatre and the Lincoln Assassination* (Alexandria, Virginia: Parks & History Association, 2001), at page 60. Sadly, at the time *Manhunt* went to press, the Park Service had removed the painting from display at Ford's Theatre, where it had hung for years.

For more on Safford, see Steers, *Blood on the Moon,* at page 123, and Kauffman, *American Brutus,* at page 19.

CHAPTER FOUR

For a description, based on period newspaper accounts, of how news raced through Washington by word of mouth after the fall of Richmond and Lee's surrender, see Swanson and Weinberg, *Lincoln's Assassins,* pages 9–11.

Lincoln described his reliance upon Stanton with a magnificent tribute: "He is

the rock on the beach of our national ocean against which the breakers dash
and roar, dash and roar without ceasing. He fights back the angry waters
and prevents them from undermining and overwhelming the land. Gentlemen, I do not see how he survives, why he is not crushed and torn to pieces.
Without him I should be destroyed."

An account of how Stanton received the news of the assassination appears in
Thomas and Hyman, *Stanton*, at page 396. For a discussion of the friendship between Lincoln and his Secretary of War, and how it grew at the president's summer retreat, see Matthew Pinsker, *Lincoln's Sanctuary: Abraham
Lincoln and the Soldiers' Home* (New York: Oxford University Press, 2003).
Also see Elizabeth Smith Brownstein, *Lincoln's Other White House: The Un-
told Story of the Man and His Presidency* (Hoboken, N.J.: John Wiley & Sons,
2005). Thomas and Hyman give an account of Stanton's evening prior to
the assassination on pages 395–396.

Seward's boast, which Lewis Powell proved to the secretary to be tragically
wrong, is from a July 15, 1862, letter to John Bigelow, and was published
in Bigelow's *Retrospectives of an Active Life* (New York: Baker and Taylor,
1909), volume 1, page 505. More conveniently for modern readers, the
relevant passage is quoted in Rhodehamel and Taper, *"Right or Wrong,"* at
page 1.

Thomas and Hyman describe how Stanton and Welles rushed to the Seward
house, then to Ford's Theatre: *Stanton*, pages 396–397. The navy secretary
also described the events in his diary: Beale, *Diary of Gideon Welles*, volume
2, pages 283–286. Brief accounts can also be found in J. E. Buckingham,
Reminiscences and Souvenirs of the Assassination of Abraham Lincoln (Washington: Press of Rufus H. Darby, 1894), at pages 21–22, and, for details not
available elsewhere, Moorefield Storey, "Dickens, Stanton, Sumner, and
Storey," *Atlantic Monthly*, April 1930, pages 463–465. The article recounts a
long ago dinner attended by the four men during which Stanton described
the wild night of April 14, 1865.

Mary Surratt's country tavern in Surrattsville (now Clinton), Maryland, still
stands, and is a splendid museum and research center maintained by the
Surratt Society.

The language from John H. Surratt's postal commission comes from a reading
of the original document, now in a private collection.

My account of the visit of Booth and Herold to the Surrattsville tavern, and
their direct quotations, come from the testimony of John Lloyd. See Poore,

The Conspiracy Trial, volume 1, pages 118–126; and Pitman, *The Assassination,* pages 86–87.

The primary source for Dr. Leale's actions is his own account, published, among other places, in Charles Leale, *Lincoln's Last Hours* (n.p.: privately printed, 1909).

Maunsell Field's abbreviated recollections were published in an article and in his memoirs, *Memories of Many Men and of Some Women* (New York: Harper & Brothers, 1874), pages 321–329.

For another account of what happened inside the Petersen house, this one by George Francis, one of the boarders, see Ralph G. Newman, "The Mystery Occupant's Eyewitness Account of the Death of Abraham Lincoln," *Chicago History,* Spring 1975, pages 32–33. Francis's May 5, 1865 letter is the source for two of Mary Lincoln's statements: "Where is my husband! Where is my husband!" and "How can it be so? Do speak to me!"

Rathbone described his fainting in Poore, *The Conspiracy Trial,* volume 1, at page 197. Also see Pitman, *Assassination of the President,* at page 79.

For more on the doctors, see Harry Read, "'A Hand to Hold While Dying': Dr. Charles A. Leale at Lincoln's Side," *Lincoln Herald,* Spring 1977, pages 21–25, and Charles Sabin Taft, "Abraham Lincoln's Last Hours: From the Note-Book of an Army Surgeon Present at the Assassination, Death, and Autopsy," *Century Magazine,* February 1895, pages 634–636.

Dr. Taft's recollections were also published in *Abraham Lincoln's Last Hours: From the Notebooks of Charles Sabin Taft, M.D., an Army Surgeon Present at the Assassination, Death and Autopsy* (Chicago: privately printed, 1934).

Welles's account appears in his diary, volume 2, at pages 283–290.

The midnight telegram to General Grant, and all other telegrams in this chapter, appear in *The War of the Rebellion: A Compilation of the Official Records of the Union and Confederate Armies* (Washington, D.C.: Government Printing Office, 1880–1901; *Official Records*). The telegrams are collected in series 1, volume 46, part 3, and appear in chronological order at pages 752–989.

For more on Corporal Tanner, see Howard H. Peckham, "James Tanner's Account of Lincoln's Death," *Abraham Lincoln Quarterly,* March 1942, pages 176–183. Tanner is the source of Mary Lincoln's statement, "Oh, my God, and have I given my husband to die?"

The quotations from Walker, Greenawalt, and Keim about George Atzerodt come from Poore, *The Conspiracy Trial,* volume 1, at, respectively, pages

391–395, 341–352, and 400–402. Hezekiah Metz's testimony appears at pages 353–357, and Sergeant Gemmill's at pages 357–361.

Dr. Abbott's statistics on the stricken president's pulse and respiration were published in all the major newspapers, including the *New York Times, New York Tribune, Philadelphia Inquirer,* and, in Washington, D.C., the *Daily Morning Chronicle* and *National Intelligencer.* They also appeared in contemporary books about the assassination, including *The Terrible Tragedy at Washington: Assassination of President Lincoln* (Philadelphia: Barclay & Co., 1865), at page 28.

The account of the first raid on Mary Surratt's Washington, D.C., boardinghouse is drawn from Floyd E. Risvold, ed., *A True History of the Assassination of Abraham Lincoln and of the Conspiracy of 1865, by Louis J. Weichmann, Chief Witness for the Government of the United States in the Prosecution of the Conspirators* (New York: Knopf, 1975), at pages 174–179. Also see Steers, *Blood on the Moon,* pages 173–174.

The sources on Dr. Mudd include his three written statements, based on interrogations of him by Lieutenant Lovett and Colonel Wells, and on the testimony of those officers at the conspiracy trial. Lovett's testimony appears in Poore, *The Conspiracy Trial,* volume 1, pages 258–272, and in Pitman, *The Assassination of President Lincoln,* pages 87–88. Wells's testimony appears in Poore at volume 1, pages 281–293, and in Pitman at pages 168–169. Joshua Lloyd's testimony appears in Poore, volume 1, at pages 273–281, and in Pitman at page 90; William Williams's testimony appears in Poore, volume 1, at pages 294–301, and in Pitman at pages 88–89; and Simon Gavacan's testimony appears in Poore, volume 1, at pages 301–304, and in Pitman at pages 89–90.

The best account of Dr. Mudd is Edward Steers Jr., *His Name Is Still Mudd: The Case Against Doctor Samuel Alexander Mudd* (Gettysburg, Pennsylvania: Thomas Publications, 1997). Steers's *Blood on the Moon* includes updated coverage on Mudd at pages 144–154. Also see Edward Steers Jr., "Dr. Mudd and the 'Colored' Witnesses," *Civil War History,* volume 46, December 2000, pages 324–336.

The material on Mudd's treatment of Booth's leg comes from the doctor's three statements, and all Mudd quotations come either from his three written statements or from the testimony of Lovett and Wells. Mudd's statements are collected in *From War Department Files: Statements Made by the Lincoln Conspirators Under Examination, 1865* (Clinton, Maryland: The Surratt Society, 1980) at pages 29 and 34.

CHAPTER FIVE

The "Sam" letter, originally published in newspapers all over the country within a few days of its discovery in Booth's hotel room, can be found in Kauffman, *American Brutus,* at pages 66–67.

Stanton's telegram to General Dix, revealing some of the content of the Sam letter, appears in the *Official Records,* as do all other telegrams quoted in this chapter.

The lock of Lincoln's hair cut by Stanton and presented by him to Mary Jane Welles, the envelope addressed by Stanton, and the dried flowers from the president's White House funeral were examined in a private collection. Most accounts of Lincoln's death quote Stanton as saying that Lincoln belongs to the "ages," not the "angels." In my view, shared by Jay Winik, the most persuasive interpretation supports "angels" and is also more consistent with Stanton's character and faith.

For an account of the removal of Lincoln's remains from the Petersen house, and the names of the men who carried him out, see Steers, *Blood on the Moon,* at pages 268–269. I obtained a typescript of William Clark's letter from the archives of the Surratt Society. For more on Clark, see W. Emerson Reck, "The Riddle of William Clark," *Lincoln Herald,* Winter 1982, pages 218–221.

Matthews's account of his reading of Booth's letter to the *National Intelligencer* is in Rhodehamel and Taper, *"Right or Wrong,"* pages 150–153.

Townsend's description of Booth's young seductress is from *The Life, Crime and Capture of John Wilkes Booth* (New York: Dick & Fitzgerald, 1865), page 24.

The breakfast conversation at Dr. Mudd's comes from Mrs. Mudd's statement taken during her interrogation. The account of the crutches comes from Dr. Mudd's three statements.

Caldwell's testimony on Atzerodt pawning his pistol is in Poore, *The Conspiracy Trial,* volume 1, page 148. Also see Pitman, *Assassination of the President,* at page 148.

The story of Dr. Mudd is one of the major controversies that has long bedeviled students of the Lincoln assassination. I agree with Steers and other historians on the nature and extent of Mudd's knowledge and culpability. Despite the claims of Mudd's defenders, he was not an innocent country physician who merely performed his Hippocratic oath, and treated an injured man he believed was a stranger. Based on a review of the evidence, I am certain that Mudd recognized Booth the moment the assassin walked through his door, and I am convinced that Mudd delayed reporting Booth's visit, thus allowing the assassin a head start from the troops at nearby Bryantown. I have chosen not to bog down the narrative by writing an analytical, legal brief arguing the pros and cons of Mudd's case. That discussion is available in other texts, and I do not rehearse it here. Instead, I have written, in real time as much as possible, what I believe happened.

My account of Thomas Jones comes primarily from his memoirs, *J. Wilkes Booth: An Account of His Sojourn in Southern Maryland After the Assassination of Abraham Lincoln, His Passage Across the Potomac, and His Death in Virginia* (Chicago: Laird & Lee, 1893). All direct quotations come from him. Booth did not live long enough to write about Jones, and David Herold, after his capture, did not reveal how the Confederate agent had helped them.

For additional material on Jones, see John M. and Roberta J. Wearmouth, *Thomas A Jones: Chief Agent of the Confederate Secret Service in Maryland* (Port Tobacco, Maryland: Stones Throw Publishing, 2000).

CHAPTER SIX

Much of the material for this chapter, and all direct quotations from Thomas Jones, come from his short memoir. Booth, Herold, and Jones were the only witnesses to their interactions, just as Jones had planned.

Somerset and James Leaman's testimony about their conversations with Azterodt are in Poore, *The Conspiracy Trial,* volume 2, page 504. Also see Pitman, *Assassination of the President,* at page 150. Asia Booth Clarke's story about John's love of nature is from her memoir, *The Unlocked Book,* pages 54 ("burrowing") and 69 ("good men's bones").

The dialogue from the second raid on Mary Surratt's Washington boardinghouse appears in Poore, *The Conspiracy Trial,* volume 2, pages 15–19 and pages 33–34, and in Pitman, *The Assassination,* pages 121–124.

The dialogue with Lewis Powell appears in Poore, volume 2, pages 9–11, and in Pitman, pages 122–123.

The letters of Madlock and Severs are in a private collection.

A number of examples of postassassination artwork, including "The Assassin's Vision" carte-de-visite, are illustrated in Swanson and Weinberg, *Lincoln's Assassins,* page 54.

Booth's notebook entry appears in Rhodehamel and Taper, *"Right or Wrong,"* at pages 154–155.

Townsend's vicious descriptions of Port Tobacco and of the Brawner Hotel come from his *Life, Crime and Capture of John Wilkes Booth*, page 52.

All telegrams are from the *Official Records*.

Booth's letter to his mother is in Rhodehamel and Taper, *"Right or Wrong,"* pages 130–131; and his "To Whom it May Concern" manifesto is on pages 124–127.

Asia Booth Clarke revealed her husband's betrayal in *The Unlocked Book*, page 91.

Richter's comment about George Atzerodt appears in Poore, *The Conspiracy Trial*, volume 2, pages 515–517. Also see Pitman, *The Assassination*, page 153. The story of Atzerodt's arrest appears in Steers, *Blood on the Moon*, at pages 169–170. Atzerodt's confessions are published in "'Lost Confession' of George A. Atzerodt," in Steers, ed., *The Trial*, pages civ–cvi, and in *From War Department Files*.

CHAPTER SEVEN

The narrative of April 20 in the pine thicket, and all direct quotations, are drawn, as before, from the memoir of Thomas Jones, the only surviving witness to the events that happened there.

For a thorough analysis of the river crossing, see William A. Tidwell, "Booth Crosses the Potomac: An Exercise in Historical Research," *Civil War History* 36, April 1990, pages 325–333.

Townsend's research appeared in George Alfred Townsend, "How Booth Crossed the Potomac," *Century Magazine*, April 1884, and is reprinted in John M. and Roberta J. Wearmouth, *Thomas A. Jones: Chief Agent of the Confederate Secret Service in Maryland* (Port Tobacco, Maryland: Stones Throw Publishing, 2000), at page 56. Wearmouth covers Townsend's correspondence with Jones at pages 45–54, and Jones's "reunion" with Captain Williams at pages 154–159.

Osborn H. Oldroyd's firsthand but frustratingly brief account of Jones's visit to his Petersen House museum is found in Oldroyd's *The Assassination of Abraham Lincoln* (Washington, D.C.: Osborn H. Oldroyd, 1901), at page 101.

Herold's remarks about partridge shooting, Davis, and Hughes all come from his statement while in custody, which is published in Hall, *On the Way*, page 8.

Booth's journal entry on being "hunted like a dog," the low point of his despair since the manhunt began, appears in Rhodehamel and Taper, *"Right or Wrong,"* page 7.

All the telegrams are from the *Official Records.*

CHAPTER EIGHT

Herold's remark about the gunboat comes from his statement while in custody on April 27, 1865, published in Hall, *On the Way,* page 7.

All the telegrams are in the *Official Records.*

Herold's encounter with the Quesenberrys was described in her May 16, 1865, statement to Colonel Wells, and is published in Hall, *On the Way,* at page 108.

The fugitives' visit to Dr. Stuart was described in his statement of May 6, 1865, and published in Hall, *On the Way,* page 114.

Bryant's statement of May 6, 1865, is published in Hall, *On the Way,* at page 116.

Lucas's statement of May 6, 1865, is published in Hall, *On the Way,* at page 122.

Both drafts of Booth's letter of complaint are in Rhodehamel and Taper, *"Right or Wrong,"* at pages 157–159.

The translation of Shakespeare's passage from Macbeth that Booth quoted in his note to Dr. Stuart comes from the definitive volume of the collected works, David Bevington's *The Complete Works of Shakespeare, Fifth Edition* (New York: Pearson, 2004), at page 1277.

Rollins's two statements of April 25, 1865, and May 20, 1865, are published in Hall, *On the Way,* at pages 126 and 127.

William Jett gave a statement on May 6, 1865, and also testified at the conspiracy trial on May 17, 1865. Both of his accounts are published in Hall, *On the Way,* at pages 135 and 139.

CHAPTER NINE

The Beckwith telegram, and all the other telegrams in this chapter, appear in the *Official Records.*

The narrative of Booth's time at Garrett's farm, and all direct quotations, are drawn from several accounts. This collection of sources includes statements, reports, and testimony, and covers the pursuit to Bowling Green, the arrival at Garrett's farm, the parley with Booth, Herold's surrender, and the shooting and death of the assassin.

Captain Edward P. Doherty's major accounts can be found in his report of April 29, 1865; his testimony at the conspiracy trial of May 22, 1865; and in his March 21, 1866, letter to Secretary of War Stanton. See Hall, *On the Way,* pages 27–36.

Colonel Everton J. Conger's accounts can be found in his statement at the inquest aboard the *Montauk* on April 27, 1865; his testimony at the conspiracy trial on May 17, 1865; at the impeachment investigation of Andrew Johnson on May 13 and 14, 1867; and at the trial of John H. Surratt on June 25, 1867. See Hall, *On the Way,* pages 40–63.

Luther Byron Baker's accounts can be found in his April 27, 1865, statement at the inquest aboard the *Montauk;* his testimony at the impeachment investigation of Andrew Johnson on May 22, 1867; and his testimony at the trial of John H. Surratt on June 25, 1867. See Hall, *On the Way,* pages 74–98.

In general, the accounts of Doherty, Conger, and Baker agree on what happened at Garrett's farm. They vary in minor details, of course, a reflection not only of the frailty of memory, but of the competition for reward money. For example, the parties disagreed about who really "captured" David Herold, pulled him from the barn door, and ordered him bound. Their accounts of Booth's dialogue vary somewhat in the actor's choice of particular words, or the sequence of some of his sentences. But they all agree on the substance of the parley with Booth, on all of the sentiments that he expressed, and on their dealings with the Garrett family.

I have not included every possible variation from their accounts. Instead, I used my best judgment and the major accounts left by the principals to construct what I believe is the most reasonable account of the climax of the manhunt.

For ease of reference for the reader, I do not cite to every page of microfilm at the National Archives, to every document, and to every report where this material can be found. Instead, I refer the reader to James O. Hall's *On the Way to Garrett's Farm: John Wilkes Booth and David E. Herold in the Northern Neck of Virginia, April 22–26, 1865* (Clinton, Maryland: The Surratt Society), an indispensable volume that collects in one place much of the significant evidence, and which refers readers interested in more to the specific microfilm reels and pages

Boston Corbett's major accounts can be found in his report of April 29, 1865; his May 17, 1865 testimony at the conspiracy trial; and an April 14, 1877 newspaper article in the *Philadelphia Weekly Times*. See Hall, *On the Way*, pages 155–162.

Members of the Garrett family left behind considerable commentary about their visitors. John M. Garrett's statement was taken at Colonel Lafayette Baker's office on May 20, 1865, and Garrett testified on June 25, 1867, at the trial of John H. Surratt. His recollections are reprinted in Hall, *On the Way*, pages 140–146. Richard H. Garrett's revealing letter of April 4, 1866, to Grandison Manning appears in Hall, *On the Way*, at page 170, and Rev. Richard Baynham Garrett's letter of October 24, 1907, appears at page 174.

Also see William H. Garrett, "True Story of the Capture of John Wilkes Booth," *Confederate Veteran*, volume xxix, number 4, April 1921, pages 129–130, and Betsy Fleet, ed., "A Chapter of Unwritten History: Richard Baynham Garrett's Account of the Flight and Death of John Wilkes Boothe," *The Virginia Magazine of History and Biography*, volume 71, number 4, October 1963, pages 387–404. This article includes Edwin Booth's letter of thanks to the Garretts and the story about John Wilkes Booth amazing the Garrett children with his pocket compass.

For a little-known but important—and eerie—retrospective based on interviews with some of the Garrett survivors, see F. A. Burr, "John Wilkes Booth: The Scene of the Assassin's Death Visited," *Boston Herald*, December 11, 1881, page 9.

CHAPTER TEN

Lucinda Holloway's description of Booth's death appears in Francis Wilson, *John Wilkes Booth: Fact and Fiction of Lincoln's Assassination* (Boston: Houghton Mifflin, 1929), at pages 209–217. It is reprinted in Hall, *On the Way*, page 178.

All George Alfred Townsend material in this chapter comes from his *The Life, Crime and Capture of John Wilkes Booth*.

The dialogue between Asia Booth Clarke and T. J. Hemphill comes from her memoir, *The Unlocked Book*, at pages 92–93.

The complete collection of Gardner's photos of the captive conspirators was published for the first time in Swanson and Weinberg, *Lincoln's Assassins*, pages 58 to 76.

The Clark Mills story was reported in the May 2, 1865, *Chicago Tribune*.

Townsend's dialogue with Lafayette Baker, and his account of the faux burial at sea, are in *The Life, Crime, and Capture of John Wilkes Booth,* pages 38–39.

Important information appears in L. B. Baker, "An Eyewitness Account of the Death and Burial of J. Wilkes Booth," *Journal of the Illinois State Historical Society,* December 1946, pages 425–446.

The U.S. Treasury warrants paid to Corbett, Doherty, Baker, and all the other recipients of reward money were uncovered recently at the National Archives and photographed for the first time.

Boston Corbett's letters repose in private collections.

Asia Booth Clarke's account of Corbett appears in her memoirs at pages 99–100.

For the most detailed modern account of the execution of the conspirators, and for the complete collection of Gardner's photographs of the hanging, see Swanson and Weinberg, *Lincoln's Assassins,* pages 98–121.

Edwin Booth's letter appealing for the return of his brother's body is in Johnson's papers. See Paul H. Bergeron, ed., *The Papers of Andrew Johnson,* volume 15, September 1868–April 1869 (Knoxville: University of Tennessee Press, 1999), at pages 431–432.

Asia Booth Clarke's book of memories concludes with this elegy. Like her assassin-brother, she could not resist quoting Shakespeare. The last line of her book, "So runs the world away," comes, unsurprisingly, from *Hamlet,* act III, scene 2: "For some must watch, while some must sleep; Thus runs the world away."

EPILOGUE

The Asia Booth Clarke letters quoted here come from the reprinted and retitled edition of her memoirs, *John Wilkes Booth: A Sister's Memoir by Asia Booth Clarke* (Jackson: University Press of Mississippi, 1996), edited by Terry Alford, at page 21.

The strange and unhappy tale of Rathbone and Harris was the subject of Thomas Mallon's eerie and compelling novel, *Henry and Clara* (New York: Ticknor & Fields, 1994).

Luther Baker's promotional brochure, his "combination picture," and his horse Buckskin's first-hoof account all appear in Swanson and Weinberg, *Lincoln's Assassins,* at page 37.

For John H. Surratt's lecture, see Clara E. Laughlin, *The Death of Lincoln: The Story of Booth's Plot, His Deed and the Penalty* (New York: Doubleday,

Page, 1909), pages 222–249. Also see "A Remarkable Lecture—John H. Surratt Tells His Story," *Lincoln Herald,* December 1949, pages 20–33, 39. The
rare broadside for Surratt's never-delivered December 30, 1870, Washington, D.C., lecture appears in Swanson and Weinberg, *Lincoln's Assassins,*
page 124.

The death of Frances Seward is discussed in Van Deusen, *William Henry
Seward,* at pages 415–416. Seward's words about Fanny's death and his "unspeakable sorrow" and broken dreams are in Van Deusen, at page 417.

Samuel Arnold's memoirs did not appear in book form until the posthumous
publication of *Defense and Prison Experiences of a Lincoln Conspirator* (Hattiesburg, Mississippi: The Book Farm, 1940).

Dr. Mudd has been the subject of several books, some quite sympathetic. The
Mudd shelf includes Nettie Mudd, *The Life of Dr. Samuel A. Mudd* (New
York: Neale Publishing Company, 1909); Hal Higdon, *The Union vs. Doctor
Mudd* (Chicago: Follett Publishing Company, 1964); Samuel Carter III, *The
Riddle of Dr. Mudd* (New York: G. P. Putnam's Sons, 1974); Elden C.
Weckesser, *His Name Was Mudd* (Jefferson, North Carolina: McFarland and
Company, 1991); John Paul Jones, ed., *Dr. Mudd and the Lincoln Assassina-
tion: The Case Reopened* (Conshohocken, Pennsylvania: Combined Books,
1995); and, finally, the best and most truthful account, Edward Steers Jr., *His
Name Is Still Mudd: The Case Against Dr. Samuel Alexander Mudd* (Gettys-
burg: Thomas Publications, 1997).

The tale of Stanton's rapid decline and sad last days is told in Thomas and Hyman, *Stanton,* at pages 627–640. Robert Lincoln's condolence letter appears
on page 638.

The bizarre, and in many ways disturbing, story of Powell's skull and funeral
honors is noted in Kauffman's *American Brutus,* at page 391.

A brief, postassassination history of Ford's Theatre appears in Victoria Grieve,
Ford's Theatre and the Lincoln Assassination (Alexandria, Virginia: Parks &
History Association, 2001), pages 84–91. George F. Olszewski's *Restoration
of Ford's Theatre* (Washington, D.C.: Government Printing Office, 1963), an
essential and fascinating account of how the dead playhouse was restored to
life, belongs in the library of anyone interested in the assassination or the
history of American theatre.

Asia Booth Clarke's conciliatory but hagiographic comments come from her
memoir, *The Unlocked Book,* page 100.

The narrative about the assassination oil paintings and wax figures draws from original advertising posters for Terry's Panorama and Colonel Orr's Museum.

The myth of the Booth who got away is worthy of a book itself, but that story is, unfortunately, beyond the scope of this one. For an introduction to the myth, and for photos of Bates's book, for oil paintings he commissioned to further his scheme, and for a letter in which he claims "I had John Wilkes Booth as my client in Western Texas from about 1875 to 1877," see Swanson and Weinberg, *Lincoln's Assassins,* pages 130–136. Also see Lloyd Lewis, *Myths After Lincoln* (New York: Harcourt, Brace and Company, 1929); George S. Bryan, *The Great American Myth* (New York: Carrick & Evans, 1940); C. Wyatt Evans, *The Legend of John Wilkes Booth: Myth, Memory, and a Mummy* (Lawrence: University Press of Kansas, 2004); and Steers, *Blood on the Moon,* at pages 245–267. Sarah Vowell's marvelous and irreverent *Assassination Vacation* (New York: Simon & Schuster, 2005) covers the Booth escape and mummy legends in her tour of the popular culture of the Lincoln, Garfield, and McKinley assassinations.

The absurd book by Booth's imposter "granddaughter" is Izola Forrester's *This One Mad Act: The Unknown Story of John Wilkes Booth and His Family* (Boston: Hale, Cushman & Flint, 1937).

My assertion that many tourists who come to Ford's Theatre overlook Booth's pocket compass is based on many hours of personal observations I conducted in the museum on a number of days. Likewise, my assertion about the popularity of Booth's Deringer pistol is based on many personal observations of museum visitors while they viewed, and talked about, the murder weapon, and also Booth's other firearms and knives.

About the author

About the book

Read (and listen) on

Insights,
Interviews
& More . . .

Meet James L. Swanson

JAMES L. SWANSON, an attorney and Lincoln scholar, has held a number of government and think-tank posts in Washington, D.C. He has written about history, the presidency, the Constitution, popular culture, books, the arts, and other subjects for a variety of publications, including the *Wall Street Journal*, the *Los Angeles Times*, *American Heritage*, and *Smithsonian* magazine. He has lectured widely at the Library of Congress, the Smithsonian, the Newberry Library, and other scholarly institutions, and at literary, historical, and arts clubs across the nation. He is the coauthor of *Lincoln's Assassins: Their Trial and Execution*, and he serves on the advisory committee of the Abraham Lincoln Bicentennial Commission.

Born on Lincoln's birthday, Swanson has studied and collected books, documents, photographs, art, and artifacts from Abraham Lincoln's life—and death—since he was ten years old. ～

© Jerry Bauer

The Chase
A Timeline

March 4, 1865. Abraham Lincoln delivers second inaugural address. John Wilkes Booth, standing nearby, says he had an "excellent chance" to kill him.

April 14. Around noon Booth learns that Lincoln is coming to Ford's Theatre that night. He has eight hours to prepare his plan.

April 14. At 10:15 P.M., Booth shoots the president, leaps to the stage, and escapes on a waiting horse.

April 14. Secretary of War Edwin Stanton orders the manhunt to begin.

April 15. About 4:00 A.M., Booth seeks treatment for a broken leg at Dr. Samuel Mudd's. Cavalry patrol heads south toward Mudd farm.

April 15. President Lincoln dies at 7:22 A.M. Booth leaves Dr. Mudd's that evening. Stanton summons more troops and detectives to join the hunt.

April 16. Confederate operative Thomas Jones hides Booth in a remote pine thicket for five days, frustrating the manhunters.

April 17. Booth's coconspirator, Lewis Powell, and other associates are arrested.

The Chase *(continued)*

April 19. Tens of thousands watch procession to U.S. Capitol, where President Lincoln lies in state. Wild rumors and stories of false sightings of Booth spread.

April 20. After hiding Booth in Maryland for five days, Jones puts him in a rowboat on the Potomac River, bound for Virginia. More than a thousand manhunters are still searching in Maryland. In the dark, Booth rows the wrong way and ends up in Maryland.

April 20–24. Booth lands in the northern neck of Virginia, and Confederate agents and sympathizers guide him to Port Conway, Virginia.

April 24. Booth befriends three Confederate soldiers who help him cross to Port Royal, and then guide him to the Garrett farm.

April 24. Union troops in Washington receive a report of a Booth sighting. They board a U.S. Navy tug and steam south, disembarking in Virginia.

April 25. The Sixteenth New York Cavalry rides right past Booth's hideout at the Garrett farm. Realizing their error, they turn around and surround the Garrett farm after midnight that night.

April 26. When Booth refuses to surrender, troops set the barn on fire, and Boston Corbett shoots the assassin. Booth dies a few hours later, at sunrise.

A Conversation with James L. Swanson

When did you first become interested in Abraham Lincoln and his assassination?

Probably the day I was born. I suppose I owe my interest to my parents for picking Lincoln's birthday, February 12, as my birthday. When I was a child, as far back as I can remember, I received Lincoln books, trinkets, medals, and souvenirs as gifts.

I became interested in the assassination when I was ten years old, when my grandmother, a veteran of the old, long-vanished Chicago tabloid newspaper scene, gave me a wonderful engraving of John Wilkes Booth's Deringer pistol. Framed with this engraving was a clipping from the *Chicago Tribune* dated April 15, 1865, the day Lincoln died. Unfortunately the clipping was incomplete, so when I was a child, I could read part of the story, but it came to an abrupt end. I remember vividly one night when I read that clipping over and over and thought, "I want to read the rest of the story." And it took a couple of decades, but one of the most thrilling things I did as part of the research for *Manhunt* was to acquire an entire run of rare, original issues of the *Chicago Tribune*—about one hundred newspapers—from the end of the Civil War through the death of Lincoln and the trial of the conspirators.

My grandmother's gift triggered my obsession with the Lincoln assassination. Later, as I got older and learned more about Lincoln, I began collecting at a more advanced level—books from the Civil ▶

> **"** I became interested in the assassination when I was ten years old, when my grandmother . . . gave me a wonderful engraving of John Wilkes Booth's Deringer pistol. **"**

A Conversation with James L. Swanson
(continued)

War, newspapers, posters announcing the death of Lincoln, original photographs, and more. I remember when in high school, instead of buying a used car, I purchased one of the rare original reward posters offering a $100,000.00 reward for the Lincoln assassins. Once I got to college, I studied the assassination of Lincoln and Lincoln's era ever more seriously. I was a student of John Hope Franklin at the University of Chicago and took his wonderful courses on the Civil War era and on the history of the American South. That's really how my interest began, grew, and continues to this day.

Having a lifetime of interest in Lincoln and the assassination, how did you approach the research specifically for Manhunt?

Manhunt was the result of a lifetime of study, plus two years of intensive research and writing. I had built up a reference library of several thousand books over the years, covering Abraham Lincoln, the presidency, the Civil War, and nineteenth-century American history. Much of what I needed for *Manhunt* had been sitting on my shelves for years, and I just needed to open these books and read them again. I also consulted my extensive collection of Civil War newspapers, and many rolls of microfilmed documents from the National Archives. Having so many sources in my home library allowed me to work deep into the night—my favorite time for research and writing. Public libraries

66 In high school, instead of buying a used car, I purchased one of the rare original reward posters offering a $100,000.00 reward for the Lincoln assassins. 99

close at night. My library was open twenty-four hours a day.

I thought I knew the story of Lincoln's assassination, and of the hunt and capture of John Wilkes Booth, very well when I started, but one of the surprises, and it turns out to have been one of the pleasures of doing the book, was to find out how much I didn't know and how much new there was to learn.

Is there anything that surprised you, or something you learned that was new or unexpected?

One of the best things was to meet the cast of characters, especially many hitherto obscure ones. I knew their names, but I didn't really know how vital each of them was to the story. One of the favorite characters I met was Asia Booth Clarke, John Wilkes Booth's wonderful, loyal, eloquent sister. She was a fascinating counterpoint to her brother. She knew that John Wilkes Booth had done wrong in murdering the president, and she knew that he was wrong to try to continue the Civil War, revive the Confederacy, and perpetuate slavery. And yet, because of her love for her brother and her loyalty to him, she fought a one-woman campaign to preserve his memory, and to—if not justify—explain and seek forgiveness for him. It was fascinating to read her once-secret memoir about her brother. I'd never read it before, and I knew I had to study it as part of the research for *Manhunt*. It was astonishing to read her stories about their ▶

66 One of the favorite characters I met was Asia Booth Clarke, John Wilkes Booth's wonderful, loyal, eloquent sister. 99

A Conversation with James L. Swanson
(continued)

childhood together and her brother's dreams and fantasies.

Another favorite character was Fannie Seward, the young daughter of Secretary of State William H. Seward. To read about her heroism the night Louis Powell tried to stab her father to death in his bed, and to read her haunting recollections in her diary, was surprising and inspiring. Her story ended sadly with her dying so young, at age twenty-one. She would have been a wonderful writer. I wish I could have known her.

Another favorite character was Thomas Jones, the Confederate courier and secret agent who helped Booth and David Herold cross the Potomac River by providing them his little boat. So for me, one of the great pleasures of researching the book was to learn much more about the characters who are often quickly passed over as fringe characters or unimportant players. But once you come to know them, they become fascinating and propel *Manhunt* forward, adding so much character and color to the book.

There is an enduring interest in Abraham Lincoln's assassination—where do you think this interest comes from? What is it about this event that makes it so fascinating to so many people?

Well, I think the interest is there for a few reasons. First, Lincoln was certainly our greatest president, so there's an immediate fascination with his death, as there is with all things Lincoln. We look to him for inspiration in times of trouble. We look to him and his words for the meaning of America.

Lincoln's assassination was a shocking event that is difficult for a modern audience to imagine. It was the first assassination of an American president, and it occurred at the climax of Union victory in the Civil War. We're children of a more jaded age— we've lived through or read about the assassinations of Presidents Garfield, McKinley, and Kennedy, of Robert Kennedy, Martin Luther King, and Malcolm X. Sadly the list goes on and on. I think we return to the Lincoln assassination because that is where this terrible progression of American political assassination began. I think we return to Lincoln and the origins to discover what lessons we can learn, or to think about how these assassinations have affected American history.

And then of course there's the drama itself. John Wilkes Booth was a great Shakespearean, and he scripted and performed the assassination. He did it expertly, with devious style. He assassinated the president and jumped to the stage before an audience of more than one thousand people. One of the most recognizable celebrities of his time, he didn't try to disguise himself. He raised his bloody dagger in his hand and cried, "Sic semper tyrannis," "The South is avenged," and "I have done it!" There's an inherent drama in the Booth story—the chase for him, his incredible ability to hide from federal ▶

> **"Lincoln's assassination was a shocking event that is difficult for a modern audience to imagine."**

A Conversation with James L. Swanson
(continued)

authorities, and his capture and death at the burning barn.

Many primary source materials are used in Manhunt—*contemporary newspaper accounts, books, relics from the assassination. How important were these types of materials in your writing of* Manhunt?

They were absolutely essential. I don't think I could have written the book without my own collection of original materials, and original materials in other collections and libraries. I wanted to immerse myself in the story to the level that when I read a newspaper story about the death of Lincoln published the morning he died, I wanted to have the original newspaper in my hands. I wanted to read the story and see it exactly as someone living at that time would have seen it when they bought the paper from a newsboy. Some of these papers are tough to find on microfilm anyway, but the microfilm gives such a dry, remote sense of history. I want to feel that rag paper in my hands. I want to turn the pages. I want to see how the stories are laid out on the page. When I wrote *Manhunt*, I wanted to read about the death of Lincoln exactly the way people who were alive then read about it, reading about events as they unfolded at the time.

The same goes for original letters, pamphlets, and photographs produced at the time. I wanted to hold the photos in my hand. See them in the exact size, the exact coloration as someone alive at the time

> " I wanted to immerse myself in the story to the level that when I read a newspaper story about the death of Lincoln published the morning he died, I wanted to have the original newspaper in my hands. "

10

might have done. I also listened to much of the music that was popular in Lincoln's time, including some of the mourning and death marches written after Lincoln's death—including a bizarre song about John Wilkes Booth. I tried to immerse myself in these materials so I could really go back in time. The great thing about these original materials is that they create a time capsule, and if you surround yourself with them, I think you can get a point of entry into the mood of the time. I knew that to transport the reader back in time, I had to go there myself first.

During most of the time I was researching *Manhunt*, I didn't have time to furnish my house. I'd moved to Washington, D.C., recently, and for more than a year, I had a table, a lamp, a desk, and a bed. No television. No stereo. No radio. It was me and hundreds of Civil War newspapers, books about Lincoln, original photographs, and documents. I think it would have been a different book if I hadn't surrounded myself with all the original materials. They were just invaluable, indispensable, to making the book what it became.

Is there anything that has been lost to time that you wish you could see?

Well, there are a couple of wonderful relics I'd sure love to find. Probably number one is Sergeant Boston Corbett's pistol —the one he used to shoot and kill John Wilkes Booth. It was a prize relic, even at the ▶

66 There are a couple of wonderful relics I'd sure love to find. Probably number one is Sergeant Boston Corbett's pistol— the one he used to shoot and kill John Wilkes Booth. 99

time. Collectors had offered Boston Corbett up to one thousand dollars for the pistol. At the time it had probably cost around fifteen dollars, though it wasn't his to sell; it had been purchased by the U.S. government and issued to him as a sergeant in the Sixteenth New York Cavalry. But soon enough it was stolen from him. Corbett fell asleep and somebody took the famous pistol, and it's now been lost to history. The person who took it surely must have known its value, but I imagine that over time as it passed from hand to hand, and generation to generation, its history and importance have been lost. So I would guess that somewhere out there, a collector owns the revolver used to kill John Wilkes Booth and he doesn't even know he has it. I would like to find that historic weapon.

I'd also like to find the gold stickpin that Colonel Conger removed from John Wilkes Booth's shirt as he lay dying at the Garrett farm. I'd love to find the missing pages that were torn out of John Wilkes Booth's diary. I don't think they contained some ultra-secret of the assassination—probably just drafts of some of Booth's notes to himself during his escape—but I'd like to know what they said. Alexander Gardner's photographs of Booth's autopsy have never been found and are presumed lost. I would love to find some of the missing John Wilkes Booth letters. People were afraid to be connected with Booth in the days after the assassination, so many people destroyed or secreted their letters from Booth.

Things are still out there. Recently

several John Wilkes Booth love letters were discovered. A teenage girlfriend had kept them hidden until her death and her family kept them secret for more than a century: They weren't discovered and published until the early 1990s. I am absolutely convinced that Sergeant Corbett's pistol is out there waiting to be found, and that there are additional John Wilkes Booth letters out there that are hidden away. The manhunt continues for me. Even though my book has been published, I'm still researching the topic, and I'm still hoping to discover other relics, letters, documents, or photographs that have been lost for more than a century. That is the most alluring thing about writing history. The story never really ends, and you never know what amazing thing you might discover tomorrow.

> 66 The manhunt continues for me. Even though my book has been published, I'm still researching the topic, and I'm still hoping to discover other relics, letters, documents, or photographs that have been lost for more than a century. 99

John Wilkes Booth's Diary

Zekiah Swamp and Nanjemoy Creek,
Charles County, Maryland,
17 and 22 April 1865

April 13th   14 Friday the Ides

Until to day nothing was ever thought of sacrificing to our country's wrongs.
For six months we had worked to capture. But our cause being almost lost,
something decisive & great must be done. But its failure is owing to others,
who did not strike for their country with a heart. I struck boldly and not as
the papers say. I walked with a firm step through a thousand of his friends,
was stopped, but pushed on. A Col- was at his side. I shouted Sic semper
before I fired. In jumping broke my leg. I passed all his pickets, rode sixty
miles that night, with the bones of my leg tearing the flesh at every jump.
I can never repent it, though we hated to kill: Our country owed all her
troubles to him, and God simply made me the instrument of his punishment.
The country is not what it was. This forced union is not what I have loved.
I care not what becomes of me. I have no desire to out-live my country. This
night (before the deed), I wrote a long article and left it for one of the Editors
of the National Inteligencer, *in which I fully set forth our reasons for our*
proceedings. He or the Govmt

Friday 21—

After being hunted like a dog through swamps, woods, and last night being
chased by gun boats till I was forced to return wet cold and starving, with
every mans hand against me, I am here in despair. And why; For doing what
Brutus was honored for, what made Tell a Hero. And yet I for striking down
a greater tyrant than they ever knew am looked upon as a common cutthroat.
My action was purer than either of theirs. One, hoped to be great himself.
The other had not only his countrys but his own wrongs to avenge. I hope for
no gain. I knew no private wrong. I struck for my country and that alone.
A country groaned beneath this tyranny and prayed for this end. Yet now
behold the cold hand they extend to me. God cannot pardon me if I have
done wrong. Yet I cannot see any wrong except in serving a degenerate people.
The little, very little I left behind to clear my name, the Govmt will not allow
to be printed. So ends all. For my country I have given up all that makes life
sweet and Holy, brought misery on my family, and am sure there is no pardon

in Heaven for me since man condemns me so. I have only heard what has been done (except what I did myself) and it fills me with horror. God try and forgive me and bless my mother. To night I will once more try the river with the intent to cross, though I have a greater desire to return to Washington and in a measure clear my name which I feel I can do. I do not repent the blow I struck. I may before God but not to man.

I think I have done well, though I am abandoned, with the curse of Cain upon me. When if the world knew my heart, that one blow would have made me great, though I did desire no greatness.

To night I try to escape these blood hounds once more. Who who can read his fate. God's will be done.

I have too great a soul to die like a criminal. Oh may he, may he spare me that and let me die bravely.

I bless the entire world. Have never hated or wronged anyone. This last was not a wrong, unless God deems it so. And its with him, to damn or bless me. And for this brave boy with me who often prays (yes before and since) with a true and sincere heart, was it a crime in him, if so why can he pray the same I do not wish to shed a drop of blood, but "I must fight the course" Tis all that's left me. ∾

Photographs and Illustrations

Ford's Theatre

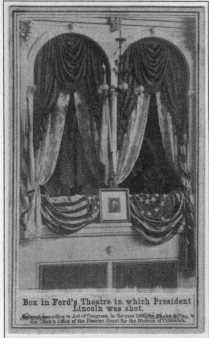

FORD'S THEATRE

TENTH STREET, ABOVE E.

SEASON II. ——— WEEK XXXI ——— NIGHT 196
WHOLE NUMBER OF NIGHTS, 457

JOHN T. FORD....................................PROPRIETOR AND MANAGER
(Also of Holliday St. Theatre, Baltimore, and Academy of Music, Phila.)
Stage Manager..J. B. WRIGHT
Treasurer..H. CLAY FORD

Friday Evening, April 14th, 1865

BENEFIT!
—AND—
LAST NIGHT
OF MISS

LAURA KEENE

THE DISTINGUISHED MANAGERESS, AUTHORESS AND ACTRESS.
Supported by
MR. JOHN DYOTT
AND
MR. HARRY HAWK.

TOM TAYLOR'S CELEBRATED ECCENTRIC COMEDY,

ONE THOUSAND NIGHTS,

ENTITLED

OUR AMERICAN

COUSIN

FLORENCE TRENCHARD ...... MISS LAURA KEENE

BENEFIT of Miss JENNIE GOURLAY

THE OCTOROON

EDWIN ADAMS

THE PRICES OF ADMISSION

Orchestra Chairs $1.00
Dress Circle and Parquette 75
Family Circle 25
Private Boxes .... $6 and $10

J. R. FORD, Business Manager.

An authentic Ford's Theatre playbill for the night of April 14, 1865

This action-packed April 22, 1865, issue of the *National Police Gazette* portrays scenes from what it calls "The Assassin's Carnival"—the assassination of Lincoln at Ford's Theatre, the attempted assassination of Secretary Seward in his bed, and the deathbed of the president.

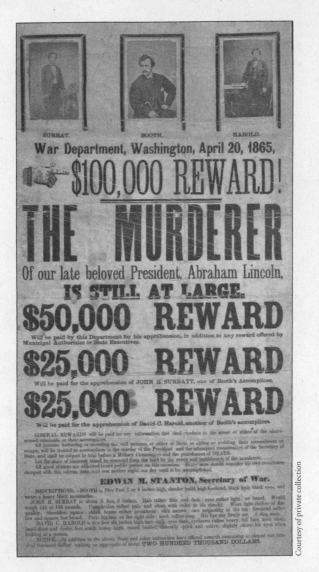

Six days after the assassination, John Wilkes Booth and his alleged accomplices, John H. Surratt and David Herold, were still on the loose. To speed their arrests, on April 20, 1865, Secretary of War Edwin Stanton offered a reward of $100,000 for their apprehension—and threatened with death anyone who gave them aid.

Photographs and Illustrations *(continued)*

Printmakers hurried to publish prints depicting the historic events at Garrett's farm. This color lithograph by Kimmel & Forster was the most popular image of the death of the assassin.

21

Photographs and Illustrations *(continued)*

Courtesy of the Library of Congress

Alexander Gardner photographed six of the alleged conspirators confined aboard the ironclads *Montauk* or *Saugus* on April 27, 1865. One by one, they were brought up to deck, seated before the gun turret, and presented to the photographer. Gardner never photographed Mary Surratt and Dr. Mudd—they were not onboard the ironclads when he photographed the other conspirators. *(Top, Lewis Powell; Bottom, David Herold)*

Courtesy of the Library of Congress

George Atzerodt

Samuel Arnold

Edman Spangler

Michael O'Laughlin

John Surratt in the Zouave uniform of the Papal Guard, where he served before his capture and return to the United States. His service in Rome fueled rumors that the assassination of Lincoln was part of a Catholic conspiracy. Copies of this photograph were sold to the public during Surratt's 1867 trial.

Photographs and Illustrations *(continued)*

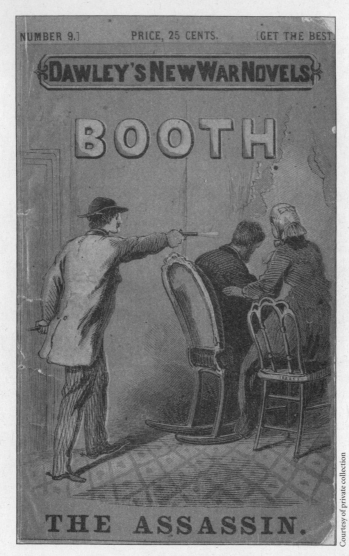

Through the summer of 1865, during the trial of the conspirators, John Wilkes Booth, even in death, continued to dominate the popular imagery of the assassination. Dion Haco novelized the life of the man he dubbed "the assassinator" in *Booth: The Assassin*, here in its original and fragile paper wrappers, one of the rarest publications from the time.

James L. Swanson on His Next Book

MANHUNT IS ABOUT JOHN WILKES BOOTH's twelve-day journey from the scene of his great crime to ambush, death, and infamy. But the chase for Lincoln's killer was not the only thrilling manhunt underway at the close of the Civil War in April 1865.

Another man was on the run that spring, desperate to save his country, his family, and his life. He was Jefferson Davis, president of the Confederate States of America. His final journey began at church on Sunday morning, April 2, where he was handed the urgent telegram from Robert E. Lee: There is no more time—the Yankees are coming—flee the capital at once. Shortly before midnight Davis boarded a railroad train—soon he would be reduced to horses and wagons—and chugged south from Richmond, vowing to fight on. Accused of plotting Lincoln's assassination, Davis, like John Wilkes Booth, became the object of a one-hundred-thousand-dollar reward and vigorous pursuit by Union cavalry. It ended a few weeks later near Irwinville, Georgia, on May 10. During the Civil War, Jefferson Davis never enjoyed the South's first love—that honor belonged to Lee and Jackson—but his final journey into captivity, and the suffering he endured, transformed him into the martyr of the Lost Cause.

During the manhunts for Booth and Davis another man undertook his last journey, too. He was Abraham Lincoln, late sixteenth president of the United States. Lincoln's final sojourn began on April 19, ▶

Read (and listen) on

66 The chase for Lincoln's killer was not the only thrilling manhunt underway at the close of the Civil War in April 1865. 99

25

James L. Swanson on His Next Book
(continued)

after the White House funeral. From there a solemn procession escorted him to the Capitol rotunda, where tens of thousands of mourners viewed him in death. It was just the beginning. On April 21, one week after he was shot, four hundred soldiers escorted him to the Baltimore and Ohio railroad depot and placed him aboard the special train that would carry him home on the nearly 1700-mile trip to Springfield. When it was over, Lincoln's corpse had been unloaded from the train ten times and placed on public view in all the great cities of the North between Washington and Springfield. More than one million Americans had looked upon their martyr's face, while several million had watched the funeral train roll by. It was the largest, most elaborate, and magnificent funeral pageant in American history, before or since, and it raised Lincoln to the pantheon of secular sainthood.

And so my next book is about final journeys, the manhunt for Jefferson Davis and the funeral of Abraham Lincoln, both martyrs to their cause.

I hope that you will receive it as kindly as you have *Manhunt*.

Author's Request
For my next book, and also for my research on other books soon to come, I ask for your help. As I learned while writing *Manhunt*, not all the important documents and relics with stories to tell repose in libraries and museums. Many items are still in private hands and remain hidden in attics, trunks,

and basements all across America. I am in search of a wide variety of material related to Abraham Lincoln's life and death, and items from the American Civil War, both Union and Confederate, including the following: ABRAHAM LINCOLN (letters, relics, photographs, campaign flags and banners, inaugural ball tickets and invitations, sculptures and busts, and oil paintings); BROADSIDES (reward posters and death announcements); JOHN WILKES BOOTH (his letters, personal possessions, and playbills announcing his performances); LINCOLN FUNERAL MATERIAL (prints, silk ribbons, mourning badges, railroad timetables, and photographs); COL. ELMER ELLSWORTH (photographs of the Marshall House where he was shot, painted ceramic pitchers depicting his death, autographs, and ephemera); NEWSPAPERS (complete runs or individual issues of Washington, New York, Philadelphia, Chicago, and Baltimore papers covering the fall of Richmond, surrender of Lee, assassination of Lincoln, death of Booth, trial and execution of the conspirators, and the trial of John H. Surratt Jr. I especially seek Washington, D.C., papers, including the *Daily Morning Chronicle*, *National Intelligencer*, and *Evening Star*, and also issues of the *National Police Gazette* and *Frank Leslie's Illustrated Newspaper*); JEFFERSON DAVIS (all material related to his escape and capture including letters, prints, and photographs); CIVIL WAR MEDICINE ▶

James L. Swanson on His Next Book
(continued)

(surgical kits and relics, medical
photographs of wounded soldiers,
salesman's samples of coffins, identified
uniforms, and personal effects); CIVIL
WAR MUSIC (especially drums, bugles,
and other items connected to the history
of military bands); and CIVIL WAR
RELICS (including swords, flags,
and uniforms, especially those with
documented histories connecting them
to individual soldiers and units).

I will be grateful to hear from readers
kind enough to assist me with my research
for future book projects.

James L. Swanson
P.O. Box 76166
Washington, DC 20013
E-mail: james@jameslswanson.com

Discussing *Manhunt*

ON THE *MANHUNT* BOOK TOUR, I had
the pleasure of meeting several thousand
readers at signings, parties, and lectures. I
was asked many interesting questions, and
at one event the leader of a book group
suggested that I share some of these with a
wider audience, to stimulate conversations
at book groups that have been kind enough
to choose *Manhunt* for discussion. Here are
some of my favorite questions:

1. What if John Wilkes Booth had missed?

2. What if not only Booth, but also Lewis
   Powell and George Atzerodt, had
   accomplished their missions? Would the
   murders of the president, vice president,
   and secretary of state have plunged the
   Union into chaos and prolonged the
   Civil War?

3. How did the Lincoln assassination change
   American history?

4. What was Mary Surratt's level of culpability
   in the assassination? Was her execution an
   injustice?

5. What of Dr. Samuel Mudd? Was he guilty,
   and of what?

6. Who is the more admirable character, the
   actress Laura Keene or the assassin's sister,
   Asia Booth Clarke?

7. Is Thomas Jones, the rebel river ghost, to be
   admired for his code of honor or
   condemned for his aid to the assassin?

Discussing *Manhunt* *(continued)*

8. Is Ford's Theatre a monument to Abraham Lincoln, or his killer?

9. In what ways, if any, is John Wilkes Booth a sympathetic character?

10. Have we, nearly 150 years after the great crime, forgiven John Wilkes Booth?

11. Who is the hero of *Manhunt*? Is there more than one?

Have You Read?
More by James L. Swanson

LINCOLN'S ASSASSINS: THEIR TRIAL AND EXECUTION

It was the crime of the nineteenth century, and it led to the most notorious trial in American history. But the story of President Abraham Lincoln's assassination didn't end with his state funeral and the death of his killer, John Wilkes Booth. In the spring and summer of 1865, a military commission tried eight people as conspirators in Booth's plot to murder Lincoln and other high officials. In *Lincoln's Assassins*, James L. Swanson and Daniel R. Weinberg resurrect these events, presenting an unprecedented visual record—with nearly three hundred photographs—that brings to light this tragic event and the perpetrators behind it.

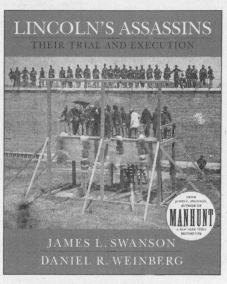

"[A] remarkable book. . . . Through an exquisite combination of vivid writing, stunning photographs, and contemporary pamphlets, letters, and documents, Swanson and Weinberg carry the reader across the boundaries of time and space, bringing the spring and summer of 1865 into brilliant focus."   —Doris Kearns Goodwin

"An authoritative and visually compelling study of the trial and execution of the conspirators."   —*Chicago Sun-Times*

"[A] fascinating book. . . . Most notably, *Lincoln's Assassins* reproduces Alexander Gardner's striking photographs of the incarcerated defendants, which convey a sense of almost surreal immediacy."

—*New York Times Book Review*

Have You Heard?

MANHUNT CD

On CD, available from HarperAudio, James L. Swanson's *Manhunt* is performed by Richard Thomas, and includes an interview with the author.

"This taut, historical account of the tense search for Lincoln's killer, actor John Wilkes Booth, is thrillingly narrated by another actor—Richard Thomas."   —*People*

Don't miss the next book by your favorite author. Sign up now for AuthorTracker by visiting www.AuthorTracker.com.